G. T. Robinson
'94

Counterclockwise

Critical Studies in Communication and in the Cultural Industries

Herbert Schiller, *Series Editor*

Counterclockwise: Perspectives on Communication, Dallas Smythe (edited by Thomas Guback)

The Panoptic Sort: A Political Economy of Personal Information, Oscar H. Gandy, Jr.

Triumph of the Image: The Media's War in the Persian Gulf—A Global Perspective, edited by Hamid Mowlana, George Gerbner, and Herbert I. Schiller

The Persian Gulf TV War, Douglas Kellner

Mass Communications and American Empire, Second Edition, Updated, Herbert I. Schiller

Forthcoming

The Social Uses of Photography: Images in the Age of Reproducibility, Hanno Hardt

Introduction to Media Studies, edited by Stuart Ewen, Elizabeth Ewen, Serafina Bathrick, and Andrew Mattson

MTV, Jack Banks

Media Transformations in the Age of Persuasion, Robin K. Andersen

A Different Road Taken: Profiles in Critical Communication, edited by John A. Lent

Hot Shots: An Alternative Video Production Handbook, Tami Gold and Kelly Anderson

Public Television for Sale: Media, the Market, and the Public Sphere, William Hoynes

Ideology, Government Broadcasting, and Global Change, Laurien Alexandre

DALLAS SMYTHE, 1990. (*Photograph by Vic Image.*)

Counterclockwise: Perspectives on Communication

Dallas Smythe

edited by Thomas Guback

Westview Press
Boulder • San Francisco • Oxford

Cover and frontispiece photo: Dallas Smythe, 1990. Photograph by Vic Image; courtesy of Centre for International Research on Communication and Information Technologies, South Melbourne, Victoria, Australia.

Critical Studies in Communication and in the Cultural Industries

Published in 1994 in the United States of America by Westview Press, Inc., 5500 Central Avenue, Boulder, Colorado 80301-2877, and in the United Kingdom by Westview Press, 36 Lonsdale Road, Summertown, Oxford OX2 7EW

Library of Congress Cataloging-in-Publication Data
Smythe, Dallas Walker, 1907–1992
Counterclockwise : perspectives on communication / Dallas Smythe ; edited by Thomas Guback.
p. cm. — (Critical studies in communication and in the cultural industries)
Includes bibliographical references and index.
ISBN 0-8133-1561-1. — ISBN 0-8133-1907-2 (pbk.)
1. Communication. I. Guback, Thomas H. II. Title. III. Series.
P91.25.S68 1993
302.2—dc20

93-24880
CIP

Printed and bound in the United States of America

The paper used in this publication meets the requirements of the American National Standard for Permanence of Paper for Printed Library Materials Z39.48-1984.

10 9 8 7 6 5 4 3 2 1

Contents

Chapter Five

Chapter Six

Chapter Seven

Chapter Eight

Chapter Nine

Acknowledgments

THERE ARE MANY DEBTS of gratitude to recognize, although I know that a few words of appreciation can hardly repay them substantially, let alone in full.

Jennie Smythe and the children—for helping to make this volume possible and for allowing me to publish for the first time so many of Dallas Smythe's manuscripts and talks. Thank you for your encouragement and for your friendship these last thirty-five years.

Bill Melody, director, Centre for International Research on Communication and Information Technologies, Australia—for interrupting an already full schedule and agreeing to write an introduction that summed up Dallas Smythe's life and work. It was a daunting task to undertake, especially under the demands of deadline and word count. I appreciate your accomplishing it so successfully.

The Research Board, University of Illinois—for funding my five-day visit with Smythe in Langley, British Columbia, in December 1991. My time with him turned out to be the key to this volume because he and I sorted through his work and career quite systematically. I also tape-recorded more than nine hours of discussions and took notes on several more hours.

The Institute of Communications Research, University of Illinois—for recognizing the importance of this project and providing crucial support. Professor Clifford Christians, the institute's director, felt from the beginning that this work was part of the institute's heritage and legacy. His encouragement of and interest in it have meant a great deal to me. Eve Munson, Carrie Wilson-Brown, and Fred Wasser, my assistants during 1992–93, contributed their help and enthusiasm. Eve dueled with computer "technology" and transferred much of Smythe's hard-copy texts to diskettes. She and Carrie proofed most of Smythe's manuscripts, and Fred verified numerous factual details—all of them worked with dedication and amazing speed. On the institute's staff, Anita Specht, tackling a harrowing job, provided the first draft of the transcription of the taped interview; Diane Tipps took care of numerous administrative details throughout the life of this project.

The Public Opinion Quarterly, The Nation, and *Canadian Journal of Political and Social Theory*—for allowing me to reprint pieces that first appeared in their pages. They helped to construct the history of communications research when they originally published Smythe's articles.

Gordon Massman, senior editor, Westview Press—for inquiring whether I would be interested in editing a collection of Smythe's work. It was a wonderful opportunity for me to repay an intellectual debt that has been on the books for three decades. I appreciate the care with which Larry Borowsky reviewed the manuscript. Aside from catching typos, he helped me improve clarity by turning murky lines into readable text.

Professors Vinny Mosco, Manji Pendakur, and Janet Wasko—for encouraging me to go forward with this work. They knew Dallas Smythe for years, often working closely with him, so they recognized how useful this collection would be.

Sylvia, my wife—for limitless love, loyalty, confidence, and patience, especially while I was working on this volume.

Thomas Guback
Urbana, Illinois

Dallas Smythe: Pioneer in the Political Economy of Communications

BILL MELODY

DALLAS SMYTHE was a Renaissance scholar, teacher, policy adviser, and activist for more than half a century. He participated in almost every major policy development in broadcasting and telecommunication in the United States and Canada during this period and in many international developments as well. He died on September 6, 1992, in Vancouver, Canada, at the age of eighty-five, leaving behind a wide range of both published and unpublished works, an incomplete manuscript on his desk, and more than sixty books to be returned to the library.

For Smythe, the primary purpose of research was to develop knowledge that would be applied in policies and practices to improve the human condition, especially for the disenfranchised and powerless. His emphasis on action and implementation has left us with a large volume of unpublished papers. Although a prodigious researcher, he was always more concerned with researching the new issues that lay ahead than with writing up all his completed work for formal publication. This volume contains some of Smythe's seminal papers that have escaped publication to date, have stood the test of time in terms of relevance and insight, and remain important contributions to the field of the political economy of communications. Thomas Guback, a former student of Smythe's and a leader among the current generation of scholars working in the Smythe tradition, has selected and introduced each of the papers to place them in context.

Although educated in economics, Smythe found mainstream economic thinking far too limiting as a basis for examining real world economic issues, especially those involving the development of human potential, the fashioning of communication policies, and the application of new technologies. At the same time, he found conventional approaches to the study of communications, drawn from other disciplines such as social psychology, sociology, engineering, and information science, to be severely restricted by their failure to consider the fundamental importance of underlying economic and policy issues. For Smythe, communication was an essential element for understanding the economy, and political economy was essential to understanding communication processes. This nexus spawned a distinct approach to the study of the political economy of communication that has provided for theoretical and policy development as well as a wide variety of empirical and descriptive research. The pioneering work of Dallas Smythe over the years was directed toward building links between political economy and communications to prepare the ground for a more comprehensive and systematic approach to both disciplines.

Smythe's approach to the study of the political economy of communications was heavily influenced by his work in Washington during the New Deal, culminating in his experience as the Federal Communication Commission's first chief economist from 1943 to 1948. At the FCC Smythe directed pioneering studies in preparation for the introduction of television. He also looked into radio spectrum allocation, the extension of telephone service to rural areas, and telegraph and telephone regulation. He was a major contributor to the landmark FCC report *Public Service Responsibility of Broadcast Licensees,* the "Blue Book" that guided U.S. broadcast regulation from the late 1940s into the 1960s. He directed the first study of television viewing and its potential social implications.

In 1948 Smythe joined the newly formed Institute of Communications Research at the University of Illinois, where he introduced the first courses on the political economy of communications. His 1960 article in *Journalism Quarterly,* "On the Political Economy of Communications," is still in widespread use as a foundation piece in the field. Smythe concluded this article by observing: "The propositions advanced concerning the policies of communication agencies may be readily converted into questions which would supply a whole generation of doctoral candidates with dissertation topics, and still leave a vista of tantalizing questions unanswered." Indeed it has!

Smythe's research helped justify the reservation of television channels for education in 1951. In 1957 he published his landmark monograph, *The Structure and Policy of Electronic Communications,* and provided research support and policy advice for Canada's Royal Commission on Broadcasting (the Fowler Commission)—one of many such advisory roles he assumed on Canadian, U.S., and international policy issues. Smythe was one of the first to publish research on the political economy and policy implications of communication satellites, beginning in 1958. He was an adviser to the U.S. Senate in the early hearings on U.S. satellite policy and participated in international satellite policy debates.

In 1963 Smythe returned to Regina (where he was born and spent his early childhood) as chairman of the Division of Social Sciences at the University of Saskatchewan, in part to take up the challenge of developing new interdisciplinary teaching and research programs in communications and related subjects. The program attracted leading scholars and students from around the world and established active links between the university and the community. In the late 1960s and early 1970s, Smythe's work with international colleagues advising the United Nations Educational, Scientific, and Cultural Organization (UNESCO) led to research on international communication flows and their implications for development as an important input to policy formation and support programs.

After his "retirement" in 1973, he moved to Simon Fraser University, Vancouver, as chairman of the Department of Communication for two years, a professor until 1980, then professor emeritus until his death. During the 1980s he was a visiting professor and lecturer at more than a dozen universities around the world and helped establish the Centre for International Research on Communication and Information Technologies (CIRCIT) in Melbourne, Australia, in 1989.

Smythe's research cut across many issues, ranging from government policy for regulating the broadcast media and telecommunications to the role of the mass media in influencing economic, political, social, and cultural activities. It included studies of the relations between the media and peace and between the media and religion. He may be the only scholar who integrated a positive role for competition within a Marxist analytical framework, just one avenue of theoretical and applied analysis he explored.

His research has opened new lines of critical inquiry in several areas. Two themes in particular recur in his work. One is the persistent probing of the power of the mass media to restrict independent thinking, channel public opinion, and assemble audiences for advertisers and the implications of these forces for consumer choice, free speech, democracy, and human rights. It is generally accepted that in authoritarian societies the population is brainwashed, noted Smythe, but it is much less well understood how, in Western societies, the population is "brain-rinsed." His research led him to conclude that the modern media reinforced de Tocqueville's earlier observation that Americans can say what they think because they don't think what they can't say. This line of research culminated in *Dependency Road: Communications, Capitalism, Consciousness and Canada* (1981), which the Canadian establishment tried to ignore for a decade but is now secretly studying in the aftermath of the North American Free Trade Agreement.

In *Dependency Road,* Smythe examined Canadian economic and political history through the lens of its communication industries and the government policies directing their development. He analyzed the implications of British and then U.S. domination of Canada's information and communication environment for Canadian economic dependency, collective consciousness, and the development of economic policy that contains desired "cultural screens." There and elsewhere he made a powerful case for cultural screens to provide breathing space for smaller nations and cultures to exercise a degree of control over their own economic, political, social, and cultural destinies. He argued that free trade always has been the policy of nations who would gain from it and always has been resisted by those who would not. Every country has had policies restricting trade at various stages in its history. When free trade policies are adopted at the national level, they are advocated most strongly for foreign consumption, whereas protectionist practices for favored industries are maintained at home. Smythe was not an isolationist but rather an unreserved advocate that smaller nations and cultures should be permitted to enter international relationships at times and on terms that they see as clearly beneficial to them, without concern from larger powers.

A second theme in Smythe's work is the contradictory character of new technologies and the tendency of those in power to expect people to adapt to new technologies rather than designing technologies to serve the real needs of people. Smythe worked to develop the institutional conditions necessary to place "needs before tools," as he frequently observed—"To focus on the tools and ignore the institutions which use them is to embark on technocratic adventurism." Smythe's work on communication technology has been particularly noteworthy, as he has marshalled the case against technological determinism in both communication and economic analysis. He has shown that communication can and should be a force for liberating human creativity, not for regimenting it.

Much of Smythe's research and writing has created discomfort for

DALLAS SMYTHE (*center*), 1951 or 1952, National Association of Educational Broadcasters TV monitoring studies, New York City. (*Photograph by Martha Krueger.*)

mainstream social science researchers, teachers, and policymakers. He challenged dogma of all kinds. He resisted deterministic and administrative theory and analyses, pointing to the need to understand and act upon the inherent contradictions in open and dynamic, not closed, systems. To him the whole point of independent research was to critically examine the major institutions in society so as to better understand their contradictions and limitations as a platform for changing them. His career was spent challenging the status quo.

Smythe's constant probing for understanding led him beyond the limits of the disciplines of economics, communications, and the social sciences. He pushed for more systemic study of the links among technologies, institutions, human needs, and public policies. He sought understanding from sources of every kind, from Mao to the principles of nonverbal communication, and he insisted on linking research and knowledge to policy and practice.

Toward the end of his life, Smythe observed that his had been a counter-clockwise career. Age and wisdom made him more radical, not more comfortable. His passion for inquiry was consuming. Driven by unquenchable curiosity, dogged determination, and a wry sense of humor, he never stopped asking the penetrating questions that forced people to think more deeply about their research, opinions, and beliefs. He was an inspiration to all who knew him. He will remain an inspiration to those whose understanding of the world is enriched by his work. This collection is an important contribution to that end.

Notes on Editing Dallas Smythe's Writings

THOMAS GUBACK

ASSEMBLING THIS COLLECTION has been a labor of love and a very enjoyable task. Putting it together has allowed me the luxury of reading most of Dallas Smythe's published and unpublished articles, reports, and speeches. Some pieces I read for the first time. Others brought memories of when I first had read them, occasionally in draft form with inserts stapled to margins like so many flapping ribbons ornamented with arrows and carets.

Readers deserve to know the grounds on which selections for this volume were made. I tried to cover Dallas Smythe's entire academic career, from his first years at the University of Illinois through his so-called retirement in British Columbia. I concentrated primarily on bringing to life his unpublished writings and talks, feeling that these deserve circulation beyond what they might have received in mimeo versions. In a few cases, such as the autobiography and notes on the press freedom doctrine, his writings have received no practical circulation at all. They would have remained stashed in neat file folders, presumably forever, which would have done no one any good and would have defeated Smythe's original intentions.

I wanted this collection to display the variety of Smythe's interests and concerns and the audiences he addressed. Therefore, I opted to include such diverse pieces as his foray into TV content studies and his challenges to nuclear weapons, his ideas on theories of press freedom and his antitrust attack on the American Telephone and Telegraph Company (AT&T). I could have included a talk to a seminary and his testimony to Congress, as well as an article on alcoholism and one on movie theatre patrons.

Another standard guided me as well. There are several pieces he wrote that practically have become legendary, and no collection could pretend even to be adequate without them. I cite "Bicycles" and "Blindspot" as works that have a unique place in the political economy of communications and therefore should be made easily accessible to new generations of students.

It was easy to select pieces for this collection; the hard part was having to drop many because of space limitations. Among the latter were "Ideology, Culture and 'Technology'" (1986), "Interview at Shanghai Advertising Corporation" (1979), "Cuban Crisis: A Failure in Our Definition of Reality" (1962), and a section of *Factors Affecting the Canadian and U.S. Spectrum Management Processes* (1985), a report he coauthored with Bill Melody for the Department of Communications in Ottawa. Fortunately, most of the other semifinalists have been published at one time or another and still can be found, although often in less-than-high-visibility journals.

Apart from selecting pieces, my other job as editor, I felt, was to present them in a way that respected Smythe's own writing style without sacrificing readability. I repaired obvious typos, reworked punctuation to improve clarity, and inserted a few words in brackets where I thought they were absolutely imperative. With the exception of two pieces, I cut nothing from Smythe's original text. In his eighty-page testimony to the FCC on Docket 14650, I abridged part I and deleted parts II and III but retained the flavor of his argument and the specifics of his conclusion. In the excerpts from his autobiography, I edited in earnest to bring the two chapters into a length suitable for this book. My deletions are indicated by ellipses in brackets. Elsewhere, I reorganized Smythe's footnotes and endnotes into a consistent style, fixed errors where I found them, and added details where they were lacking.

During the several days I spent with Smythe in December 1991 and in correspondence the following year, we picked out items for this collection. Typically I proposed pieces and he acceded. In a few instances, my ideas moderately surprised him. Nonetheless, he was enthusiastic about the final list and agreed entirely with every selection.

A reader might well ask why nothing is included from the pre-1948 period, especially from Smythe's years at the Federal Communications Commission. My answer is that government work is not always the product of a sole author nor entirely the conception of the author. Beyond that, some key documents he worked on were published by the commission and still are available in major university libraries—documents such as *An Economic Study of Standard Broadcasting* (1947) and *Public Service*

Responsibility of Broadcast Licensees (1946), to which Smythe contributed only the economic section. What may surprise many is Smythe's own appraisal of his work at the commission. He wrote to me that "possibly the most meaningful study I did while at the FCC was the short memorandum on farm telephone service [October 1944], of which I have no copy, but which was instrumental in the ultimate creation of the telephone program of the REA [Rural Electrification Administration]. But who am I to evaluate the effects of all that pre-1948 (July) work?"

This reflection speaks to an important aspect of his professional career and his writings. Smythe was an economist of the old school—that is, a political economist—but by *old* I do not mean *dated* or *irrelevant.* Indeed, the old school is more relevant now than ever before. I do mean *old* in the sense that it is the *root,* which is the basic definition of *radical.* His approach was *fundamental* and openly engaged. One thing I noticed while going through so much of Smythe's work is that he wrote accessible text that could be read. I have yet to discover in his published or unpublished writings any formulas or equations. I suppose this method of analysis is out of favor in the economics profession these days. Furthermore, he was presumptuous enough to make value judgments. I am reminded of his 1964 testimony to the FCC on AT&T's predatory tactics against Western Union. He produced a lengthy, complex antitrust attack against AT&T with hardly a number in the whole thing, except for dollar values and a few percentages. Would that economists' writings could be so readable today.

When I surveyed Smythe's bibliography, I discovered that he did not write for the journals in public policy or economics. The few early pieces in *Current Economic Comment* and *Illinois Business Review* probably appeared because those periodicals were published at the University of Illinois. I also noticed that he did not often write for what some communications academics call "the major journals in the field." A good deal of what he did produce was published in relatively obscure periodicals.

Much of what he wrote was confrontational, if not unpopular, and would not have met what some claim to be the rigorous academic standards of economics and public policy science. His work was not supported by lavish, or even not-so-lavish, grants from the prestigious funding agencies that many other academics court (and covet). He did not hop on bandwagons, follow the latest fads, or punctuate his writings with clichés, obscurantist terminology, or trendy lingo. He did not produce a string of books, either. Only his second and last, in 1981, dealt squarely with political economy, and a good part of it was a revision of material used earlier.

His classic 1957 monograph, *The Structure and Policy of Electronic Communications,* was published as a University of Illinois bulletin from the College of Commerce and Business Administration. He was not a contender for the Nobel Prize in economics, especially in view of the string of recent recipients. He was concerned with equity, not efficiency.

Dallas Smythe's impact came from quality topical work, talks, and teaching. He was personally influential. I am convinced I learned more as an assistant working for and with him than in my graduate courses. Several were important, and I would not want to diminish their value. But being associated closely with Smythe for three years, even though we did not see eye to eye on everything, was an indelible formative experience. In retrospect, I feel it is something every professor who has an assistant needs to keep in mind.

Although a casual reader might see Smythe's career and writings as eclectic, that would not be a fair comment on his work. It is very true that his apparent focus did shift from time to time, as after his sabbatical to Europe in 1959 when he began writing about, in his words, "international or global relations of resources, peoples, nations, organizations, and policy." But we have to understand that his subjects were only different ways of expressing a profound commitment to a point of view. His work does have unity and continuity, which I noticed in going through piles of talks and papers. Certain themes came up in pieces separated by fifteen and even twenty years. His last comments to me were about a monumental theory of information and communication that would embrace and build upon everything he had already done. He said this study was "a natural outgrowth of all the preceding ones" and pointed out that "it's in this sense that Bill [Melody] was right that I wasn't ready to write it at an earlier point, and now I am." I could say that everything in Smythe's professional life was leading to this (perhaps final?) opus, which he was never able to complete.

Does this mean his was an incomplete life, a life without a conclusion? Not at all. There is now a whole generation or two, perhaps even three, of political economists who are walking in the path Smythe pointed out. Maybe they do not call themselves political economists—after all, how popular or understood is that term today?—but political economy is what they are doing. If it had not been for Dallas Smythe, the study of communication would be very different these days and certainly less relevant and adversarial.

As I observed above, Smythe's writing does show shifts in themes. For example, by 1960 or so he had left the structure and policy of U.S. broadcasting, never to return in published articles. He did continue to work in this field in pragmatic consulting studies, such as the one in 1962 on deintermixture of UHF and VHF television channels in central Illinois. His research into television content largely was concluded by 1955. Smythe's work on religion and the media drew to an end around 1960, as did his critique of the "freedom of the press" doctrine. After that, he turned outward from academic and intellectual issues to world issues centering on peace, nuclear weapons, and the political process and their relation to the mass media. It was at this time that he also began his studies of satellite communication in a global context. His subjects changed, but his political perspective did not.

In December 1991 I visited Smythe and sat talking with him in his living room and over a few dinners in restaurants. I recorded much of those rambling discussions, which sometimes bounced from topic to topic like a billiard ball making its circuit of the table. We reminisced a lot; after all, there were close to thirty-five years to make sense of. Mostly I let Smythe speak at length about his career, work, and writing, which was the main reason for my visit. There are excerpts from the conversations throughout this collection. Yet many of his observations are not included because of space limitations. As well, I have reserved the right to respect his privacy on some matters, as every person deserves moments out of public view, moments when things are said in confidence among friends.

It is fair to say that Smythe and I spent more time coming up with a title for this collection than debating over the contents. The proposed working title was *The Dallas Smythe Reader.* Smythe said it reminded him of a grade school text. We knew this was nothing more than a provisional title, but because neither he nor I liked it, we felt we had to come up with something better. In our discussions about a new title, I introduced one comment he had made about his whole life. He had said it ran *counterclockwise*—that is, it started in Regina, went to Berkeley, then to Washington and Urbana, back to Regina, and then on to British Columbia. He even used that term when he described the structure of his autobiography, which he likened to several circus elephants joined tail to trunk walking in a circle. Quite apart from the geographic trajectory of his life, *counterclockwise* has another significance, I think: It suggests leftward progress, out of step with the mainstream, something of which Smythe would approve.

I suggested that the title might incorporate that idea—something like *Counterclockwise Perspectives on* such and so. In his last letter to me, Smythe wrote: "I *do* like the idea you suggested of using 'Counterclockwise' in the title. One tentative suggestion: 'Counterclockwise: Perspectives on....from Dallas Smythe.' As to the four dots, I don't like anything I've tried for that spot. 'Policy and Structure' simply turn off non–political economists not of our kind. Maybe simple 'Communication' there would be best. [...] The reason I'd like to feature Counterclockwise is because this may well be the only thing published which contains at least some of the content of my autobio. Now that you've started me thinking about it, I'll try to find my draft copy of the short preface which I originally wrote when I began the autobio: it explains several of the senses in which it reflects my life. Will send it to you if I find it (or else try to reconstruct it from memory)."

Dallas Smythe never had time to do that.

1

"In 1948–49, I began teaching what was almost certainly the first course anywhere in the political economy of communications"

EDITOR'S NOTE: When you have lived a full and influential life, when you have prompted people to think in new ways about familiar subjects, when you have created a discipline, when you have received international renown, you have the right to pen an autobiography in any way you want.

Because Dallas Smythe's life was unusual, so is his autobiography. We expect to read about his remarkable work in Washington, then how he established the political economy of communication in a not-too-friendly academic environment, then how he charted the field of communications research. But a reader is not prepared for the structure of the autobiography. The layout of the work is unconventional. Compared to the form of the typical self-written history, Smythe's is backwards. Chapter 4, modestly called "Mature Immaturity," describes the 1948-to-1963 period in Urbana, whereas Chapter 5, "Immature Maturity," tells about the 1937-to-1948 period in Washington. The subsequent chapters proceed further back into his story until we come to Chapter 8, the final one, which marks the beginning of his life. Chapters 1, 2, and 3, which were never completed, were to relate in similar reverse chronology the post-1963 period, with the first chapter of the work devoted to the most recent events of his life.

This rearview mirror approach, if I may call it that, demanded an inventive way to connect the chapters, as the normal flow of time was turned around. Smythe did so in another unusual way—by beginning each chapter the way he ended it. For example, Chapter 4, on the 1948-to-1963 period at the University of Illinois, starts with the Smythe family *leaving* Urbana in August 1963 and heading to Saskatchewan. This technique provided the necessary link to the preceding Chapter 3, which was to have dealt with his Regina experiences. Chapter 4 ends, in proper internal chronology, with the family concluding its years in Urbana and driving away to Canada. It was an unconventional sequential approach to autobiography. But could we have expected less from Dallas Smythe?

In our talks in December 1991, Smythe gave me a rollicking description of this unlikely approach. He clearly had a lot of fun writing the autobiography this way, and he obviously enjoyed explaining to me this somewhat bizarre system. With much glee he likened all the chapters to a chain of circus elephants walking in a circle, the tail of one held by the trunk of the next. The circle had significance as well, as I explained in this volume's introduction.

From our conversations and from letters he wrote to me until shortly before he passed away, I understood that Smythe knew he would never have time to finish his autobiography. There were too many other pressing demands, such as his work on a general theory of information and communication, some of which he already had committed to paper. Quite simply, there were not enough hours in the day to do everything he wanted and still swim a few laps. He was enthusiastic about my editing and publishing excerpts from the chapters he had completed. I told him, though, that for the purposes of this volume the most important chapters were those on his years in Washington and Urbana. In an exchange of letters, I said that those two chapters were much too long to be included without cuts. Indeed, the original version of Chapter 4 was over 19,000 words, that of Chapter 5 about 22,000 words. Together they would have accounted for more than two-fifths of this volume. So I relayed to Smythe my general plans for editing—what I intended to cut and what I intended to retain.

In one of his final letters to me, less than a month before he passed away, he wrote: "I'll be interested to see what you select from my autobiography. I hope it will include my treatment of my relations with Schramm. [...] Including my footnote references to the FBI! Why I became a PAF [premature antifascist] and its consequences (incl. loss of imminent commission as Lt. Commander, U.S. Navy in 1943 or '44). I hope you'll pluck out the pieces on the League for Peace and Democracy and the HUAC [House Un-American Activities Committee] treatment. All this because I'll probably never finish or publish the autobiography." Not surprisingly, our ideas about what to include coincided exactly. I have every reason to believe that Smythe would have approved the excerpts had he seen my final editing.

I found the task of abridging the two chapters I selected immensely difficult. An autobiography is a record of a life, and editing such a record is editing a life. Aside from a few stylistic changes and correction of obvious typos, I tried to preserve the sense and flavor of what Smythe had written. My rule of thumb was to retain as much as possible of his professional and public life and to cut passages about purely personal and family matters. I figured that private life should be just that, until such time as his family decides to authorize publication of the unabridged autobiography. Moreover, it is Smythe's contribution to radical thought and to the political economy of communications that concerns us in this volume, and those aspects ought to have sole priority.

I have made one concession to convention that Smythe probably would have found amusing. The two chapters presented here are in *reverse* order from the way they originally fit into his overall plan. That is, the Washington years now precede the Urbana years, although I have retained the original chapter numbers. I have taken another liberty, a small one, to improve the continuity of the material: I have moved each chapter's beginning paragraphs to the end, where they fit better into the chronology of the abridgment I have made. I felt comfortable making these revisions because the flavor of Smythe's elephants-in-a-circle analogy simply did not come across in excerpts from just two of his chapters.

How did Dallas Smythe sum up his career? He told me: "This has been a dialectical, skeptical, politicized, counterclockwise career throughout. It's an enjoyable development of theory and practice, done with zest and curiosity. [...] I'll probably use this formulation in writing Chapter 1 of my autobiography if I ever get that far."

Excerpts from Autobiography, "Chapter 5: Immature Maturity: Washington, 1937–1948"

[...] My professional/intellectual/political development was steady and progressive during my years in Washington. [...] My first job was Associate Economist, Central Statistical Board—a civil service appointment beginning at $3,200 a year in April, 1937. The CSB was then a temporary agency existing under an Executive order. It had been formed several years earlier to coordinate federal statistical activities. With a Board broadly representative of government agencies, it operated with a small staff of some 15 statisticians, economists and sociologists. [...]

The fact was (and is) that my abilities as statistician were those of a critical user of the results of statistical procedures. I knew or quickly learned on that job the logic (but not the mechanics) of sampling theory, variance analysis and such quicksand concepts as index numbers and time series analysis. When discussion turned on latin squares, orthagonal factor analysis, etc., I remained discreetly silent and listened for the moment when people have to say, "In other words, it means..."—at which point I picked up the implications of the preceding argument. I was to find that the same tactic served also to permit me to understand electronics and radio frequency allocation policy when I became Chief Economist at the Federal Communications Commission later on.

The staff of the CSB, I quickly learned, consisted of specialists in the various areas into which the statistical activities of the federal government could be classified. [...] Mine was to be the Department of Agriculture!

The program of the CSB was simple in theory but very complex in practice. It rested on the principle that before a federal agency could print and use any piece of paper with which information was to be collected from the public, it had to be reviewed and approved by the Central Statistical Board. This would include not only questionnaires intended for research purposes (e.g., the forms and instructions to be used by the Bureau of Labor Statistics to conduct a cost of living study) but forms used for administrative purposes (e.g., income tax report forms and instructions, forms for reporting goods imported to the country, etc.). The essence of the review by the CSB was to find answers to two questions: (1) Is the form efficient in relation to its purpose (i.e., did it embody acceptable statistical standards and common sense)? (2) Does the form involve duplication with the collection of the same or similar information by other parts of the government, either within the originating agency or in other agencies? If it did, then either the duplication had to be justified on some rational grounds (perhaps two agencies could jointly share the results rather than issue two reporting requirements on the public) or it was indefensible, in which case the CSB would not approve it. [...]

On the whole my professional work in the year and a half I was with the CSB was not demanding and left me with off-hours free to do other kinds of work. I was promoted to Economist by the CSB ($3,800) in the fall of 1938. [...]

I organized a local of the new and radical public workers union, the CIO United Federal Workers, in the Central Statistical Board staff. While our local had only five or six members, it did exist. The UFW organized an extension school for federal workers in the spring of 1938, and in the ensuing academic year I taught an elementary course in economics to a handful of students. It was there that I met Daniel Driesen and Joe Kehoe when they came to my class and asked permission to make an announcement about a telegraph union meeting. Danny [...] was the legislative representative of the American Communications Association. ACA was a CIO union that then represented all the Postal Telegraph Company workers and those in New York and Detroit of the Western Union Telegraph Company. He came from New York, as did Joe Kehoe. [...] Both were supremely intelligent, sensitive and Marxist. Besides, they loved life and people. We were good for each other and had a very close relationship from 1938 on. I learned much from them both.

By the winter of 1937–38 the Spanish Civil War was in its climactic phase, and the government forces were being attacked by the Nazi Condor Legion and large Italian fascist forces well equipped with tanks and aircraft. Under the hypocritical guise of the "Non-Intervention" blockade, England and France effectively denied the Spanish government its right to buy arms with which to defend itself against the fascists. Roosevelt, pressed hard by isolationist influences, especially those from the Roman Catholic Church, prevented the Spanish government from buying arms and supplies from the United States. In 1932 at Amsterdam the popular front movement known as the League Against War and Fascism had been organized by Bernard Shaw, Madame Sun Yat Sen, Theodore Dreiser, Albert Einstein, Maxim Gorky, and Heinrich Mann. It was reorganized in the United States as the American League for Peace and Democracy in 1936. With individual and union memberships representing 5 or 6 million people, it conducted nationwide activities to get the embargo on the shipment of arms to Spain lifted. A magazine was published, local chapters organized, mass meetings held, petitions signed. I was asked by people I had met in the United Federal Workers to attend an organizational meeting in

January or February, 1938, [...] and was elected vice-chairman of the Washington Branch of the ALPD. Chairman of it was Harry Lamberton, Associate General Counsel for the Rural Electrification Administration. Among our board members were Oscar Chapman, Assistant Secretary of the Interior, Fred Silcox, head of the U.S. Forest Service, Robert Marshall, Chief of the Public Lands Division of the Forest Service, and others equally distinguished. We became active, established an office, planned and conducted leaflet campaigns and public rallies.

In May, 1938, Congressman Martin Dies became chairman of the House Unamerican Activities Committee, which immediately became the center of a campaign by reactionary forces in the United States to smear as "Communist" public officials at the local and state level, as well as at the federal level, who supported relief programs for the destitute, organizing activities by the CIO (then just starting), etc. It was the breeding ground for people like Richard Nixon (then just a young man). Because we were good headline material, the Dies Committee gave priority to smearing the ALPD. On successive days at the Dies Committee's first series of hearings in mid-August, 1938, the ALPD was tagged as a "communist front" organization, and the charge was made that eight high government officials were members of the communist-dominated Washington branch of the ALPD. The eight named included, in addition to Lamberton, Alice Barrows and myself, Chapman, Silcox and Marshall—all of whom were officers or on the Board—and John Carmody, Administrator of the Rural Electrification Administration, and Mary Anderson, director of the Woman's Bureau, who were not. Scare headlines appeared magically in newspapers in all major cities on 18 August. My telephone was busy with wire service reporters asking my comments.[1] Press photographers took my picture, which appeared in papers across the country. [...]

The League continued its campaign to get the embargo lifted and became so focal an issue that both Harold Ickes and Mrs. Eleanor Roosevelt found themselves torn between giving public support to us and remaining discreetly silent. It appeared that we had nearly accomplished our objective when an article appeared on the front page of *The New York Times* quoting unnamed sources in the State Department as saying that it appeared that public opinion wanted the embargo lifted, citing the ALPD, the North American Committee for Medical Aid to Spain, and the expressions of the large CIO unions on the matter. It was only later that we realized that this had been a calculated stimulus to the Roman Catholic Church and other reactionary lobbies to produce further support from them for the embargo. At about this time the Dies Committee raided our office and stole our files (no subpoena was used), leading to a session before the Committee in which Harry Lamberton demanded redress, Dies threatened him with a contempt citation and Harry responded, "I have only respect for your office, Mr. Chairman."

The Spanish Civil War was lost by the spring of 1939, but during the 15 months of heavy activity in the ALPD I spent a great deal of time in meetings, during lunch hours and evenings, and on the telephone both at the office and at home. As well as working in the union, teaching at the UFW extension school, and working in the ALPD in 1938–39, I attended many fund raising events (meetings and cocktail parties) to help (1) organize farm workers, (2) organize to fight the poll tax that disenfranchised southern Blacks, (3) organize a left-wing cooperative bookshop in Washington, (4) raise funds for purchase of medical aid to Spain.

Apart from my work associations in the CSB (and later the Wage and Hour Division and Bureau of the Budget), which were warm and correct, I enjoyed the life of the left. [...] They were exciting times in the New Deal period, and I averaged two or three nights a week with my left friends. [...]

I enrolled in an extension course, conducted by the War Department, that would lead to a commission as Lieutenant in the U.S. Army in September 1938. I did this within weeks after the Munich agreement by which England, France and the United States gave Hitler the green light to destroy the independence of Czechoslovakia. It was then my view that World War II was inevitable and that I should prepare myself to take part in it. I was 31 years old—too old to enter a training program for an officer's commission in any combat arm of the U.S. military, but not too old to get a commission in the Quartermaster Corps. [...] I never touched a weapon or donned a uniform, but I received my commission as 2nd Lieutenant, U.S. Army, Organized Reserves, in the early summer of 1939. It was required, however, that I attend for two weeks a training camp, and that was supposed to be in June, 1939. [...]

I left the Central Statistical Board in November, 1938. On October 24, 1938 the Fair Labor Standards Act was signed, which for the first time set minimum wage rates (25 cents an hour) and maximum hours for workers engaged in industries which were interstate commerce, and created in the Labor Department a Wage and Hour Division to enforce the law. Here was a program that touched my concerns with the Okies and Arkies and the dispossessed in general. [...] Through the network of left-liberal economists of which I had become a part, I had information and support for a job there. In this career change I was moving into more challenging work at higher rank and salary (Senior Economist, $4,600). It was a friendly departure from the CSB, and I was later to return there when it had been absorbed in the Bureau of the Budget.

There were two wings in the Economics Division: one wing contained the economists who would be supplying the staff work for the industry committees (labor and management both being represented on the committees) that would establish wage and hour standards [...] for the nation as a whole (e.g., "Textiles"). I was not much interested in that wing. The other wing specialized in studies bearing on the interpretation to be placed in practice on various provisions of the Act. Three such aspects of the Act concerned me for the next three years. Because under the constitutional system of the United States the courts ultimately determine the limits of a law's enforcement, the meaning of "interstate commerce" as a practical matter was of crucial importance in determining what workers could benefit from the wage and hour standards. In an industry such as railroads, for instance, the scope of federal regulatory authority had been established as well nigh universal, and no new economic studies were necessary in order to establish that railroad right-of-way maintenance workers, for example, were engaged in interstate commerce. But for large newspapers such studies were necessary. Not only was there the challenge from the newspaper publishers that they were not engaged in interstate commerce, but the further challenge that newspaper delivery boys were "independent contractors" and not employees and hence beyond the protection of the minimum wage law. Similarly, railroads contended that redcap service to passengers at terminals was not performed by their employees but by independent contractors. The same argument was presented by the telegraph companies with regard to the messengers who picked up and delivered telegrams. Another interesting problem was presented in connection with "company stores" and "company towns." The Fair Labor Standards Act permitted employers to count as part of the minimum wage the "reasonable cost" of services supplied to their employees through company-owned housing, stores and other community facilities. Most employers who provided such services abused this provision by arbitrarily assigning higher values to such services than the cost to them of providing the services and counting such values as increases in wage rates to meet the 25-cent-an-hour minimum wage required by the law. Finally, there were problems connected with "sheltered workshops." This term covered a wide range of productive business establishments in which were employed "handicapped" workers—the blind, the paraplegics, mentally defectives, and those orphans and marginal delinquents who were living and working in shops run by a variety of "homes" maintained by charitable institutions and churches. The problem for us was to weigh the degree of handicap with which all such workers worked. We found that in some cases the workshops were run honestly, and the degree of handicap was reasonably reflected in the wages and hours of the workers. But in some cases the sponsoring institutions (churches and others) were exploiting a source of cheap labor for the profit they made in the shops. [...]

The economic study of the newspaper industry that [Philip] Arnow and I did in the spring of 1939 was a 195-page report—which would have been a publishable master's thesis in a university. Apart from a substantial analysis of the operations of the newspaper industry from the standpoint of interstate commerce, the issue of professionalism of news staffs (publishers argued that news staffs, as "professionals," should be exempt from minimum wage and maximum hour standards applied to "employees") and the issue of the "little contractor" newsboys were covered. [...] This report became the basis of policy statements by the Division, interpreting the Act as it related to newspapers. It also indirectly led to my assignment, in 1940–41, to work with litigation lawyers who tried the case of the *Dallas Morning News*. All of the issues covered in my newspaper study arose in this case, and I spent a month in Dallas to testify in Federal District Court and to advise our attorney. We won the case.

The question whether workers in a particular occupation and industry were engaged in interstate commerce also arose in many other ways, and I did studies and testified in Federal District Courts in such cases a number of times before I left the Wage and Hour Division in December, 1941. Such studies and testimony took me to Detroit, Michigan, and to Wichita Falls, Texas, for cases involving petroleum production, and to northern Georgia for a case involving small scale production of chenille bedspreads.[...]

The last occupational study I did concerned telegraph messengers and indirectly led to my moving to the Federal Communications Commission a few years later. For this study I went to New York and interviewed senior officers of the Western Union Telegraph Company and Postal Telegraph Company, then competitors nationwide. I also interviewed officers of the AFL and the CIO unions of telegraph workers. In this study I was coached by Danny Driesen and Joe Kehoe. My report, made in February, 1940, revealed that the *average* wage rate of the some 20,000 telegraph messengers was about 11 cents an hour. It led to the interpretation of the Wage and Hour Division as covering such workers. [...]

By far the most interesting and rich-in-learning experience of all my work in the Wage and Hour Division was the group of studies I made on the "reasonable cost" of facilities furnished by employers to their workers.

The first of these was the Atlantic Coast Line case. It arose from the fact that that railroad (which ran from Richmond, Virginia, to the Everglades) paid its Black maintenance-of-way workers much less than the required 25 cents an hour and contended that the difference was more than made up by the cost of company housing, fuel, water, landscape horticulture, and police protection which it provided them. We received many complaints from the workers. Then an "employee suit" was filed in Raleigh District Court by five such workers (the Wage and Hour law permits recovery of damages from successful lawsuits waged by workers to enforce the law). I was assigned to work with Robert Stern, a Justice Department lawyer, who because of the constitutional aspect of the case was assigned to try the case. I drove to Fayetteville, North Carolina, where the five complaining workers lived, interviewed each of them and inspected the facilities the Coast Line provided them.

Accompanied by a Wage and Hour lawyer I visited the head offices of the railroad in Wilmington, N.C. The dominant figure there was one Willoughby, the operating vice president, who was a tough, ruthless man, cut in the mold of Cecil Rhodes—the stereotypical 19th century white man who would build a railroad across "darkest Africa." The railroad's general counsel, Davis, was a whiskey-eroded bureaucrat. My investigation disclosed that the "housing" the company provided the maintenance-of-way workers were abandoned box cars and in some cases abandoned station buildings, but the company's accountants were charging the workers with the capital costs of the boxcars and stations as if they were still usable assets. The "firewood" provided the workers were the discarded, worn-out railroad cross-ties that would have to be collected and burned at company expense if the workers did not take them away as firewood. The water was from station pumps. The landscaping was the operating cost of casual care of station grounds. And the "police protection" was the operating cost of the company police charged with the duty to protect company property against pilfering and damage. The company's argument was fraudulent.

The case was tried before Judge Meeker in Raleigh. My economic testimony went in unchallenged. The argument on the constitutionality of the Wage and Hour law was offered first by Davis, for the company. He stumbled through a printed brief, reading some passages and paraphrasing others clumsily. Then Bob Stern gave his, without notes, tracing the constitutional history of the law on interstate commerce and the legislative history of the Fair Labor Standards Act, quoting extensively from court opinions (with page citations and dates). It was a brilliant performance and the Judge sat watching and listening with barely concealed admiration. Stern won the case. There were several consequent events. Bob Stern went on to become one of the youngest Solicitors General in U.S. history. And some thousands of Atlantic Coast Line maintenance-of-way employees received about $250,000 in retroactive wages. The latter happened because, having won the test case involving five employees, the Wage and Hour Division filed suit on behalf of all Atlantic Coast Line maintenance-of-way workers from Richmond to the Everglades. In preparation for this trial I organized a team of junior economists (including Phil Arnow) and sent them to various sections of the ACL equipped with 35 mm. cameras to take pictures of housing and privies provided by the ACL to these workers. The resulting pictures were horrible and wonderful—including pictures of privies literally overflowing. I could hardly wait to get into court. But our case was so airtight that ACL caved in and agreed to pay the retroactive wages without going through the trial. None of this, of course, even merited a paragraph in the press. But it was gratifying to see results from my work. [...]

My health had been variable in the late 1930s. [...] But in the winter of 1938–39 I had a persistent soreness under my right ribs. Knowing that Army camp would mean exercise and no controlled diet, I went to the Group Health clinic [...] to get a diagnosis. [...] X-rays showed a single large gall stone—so large it appeared improbable. I asked the Group Health doctor what it meant. He said, probably an operation, but perhaps it could be controlled with medication. I told him that I was due to go to camp in connection with military service. He replied, "Impossible. I'll give you a note to the Army." I took his x-rays of my gall stone and his note to the Munitions Building and showed them to a very senior officer who was very bored when I entered but perked up considerably when he looked at the x-rays, taking about 10 minutes to study them and question me. Finally he turned and said shortly, "I'll recommend that you go in the inactive reserves." So it was that I never became a full-fledged soldier even though I did receive my commission.

The outbreak of World War II in September, 1939, thus found me in an ambiguous position in relation to the military: inactive reserve. For the next five months I tried medication and diet to control the soreness under my right ribs. It became obvious that I could not go through the rest of my life under these conditions when an operation could remedy the situation. Because gall bladder operations in 1939 were not as routine as in later years, I was frightened. I went to a famous New York hospital to have the diagnosis confirmed; it was. I chose a surgeon in Washington, and the operation was in February, 1940, in Doctors' Hospital, then recently opened. [...] The surgeon removed my gall bladder and a stone about the size of a small hen's egg. [...] I was still considered ineligible for an active reserve commission in the Army—a status that existed until the military draft was put into effect in 1940. Shortly thereafter I resigned the inactive reserve commission and registered for the draft.

The gall bladder problem and its resolution by the operation was one of those events in the absence of which my life would have been completely different, and very possibly much shorter. For example, my instructor in the evening extension course by which I earned the commission, a Captain Kalakuka, within two years was killed in the Bataan death march when the Japanese captured Corregidor. I never did get into the military during World War II. I was called for the draft after I had joined the staff of the FCC in 1943–44, but the agency requested my deferment because of my essentiality. Also in 1943 I tried to get a commission in the Navy. I was appointed a Lt. Commander but flunked the security check. When the Navy people saw my FBI report they turned me down flat. So I stayed a civilian.

The timing of my gall bladder operation also had an unintended but powerful effect on me in the political area. The outbreak of war in 1939 had been preceded by the non-aggression pact between the Soviet Union and Nazi Germany. [...]

The effect of this on the Left in the United States was very upsetting. Clearly the "united front" strategy to oppose war and fascism was no longer appropriate. As for me, I considered that the main target of the Nazis had been and must in the future be the first Socialist country. Hitler had made no secret of this from his first campaign for office. Churchill and other public and private leaders in England and France likewise wanted control of the natural resources of the Soviet Union. I considered the Soviet participation in the non-aggression pact with the Nazis a justified breathing space in which to prepare to defend itself against the West. [...] And I was fearful that efforts to align the United States with England and France against Germany at that time might lead the West into a peace settlement with the Nazis and our subsequent support with them of an attack on the Soviet Union. While most of my left friends agreed with me, those with more social democratic (rightist) tendencies split sharply from us. The American League for Peace and Democracy was based on a united front against war and fascism—but now that war had come in very ambiguous forms, the organization fell apart for obvious reasons. But if not the ALPD, then what form should our political activity take?

The consensus in the Washington left was to form a new organization, the Washington Committee for Democratic Action, dedicated to the sole and explicit objective of defending and extending the democratic process and civil rights on a non-partisan basis. I attended the meeting that dissolved the ALPD and initiated this organization and intended to work in it. This was a few days before I went into the hospital for my gall bladder operation. By the time I had recuperated from the operation—in late March—the new organization had already been labelled a "communist front" by the Dies Committee, and its officers, chosen during my illness, but excluding me, were under fire. Early that summer [...] [I went] to California for a vacation and further rest and recuperation. Inevitably my medical problem had separated me from the Washington Committee, as it came to be called, which had a very short life. As an accidental result of all these circumstances, when succeeding waves of political oppression of the left took place during the 1940s, there could be no evidence that I had "followed the Party line" subsequent to the end of the Spanish Civil War and the dissolution of the American League for Peace and Democracy. When I was interrogated by the FBI in March, 1941, I could honestly say I had not been active in the Washington Committee, and their stool pigeons within that organization could not contradict me. The results were far-reaching. My security file was reviewed by the Bureau of the Budget in 1942 when I was working there and I was given a clearance of charges that I was subversive by the Director of that organization. When I joined the staff of the FCC and needed security clearance because I was working also for the Board of War Communications, I received such clearance for "secret information." And when I moved to the University of Illinois, a challenge to my appointment narrowly failed because of this feature in my political record. [...]

By Pearl Harbor in December, 1941, it was clear to me that I should get out of Wage and Hour. I had kept excellent relations with friends on the staff of the Central Statistical Board, which by that time had been absorbed into the Bureau of the Budget as the Division of Statistical Standards. They offered me a promotion to Principal Economist ($5,600) to come back, but this time as their specialist in labor statistics. I accepted and began work there immediately. My time was mostly taken up in 1942 with helping to design the organizational structures and data collection programmes of the war agencies then being created to manage the labor problems in the war-mobilized economy. [...] The National War Labor Board and the War Manpower Commission took most of my time. [...] And so did the Board of War Communications. It was the last that got my special attention.

Danny Driesen was largely responsible for this. He it was who had helped me immensely in my 1938 study of telegraph messengers under the Wage and Hour Law. He it was who had arranged for me to present that study as testimony before the Senate Committee on Interstate Commerce in 1941 when it was conducting hearings to determine whether the antitrust laws should be amended to permit the merger of Western Union Telegraph Company and the Postal Telegraph Company. And he it was who provided the liaison between the FCC and the Division of Statistical Standards in connection with the 1942–43 budget estimates that brought me to the FCC.

[...] Before and during my time at FCC the staff was organized into Law, Engineering, and Accounting departments, each headed by a chief. They had no economists on the staff. And there was growing awareness that they needed some, especially economists able to understand labor economics. Then and for decades afterward there were no university programmes in the United States where a young person could study communications in a way which would prepare him to enter the FCC staff. My doctorate in the economics of transportation had at least familiarized me in general with the structure and policy of the FCC, even though I knew nothing of physics and electronics.

Danny arranged for me to meet a young lawyer, Sidney Spear, in the Law Department who was trying to do a study of manpower supply problems in the communications industries as they related to selective service policy, and a sorry study plan it was. The Board of Communications needed that sort of information as a basis for representations to Selective Service, the War Manpower Commission, and the National War Labor Board in order to ensure that essential communications services be continued during the war period. Spear wanted out of the FCC and left when I joined it. [...] Danny also arranged for me to meet the FCC's General Counsel, Telford Taylor, its Chief Engineer, E. K. Jett, and its Chairman, James Lawrence Fly. As a result, I was offered the job of Chief Economist ($6,500—later raised to about $9,800 before I left in 1948) beginning January 2, 1943.

[...] Why did I want to go to the FCC rather than to one of the War agencies or to stay in the Bureau of the Budget? I felt that while the war agencies were important at the time they offered no long-term career prospect. As a graduate student I had thought seriously of making a career as an economist for the Interstate Commerce Commission, where railroads were the principal concern. By 1942 I realized that the ICC was a tool of the railroads and hopelessly sterile. The FCC, under New Deal leadership, however, was a place where the public interest might be served.

Moreover I was interested to see what I could do to influence policy toward communication monopolies. The Board of War Communications, which was staffed by the FCC staff, was an important, if small, war agency. And my initial responsibility at the FCC was to be labor relations adviser to the Board of War Communications.

My first six months with the FCC were discouraging (and for a time in March I seriously considered going back to the Division of Statistical Standards). By the time I had joined its staff Tel Taylor had resigned as General Counsel, going into the Army, where he stayed after 1945 as a top war-crimes prosecutor at Nuremberg. The General Counsel to whom I reported was Charles R. Denny, a glib, glittering, very facile lawyer whom I never liked or trusted, with moral standards not much above those of Richard M. Nixon. He was uncomfortable with economists in his department and managed six months later to arrange our transfer to the Accounting Department, which from my standpoint was even worse than the Law Department. The Chief Accountant was William J. Norfleet, a southerner who showed courtesy to women (whom he politely addressed as "Madam") and servility to the bosses of the communications industry whose good will he wanted and earned. [...]

If my programme had been at the mercy of Denny and Norfleet, it would never have gone anywhere but down, but the Commissioners themselves were my best supporters. Not that all of them were, but enough. Fly was very much the dominant figure as long as he stayed with the Commission—until 1944—and he was a staunch supporter of mine. Fly was a trusted friend of President Roosevelt's and had been General Counsel for the TVA [Tennessee Valley Authority] before coming to the FCC. A lawyer, he had graduated from the Naval Academy but never served in the Navy. Tough, hard, decent, and subtle, he was a commanding chairman who liked it best when he could make an industry boss squirm. His example rubbed off on me considerably. [...] Clifford J. Durr was a second commissioner who was supporter and friend (and Jennie and I gave his first name to our son Pat). Durr was one of the sweetest, finest men I have known. From Alabama, he represented the best qualities of southern men. Politically he was a liberal southern democrat who followed Jeffersonian philosophy and principles. He had been a Rhodes Scholar at Oxford, returned to work for the Alabama Power & Light Company briefly, and then joined the staff of Jesse Jones at the Reconstruction Finance Corporation, a New Deal depression agency. Charles Wakefield, a California Democrat, was a third supporter, though a weak one. Wakefield was a timid man, uncomfortable in conflict. He left the Commission in

1947 and shortly after committed suicide. Commissioner Paul Walker was the fourth of the Democrats on the Commission. He was from Oklahoma and I doubt if he was ever very bright. By 1943 he was becoming senile and had a habit when he wanted to say something on the bench of raising his hand to get attention; having gotten the floor he would open his mouth and we would all wait—finally he would say something. [...]

The three Republicans on the FCC when I joined its staff were [Thomas A.M.] Craven, [Norman S.] Case, and [George Henry] Payne. Craven was a durable bastard who stayed on the Commission into the 1960s, when age and heavy alcoholic intake forced his retirement. Descendant of a navy family, he had gone through Annapolis but had been unable to take a seagoing post because of seasickness! Commander Craven, as he preferred to be called, took his orders from industry: In the Western Union–Postal merger hearings, when I was on the stand he took eye-coaching from the Western Union labor relations vice president when asking me questions the latter wanted asked from the bench (I watched them from the witness stand while parrying his stupid questions without difficulty). I could always count on him to be a staunch and open opponent of anything I proposed to the Commission. Case was a Rhode Island former governor, an easy-going cigar-smoking man who always reminded me of Warren G. Harding. I found him an honest man for whom I could readily work. Vaguely identified with the industry point of view, he listened to facts and respected a professional like myself who provided them, even if he didn't always like the conclusions to which they led. The last, Payne, in the year he stayed on the Commission after I joined it, was a nonentity, a reactionary vote tied to Craven, but of no further consequence.

My first problems at the FCC were to recruit a small staff to work with, to complete Sid Spear's misbegotten manpower study, and to begin work on the proposed merger of Western Union and Postal Telegraph. [...] The year 1943 was not one in which to try to recruit economists knowledgeable about communications. We could not offer draft exemptions as bait. Nor were we one of the big glamorous war agencies like WPB or WMC (which did offer some draft exemptions). [...] I scoured my telephone lists from Budget Bureau and Wage and Hour days in vain. I scoured the lists from the Civil Service Commission and found four people. Hy Goldin was one of the first and best. An economist from New York, he had come under the influence and example of Greg Silvermaster when he was a senior officer in the Rural Resettlement Administration in Washington, and he came to me with Greg's recommendation. He had a natural flair for historical economic analysis and helped a lot with our common carrier problems, including the labour protection provisions of the merger legislation. After little more than a year he went to Harvard and obtained his doctorate with a thesis on the history of the telegraph industry. Returning to the FCC, he rejoined our Division, and when I left it in 1948 I recommended that he be named my successor as chief economist. It didn't work out that way because the Commission reorganized the staff shortly thereafter, breaking up the three operational "departments" and substituting a line organization of "bureaus," one for broadcasting, one for common carriers, and one for safety and special services. From that point on, when the FCC has had economists on its staff they have been confined to one or another of these bureaus. Goldin elected to go with the Broadcast Bureau and worked there until his retirement, [...] [after which he was] on the faculty of Boston University, specializing in broadcast matters. Another was G. Barr King, a young economist from Berkeley whose eyes were so bad he could see practically nothing without glasses, and hence he was "4-F." He stayed for a year or so, then resigned to join the American Friends Field Service as an ambulance driver. Wounded in Italy, he returned to the FCC in 1945. Barr was a good man, but not one to operate solo in our agency. He was and is still a good friend. The third was Carrie Glasser, a woman economist of a very conservative sort but competent and capable of doing scholarly studies—again not someone to send to a meeting of the Commission alone. Both Barr and Carrie lived in Washington and came in for job interviews. The fourth person I hired was one whose name came off a civil service certificate and I had to make a trip to Chapel Hill, North Carolina, to interview her—an indication of how desperate our job situation was in wartime, when I could ill spare the time for the trip. It was Jennie Newsome Pitts. I interviewed her in June, noting her energy, intelligence, articulateness and poise, as well as her great physical attractiveness. I thought we should hire her, and her appointment became effective about 1 September, 1943. [...]

Later we also recruited several more staff. Richard Gabel came to us as a junior economist and worked on a study of farm telephone service in 1946. He left the Commission about when I did, went to the Rural Electrification Administration to work on the farm telephone programme, and rose to a position of deserved prominence in telecommunications economics in the Department of Commerce and White House secretariat in the 1960s and 1970s. When he was with me, he was a philosophical anarchist who could hardly take seriously the matter of national policies on communications or anything else. [...]

My five years of intense work at the FCC may be summarized under two heads: the labor relations function that ended when the war did, and the economic one that began during the war and was my sole function after the war.

The labor relations function had three types of problems: the manpower problem, the problems derived from the telegraph merger, and telephone strike problems. The selective service problem was a top priority manpower function in January, 1943. [...]

My work as a general economist (as distinct from labor economist) ran concurrently with the labour work during the war. We began economic analysis of the telegraph industry during the merger hearings and produced a number of reports, some of which were used as testimony in hearings on telegraph company applications to close offices and to raise rates—testimony that was given either by me or by Jennie. Our studies indicated that the demand for message telegraph service was not as inelastic as the company believed it was and that therefore a policy of improving and extending service and maintaining low rates would lead to greater traffic, better service, and higher profits for the company. The company's policy was the opposite: Reduced service because of closing of offices and rate increases led to lower profits and demands to permit further reductions and service—a downward spiral. We tried to get the Commission authority to hold a special investigation of telegraph service and rates in 1947–48, but the Bureau of the Budget, then firmly under the control of industry, refused to recommend our special budget for that purpose.

Our first non-labor contact with telephone problems came in the early fall of 1944 one day when Commissioner Durr phoned me to ask if we could pull together what information was readily available about the extent of farm telephone service. A friend of his, a Senator for Alabama, was preparing a bill which would set up a Rural Telephone Administration to provide technical and financial assistance to cooperative and other organizations interested in providing farm telephone service. We did a little analysis of census information and pulled some material out of the files of the Special Telephone Investigation by the FCC in the late 1930s, and sent a small report to him. It had some startling information. In 1920, some 40 percent of farms had telephone service, in 1930 24 percent, and the percentage had not risen substantially since then. The indications were that the Bell telephone monopoly and the other large commercial telephone companies had avoided farm telephone service as far as possible because capital and other costs of providing it were so much higher than in urban areas. Durr made quite a speech in the Commission meeting the following week, and as a result our little report was published: I gave it the very modest title, "Preliminary Studies of Some Aspects of the Availability of Landline Wire Communications Service." A week later legislation was introduced into both houses of Congress by Durr's friends, proposing to set up an RTA and proposing a capital loan fund of $200 million for post-war expansion of farm telephone service. Two days later came the Bell System riposte: a 15-page letter to each Commissioner detailing their criticisms of our little report (example: we had not included in it the fact that telephone service in Europe wasn't so hot either) and requesting a meeting with the full Commission to rebut our report, and secondly the use of all commercial announcement slots in the Bell Telephone Radio Hour (this was before the days of TV) the following Monday night to announce that the industry was going to devote $200 million to postwar expansion of farm telephone service. As the trade magazine, *Telephony,* said, the farm telephone legislation might mean that the camel's nose of government ownership would get under the tent of private ownership of telephones. After a reasonably short period, i.e., by about 1948, the technical aid and loan provisions of the original legislation were assigned to the Rural Electrification Administration. The resulting program was extremely successful in extending farm telephone service.

Apart from that study we really did nothing significant about telephones. The Commission was then and later (until the mid-1960s) unwilling to take on the Bell System in a full scale rate hearing. Whenever profits got too large (on the Bell System's own accounting for them), the Commission would make noises as if it were going to hold a general rate hearing. Whereupon the Bell System would come in and offer to reduce long distance rates sufficiently to bring their profits within "reason." We used to call it "shaking the apple tree." So elastic was the demand for telephone service that no sooner had there been a rate reduction than service volume and traffic rose, as did earnings and profits, and we would be back again to shake the apple tree 6 to 12 months later. This process continued until the FCC was embarrassed by the fact that long distance interstate rates had been reduced so much that they were becoming discriminatory as against intrastate rates, which were not within our regulatory jurisdiction and were carefully protected by the state public utility commissions which were well cared for by the Bell System.

The FCC was not so busy with war-related problems that it could not spare the time to hold public hearings beginning in 1944 on the post-war reallocation of the radio spectrum[.] [The hearings were] required because of the development of new electronic equipment for a wide range of applications ranging from radar and loran through the safety and special services (land mobile, for example) to FM and TV broadcasting. When war came, there were only eight experimental TV stations on the air and an insignificant number of receivers in public hands. Should the same engineering standards and frequency bands be used for the postwar expansion of TV, or should TV be changed from the VHF frequencies to the UHF frequencies, and perhaps made exclusively colour TV? The Commission delegated the spade work on all this to the industry committees established by the Radio Television Manufacturers' Association. While the Economics Division was called on to do several pedestrian research jobs concerning equipment investment and costs for FM broadcasting, we had no central role to play in those hearings. I listened to all the hearings and some of the industry panels and learned a lot about the relation of telecommunications allocation procedure to the structure of power and to imperialism. I witnessed, for instance, how Chairman Denny, in the later stages of the hearings, played RCA's game in moving FM from its pre-war band (below 50 MHz) to a new and untried band (88 to 108 MHz), thus effectively preventing FM from becoming a substitute for AM as the popular basis for sound broadcasting. It was a rigged game[2] involving propagation evidence of very dubious validity and intent taken in meetings closed under the guise of "national security" (shades of Watergate).

Another object lesson: I observed Columbia Broadcasting System's strong first try at getting colour TV adopted *instead* of black and white. At the time RCA had no colour system to propose, but it had an admirably located string of assembly plants (financed by the government for the war as shell-loading plants) which it had planned to use for monochrome TV set manufacture and assembly. CBS had not previously owned any set-manufacturing plants, but it was ready to buy or build them if its colour standards were approved. Its colour system was a partly mechanical system requiring use of a colour wheel, but capable of rendering excellent colour pictures. [...] Given the fact of this rivalry, the FCC could and did give a hearing to both sides. That it decided in favour of RCA was the result of the bias of most of the industry, with which the FCC went along. Three years later the same issue broke into the open again when it became evident that the mileage separation that the FCC's first postwar regulations had established, as between TV stations on the same frequency, was too small and the allocation plan would have to be reconsidered. A CBS push via the Senate Committee on Interstate Commerce forced the Commission to reopen the hearings. Shortly before I left the Commission, we were shown the CBS colour system in trial operation, and beautiful it was.[3] Later the Commission after lengthy hearings approved the CBS colour TV system. The outbreak of the Korean War in 1950 provided the excuse of shortage of essential materials, and the FCC suspended and later revoked its approval of the standards when RCA came up with the colour standards that are those presently used.

As is now clear our work in broadcast economics began in this way via allocations. Ultimately, before I left the FCC, we had done a number of odd job studies on various aspects of AM broadcasting. But the most ambitious came about through the Clear Channel hearing. Under the allocation policy for AM broadcasting that had developed, there were three classes of stations: (1) local stations with low power, some of which were restricted to daytime-only broadcasting—in order to minimize interference between stations on the same frequency. They were the most numerous. (2) Regional stations with power of from 1 kw to 10 kw, intended to serve larger areas; because of co-channel interference they were much smaller in number. (3) Clear Channel stations that in theory were to be given exclusive use of a frequency in the United States and that had been permitted to broadcast with 50 kw of effective radiated power. The total number of AM stations in 1944 was about 700 and represented a full use of the broadcast band of frequencies, given the standards then existing.

During the war no new station construction had been permitted and the FCC had a very large number of applications pending for consideration for station licenses after the war. There was keen pressure from the local group and regional group to break down the clear channel monopolies of their frequencies and to protect their own more limited service areas. There was equally heavy pressure from the then licensees of the Clear Channel stations to get even greater power assigned to them—as much as 500 or even 1,000 kw. And certainly in their view the public interest would suffer if additional stations were to be licensed on the clear channels.

The FCC began a hearing to resolve these tangled issues in the 1944–45 fiscal year. Whatever their positions, all the three classes of stations were sure that the public would support their particular demands. And all three proposed to conduct audience surveys to prove it. In order to avoid confusion over survey standards, the FCC asked me to chair a committee, on which sat lawyers representing all the parties to the hearing, with a mandate to bring about such surveys as would serve all the parties' interests. It was a fascinating exercise that in one form or another absorbed my attention for several years.

It was not too hard to get all parties to agree in principle that they wanted two types of surveys: (1) surveys that would get directly at the attitudes of rural people toward the service rendered by each of the three classes of stations, and (2) a survey that would find out just how far from a particular station its signal could be heard without or with difficulty. [...]

Louis Caldwell was counsel for the Clear Channel group (and Col. McCormick's *Chicago Tribune* station), a very conservative, tough man. [...] As an unanticipated benefit to me, the mutual respect that Louis Caldwell and I developed during those meetings led him to volunteer valuable help for me when my appointment at Illinois was challenged on loyalty grounds several years later.

The Division of Program Surveys in the Department of Agriculture, headed by Rensis Likert and Angus Campbell, was selected to do the first type of survey. [...] That survey cost us about $50,000.

The Census Bureau survey was a nightmare, costing more than $500,000 and consisting of thousands of statistical tables even to summarize the results (a total of more than 50,000 basic tables were prepared but never even transcribed from the Hollerith printout sheets). The complexity of that study arose from the need to cover the situation of *all* the stations, in their geographically unique situations. But it too was put in evidence in the spring of 1946. It was all great fun. And nothing but fun. For the FCC never rendered a decision in that Clear Channel case. Meanwhile, of course, the factual situation long since made the record of that hearing quite obsolete. By 1950, the FCC had licensed about 2,000 AM stations, and the total by the 1970s was upward of 4,000. As with all frequency allocation problems, the trick in solving it is like putting two quarts of ripe strawberries into a one-quart container. Optimally one does it by weeding out the inferior strawberries. In the Clear Channel case, the de facto policy adopted was to squeeze all the berries into the container.

About 1946, I got interested in analyzing the market for broadcasting. My first step was to prepare a report (published by the FCC), "An Economic Study of Standard Broadcasting" (1947), that tried to analyze the impact of the vast numbers of prospective new broadcast stations on revenues, costs, and quality of service. This area continues to fascinate me as the locus of the unpaid work that audiences perform in the interest of consciousness industry. A more significant little study of broadcast economics was the chapter I contributed to the FCC's controversial report, *Public Service Responsibility of Broadcast Licensees* (1946). That report, which seems innocuous now, was regarded as very subversive in 1946. My connection with Durr in the writing of the report (he was largely responsible for the report) was to be cited by enemies of us both in their attempt to prevent me from getting my job at Illinois in 1948. [...]

Because the loyalty/security issue runs through these years as a constant theme, I want to try to clarify my political position up to then. As noted above, I had engaged in popular front political activities in the government workers' union and committees such as the ALPD prior to my gall bladder operation. After that event, I took no part in such activities, reserving my political work to the FCC arena. What was my relation to the Communist Party? In Berkeley, [my then wife] Bee and I had attended one or two public meetings sponsored by the Party on the invitation of our good friends the Cohees, who were open members. But no one in Berkeley tried to recruit us into the Party. Hardly had I become active in union and political affairs in Washington than I was invited to become a member of the Party. For reasons never clear to me, I declined. When I became close to the ACA people the same question was in our minds, but they never asked me to become a member of the Party, nor did I ever do so. Even in the days when [Earl] Browder and the CPUSA were following a reformist line and totally supporting the war effort, it was obvious that the Party contained many FBI agents. Why should I be exposed to the risk? was their attitude, and mine as well. The onset of the cold war in 1947 and the government's new and tougher loyalty programme all served to make the issue salient. Clifford Durr refused to accept re-appointment to the FCC in the spring of 1948 when it was tendered to him via Felix Frankfurter because he could not in conscience serve a President (Truman) who was supporting the government loyalty programme, which Durr considered unconstitutional and immoral. And Durr was never a Communist.

It was a time that suggested I should leave government service. I might or might not have survived the loyalty programme inquisition of the 1950s. But why should I try to do so? The policy of the Truman Administration was a big-business policy—a far cry from the New Deal of FDR. And the signs of the policy times were evident to me in the workings of the FCC. So where to go? I considered going into private business. Ed Murrow (the famous CBS newsman) interviewed me for a job with CBS. An advertising agency, hearing via the grapevine that I might leave the FCC, invited me to New York for an interview. The very prestigious public relations firm Earl Newsom invited me to New York for an interview. None of these Madison Avenue jobs ever materialised; probably I was insufficiently persistent or greedy for money—and Madison Avenue would smell that.

At that point an attractive possibility appeared to return to university life. In connection with my work in the Division of Statistical Standards, I had become acquainted with Harry Magdoff, an economist working with senior officers of the War Production Board, where he was implementing very sophisticated methods of planning the flow of materials and partially processed goods through the industrial structure of the country, using Hollerith calculating machines and input-output theory. Among our mutual friends was Robert Heller, then a leader in Columbia Broadcasting System's radio documentary department. At about the same time both of them told me that the University of Illinois was forming an Institute of Communications Research under Wilbur Schramm (whom Heller characterized disgustedly as a "lousy social democrat"). Magdoff told me that Howard Bowen, an economist friend of his, was going to Illinois to be Dean of Commerce and Economics. Through Magdoff, [Paul] Lazarsfeld, and Heller the word was passed to Schramm and Bowen that I might be a good person to hire.

I was invited to Champaign-Urbana for interviews. In one short day I was introduced to the senior staff of the Economics Department, the Journalism faculty and Provost [Coleman R.] Griffith. Then I was taken to the Urbana Lincoln Hotel for a drink by Bowen and Schramm. They offered me a professorship at $8,000 a year (I was then getting about $9,800 at the FCC) and assured me that with summer teaching I could earn as much as I was getting in Washington. My reply was: "Before you make me a serious offer you should know that it is very possible, this being an election year, my being a New Deal Democratic Chief Economist for a politically sensitive agency like the FCC, and my being associated with Commissioner Durr in the eyes of the industry, that if you appoint me the appointment may be attacked as that of a Communist." To which Schramm shook his head with a complacent grin and said, "Don't worry about that." And Bowen said, "Only if it were shown that you were a card-carrying member of the Party would it be significant, and even then we'd win." I then explained about my being on the Dies Committee "list" because of my involvement with the ALPD and my membership in the Washington Cooperative Bookstore. They dismissed the matter as unimportant. My appointment as Professor of Economics and Research Professor, Institute of Communications Research, reached me by telegram in late June, 1948. I submitted my resignation to Wayne Coy, Chairman of the FCC, effective 6 July, 1948. [...]

Washington, D.C., in 1948 was a good place for a New Dealer left-wing economist to leave. My friends said I was about the last one to leave—and still get a university appointment; the few who stayed suffered the pains of the anticommunist hysteria, sometimes known as the "new inquisition." When I resigned as Chief Economist for the Federal Communications Commission, there was uncertainty whether I had indeed escaped it.

Notes to "Autobiography, 'Chapter 5 . . .'"

1. I was quoted by *The New York Times* on 17 August, 1938, as saying that it is a "'matter of common knowledge that the league is not a Communist organization.' He said he is 'proud' to be a league member and its local vice president."

2. Denny was rewarded with a lifetime salary beginning at $50,000 a year and the title Vice-President and General Counsel for RCA. See Lessing, Lawrence, *Man of High Fidelity*.

3. The fact that when we saw it we had already drunk 8 or 10 drinks may have biased our perceptions. The Commissioners and senior staff went to New York one afternoon and after seeing Western Electric's "show ponies" were guests of Walter Gifford, then President of ATT, at the Links Club—a particularly gorgeous meal in his private club, preceded by a cocktail party. The next morning we were taken to the Dumont Studios in [New] Jersey where, after a look at their hardware, we had more drinks (mid-afternoon). Then we were put in Cadillacs and driven to Tarrytown some 30 miles away, where in a lovely rustic club-house we had more drinks—and watched a colour TV transmission from Manhattan, after which we had a steak dinner with sparkling burgundy, after-dinner liqueurs, cigars, and more drinks, ending up back at the 21 Club in Manhattan for a final drink. [The next day,] I tried to count the drinks we'd taken in on the trip and made it 32 for me. The hangover was mild, considering, which I attributed to the fact we also had eaten constantly.

Excerpts from Autobiography, "Chapter 4: Mature Immaturity: The Urbana Years, 1948–1963"

By early September [1948] I was living at the Faculty Club in Urbana, where I stayed until the next January, when Jennie and I were married. After the wedding in Chapel Hill, we drove to Urbana. [...] The housing we found was a "zero bedroom" (i.e., one room) apartment in a student housing building, from which we moved to a one bedroom and living room apartment about a year later. [...]

Summer school teaching appointments took us to Claremont College (1951), and the University of Southern California (1953 and 1956). There we rented houses, enjoyed the beaches and entertained old friends of mine from the 1920s, and George and Ilona Gerbner, whom I had met at USC in 1953. [...]

After teaching economic history of Europe for five years as an assistant to M. M. Knight, Europe lured me. In 1959 I took a sabbatical. We ordered a Mercedes 219 Sedan for factory delivery at Stuttgart and enjoyed crossing in the Holland-America's *Maasdam*. [...] A sabbatical involves a study plan: mine was to do reconnaissance on the communications systems in Europe. This meant a stay of from a week to 10 days in a capital city and sometimes other cities, where I interviewed senior policy people in the telecommunications and broadcasting organizations. [...]

[Back in Urbana, we] gradually developed a group of friends whose political views were consonant with ours. It began with John DeBoer (Education) and his frisky and exuberant wife, Henrietta. They had suffered political repercussions from his signing the Waldorf Peace statement about 1947 (in opposition to the start of the Cold War). Through them we met the Levys and Joe and Esther Landin (Mathematics). On my recommendation, the Institute of Communication Research appointed George Gerbner; he and Ilona were welcome additions to our circle of friends. When Joe and Jen Phillips and Herb and Anita Schiller came to Urbana they were congenial. We discovered Oscar and Ruth Lewis (Anthropology) in the mid-1950s.

By the late 1950s our "group" was meeting for dinners (sometimes picnics) about once a month. We never had any formal organization, and our conversations ranged widely from national and international affairs to capital punishment. We never had an action program of any kind. It was interesting therefore to find our group caricatured in the files of the FBI when I obtained my FBI file under the Freedom of Information Act in the 1970s. In reaction to the Bay of Pigs invasion in 1961, some of us may have signed a petition to Attorney-General Robert Kennedy protesting the violation of U.S. Neutrality laws and international law in conducting clandestine military operations against Cuba. On 23 June 1961, an FBI "confidential informant" reported that this petition was part of a campaign in Urbana that was "'a fully Party line job' with a high degree of prior preparation and organization." Responsible for this campaign was "a Marxist study group," initiated by five individuals of whom I was one. The proof that we were a Communist cell was that we "...were very careful to give the impression that we were affiliated with no organization."[1] While we never mentioned such things, I believed that none of our group might have been Party members or associates in the 1950s.

Before discussing our Urbana political activities, because they were conditioned by my professional political situation, I turn to the latter. When I joined the University of Illinois faculty, I wanted to learn as much as possible about how mass communications and the capitalist system achieved a large measure of "the engineering of consent." My work at the FCC, in particular, had impressed me with the power of the propaganda campaigns used before, during, and after World War II, and I wanted to find out the "secrets" of effective propaganda. I gave priority from 1948 to about 1955 to learning all I could from the research literature in social psychology, experimental psychology, and political sociology that might answer my question. Of course, I learned that there was no "black box" of secrets about propaganda. But during the worst of the New Inquisition years, my focus on learning those disciplines to some extent kept my head down out of the political arena. What I learned from all that reading was that I should concentrate on the "macro" relations of people in institutions that generated and steered the propaganda. Not until 1981 did my book, *Dependency Road,* pull together much that I learned about propaganda. So it was with no driving intent to be politically active that I came to Urbana to teach in September 1948.

But at the threshold it seemed doubtful whether I even had a job, despite a signed contract with tenure. True, I had in my first visit to Urbana warned Wilbur Schramm (Director, Institute of Communications Research) and Howard Bowen (Dean, College of Commerce), who were to be my two bosses, that my anti-fascist activities, 1937–1948, and my association with Commissioner Clifford J. Durr at the FCC might well result during the 1948 presidential election in my appointment being denounced as that of an "Unamerican." True, they had scoffed at that possibility. But when I was in Reno in August, I received a letter from Schramm who said that in the Board of Trustees meeting where my appointment by the university president was to be confirmed, one trustee had objected and made that charge. The statement that he distributed to the Board (I learned later) came from the House Unamerican Activities Committee. It charged that I had associated with Cliff Durr, especially in helping write an FCC report, *Public Service Responsibility of Broadcast Licensees* (1946), which had asserted that broadcasters had public service responsibilities because they were using publicly owned radio frequencies. It also said that I had tried to deny the FBI access to the fingerprints of radio operators (referring to a dispute between the Commission and the FBI that had been concluded a year or more *before* I joined the FCC staff). It said that I had a Black secretary (true, and she was the first in the Commission's history), had impregnated her, paid her hospital bills, and visited her in the hospital (all untrue). The Board of Trustees had referred the matter back to university officers to investigate. Schramm concluded his brief letter, which did not detail these charges, by saying that he was shocked "that there was anything in my background sufficient to cause this." However, he added, I should stay calm; he would get in touch with me later.

I was furious and desperate. A phone call to Jennie (still employed at the FCC) and to Charlie Clift (Durr's assistant) yielded me a copy of the HUAC letter and the news that the Academic Vice-President had asked my referees to comment on it. I learned later (but not from Schramm) that my referees had responded with splendid letters. James Lawrence Fly's letter glowed with anger, and Charles Denny (then General Counsel and Vice-President of RCA) said, "I am shocked almost beyond words by the inaccurate and libelous memorandum." My other referees were Paul F. Lazarsfeld, the sociologist; Frank Stanton, President, Columbia Broadcasting System; Stuart Daggett, economist; and Stuart A. Rice of the Bureau of the Budget. Rejecting Schramm's suggestion that I stay away from Urbana until after registration and the start of classes (which might well have put *me* in violation of my contract), I showed up in Urbana in due time. Upon my arrival both Bowen and Schramm assured me that my absence for a week would not jeopardize my contract and said that if I were unavailable to the local press, there was less probability that the issue would become public. Fred Siebert, Dean of Journalism, and much more knowledgeable politically than Schramm and Bowen, asked me if there was any way that I could ascertain whether or not the *Chicago Tribune* was going to make a public issue of my appointment. I recalled that Louis Caldwell, Washington attorney for the *Tribune* (and the Clear Channel stations), only a few months before, had offered to help me if I ever had a "loyalty" problem. I phoned Caldwell in Washington and relayed Siebert's question to him. He phoned back within an hour to say that he had talked to "Chicago" and that, while the *Tribune* people were aware of the HUAC attack, they did not intend to exploit the issue; they had bigger fish to catch (referring to George Stoddard, president of the university, who was then active in the formative stages of creating UNESCO, which the *Tribune* considered dangerous to the U.S.). I immediately went to Chicago where Jennie had come to see me. We had dinner in the Pump Room, and the next day Howard Bowen phoned to tell me that he had just come from a meeting with President Stoddard, Schramm and the Provost, where it had been decided that I should be put to work like any other employed professor.

What happened to resolve the issue began to become clear to me only when Schramm resigned from Illinois some years later, leaving his file on me behind, whereupon Siebert's secretary handed it to me. The full context involved the FBI, and that was clarified when I obtained its file on me 28 years later. I have no way of knowing whether major parts of my FBI file were kept back from me, and the parts they sent me were heavily expurgated with thick black lines. On the basis of the "To," "From," date, and city shown on what I did receive, plus the small amount of unexpurgated text, however, it is possible to distinguish five periods when I was under FBI investigation and/or surveillance. The first period concerned my activity in the American League for Peace and Democracy and the Washington Co-Op Bookstore, when the FBI thought I might have violated the Hatch Act and possibly other statutes passed to catch and punish "premature anti-fascists" (i.e., people who had openly opposed Hitler, Mussolini, and Japan before Pearl Harbor). The file shows that its report on that investigation was resolved by replies from the Director of the Budget (in 1942) and the Board of War Communication (in 1944) to the effect that they intended to continue to employ me. A second minor flap arose in 1947 when an unidentified female FCC employee visited J. Edgar Hoover's office and told his top deputy that I, along with Durr and all members of the Economics Division, were pinkos.[2]

A major investigation of me was done in connection with the Loyalty Program in March and April 1948. The report of that investigation runs to 34 single-spaced typed pages and embraces reports from eight FBI offices: Washington "field" staff (re: my FCC associations), New York (spies within the CPUSA), Los Angeles (concerning my home in Pasadena and my school years in Southern California), Philadelphia (where the Immigration and Naturalization people hunted out records), Boston (for reasons I cannot fathom), Richmond, Virginia (covering my neighbours at my homes in Arlington and East Falls Church), Cincinnati (where someone I had known had moved), and San Francisco (covering eight people employed in the Agricultural Extension Service, faculty in the Economics Department, five employees of the Key System transit company—where I had gathered thesis material—and neighbours to four houses that Bee and I had occupied in Berkeley). A number of names of other suspected "Communists" were linked to me, scattered through the field agents' reports. Some were friends (Silvermaster, Magdoff, Bassie, Driesen, Kehoe, Shandros, Selly, Ed Warren, Palmer Weber), but some were references to people and the "Gregory case," of which I have never heard. A large number of interviewees had nothing but nice things to say about me. The FBI reported that my "criminal" record consisted of two vehicle traffic tickets in Washington, two in Arlington County, and one in Long Beach, California. Coming on the heels of the loyalty investigation were interviews made in connection with the HUAC charges in Illinois. The remaining waves of reports concern my peace-related activities in Urbana from the late 1950s until we moved to Canada in 1963, and the reports interchanged between the RCMP and FBI after 1963.

Stoddard had asked U.S. Attorney General Tom Clark for information on my loyalty, having been denied it by J. Edgar Hoover. Clark had told him by telephone, according to a confidential memorandum by Stoddard, that "...there is no evidence, past or present, concerning Doctor Smythe which would interfere with his holding a high office in the Federal Government."[3] Stoddard then reported to the Board on the responses of my referees and his conversation with Clark and recommended that my appointment "be considered proper and in good order, requiring no action by the Board of Trustees." On that basis I began work.

But the matter was far from settled. The Springfield FBI office telegraphed Hoover on 21 September 1948 that prior to the Clark telephone call confidential informants in the university administration "...indicated that the appointment would be dropped." He also broke the distasteful news to Hoover that his boss, Clark, had "quote cleared unquote Smythe." Moreover, the Board meeting to consider Stoddard's memorandum was not until 22 September. On 13 October and again on 4 November 1948, reports from the Springfield FBI to Hoover emphasized that it had an "excellent contact" close to Stoddard. This source "...maintained a very friendly attitude, indicated he had a great deal of respect for the Bureau. ... [He] advised that some day in the future there may possibly be a very loud explosion in the press with regard to the subject's appointment." My appointment was said to be for two years, and I was going to be under surveillance.[4] Of course the source close to Stoddard was obscured with black ink. However, it was a seven-letter name.[5] The names of Bowen and Griffith (officers close to Stoddard on this issue) have five and nine letters. Schramm was Assistant to the President, and his has seven. The FBI's position was delicate. The Springfield special agent sought to protect himself from Hoover's anger regarding the Clark "clearance."[6] He:

> ...recommended that this information regarding President Stoddard's alleged contact with Attorney General Clark not be furnished to the Attorney General for the reasons that (a) in furnishing such information it would appear that the Bureau has an interest in the local difficulties at the University which the Bureau does not have; and (b) the furnishing of such information to the Attorney General would jeopardize the excellent contact [seven-letter name obliterated] that the Springfield Office presently has at the University of Illinois; and
>
> (2) It is further recommended that the Springfield Office be permitted to make limited discreet inquiries only through established reliable contacts and confidential informants to keep abreast of Smythe's Communist activities [sic]....

The latter recommendation in November was approved the same day.

None of this was ever mentioned by Schramm to me.[7] And for many years thereafter, whenever he had occasion to speak to me, his chronic occasional stammer was very pronounced. The auspices for my job at Illinois were not good.

In 1948–49, I began teaching what was almost certainly the first course anywhere in the political economy of communications—an advanced undergraduate course to which graduate students were admitted. To give the College of Commerce full credit, it permitted me to teach that and another course (a section of the course in introductory economics) for that and eight more years, although tact dictated that I call my course on the political economy of communications, the economics of communications during that period). In that nine year period, serving two colleges, my salary, which started at $8,000 a year, increased to $8,800 by 1956–57—appreciably less than I had been paid at the FCC. [...]

The development of the communication program at Urbana rested on a research wing and a teaching wing. The former was the Institute of Communications Research, which was a vehicle to hire from two to perhaps a half dozen people between 1948 and 1963 with split appointments with all the social sciences—but it never developed that way. In 1948 I was the only person on its staff (other than Schramm, the Director). The next year Charles E. Osgood was hired, as a split appointment between the Institute and the Psychology Department. No effort was made to create split appointments with Sociology, Anthropology, Political Science, or History. In my years there, the Institute attempted no interdisciplinary projects. In 1948–49 Schramm held a series of meetings to discuss the [Robert M.] Hutchins [Commission] report—a genuinely critical analysis of the economic concentration in the U.S. mass media, and its journalistic performance—but no program consequences flowed from the meetings. In the early 1950s another series of seminars was organized to present papers appraising Osgood's "mediational hypothesis"—an exercise in social psychology that tried to meld into social theory an application of the Shannon-Weaver information theory—a spin-off from Bell Laboratories electronic research to aid in engineering a telephone network with broadband capacity. This was connected with Osgood's development of the semantic differential technique and the employment of a number of psychologists and a few anthropologists who administered the headquarters phase of Osgood's cross-cultural study of values, financed by a foundation that later was revealed to be a conduit for the CIA. I participated in the Institute general meetings on Osgood's work and found use for it in my later research on content and effects, but had no connection with his CIA project.

As indicated above, Schramm brought no outside money to the Institute program. In my period in Illinois it was simply a holding company to house its Director and a few faculty connected with Psychology, Journalism, and me, in Economics.

The other wing of the Communications Program was the Ph.D. Program—the first of its kind anywhere. It began in 1949–50, through an interdepartmental committee appointed by the Dean of the Graduate College. The program consisted of requirements to study specific courses dealing with communications offered in the conventional departments, plus one interdisciplinary seminar offered by the administrative committee. Fred Siebert was chair of that committee until his departure in 1957, followed by me. [...] It was run on virtually no budget of its own. In 1958 on his own initiative, the Dean of the Graduate Faculty, a very decent fellow named Fred Wall, arranged the transfer of the "half" of me that had been in Economics to the Graduate College, where I became half-time Research Professor. My salary income, which had increased by a total of 10% between 1948 and 1955, rose by a total of 50% in the next seven years.

My first research priority in 1948 was what I thought of as my "black box" study, which I identified as follows:

> To ascertain the direction and magnitude of changes in family and individual culture patterns, and the psychological bases thereof, resulting from television viewing in the home; to determine the effect television may have on the relation of the individual to the state, on the relation between freedom and authority.

[...] I describe this effort in some detail for several reasons. It firmly disabused me of any illusions about a "black box" for manipulation of which psychologists knew or were about to know the secrets. Of course this did not mean that practical programmers of the mass media might not have small manipulative secrets. This experience is reflected in the last two chapters of *Dependency Road.* And finally, the effort to do that research had an unanticipated spin-off: my involvement for the next 11 years in religious broadcasting policy research. But first came the educators.

When I began working at Illinois, I was asked to become Director of Studies for the National Association of Educational Broadcasters, who then were using only radio broadcasting. The some 25 or 30 member institutions in the NAEB were the remainder of a once major part of U.S. radio broadcasting. Educational institutions had operated more radio broadcast stations than did newspapers in 1922, but they were forced out by commercial operators until only a lonely remnant remained. With a few conspicuous exceptions (University of Wisconsin, University of Minnesota, New York City), their broadcast policy was anemic and they mostly functioned as training grounds for commercial station employees. I did content analyses of their programs and released the results in 1949 and 1951.

By 1950 there appeared to be no possibility of non-commercial TV stations getting licenses, so great was the rush to get commercial TV stations on the air. But for several reasons unrelated to the merits of non-commercial TV broadcasting, an opening appeared. The FCC announced a rule-making for frequency allocations in both the VHF and UHF bands, to begin with a public hearing in January 1951. The Board of the NAEB met just after Christmas 1950 in the Waldorf-Astoria Hotel in New York to consider asking the FCC to reserve frequency assignments for non-commercial/educational TV stations. Telford Taylor, former General Counsel for the FCC, was our lawyer. He and Seymour Siegel, director of WNYC, New York, led the argument for reservations, and the Board agreed that the NAEB make such a request at the FCC hearings.

What kind of evidence could we offer to counter the hard pressures of the commercial networks and stations? Taylor looked at me and reminded us all that I had done content analysis at the FCC: why couldn't we analyze the existing commercial station programs and show the FCC how lacking in public service content they were? The decision was taken to do a content analysis of all seven New York City commercial station programs for the first full week of January 1951. We would present the results to the FCC. I was an obvious person to direct the study, but George Probst (University of Chicago) insisted that there should be a co-director and he favoured Don Horton, an anthropologist on the University of Chicago campus, for the job. So it was agreed.[8]

It was the fastest-organized study I ever saw. In less than a week we rented adjoining suites in the Waldorf-Astoria, rented seven TV sets, designed and had printed the forms the monitors would use. I got the loan of Western Union clocks with large faces and sweep-second hands to put on the walls, bought stop-watches with which to time the advertisements, and arranged through Bob Heller (soon to be CBS vice-president in charge of TV before the HUAC auxiliary, *Red Channels,* charged him with being a Communist, whereupon he resigned from CBS and thereafter worked first in Mexican TV and for decades as a producer for Grenada TV in Britain) and Oscar Katz (then and for a long time research director for CBS) to find us writers, actresses and actors who could serve as monitors. Much publicity was given in the press to our study (thanks to Sy Siegel of WNYC) and *Time* magazine ran a column on our study, with pictures of Horton and me. When the week's monitoring was done we moved to a double suite in the Algonquin Hotel to do the coding and tabulations and to prepare the testimony that Horton and I would give when the FCC hearings opened about 20 January 1951. It was a pleasure to work with Don and our testimony was well received at the FCC.

With the support of one commissioner, Frieda Hennock, the reservation of educational channels was adopted in the same year. The resulting growth of educational TV broadcasting was slow in the 1950s for two reasons. Almost all the frequency assignments reserved for educational use were in the UHF band, and it was many years before set manufacturers got around to building UHF capacity into all TV sets. Also, it was difficult for educational institutions to obtain the necessary funds to build and operate their own stations. The Ford Foundation helped with generous grants, and by the 1960s educational TV began to take the shape and stature it had in the 1980s. In light of the attendant helpful publicity, the NAEB, with Ford Foundation funds, repeated the monitoring in New York for the same weeks of 1952 through 1954. I was responsible for the 1952 and 1953 studies; in 1952 Professor Robert K. Merton was a consultant to me and wrote an interpretive foreword to the report. In 1952 and 1953 we added a count of acts [of violence], and threats of acts, and tabulated them, as well as advertising time by class of programs. In 1953 we also added an analysis of the characters in indigenous TV drama programs (as distinct from theatrical movies), and used Osgood's semantic differential to analyze the villains, heroes, heroines and all other characters in terms of their values (e.g., brave/cowardly), their power or potency (e.g., strong/weak), and their activity (e.g., quick/slow). And all of this was tabulated according to the characters' occupations, race, sex, roles, and whether they were engaged in legal or illegal business. [...] By comparing the characters' occupations, sex and race with U.S. census data, we were able to contrast the world of TV drama with the real world.

In addition to the New York studies, the NAEB also conducted similar studies of the seven Los Angeles commercial TV stations' programs in May 1951 (in that study Angus Campbell, Survey Research Center, University of Michigan, was a consultant to me); one of the four Chicago TV stations, July–August 1951, directed by Don Horton, Hans O. Mauksch and Kurt Lang; one in New Haven in May 1953 (directed by me); and the final one in New York in 1954, directed by the Purdue University Opinion Panel. While there were unique features in each of these studies, the basic procedures were maintained so that the results might be compared over time and between cities. [...]

While at the FCC I had met Everett C. Parker, then Director of the Protestant Radio Commission. In 1951 he invited Dr. David W. Barry and me to join him to plan and conduct a study for the Broadcasting and Film Commission of the National Council of Churches of Christ (U.S.A.). It was a study of the nature and effect of TV and radio programs and films produced by the churches. Did they become a substitute for church attendance? To what extent did they reach non-churchgoers and with what effect? Did they build character, improve society? Did they convey the Christian Gospel in faithful or distorted form? [...]

We rejected the idea of a national sample and focussed on New Haven, Connecticut, where the study was housed in the Divinity School of Yale University. [...] The report on the New Haven study was a published book[9] that led in turn to membership on committees at both national and state levels, of the National Council of Churches, a series of speeches at their meetings, and authorship of a chapter on "The Mass Media and the Churches" in a book by theologians and church administrators.[10] I had found an area where political activity had substantial freedom in the 1950s. Indeed, it was only at lectures in Divinity Schools where theologians were not afraid to discuss capitalism, socialism and communism frankly and with enthusiasm and self-confidence.

Two other studies in which I did not wear a political economist's cap began in the mid-50s. As a reader of *Variety*, I had noticed that Canada had set up a Royal Commission to study TV and radio broadcasting but I was surprised one day in March 1956 to receive a phone call from Robert M. Fowler, its chairman, [who] invited me to go to Montreal to discuss content analyses that they expected to need. He met me at the railroad station, took me to my hotel, and then to his club for dinner where we were joined by Paul Pelletier, secretary of the Royal Commission. Bob explained that I might think that he, being president of the Canadian Pulp and Paper Manufacturers Association, would be biased in favour of the private (commercial) broadcasters (a high proportion of which were newspaper-owned), as against the Canadian Broadcasting Corporation, but that he had no such bias. He then described a study he wanted me to plan and conduct that was to cover a week's programming of *all* Canadian TV and radio stations.

Before accepting, I made the same declaration that I had made to Schramm and Bowen before accepting the Illinois job, mentioning the American League for Peace and Democracy, the Washington Cooperative Bookstore, my subsequent characterization by the House Unamerican Activities Committee and the FBI as a "premature antifascist," and warned him that if his Commission became politically controversial he might be embarrassed by my being an ex-New Dealer. At that point he grinned and said, "'New Dealer' is not a dirty word in Canada. Besides, if you accept our invitation, you may find yourself embarrassed because I have been president of the Council on Pacific Relations, which was attacked by the Unamerican Activities committees, and I have tangled with Senator [William] Jenner, so the record is clear where I stand."

What followed was a very comfortable relationship. Using program logs rather than viewing/listening, we monitored all 33 TV stations then operating in Canada, a sample of U.S. border TV stations, and a sample of 62 radio stations for the week, 15–21 January 1956. The actual detailed analysis was done in Urbana with a staff built around my research assistant, F. Earle Barcus, who had helped me conduct some of the NAEB TV studies. I wrote chapter 3 of the Royal Commission's report ("The Programme Fare") and the Commission published a full analysis of our program findings as volume 2 of the report (*Programme Analysis*) and, amazingly, all our basic tabulations (some 267 pages, *Basic Tables*). Throughout, I was treated with sensitive courtesy and generosity and participated in executive sessions of the Commission, including the final session, when the plan and first draft of its report (done, to my surprise, by Fowler himself) was modestly presented and discussed. My experience with the Fowler Commission raised in my mind the possibility of migrating back to Canada. [...]

The other study was pure scientism: a controlled experiment to try to determine the effects on reading readiness of pre-school-age children in Urbana (where no TV service was then available), using the Disney Mickey Mouse Club TV program as stimulus. I designed the study and obtained a very small grant from the Educational TV-Radio Center to pay for it. We found significant effects. Having proved I could do logical positivist style "science" I was glad to drop it forever.

While my work as a political economist was not centre-stage stuff in the 1950s, it was not absent either. Looking back, several pieces are worth recalling. [...] [One] of those politico-economic pieces was an attack on the University of Chicago's ideological neo-conservative initiative to promote "market forces" as a preferable alternative to government regulation of the use of the electromagnetic radio spectrum. A University of Chicago Law School student published an article proposing that the market was preferable to government as regulator of the use of the radio spectrum, using the then current dispute between RCA and CBS over colour TV standards as a case in point. I replied with an article that I could not have improved 35 years later. Both papers[11] regularly appear in the bibliographies in the subsequent literature on this facet of the neo-conservative offensive against economic democracy.

[Another] of these major politico-economic efforts in the 1950s was my monograph on electronic communication.[12] It began with Robert A. Brady sending me a manuscript for criticism in 1955. He was writing on the development of standardization (as part of his work on the rationalization/bureaucratic movement) and its politico-economic consequences. I wrote to him, pointing out he had made certain erroneous statements about standardization in telegraphy and telephony. He replied with interest in my views as to how the manuscript should be modified. I then proposed a joint book in which I would deal with the standardization movement in telecommunications and he with other areas of industry. He suggested that we write our pieces independently. My first book-length treatment of the political economy of telecommunications was the result. It was published as a monograph by the Bureau of Economic and Business Research, University of Illinois, in 1957, and totally ignored by the economics journals, while getting a short favourable review in a sociology journal—that to my amusement praised it as a study in political sociology.

This report on my scholarly efforts in the first decade at Illinois may be concluded with the confession that by 1954–55, I was outlining a proposed book on communications in political economies. For a whole year, my research assistant, Earle Barcus, dug up and organized materials on the development of the book industry, in that context. When I considered Earle's work on it, I concluded that the book industry alone would require a whole volume; and that I was looking at a whole series of books on telegraphy, telephony, the radio spectrum, radio broadcasting, TV, cinema, and popular culture. Only then could I integrate the analysis into a single volume on the political economy of communications. I concluded that, at the pace at which I worked, and with the distractions to which such a commitment would be subject, it would be enough work for two lifetimes. I had only one and it was at about the half-century mark. I had better confine myself to exploratory studies in the political economy of communications, and try to interest future colleagues and students to pursue them. I returned to writing a comprehensive book only in the mid-1970s because by that time I had acquired sufficient theoretical command of the subject matter from a Marxist/Institutional perspective to be able to do it—and *Dependency Road* was the result. Considering that I had close contact with dozens of Ph.D. candidates and six research assistants in that first decade, I certainly did not inspire many towards work on the critical side of political-economy of communications, [but] two stand out: Thomas Guback and

Mike Kittross. [...] By a strange quirk of fate, [a] near-contemporary of mine [became interested in communications,] and the fire has not quieted. Herbert I. Schiller came to Illinois as a political economist concerned with resource industries. When I resigned from Illinois in 1963 to go to Canada, it left a vacant slot in the Illinois communications teaching program. Schiller filled it and within six years had capped a series of excellent critical journal articles with a book, *Mass Communication and American Empire,* that launched a career that established him among the world leaders in the field.

While the great bulk of my energies in that first decade at Urbana was directed at educational, religious, and political-economic studies, I did a small but continuing sequence of consulting studies for the business world. It was amusing, in light of the radio and TV industry attacks on my FCC work, to be approached by the TV broadcasters' trade association to design and conduct a massive study for them. It was shortly after our successful TV content analyses on behalf of educational TV. The TV and radio industries were in their perennial struggle with ASCAP [American Society of Composers, Authors and Publishers] over the amount of royalties to be paid for music used in broadcasts. [...] In late spring of 1953, counsel for the All-Industry Local TV Music License Committee asked me to design and conduct a content analysis intended to furnish information on certain aspects of the use of music by TV and radio stations in the U.S. The study as planned was meticulous (accuracy down to the hours, minutes *and seconds* was required). Music by category ("featured music," "theme music," "background and bridge music," "jingle music," and "public events, sports and parade music") was to be measured and expressed as percentages of station program time (as between "sustaining programs" or "commercial programs"). All of this was to be broken down according to the form and origin of the program (local-live; local-TV film; local-other film, network-cable, network-kine [kinescope recording]), and presented separately for four precisely defined time segments of the day and night, for both TV and AM radio stations. [...] Field work monitoring ten pairs of stations was completed in November–December 1953. At that point the parties settled the dispute, and we terminated further monitoring, analyzed the material we had obtained, and wrote a report for the Committee, summarizing the work done, in the event the issue was reopened in the future. [...]

My 1950 article raising questions about the various possible economic bases for TV indirectly led to my involvement in a controversy over Pay-TV in 1955. A Joint Committee representative of all major motion picture theatre associations engaged as counsel Marcus Cohen, a colleague and friend of mine from the staff of the FCC, and me as their economist. We prepared a brief and comments for the FCC proceeding to act on petitions from Paramount Pictures, Zenith Radio Corporation and Skiatron, all of which proposed to innovate Pay-TV on channels licensed for advertiser-sponsored TV, using various scrambling devices to police the systems. We did not oppose the use of cable to distribute movies or other program material to home TV receivers. But we opposed Pay-TV from TV broadcast stations because it would result in siphoning all mass audience TV programming through the tollgate of the descrambler, with no assurance that the resulting programs would be free of advertising material.[13]

There was also a consulting relationship, again involving the use of music copyright by ASCAP, but this time music broadcast by FM stations to retail institutions that blocked out the commercial announcements and used the programs as background music (1957–58). Like the All-Industry music study, this study was aborted by the settlement of the law suit between ASCAP and the FM background music people. Other consulting studies included a report for a nationwide Committee for Competitive Television (a committee of UHF TV broadcasters whose station potentials were suppressed by the combination of VHF station competition and the reluctance of TV set manufacturers to build receivers capable of receiving UHF TV signals, 1961–62). Eventually pressures such as that study prompted Congress to require TV manufacturers to build receivers capable of receiving both VHF and UHF signals; the FCC was too dominated by the VHF oligopolist to adopt such a rule.

I also dabbled in the business world. [...] It was when the FCC was about to lift the "freeze" on construction of new TV stations. Champaign-Urbana lay in rich corn-hog country, in the centre of a triangle the points of which were Chicago, Indianapolis and St. Louis. Each of those metropolitan areas had VHF TV stations, but their signals were not receivable in Urbana. Caught up in the freeze was one VHF TV channel assignment for Champaign-Urbana, for which the two newspapers in the twin cities had filed competitive applications. It was common knowledge that deep family rivalries prevented the two newspapers from merging (it was one of a tiny minority of communities with competitive newspaper ownerships). It seemed to me and my associates (Phil Zimmerly, an attorney; Don Holshouser, an electronics engineer at the University; and Vernon Fryburger, a recent Ph.D. in advertising from the University) that the chances were very good that we might be able to get our own commercial TV station—a UHF station—on the air and firmly established while the *News*

Gazette and the *Courier* newspapers were slugging out their competitive hearing for the lone VHF station. If we could get the UHF construction permit for Champaign-Urbana and get the station on the air promptly, the public would demand, and the TV set retailers would supply, receivers capable of receiving UHF signals (all channel receivers). The bait was the fact that we could offer programs that were sure audience-pleasers (the World Series, the Rose Bowl and Orange Bowl, and many drama and comedy programs that were being offered as the free lunch to build audiences for the TV broadcasting industry to sell to advertisers in what was properly called "the golden age" of TV programming). All that we needed were: (1) pledges of capital sufficient to build a slim-equity corporation that could buy its studio equipment, transmitter, tower and antenna on a long-term installment contract from equipment manufacturers eager to sell the stuff. We estimated that we needed no more than $175,000 to get the station operational because initially we would not be producing much local programming. (2) A good network contract, and I had excellent contacts for obtaining one. (3) A suitable antenna site, conforming to restrictions imposed by aviation authorities, and Holshouser was an expert on such matters. (4) Contacts with advertising agencies, and a rate card appropriate to our conditions, and Fryburger was our expert in that area. (5) A prestigious Washington law firm to represent us before the FCC, and I was sure I could get James Lawrence Fly, former FCC chairman, in that capacity. Don Zimmerly and I would co-ordinate and manage the promotion of the enterprise. Why did we want to do it? Mostly to prove we could. All of us wanted to have an independent and liberal political instrument. All of us needed additional income, but none of us aspired to be millionaires.

My particular job was to raise capital. I did obtain tentative pledges amounting to about $100,000 from prosperous professionals, retired farmers, and urban businessmen in Champaign. One of the most enthusiastic of these suggested that I talk to his banker in Champaign; if I could convince him it was a good investment, his other clients would hasten to pledge the needed capital. I had serious doubts about seeing the banker: he was too close to the local power structure in the twin cities. But after discussing the hazards with Phil Zimmerly, I did talk to him. He thought our plan was excellent, but said he was not an expert on TV and wanted to talk to some banker friends of his in St. Louis. If they concurred, he would back me 100%. He was going to see them the next day and promised to phone me the following day. I never did hear from him but two days later the local newspapers carried the story that the competitive VHF applications had been withdrawn by the two newspaper publishers. A new application for the vacant VHF channel had been filed by a new corporation in which the two newspapers jointly held stock. With amazing speed the FCC had approved the new application within two days of the withdrawal of the competitive applications. I was later told by a friend familiar with both the FCC and the way influence peddlers use their senators, that it had cost the promoter of the new TV station $50,000 to grease the necessary wheels via the office of Senator [Everett] Dirksen of Illinois.

What followed was anti-climactic and farcical. It would still be possible for our UHF station to prosper if it could match the construction schedule of the new VHF station. But we still needed the $175,000 capital, and I doubted that my pledges would hold up in the face of the successful local initiative for the VHF station. Through Palmer Weber, I met one Gerald Schaflander, an account executive for a Manhattan advertising agency. He promised to find the needed capital for our Champaign station. The next stage was hilarious. Gerald introduced me to Mr. B who in turn promised to find all the necessary capital. Then I would be invited to New York by Mr. B to meet Mr. C who would find all the capital we needed. And so on, until we reached a man (Norman Blankman) who "owned" the General Motors Building on Broadway. He did undertake to raise the capital. But by then, each of the line of "finders" claimed his slice of the equity capital. As the proposal finally jelled, it offered the original four promoters (us) only about 8% of the capital stock as compared to the 49% we originally expected. At that point, we four dropped the plan in disgust. We watched with wry amusement as Blankman's unopposed UHF application for the Urbana channel assignment (our proposal) was delayed for many months by an FBI investigation of its backers that had been caused by an anonymous telegram to the FCC, warning that subversive influences were behind our proposal. Circumstantial evidence pointed to the managing director of the new VHF permit-holder as the author of the telegram. [...]

Compared to the menace of nuclear and CBR [chemical, biological, radiological] weapons that the Military Industrial Complex was innovating in the 1950s, the existing peace movement was fragmented, stunted, and except in the case of the American Friends Service Committee, dedicated to individualistic pacifist actions. Practically every American was implicated directly or indirectly in the MIC, and an idealist approach that shunned massive institutional change was weak. Beginning in the 1950s, efforts to make war and weapons the focus of campaigns were directed at the MIC. Mass demonstrations, silent vigils at weapons sites, were stimulated by people from the AFSC. With non-violent penetration of military sites, peace activists began to learn the lessons of Ghandi's non-violent mass actions aimed directly at changes in policies and structures.

Jennie was one of three organizers of a Champaign-Urbana chapter of Women Strike for Peace in 1961. The next summer she participated in the demonstration at the Mercury test site near Las Vegas to protest atmospheric bomb testing. We both helped organize and participate in a mass meeting at McCormick Auditorium in Chicago in February 1963. She was particularly active during the week in October 1962, when nuclear war over the Cuban missile sites was imminent and both Super Powers were on "Red Alert." [...]

When we returned from our European sabbatical in January 1960, my political activity accelerated and took several lines. I gave an impassioned polemic, "The Spiral of Terror and the Mass Media" as a public lecture at the University of Pennsylvania in September 1960. Invitations to give variants of it took me to the Adult Educational Council in Chattanooga, Tennessee, that November, Michigan State University, and theological schools at Chicago, New York, Rochester, Louisville—the sponsoring institutions ranging from the United Church of Christ to Southern Baptist—in the next 12 months. I gave it to the American Psychiatric Association's national conference in Washington, D.C. in May 1961, and as university lectures at the University of Maryland (June 1961), and the University of Illinois (April 1962).

Less explicitly political was my work on communications satellites. I gave a paper on the social and political implications of the satellites at the American Sociological Association meetings in September 1961. And within the 12 months beginning June 1961, five journals in the U.S. published papers by me on the basic issue: who should own, control and use the satellites: transnational corporations [TNC], or some international public body, perhaps affiliated with the UN? The U.S. telecommunications carriers were determined to own and control them. The Bell System originally hoped to be the sole owner. Other telecommunications carriers objected as did the aerospace TNCs (Hughes, Lockheed, General Electric, Ford Motors), because they too wished to own and control them. The first battle site was the FCC, which obligingly obtained an anti-trust exemption and under its "aegis" brought the rival telecommunications carriers (ATT, ITT, Western Union, etc.) to accept a proposed consortium in which they would all participate to build, deploy, operate and own the first communication satellite. This was a strategic defeat for the aerospace TNCs who fueled the growing opposition. The Senate Subcommittee on Monopoly of the Select Committee on Small Business under Senator Long held public meetings. I testified as a Committee witness on 3 August 1961, and was gratified the next day to find on the front page of *The New York Times* a fair summary of my point of view [as well as] the testimony of the aerospace companies that were still unsatisfied with their pieces of the possible pie.

The upshot of the Long Subcommittee hearings was that the FCC-sponsored "consortium" was abandoned and the Kennedy administration turned the problem over to its National Aeronautics and Space Council. It proceeded to develop a plan that became the Act that created the Communications Satellite Corporation—a corporation with mixed private and public capital and control of the proposed satellite. It was understood that as a consolation prize the aerospace TNCs might enjoy some of the contracts to design and build the satellites and associated ground stations. It was a hectic summer. ATT, sparing no expense, pushed its development of a prototype communications satellite—naming it "Telstar"—and mounted an all-out public relations campaign in its support (including, as I noted at Disneyland that summer, a lavish display of how it would work). Telstar was nothing but a publicity gimmick—it was only a passive sphere lofted into a low orbit and therefore needing to be "tracked" by highly sophisticated ground stations if signals were to be bounced off it back to earth.

Meanwhile the Kennedy bill was submitted to the appropriate committees of both houses of Congress. That bill was opposed by the AFL-CIO (except for the Communications Workers of America whose president, Joseph Beirne, under Committee examination admitted that he sounded like a "company stooge"). Thirty-five members of Congress formed a bloc to try to prevent passage of the bill, and indeed there was evidence that the ruling circles in Washington were divided: the Deputy Assistant Secretary of State for International Organization Affairs in 1962 later wrote that U.S. national interest would be served by a communication satellite program under UN auspices in light of the promised co-operation between the USA and the USSR in such matters, saying "...it can help widen and deepen co-operation on a free-world basis. ..."[14] I deliberately avoided testifying before the Kennedy-dominated Congressional committees. I was, however, asked to testify before the Senate Subcommittee on Antitrust and Monopoly of the Committee of the Judiciary on 5 April 1962, where I tried to dispel the illusion, fostered by the bill's advocates, that the FCC would be an effective guardian of the public interest in the operation of the proposed COMSAT Corporation. The contending forces reached a climax in a filibuster in which the opponents of the bill hoped to rally support for its defeat in August 1962. Aides of Senator [Russell] Long asked me to write a speech lasting two hours that he used as part of his filibuster effort. [...]

The Administration forces were too strong, and the filibuster failed. At least, however, we had made a good fight. And the other nations, when they came to negotiate with COMSAT and the State Department, could know the weak spots in the U.S. position, for it must be remembered that the other nations *had* to acquiesce before COMSAT could operate at all. I tried to give them some help with an article in the International Telecommunications Union *Journal* in September 1962, which appeared at the time when COMSAT was beginning to try to sign them up to work with a U.S.-dominated international organization to own the satellites, outside the UN family. This line of work was the basis for my specializing in international communications thereafter.

There were other wings of that drive, even as early as 1961 when I obtained a substantial grant from the Graduate College to finance a study of post-1945 U.S. motion picture industry activity in Europe. I turned the money over to Thomas Guback, one of my most brilliant Ph.D. candidates, and an invaluable research assistant. Tom, having gleaned from past issues of *Variety* names and events in that area, went to Europe and interviewed the people named in the stories. After a year he returned to Illinois and wrote a thesis that was soon published. [...]

In the aftermath of the Cuban Crisis, Jennie and I evaluated our situation. The efforts of the peace movement to influence U.S. policy had proved ineffective—despite developing public opinion to halt atmospheric bomb testing (1962), underground testing was proceeding apace. The Kennedy government in the Bay of Pigs, the Berlin Wall crisis, and Missile Crisis had shown a belligerent stance. By contrast, the efforts of the Blacks to build an effective popular movement to tackle the problem of racial discrimination had been spectacularly successful (bus boycotts, sit-ins at public facilities, intensive lobbying [of] Congress and the White House, etc.). We concluded that, by comparison, we could do little as white middle class and professionals. And our assessment, in the midst of the intense campaign to build bomb shelters in backyards and basements, was pessimistic. [...]

Frazzled by the struggle over the Berlin Wall hysteria, Jennie and I began seriously considering leaving the U.S. If we and our two children were to die in a nuclear war, we didn't want to do it as Americans. I had been tempted by my work with the Fowler Royal Commission in Canada to look for a job in Canada. But we also considered New Zealand. [...] Jennie and I decided to make our own exploratory trip there, but our request for a visa was denied (I think because I had stated on the application for the visitor's visa that we wanted to consider settling there and the consulate checked me out with the FBI before denying the request). Why we did not consider migrating to Australia I don't know, because when I later visited that country in 1977, I wished we had moved there instead of to Canada. [...]

On a hot sunny day in late August 1963, two cars drove into Regina, Saskatchewan. One, a Ford, contained Jennie and our daughter, Carol, then a little more than two years old. In the other, a Mercedes, were our son, Pat, then nine, and me. We were arriving to start a new life in the city where I had been born, 56 years before. I was coming to be the first Chairman of the Division of the Social Sciences, University of Saskatchewan, Regina Campus. We were a close knit family. We had rejected the United States as a country to respect or to live in, and looked forward eagerly to a better life in Canada. [...]

Notes to "Autobiography, 'Chapter 4 . . .'"

1. From a report dated 10 October 1963, for the RCMP in Canada, p. 2.

2. Her evidence: Durr had publicly opposed the Truman Loyalty Investigation on First Amendment grounds. In opposing Hoover, Durr was trying to build a fifth column. As to me, I was one of Durr's "closest friends,...that Smythe and the Durrs have given political parties out in Virginia where colored women were invited." And all members of my Economics Division were union members.

3. Memorandum to the Board of Trustees, 9 September 1948.

4. Memorandum, 13 October 1948.

5. Those were the days before typewriters had proportional spacing and justified margins.

6. "The Bureau has in no manner been involved in the disputes which have arisen and the information which the Springfield Office has furnished the Bureau has come to that office through established reliable contacts and the Springfield Office is in no manner involved" (4 November 1985).

7. Schramm stayed at Illinois until 1955, and I wondered during Institute seminars on Institute members' research what his consulting work for the U.S. government was about because he never mentioned it. I was aware that his book, *The Reds Take a City* (1952), was based on interviews made while the U.S. armed forces were "liberating" Seoul, Korea, from North Korean control, and it was obvious that he could only do this as part of a military intelligence operation. Not until I began writing this chapter did I look up his record in *Who's Who in America.* There I learned that he had been a consultant on psychological warfare since 1943 and his clients were the War Department, the U.S. Air Force, the State Department, the U.S. Army Operations Research Office, the U.S. Information Agency, and the U.S. Department of Defense.

8. I learned soon after that Probst knew of my brush with the House Unamerican Activities Committee two years before and wanted "insurance" in the form of an unassailable co-director. Don Horton had worked for the Columbia Broadcasting System and

was an obvious choice. The irony of the situation lay in the fact that when the HUAC held public hearings to investigate the University of Chicago "pinkos" a year later, Horton, who had not been summoned by HUAC to appear, did appear on his own initiative to confess that while employed by CBS he had been a member of the Communist Party, whereas HUAC never openly attacked me.

9. Parker, Everett C., Barry, David W., and Smythe, Dallas W., *The Television-Radio Audience and Religion.* New York: Harper, 1955, 464 pp.

10. Rian, Edwin H. (ed.), *Christianity and World Revolution.* New York: Harper & Row, 1963.

11. Herzel, Leo, "'Public Interest' and the Market in Color Television Regulation," *The University of Chicago Law Review,* Vol. 18, 1951, pp. 802–816. Smythe, Dallas W., "Facing Facts About the Broadcast Business," published with a rejoinder by Leo Herzel, *The University of Chicago Law Review,* Vol. 20, No. 1, Autumn 1952, pp. 96–107.

12. Smythe, Dallas W., *The Structure and Policy of Electronic Communication.* Urbana: University of Illinois Press, 1957, 106 pp. Reprinted in Kittross, J. M. (ed.), *Documents in American Telecommunications Policy,* Vol. II. New York: Arno Press, 1975.

13. Although Jennie helped me with many research projects, the article that was published under both our names on this controversy was the only time we co-authored anything: Smythe, Dallas W., and Smythe, Jennie N., "The Menace of Pay-TV," *The Nation,* Vol. 186, No. 1, 4 January 1958, pp. 5–9. The *Comments* and *Reply* of the Joint Committee are in Federal Communications Commission, Docket No. 11279.

14. Gardner, Richard N., "Cooperation in Outer Space," *Foreign Affairs,* January 1963, p. 344, et seq.

2

"The most basic and subtle dimension of television's 'reality' is the commercial context in which it is presented"

EDITOR'S NOTE: In September 1948, the Federal Communications Commission announced it was halting temporarily the licensing of new television stations. The FCC wanted to sort out problems in its allocation plan, which it had said from the beginning would not permit a nationwide, competitive television system. The freeze on licensing was to last until April 1952, when the FCC issued its *Sixth Report and Order,* which changed certain technical characteristics of television channel allocations and opened the UHF portion of the spectrum to TV station assignments.

The *Report* also reserved a limited number of channels for noncommercial broadcasting, an achievement of no small dimension, given the demands and lobbying of private companies eager to mine the television bonanza. Dallas Smythe was instrumental in helping noncommercial educational interests establish the principle of channel reservations.

Prior to the licensing freeze commercial parties gobbled up television channels, and educational interests, suffering from minuscule financial resources, seemed destined to be shut out from the new medium. However, the freeze unintentionally provided noncommercial forces a window in which to get organized and make their case.

When Smythe was appointed to the Institute of Communications Research at the University of Illinois in 1948, he was asked by the National Association of Educational Broadcasters to become its director of studies. In that capacity he did content analyses of noncommercial radio stations. When the NAEB board met late in December 1950, it decided to participate in the FCC hearings on TV allocations and to petition for channel reservations to give educational broadcasters a chance to get stations on the air. To support its claim that noncommercial stations were in the public interest, the NAEB board needed evidence that profit-motivated stations were not providing a well-rounded program service. Smythe, who was at the board meeting, was called on to conduct a content analysis of commercial stations. He already had suggested the need for a noncommercial broadcasting service in "A National Policy on Television?" published in the Fall 1950 issue of *The Public Opinion Quarterly.*

As Smythe explained in his autobiography, he organized the study quickly. The board was meeting in New York City, which had seven commercial stations on the air, so that seemed the logical site for the content analysis. The first full week of January 1951 became the test period. Smythe and his principal collaborator, Donald Horton, presented their findings to the FCC later that month (see *Time* magazine, February 5, 1951). Over the opposition of commercial interests, the FCC, led by Commissioner Frieda Hennock, approved channel reservations for noncommercial broadcasting.

The January 1951 content analysis was so revealing that the NAEB sponsored further studies in New York, as well as in New Haven, Chicago, and Los Angeles, most of which Smythe worked on. These content analyses are the earliest and most extensive reports on TV programming and became the benchmark for further research by other scholars.

"Reality as Presented by Television," published in *The Public Opinion Quarterly,* Summer 1954, summarizes the content analyses of TV in New York (1951, 1952, and 1953), Los Angeles (1951), and New Haven (1952). Smythe liked this piece because he felt it was the best roundup of the studies he had done. For readers familiar only with his later, overtly political writings, this article is revealing because it shows Smythe's capacity for quantitative, empirical research. Yet he never passed beyond that into interpretation of the programming's messages. He explained, "It has always seemed to me that the textual approach, the exegesis of text in media, is an excellent way of devoting an awful lot of energy, from an awful lot of people, for no purpose worth a damn—because it ends up where it began, with speculation. It doesn't have any relation to behavior—and I'm not a behaviorist in the psychological special use of that term—but I do think that action is the name of the game. And I guess I should say, it doesn't give rise to any action, except

the waste of energy on the part of the people who do it. [...] If I'm silent [in 1991] on the work of the textualists, it's out of politeness or indifference on my part. I don't think they matter that much, except that I hate to see a lot of bright people wasting their time."

Reality as Presented by Television [1954]

REALITY IS TOO ELUSIVE a concept to be pinned down definitively. "Reality" as used here, refers to the body of knowledge or, to put it less ambiguously, the flow of representations of the human condition. In referring to the representations of the human condition which appear on television, we should understand what we mean by categories of television program content. Program material on television (and in other media) should be thought of as a group of symbols which serve as a medium of exchange between the mass media and the audience. This is a transactionist view of the relation between mass media content and audience members (and producers too). In this view of the communications process it is important to understand that audience members act on the program content. They take it and mold it in the image of their individual needs and values. In so doing they utilize not only the explicit layer of meaning in the content but also innumerable latent or contextual dimensions of meaning. On the producers' side, both contextual and explicit layers of meaning are consciously or unconsciously built into the content through the artistic process of program production. The produced program is, then, more than the sum of the program ingredients.

Content analysis may then be thought of as the study of the stimulus field for "effects" studies (of the audience), or as the study of the effects field for intention studies (of the production process). This frame of reference for content analysis has the implication that *all* of the categories relevant to studies of perception, motivation and learning are equally applicable in the measurement of content.

While the relevance of such a widely diversified kit of analytical categories seems indisputable, it presents a nice problem of choice and significance to the content analyst. This conception of content categories, if accepted,

---

This article was originally published in *The Public Opinion Quarterly*, volume 18, number 2 (Summer 1954), pp. 143–156, and is reprinted here with the permission of The University of Chicago Press.

supersedes in large part the formula of "manifest content" and the related notions of content analysis as formulated in the Lasswell tradition by Berelson, Lazarsfeld and others.[1] Seen in terms of the present frame of reference only a delusory validity inheres in their insistence on "objective," "quantitative" measurement of "manifest content."[2] The sterility of the alleged dichotomy between quantitative and qualitative, between objective and subjective content analysis is exposed. The validity (in the statistical sense) of a content analysis of modern poems (an event cited by Berelson as being at the non-manifest end of a continuum) may be as high as that of a content analysis of reports of train wrecks (an event cited as being at the manifest end of the continuum) provided in both cases meaningful categories have been selected to measure contextual and superficial meanings.

The significance of conceiving content categories as integrally related to perception, motivation and learning hypotheses is at once perceived in the present context where we are concerned with the interpretations of reality afforded by television. Before we may definitely say *what* the reality is we must make some assumptions as to the nature of the interpretive process by which audience members give their more or less unique meanings to the stimulus fields. To illustrate: a televised wrestling program is an ambiguous stimulus field. Superficially it is often thought of as a sport. If it is perceived as a sport, what representation of the human condition does it provide? An image of skillful use of trained bodies? An image of resplendent or gross sex aggression in a sexually deviant context, e.g. against a person of the same sex? An image of "natural man" competing for survival without the benefit of accepted law? Or "n" other interpretations of reality? But wrestling may also be perceived as a form of folk-drama. As such does it provide the material from which an audience member fills his need for a sardonic morality story in which virtue is cruelly mistreated by evil cunning until finally by superior skill virtue wins in the end? Or an image of a more cynical kind of how "you can't win by being honest"—where as more frequently happens, the villain who has "got by" with unfair practices in the end wins over the stubbornly honest hero? Still others in the audience perceive wrestling from yet another dimension of meaning. These embittered souls "know" wrestling is "fixed." They watch it as if to repeatedly build up their damaged self respect by observing that the ringside audience and presumably the "they" who are watching the match on television are inferior beings who believe wrestling to be "on the level."

Psychologists are still far from general agreement as to the nature of the interpretive process. While promising efforts towards developing such theory are underway, the fact is that as yet we don't have it. The program for research in content analysis seems to be to work with the categories in the more promising hypothetical theories. In this fashion we may move closer to valid measurements of reality as perceived by man, including quite incidentally, the reality presented by television.

Categories of Content

In the meantime what kinds of categories of television content are available to us? And what can we say about the reality they represent? One-week inventories of television programs have been conducted for all of the seven stations serving New York in January of each of the past three years. Similar studies were conducted in Los Angeles in May of 1951 and in New Haven in May of 1952. All of these studies were conducted with comparable techniques and concepts by the National Association of Educational Broadcasters.[3] Funds were provided by the Fund for Adult Education, an independent organization created by the Ford Foundation.

In each of these studies the total television program time was classified by program units into one or another of 17 major classes of programs. Of these, 15 major classes were classifications of programs designed for the general audience while two were used to identify domestic-interest programs and children's interest programs. Two of the seven sub-classes of domestic-interest programs are convertible into the 15 general interest program classes, while the same is true of five of the six sub-classes of children's programs. The remainder of the domestic- and children's-interest sub-classes are distinct from all of the 15 general-interest classes. Thus in these studies we have distinguished the following 21 different substantive classes of programs:

Classification	*Basis of Classification*
Drama (general and children's)	Form
Variety (general, domestic and children's)	Form
Dance	Form
Music (general and domestic)	Form
Personalities	Form
Quiz, stunts and contests (general and children)	Form
Fine arts	Substance
Sports	Substance
News	Form and Substance
Weather	Substance
Information (general and children's)	Form and Substance

Cooking	Substance
Arts, crafts and hobbies	Substance
Shopping and merchandise	Form
Personal care	Substance
Public issues	Substance
Public events	Substance
Public institutional	Source
Religion	Substance
Personal relations	Substance
Pre-school entertainment	Substance

Still in our quest for the nature of the reality presented by television, we should more closely examine the basis of these program classifications. Opposite each of the class titles are the author's interpretations of the basis of classification. Of the 21 substantive program classes, eleven seem to be based on substance, seven on form, two equally on form and substance and one on source. It will be noted that none are based on effects and hence there is no program class called educational.

The apparently heavy reliance on form in this classification structure relates only to the broad program classes. Of the nine program classes for which form is part or all of the basis of classification, six (drama, variety, music, quiz, stunt and contest, information, and news) are broken down into sub-classes, each of which is determined on the basis of substance or substance and form combined. Thus drama is sub-classified into domestic (serial and other), crime, western, action, comedy, romance, classics and other. Of the eleven classes based on substance only two are broken down into sub-classes. One of these, sports, is further broken down on the basis of substance (into spectator sports, participant sports and recreation, and sports news and interviews). The other, public issues, is broken into formal sub-classes (individual views and discussion and debate). The single major class which rests on the source of program material, public institutional (meaning programs presented in the interest of the armed forces, cerebral palsy drive, etc.), is also broken down into formal sub-classes (expository: dramatization).

The classification structure employed in the National Association of Educational Broadcasters' television studies has one other element. We have grouped the program classes into three broad *types* of programs: entertainment, information and orientation. The orientation-type group includes program classes the content of which is structured by the producers in terms of changing attitudes and values. Here we place religion, public issues, public institutional, public events, personal relations, and pre-school entertainment. The information-type group includes those program classes ostensibly devoted to conveying information—the raw material for building values and attitudes. In this group we place news, weather, and information for the general, the domestic, and the children audiences. The third group—the entertainment-type programs are pragmatically taken to be those whose ostensible purpose is only to amuse, entertain and otherwise occupy the attention of the audience.

This three-fold classification of goals is useful, but its limitations should be clearly understood. Information-type programs surely are also orientational and vice-versa. Entertainment-type programs surely color attitudes and values while imparting information of a sort. Conversely, orientation-type and information-type programs which fail to "entertain" and interest a suitable portion of the audience, will not long be telecast.

It is possible to relate this analysis of television program categories to our earlier observation that content categories must be thought of as related to categories and hypotheses relevant to perception, motivation, and learning. The relative crudeness of contemporary content analysis categories stands nakedly exposed as soon as we ask what relation there is between the material classified as, for instance, drama, or sports, and audience members' perceptual, need-value, or learning processes. We have experimental evidence that audience members re-structure the content of a given drama program to meet their own needs.[4] While this evidence is not directly to the present point it seems safe to assume that such re-structuring might result in some audience members perceiving a given drama as a crime drama, while others might perceive it as a domestic drama, others as an action drama, and so forth. No evidence has yet been reported as to whether such audience re-structuring bridges between two or more major classes of television content, as distinct from bridging between sub-classes of the same program class. For radio, quasi-clinical research on soap operas has established that for some housewives such programs are perceived as fictional drama, while for others they are perceived as personal relations programs, programs which seriously offer advice on interpersonal relations.[5] Further research is needed on the patterns of re-structuring which are practiced by audience members. It seems reasonable to assume that when such research has been conducted certain patterns will be found to represent central tendencies in content use but there will be a wide spread of variance over very different patterns found within the audience population. At such a time we might look forward to formulating program content categories which correspond both to the modal patterns and to the deviant patterns of use. Until that time, we will be forced to limp along with existing structures of content classification. For special purposes, such as those of propaganda analysts, the categories developed by Lasswell and his followers may work well empirically. For general research purposes, however, categories which have general theoretical significance are needed. Until they are available about all that can safely be said about the reality represented by television is that such and such quantities and proportions of television content fall into categories of program content which seem intuitively to represent reality in certain formal and substantive modes such as those presented above.

Macro-Analysis

If the conventional program categories are used, with full understanding of their theoretical weaknesses, it is still possible to state tentatively the reality dimensions of television program content. For this purpose the author draws on the NAEB program inventories referred to above. In thinking about the following material, however, it is well to keep in mind that here we are trying to say something significant about the totality of television program content—hence the subtitle "macro-analysis."

The most basic and subtle dimension of television's "reality" is the commercial context in which it is presented. All programs on commercial stations are presented in an implicitly commercial context which more or less subtly conditions even the non-advertising content of programs. In addition, advertising overtly occupies about one of every five minutes of big city television program time and about one of every four minutes of smaller-city program time. Roughly half of this advertising time consists of commercial announcements which interrupt the ostensible program content and the remainder includes commercial messages tightly integrated with program content and even commercial messages (such as those of the pitchmen) which *are* the program content.

On the dimension of program content (for advertising time being dispersed in program time is not itself a program class), entertainment-type programming constitutes three out of four minutes of total time. One might say that the chief element in television programs is the representation of reality as entertainment—a matter of diversion, of occupying time. Whatever the motives, whatever the real gratifications from its use, three-fourths of television programs are ostensibly "for fun." Information-type programs amount to slightly less than one-fifth of total program time. And orientation-type programs constitute the remainder or slightly more than one-twentieth of total time.

By all odds the largest program class is found in the entertainment-type group: drama. In the largest cities, drama seems to be increasing as a proportion of the growing volume of television program time. In 1951 it amounted to 33 per cent of total time in both New York and Los Angeles. A year later in New York it was 42 per cent. In 1953 it was 47 per cent. The largest single subclass of drama is crime drama which alone provided just short of one minute out of six of all television programs in New York in 1953. This type of drama seems to be increasing for it amounted to only one minute in ten of total program time in 1951 in New York. Western drama consistently occupies second place in New York with 7 per cent of total time in 1953. Domestic drama has shown the fastest rate of increase of all the sub-classes of drama in New York; in 1953 it amounted to 6 per cent as compared with 1 per cent in 1951.

Consistently in all the time segments of the week (we have divided the week into the children-hours, the adult-hours, the domestic-hours and the late-hours), drama is the most common type of television program. It provided 57 per cent of children-hour, 50 per cent of adult-hour, 33 per cent of domestic-hour, and 58 per cent of late-hour program fare in New York in 1953. The 57 per cent of children-hour time given to drama was 6 per cent drama aimed at the child audience and 51 per cent drama manifestly programmed for the general audience.

The limited data on small city television indicate that drama is relatively less important there than in the big cities—for in New Haven in 1952 drama amounted to only 29 per cent. There too, however, crime drama was the largest sub-class, followed by domestic drama.

Variety is the second largest class of program on television. In New York in 1953 this class provided 12 per cent of total program time; in New Haven it amounted to 20 per cent the year before. Four other classes of entertainment programs are important. These are quiz, stunt and contest programs (6 per cent in New York in 1953); sports events (6 per cent); music programs (4 per cent); and personalities programs (3 per cent). Larger proportions of sports events and quiz, stunts and contests were also found in New Haven.

Traces of certain time-honored entertainment categories were found in the television studies. Fine arts (painting, sculpture, architecture, etc.) and literature were represented in the 1953 New York study by 0.3 per cent of all program time, while 0.1 per cent of the time was devoted to the dance (ballet and other non–vaudeville style dancing). None of either of these classes were observed in Los Angeles or New Haven.

The American television-using public receives its information-type programs within one-fifth of television program time. The largest single class of program in this group is news (8 per cent in New York in 1953). About half of this time is given to news reports and the remainder to special events (such as [Dave] Garroway's and [Edward R.] Murrow's programs) and sports news and interviews. Under the heading of domestic information, cooking programs amount to 3 per cent, shopping and merchandising programs to 2 per cent, with less than 1 per cent in arts, crafts and hobbies and personal care programs. Information of a general sort for the whole audience (science, travel, etc.) is contained in about 2 per cent of program time, while similar programs aimed at the child audience amount to less than 1 per cent. Weather programs run consistently at about half of one per cent.

Orientation-type program classes are present in small quantities, as might be inferred from the fact that altogether they accounted for only 5 per cent of New York television time in 1953. Religion, with 1.7 per cent, was the largest of this group. Public issues programs followed closely with 1.5 per cent. Personal relations programs and pre-school entertainment programs were represented by less than 1 per cent of total time. There were no public events telecast in the 1953 New York study week, though traces had been observed in earlier years.

Quite apart from the evidence as to the nature of the reality represented through kinds of television programs, the National Association of Educational Broadcasters studies have also provided information concerning the extent to which the television world is characterized by violence. The number of acts and threats of violence in 85 per cent of television program time (all except sports, news, weather, public issues and public events programs) was measured and analyzed in New York and New Haven. For the full week in New York 3,421 acts and threats were observed in 1953—an increase of 15 per cent above 1952. This number equalled an average of 6.2 acts and threats per hour in 1953.

Entertainment-type programs accounted for 98 per cent of all acts and threats of violence. Drama itself contained 87 per cent of the total and averaged about 10 per hour. Crime drama contributed 28 per cent of all acts and threats; western drama contributed 23 per cent. The highest frequency of violence (in a whole drama subclass) was in westerns (17.0 acts or threats per hour). Children's drama had more than three times the frequency of violent acts and threats which was found in general audience drama (22.4 as against 6.0 per hour). The highest average was found in children's comedy drama (36.6 acts or threats per hour). About one-fourth of all acts and threats of violence were committed in a humorous context, and humorous violence was more common in programs for children than in those for the general audience. About one-sixth of the acts and threats were committed in the interest of "law and order." The proportion of "law and order" acts and threats was slightly higher in most program classes for programs designed for children than in those for the general audience.

The hours of the week when children might be expected to see most of their television had proportionately more violence than the rest of the week. In the children-hours in 1953 there was an average of 9.6 acts or threats per hour, as compared with 5 per hour in other hours.

The world presented to American television viewers has little participation from educational institutions. In the full week of programming from seven New York stations in 1953 there were 12 programs identified with recognized educational institutions for a total of less than 1 per cent of total program time.

Micro-Analysis

The 1953 New York television study included a detailed analysis of drama programs produced for television (as distinct from drama produced on film for other purposes). The purpose was to examine the nature of character stereotyping in these indigenous drama programs. A total of 476 characters in 86 drama programs representing more than one-fifth of all drama program time was studied.

In the world of indigenous television characters, males outnumbered females by a ratio of two to one. This population was concentrated in the age brackets of peak sexual attractiveness. The average age of all of them was 37, with males averaging 38 and females 33. More than half of the United States population was less than 20 and more than 50 years of age; yet only one-fourth of the television population was in those age brackets. Television drama heroes averaged 32 years of age, villains, 43, and supporting characters, 37. Men averaged older than women as heroes (34 as against 29) and as supporting characters. However, as villains the average woman was older than the man (47 as against 42). The hypothesis is reasonable that for television drama, heroes are identified with younger, attractive people, while villains are representative of the menace of an older generation with more social power but physically and sexually on the wane.

Indigenous television drama characters were white Americans four times out of five, with males being relatively more common among the white Americans and females being relatively more numerous among the characters of other nationalities. As compared with both their representation among Americans according to nationality of birth, and in the world population, Europeans were over-represented on indigenous television drama. American Negroes were two per cent of all characters. Russians (White) amounted to one per cent. There were no Jews identified. English were the most numerous non-American group (five per cent), followed by Italians (three per cent) and French (two per cent). Nationalities with more than one-third of the world population (India, Africa and Asia other than China) were entirely unrepresented in indigenous television drama, while China with 22 per cent of the world population provided only 0.2 per cent of the television population.

Proportionately more of the heroes were white Americans and fewer of them were villains than their numbers would lead one to expect on a chance basis. They were 83 per cent of the heroes but only 69 per cent of the villains. Europeans, who made up 14 per cent of the total television population, provided 10 per cent of the heroes but 24 per cent of the villains. A latent selective process seemed to favor American white males and females from other nationalities in the selection of heroes. Heroes from among American whites were males rather than females by a ratio of three to one, while heroes from other nationalities were females rather than males by a ratio of almost two to one. Such results could happen by chance less than two times in 100.

Television over-represented people who work as against people at home, and among those who work, managers and service personnel were most over-represented. Almost three-fourths of the television population was employed or employable, while this was true of only two-fifths of the United States population. Television reflects a culture which values highly managerial and service activities and rates low physical production work. Professionals, managers, officials and proprietors, service workers and private household workers were 51 per cent of the television population but only 11 per cent of the United States population.

The largest single occupation for women in the television world, as in the real world, was that of housewife, and in this pursuit, women on television were only slightly under-represented as compared to the whole population (37 per cent as against 42 per cent). The under-representation on television of the non-labor-force population, both males and females, lay in the children, the superannuated, the institutionalized, and the like.

More television villains than heroes were employed or employable. The chances of a villain being in the labor force were more than six to one, while for a hero the chances were a little more than two to one. Housewives were less after [sic—often?] shown as villains than were women in the labor force, while they as well as other non-labor force women had much better chances of appearing as heroes than did women who worked or were employable.

Four-fifths of all television characters were law-abiding, one-fifth were law-breakers. In each major occupational category men were portrayed as more law-abiding than women. However, because men outnumbered women, especially in the labor force, and because the employed persons were much more often shown as law-breakers than those not in the labor force, in the aggregate men on television were more often pictured as law-breakers than were women.

It is interesting, in the light of the 1952 presidential campaign, to note that in television drama public officials are shown as more respectful of law than were private business officials. Of the public officers (including politicians) 92 per cent were shown as law-abiding, as compared with 73 per cent of the legitimate businessmen.

American white characters were slightly more law-abiding than were other television characters. The largest proportions of law-breakers were found among Italians (44 per cent were law-abiding). The small number of Negroes, American Indians, Latin Americans, Irish, Danish, Norwegian, Scottish, and Polynesians were all law-abiding.

Of all television characters, 94 per cent appeared to be normal in health and sanity. In the once-a-week dramas, 95 per cent of the characters were normal while in the serial dramas this was true of 91 per cent. Over-all, 2.5 per cent of the characters were "unhealthy," while 2.1 per cent were insane. The once-a-week characters were less frequently "unhealthy" than were serial characters (2.4 per cent as against 2.9), and less often insane (1.5 per cent as against 5.8). One per cent of the characters were observed to be super-healthy ("brimming over with good health, energy"). These "supermen" were all male and all found in once-a-week drama.

For the first time in the same study it was possible to approach the identification of stereotypical characteristics through the use of a semantic differential. This method involves measuring character portrayal on evaluative, potency and activity seven-point scales where the object is to determine the inward meaning of the portrayals—the connotative as distinct from the denotative content.[6] Each of the characters observed in the indigenous television drama in 1953 was measured by as many as three observers independently. Analysis of these scale ratings permitted determination of both the mean ratings for different groups of television characters (e.g. determinations of the stereotypes), and of variance from the average ratings (e.g. determination of degree of stereotyping).

The average pattern of character or personality stereotype of all heroes was found to correspond closely with the values held by our culture, while that for villains was generally antithetical to those values. The potency and activity attributes of the characters of villains were, however, not too different from those of heroes. Male heroes were closer to community ideals than were female heroes, but further from these ideals when they were villains. As between American-white and other nationality and race groups, American-white males, when they were heroes, were pictured as closer to the community ideals than were the others. This was especially true of the potency and activity scales. Conversely, as villains, foreign and minority race males were shown as more potent and active than were American-whites. Females from the other nationality-race groups, when they were heroes, had potency and activity attributes approaching in magnitude those of the American-white male heroes. American-white women, as heroes, fell far short of the other women in these respects. No significant character difference appeared between the two groups of women as villains.

Public officers were pictured as approximating socially desired value standards more closely than executives of legitimate businesses, who in turn were closer to them than executives of illegal businesses. On the potency and activity scales, illegal business executives were not too different from public officers and legitimate businessmen. The second echelon under each of these groups was presented on television in character values more consonant with the prevailing mores than was the top echelon, although they were less positive on the potency and activity scales. Each of the three groups in the second echelon bore the same general relation to each other as did their superior officers in the top echelon. Farmers and farm managers were typically represented [as] closer to the community ideal of personality values than were the legitimate business executives, as well as more positive on the potency and activity scales.

Among the professional groups shown on television, the journalists were generally closer to community ideals and scientists generally most distant from them in character attributes. Teachers were typically shown as the cleanest, kindest, and fairest of the professional groups, while journalists were the most honest. Scientists were portrayed as the least honest, least kind and most unfair, while lawyers were shown as the dirtiest of the character types. On the potency scales journalists were the sharpest, strongest and quickest, while lawyers were the hardest. Teachers were pictured as the weakest, softest and slowest, while lawyers were the dullest of the professional character types.

Housewives were shown with personality patterns basically like those of female American heroes, although the former were slightly less honest, clean, and fair, and more kind, strong, sharp, hard and quick than were those heroes. On all valuative scales, private household workers were farther from community ideals than were the housewives, and they were distinguished for the degree of dullness and softness of their characters. The unemployed (but employable) were endowed with less honesty and cleanness than any other non-criminal group and were the weakest of all groups, though rated slightly positive on the potency and activity scales.

The concentration of the true character ratings (after extracting variations due to monitors) around the means, i.e. the amount of stereotyping, was greater for male American-white heroes than for male American-white villains, and for heroes of both sexes from other nationality and racial groups. All male villains were less stereotyped than were female villains and heroes of both sexes. No significant difference existed between the amount of stereotyping for *all* heroes and *all* villains.

The concentration of character variations around the mean was found to be the greatest in the journalists portrayed on New York television, and least for the unemployed (but employable) and doctors. Lawyers, teachers, and law-enforcement officers were also highly stereotyped.

The semantic differential and sociometric measurements which were used in the 1953 television study in New York are equally applicable to other media of communication. As other studies extend our knowledge of the characteristics of mass media content, studies of the audience members and studies of content may be brought together. As one promising approach to this state of affairs we look forward to application of the semantic differential to audience members. We can ask them to rate characters and program material on *the same scales* as are employed in content analysis. By comparison of the sociometric and psychological groups of the audience with information about mass media content, we will then better understand how and for what purpose what kinds of audience members use what dimensions of content. That way seems to be the road to an adequate comprehension of the reality presented by our mass media of communications, including television.

Notes to "Reality as Presented by Television"

1. See, for instance, Bernard J. Berelson, *Content Analysis in Communications Research* (Glencoe, Illinois: The Free Press, 1952).

2. My objections to their formulations have much in common with those of S. Kracauer, "The Challenge of Qualitative Content Analysis," *Public Opinion Quarterly*, Winter, 1952–53, pp. 631–642.

3. Dallas W. Smythe and Angus Campbell, *Los Angeles Television, May 23–29, 1951* (Urbana: National Association of Educational Broadcasters, 1951); Dallas W. Smythe, with introduction by Robert K. Merton, *New York Television, January 4–10, 1951–1952* (Urbana: National Association of Educational Broadcasters, 1952); Dallas W. Smythe, *New Haven Television, May 15–21, 1952* (Urbana: National Association of Educational Broadcasters, 1952); Dallas W. Smythe, *Three Years of New York Television, 1951–1953* (Urbana: National Association of Educational Broadcasters, 1953). In addition one study was conducted with non-comparable concepts: Donald Horton, Hans O. Mauksch, and Kurt Lang, *Chicago Summer Television, July 30–August 5, 1951* (Urbana: National Association of Educational Broadcasters, 1952).

4. *The Quarterly of Film, Radio and Television* published an excellent annotated bibliography in its vol. 6, Spring, 1952 issue. See pp. 284–292 especially.

5. See particularly the studies by W. Lloyd Warner and William E. Henry, and Herta Herzog summarized in the bibliography referred to in note 4.

6. Charles E. Osgood and George J. Suci, "A Measure of Relation Determined by Both Mean Difference and Profile Information," *Psychological Bulletin*, vol. 49, no. 3, pp. 251–262, May 1952; Charles E. Osgood, "The Nature and Measurement of Meaning," *Psychological Bulletin*, vol. 49, no. 3, pp. 197–237, May 1952.

3

"The intellectuals are evidently mistaken in expecting pay-TV to serve their unique needs"

EDITOR'S NOTE: When the FCC halted the licensing of TV stations from September 1948 to April 1952, Dallas Smythe used the period to raise questions about how the new medium should develop, especially how it should be financed. "A National Policy on Television?" published in the Fall 1950 issue of *The Public Opinion Quarterly,* examined sources of support other than advertising and, as Smythe points out in his autobiography, indirectly led to his involvement in the pay-TV controversy. Motion picture theatre interests engaged Smythe to prepare a study opposing the use of commercial TV channels for pay-TV. The FCC in the mid-1950s was considering petitions from several parties that wanted to launch pay-TV on those channels. The signals were to be scrambled, and subscribers would need decoders to receive the broadcasts.

Carey McWilliams, a close friend of Smythe's, was then editor of *The Nation,* a liberal-left magazine that frequently dealt with Cold War issues and public policy matters in terms accessible to nonspecialists. McWilliams encouraged Smythe to write a piece for *The Nation* that would demonstrate the dangers of pay-TV.

In the 1950s intellectuals scoffed at commercial television, as they had earlier at radio, for the abysmal level of its content. They believed advertising was the root of the problem and that if it could be gotten rid of, broadcasting content automatically would improve. Pay-TV, directly responsive to consumers, would be the answer, many intellectuals felt. This myopic view neglected to address the institutional matter of ownership—that pay-TV, like commercial TV, would be situated in the capitalist sector of the economy, privately owned and profit-driven, and that *this* would condition the kind of program service. Smythe argued that the revenue potential of pay-TV ultimately would siphon programs from commercial TV, and the public would wind up paying directly for a broadcasting service it had been receiving without additional cost. Pay-TV companies, furthermore, did not guarantee that their programs would be transmitted without advertising spots.

Although "Menace of Pay-TV" was written more than three decades ago, the assessment still is worth considering. For example, pay-TV (like other cable services) has had a significant impact on commercial networks and stations by siphoning recent theatrical films. As well, the network audience has been diluted, which has adversely affected network advertising revenue. This revenue loss has translated into employee layoffs at the networks, a keener search for cheaply made programs, and ever greater obsessions with efficiency and with producing just the right kinds of audiences advertisers want to buy. Cable networks, of course, carry advertising.

Jennie Smythe co-authored "Menace of Pay-TV." This was the only time she received credit for collaboration, even though, as Dallas Smythe told me, "she contributed via discussions to many of my articles, e.g., 'After Bicycles, What?' and 'Interview at Shanghai Advertising Corporation,'" the latter stemming from their visit to China in 1979. Jennie helped with many research projects and also worked closely with Dallas on speeches and papers dealing with the Cold War, the military-industrial complex, and nuclear weapons.

Menace of Pay-TV [1958]

One of the most skillfully conducted public-relations campaigns of modern times has brought pay-TV to the verge of acceptance. It is understandable that support for pay-TV should come from those whose self-interest would be served by it—namely, the writers, actors, directors and front offices of Hollywood and Broadway. For them and for sports

---

This article, "The Menace of Pay-TV," by Dallas W. Smythe and Jennie N. Smythe, *The Nation*, January 4, 1958 (pp. 5–9), is reprinted with permission from *The Nation*.

promoters, the attraction is the tremendous revenue potential of box offices located in the living rooms of millions of American families who, on the average, spend five hours a day watching TV.

But without the support or at least friendly neutrality of intellectuals, pay-TV would have made little headway. Intellectuals, however, have fallen easy prey to the pay-TV merchants. This is regrettable on two counts. First, they have not pursued their own self-interest; second, they have failed to recognize their social responsibility for the welfare of the larger population of less education and sophistication.

Let us examine the self-interest of intellectuals, who are genuinely frustrated in their need for mature, original entertainment. They are offended by repetitive, formula-ridden material and resent being manipulated and cajoled by advertising. It is good that they feel this way. But such is their despair with the current product that they have grasped at the first alternative which seemed to promise Bach, Beethoven and Bartok concerts and "Broadway plays"—especially when it is suggested that pay-TV would be free of crass commercial announcements.

Looking only at the absolute economics of pay-TV, the "eggheads" are impressed by what they think are the advantages of the "box office" approach. It might be profitable, they say, for a pay-TV operator to broadcast a chamber music concert free of advertising. Because they would like to watch such a program, for a price, they conclude that pay-TV would be a worthwhile *addition* to free TV. Let us, so they argue, pay for what we like; others could continue to enjoy free the $64,000 Question.

This line of reasoning has been skillfully spread by the pay-TV promoters. The facts, however, don't square with it. First of all, there is good reason to suppose that pay-TV would carry advertising just as does free TV. As *Life* said (on October 14): "Once [pay-TV] gains wide acceptance, what is to prevent a franchise-holder from selling commercial time?" Occasionally, an advertising man says it more directly. William Lewis, president of Kenyon and Eckhardt, recently told a broadcasters' club in Boston: "There is no reason why TV, like the print media, should not receive income both from commercial interests and the general public which the producers are serving."

Deprived of the lure of no-advertising, the intellectual falls back to what he thinks is more secure ground. Won't pay-TV provide finer entertainment than free TV? To this there are answers on several levels. One is: Look at the movies! There is no reason why even a big movie theatre couldn't cover its cost and make a profit by offering a film version of a La Scala performance. But how often do they?

The more basic answer is that in our commercial culture, a box office attached to a mass-production line provides a mass-produced product. And pay-TV, when it uses the air waves, will have a built-in mass-production line just as does free TV. After all, the reason which makes the use of the air waves more attractive than wire lines to pay-TV promoters is the cheapness with which a broadcast signal can reach millions of homes.

"But," you may say, "if it is possible to broadcast profitably programs which would satisfy a minority audience, why would this not be done on pay-TV?" The answer is the same as that which must be given to the parallel question concerning the automobile industry. Why does Detroit not make cars like those European imports which appeal to minority automobile tastes because of their smallness, maneuverability and economy? Detroit could do so, and at a profit. The explanation lies at the root of mass production. Mass production is always concentrated on the product where the *largest* profit will be earned. Catering to a minority may yield a profit; it can never yield the largest profit.

Pay-TV may offer some genuinely cultural programs, especially at the outset, in order to cultivate the support of intellectuals who, by their acceptance of the new idea, may help to "sell" it to the general public. It may also offer cultural programs as "loss leaders" to ward off public criticism and control. But the staple article which pay-TV will offer will be determined, as one of its chief promoters frankly says, by the fact that "the arithmetic of low-cost mass distribution will also apply to subscription television."

If pay-TV offers—as it must under existing conditions—much the same sort of fare as is now provided by free TV, what happens to the latter? Will the public want to pay to see the same kind of entertainment they now receive free? Obviously not. But the conclusion does not follow that pay-TV will have to offer substantially different fare in order to be successful. *A more realistic conclusion is that the public will be given no choice but to pay for substantially the same thing it now receives free.* For talent would rapidly be removed from free TV by the inexorable process of the market-place. The clearest example is offered by sports programs. Already the Los Angeles Dodgers and the San Francisco Giants are unavailable for free TV, because the broadcast rights to their games have been bought by pay-TV promoters. Here the mere prospect (not the actuality) of pay-TV is depriving free TV of talent. As soon as sports events begin to be broadcast on pay-TV, they will be preempted generally for this market. The bait held out to the public by pay-TV promoters is that the occasional sporting event—a championship prize fight, for instance—not now available to free TV, would be brought to the living room screen for a reasonable price. While the cost of viewing these occasional events may be nominal, the *real* price will be the aggregate pay-TV expenditure for watching all the football, baseball, tennis, horse racing, basketball, golf and other sports which are now available free. Moreover, even the *radio* broadcast of sports events will stop in order to protect the market for pay-TV broadcasts.

As for sports, so with the most popular TV dramatic shows. *Gunsmoke* now is the most widely watched regular TV program. Its star (James Arness), its producer and its writers will inevitably withdraw from free TV if larger profits are in prospect from pay-TV. This siphoning process follows from the fact that pay-TV will be in a position to outbid free broadcasting for talent. For example, in the spring of 1957, *Gunsmoke* was watched in more than 13.5 million homes each week. The sponsors paid $38,000 for talent and $52,200 for station time, or a total of $90,200 per week. Now assume that only one-fourth, or 3,385,000, of the 13.5 million families who watched *Gunsmoke* weekly were equipped to receive pay-TV. Assume that only one-fourth, or 846,000, of the equipped homes bought *Gunsmoke* (on free TV the show had an audience rating of 36 per cent). Assume that the very moderate price of 25 cents was paid per viewing. This would yield a weekly gross of $212,000. Our assumptions have been conservative; yet the result is a gross pay-TV revenue more than twice as large as the present total cost to its sponsors of the free program.

The crushing effect of pay-TV on free TV is discernible in other directions. Only about twenty cities in the United States have four or more TV stations. In all other cities, and in virtually all rural areas, the substitution of pay for free TV programs would preclude one or more of the networks from bringing free TV programs to the stations. The clearest illustration of this would be in the one-station community, where each hour of pay-TV operation would black out free TV for that hour. Free TV network programming depends on the availability of station time; this is what the networks basically sell to advertisers. If pay-TV spreads to the three-or-less-TV-station communities, it will cripple networks both because of station unavailability and declining audiences. Advertisers will turn from free to pay-TV or to other media. In addition to diverting programs, therefore, pay-TV would dry up the economic support of free TV. Faced with this prospect, the management of free TV networks would themselves go over to pay-TV.

What, then, do viewers stand to gain from pay-TV? Championship prize fights and perhaps some "first run" movies would become available to "middle-brow" and "low-brow" viewers. For the "eggheads," the main attraction would be the largely illusory expectation of genuinely cultural programs. To gratify this expectation, the egghead supporters of pay-TV seem ready to deprive the general public not only of the trite programs on free TV, but of the many finer programs which it also affords. Leaving aside entertainment such as *Peter Pan, Blithe Spirit,* NBC opera, etc., it is to be noted that free TV does produce *See It Now* and other programs in the area of public affairs, as well as many non-entertainment shows of outstanding value. Pay-TV could not be expected to provide as much of this kind of material. As CBS put it, "While there are some advertisers who are interested in institutional advertising [to support such programs], there would be no coin-machine operators interested in institutional dimes when they can collect commercial dollars." In this connection the performance of the motion-picture theatres is revealing evidence of the almost total disinterest of box-office operators in cultural material for minority audiences. The intellectuals are evidently mistaken in expecting pay-TV to serve their unique needs.

They have also been oblivious to the hardship pay-TV would bring to the low-income part of the population. To say, as some do, that the "low-" and "middle-brow" groups needn't be deprived of their entertainment for they can buy it on pay-TV, is to reveal the essential vice of pay-TV. For it cynically assumes that what is for the low-income viewer a "free good" should be made over into an "economic good." Presently the total direct cost to the viewer of free TV is the sum of his set depreciation, service calls, replacement parts and electric-power—a total of about $80 per annum. That advertising (on TV and otherwise) may indirectly be paid for by the consumer is irrelevant. The consumers' cost of living would not be reduced by pay-TV.

Well over half of all TV homes have incomes of less than $5,000. And *Life's* consumer-expenditure study in 1956 shows that the total expenditure for recreation and recreation equipment in households with incomes from $4,000 to $4,999 was $233—with substantially small amounts for those with less income. The average household now spends much less than $100 a year on motion-picture attendance. No one knows just how much the middle- and lower-income groups would spend on pay-TV. But, with payment by the program, the individual and family pressures might well result in larger total expenditures on pay-TV than now go for TV set maintenance and depreciation plus motion-picture attendance. If as little as 25 cents an hour were paid for only half of the present average TV viewing time (more than five hours per day), the annual cost would be $228. Unless the intellectuals adopt a "let 'em eat cake" point of view, they must be concerned over the potential hardship pay-TV would visit on the non-egghead population.

If viewers stand to lose from pay-TV, who stands to gain from it? The answer is that the holders of the patents on the unscrambling devices necessary for pay-TV expect fabulous profits. Telemeter, a Paramount subsidiary, estimated two years ago that total pay-TV revenue in 1960 would be about $4.5 billion, assuming 75 per cent conversion and weekly payments per home of $2.50 (or a mere 36 cents a day). Of this total, perhaps one-third would go to the pay-TV operator as distinct from the TV *station* and the program producer.

Pay-TV would create an industry rivaling in size the Bell System, and it would inevitably be a monopoly. While presently three different systems are proposed, it is inconceivable that more than one would be authorized for commercial development in a country with as much population mobility as ours, and in light of the tradition of standardized engineering specifications for broadcast services. According to all three principal promoters, the operating plan would be like this: The patent-holder would license a local pay-TV operator. This operator, under the control of the patent-holder, would sell or rent encoding and decoding equipment to station viewers. He would buy time on the stations, determine what pay programs to broadcast, promote the business and collect revenues from the public. He would also pay license fees to the patent-holder. The patent-holder would establish a program distribution company which would become a nation-wide pay-TV program network.

Control of program policy and the profits which would go with a nation-wide monopoly of program *distribution* would thus rest with the patent-holder. It is quite correct to say, as pay-TV promoters often do, that the promoters would *not* monopolize program production. The program network would probably buy and distribute a substantial proportion of "independently produced" program material. But the pay-TV program monopoly would have the power to determine what Americans can view—and the unrestricted power to set prices as it pleased. In contrast to the stark monopoly of program distribution which pay-TV involves, the shortcomings of the three free TV networks look to many people like a relatively beneficent oligopoly.

We pointed out earlier that, where commercial stations are concerned, public service or educational material would have less chance than on free TV. What about educational stations? If the cost of education is to be assessed against the beneficiary of the education, educational TV stations could follow the pattern of private schools (except for the fact that the profit for the pay-TV patent-holder has no precedent in private schools). However, in view of the tax-supported public education tradition and the fact that the TV waves are public property, there is serious objection to placing a price tag on educational broadcasting. The objection is based on the fact that those who stand to benefit most from it may well be those least able to pay and least aware of the benefits to be derived from educational broadcasts.

Pay-TV would not help the UHF-TV stations. Their problems are soluble by more direct means. Nor is it likely that pay-TV will result in many "art theatre" type of stations.

The principal economic characteristic of an "art theatre" is its relatively small physical plant costs and seating capacity, both conducive to long and profitable "runs" when word-of-mouth advertising produces a sustained audience flow. By its very nature, a TV station has a mass-market capacity for viewers. And the pressures, both from the mass-market side and from the patent-holder side, would make an "art-theatre" pay-TV station an anomaly.

The push for pay-TV has been chiefly directed toward pay-TV on the airwaves. But while its promoters have pressed for the use of broadcast pay-TV, a less noticed development has provided an alternative more palatable to the public. Wired pay-TV has been planned for by some ninety-six applicants for franchises in some sixty-six cities. For quite different reasons, motion-picture theatre interests and two of the three promoters of broadcast pay-TV have pushed it. Wired TV involves distributing programs from a central location by telephone cables directly to the TV receiver in the home. It does not displace any broadcast station because there are enough unused channels in every TV receiver to permit the reception of both free and wired pay-programs.

Since last September, the first actual wired TV system has been operating in Bartlesville, Oklahoma, where twenty-six different films are delivered for twelve hours a day for a monthly price of $9.50 per home. Half of these films are first-run and half re-runs. Whether charged for on a monthly or per-attraction basis, the same plan is contemplated for sports as well as movies. Skiatron (which has bought TV rights for both the Dodgers and the Giants) and Paramount's Telemeter have been active in obtaining franchises and making other preparations for using wired TV.

Wired TV has many advantages for the public as compared with broadcast pay-TV. It would offer competition to free TV without preempting the channels or disrupting the structure of station-network relations. Because cables can carry not one but three or four simultaneous programs, wired

TV offers much more service than broadcast pay-TV. The technical quality of wired TV pictures is superior to that of broadcast TV. Wired TV requires no complex encoding or decoding equipment and avoids the many problems created by building a decoder into the home receiver. It would thus avoid the tendency towards monopoly in TV-set maintenance which broadcast pay-TV threatens. Possibly most attractive is the fact that whereas a nation-wide program monopoly would rest on the patents for encoder-decoder equipment for broadcast pay-TV, the equipment for wired TV is readily available, requires no exclusive patents and would permit competition. While capital investment for both wired and broadcast pay-TV will be enormous, the public would have to put up directly a large part of the sums required for broadcast pay-TV (through purchase and installation charges for decoders), while the promoters of wired TV would have to bear the risks attending the large investment in cable lines. While wired TV would compete for program material against free TV, there would not be the fast siphoning process which preemption of broadcast channels would trigger. As a result of the greater cost of wire-line operation, competition for program material would also be reduced by a lesser ability to outbid free TV. And the public, especially the low-income public, would be protected considerably against the dangers of a wired TV monopoly by the continued availability of free TV service.

The Bartlesville wired TV experiment already demonstrates that the airwaves are not necessary for pay-TV. Indeed, by developing wired TV plans of their own, two of the three chief promoters of broadcast pay-TV have undercut the case for it. Congressman [Emanuel] Celler and others have introduced bills to prohibit the use of broadcast frequencies for pay-TV. Nevertheless, in October, the Federal Communications Commission authorized trials of broadcast pay-TV over a three-year period, with the proviso that no licenses would be granted prior to March, 1958. These trials would be limited to some twenty cities, each having four or more TV stations. Hearings are scheduled on the Celler bill this month and it is quite possible that Congressional action may stop the broadcast pay-TV trials before they can be started.

Those concerned with a resolution of the pay-TV issue in the public interest must rely on Congress. For the FCC has abdicated its responsibility. It has not held an evidentiary hearing, without which no equivalent revolutionary change has ever previously been authorized in *any* broadcast service. Instead, it has given a green light for "experiments" which Congressman Celler correctly says must "be regarded as potential commitment to a course from which there may be no return."

4

"Apply revenue from the rental of frequencies to commercial broadcasters to the support of a public service broadcasting agency"

Editor's Note: Dallas Smythe's experience on the Federal Communications Commission led him to be an outspoken critic of broadcasting policy and the broadcasting industry. In the 1950s, 1960s, and even later, he struggled with the issue of private ownership of the medium and constantly pointed to alternative forms of ownership, organization, and finance. He was a realist in that he knew broadcasting in the United States could never be taken out of the capitalist sector, so he searched for ways of strengthening oppositional forms and supporting broadcast organizations that met commercial forces head on.

"A National Policy on Television?" in the Fall 1950 issue of *The Public Opinion Quarterly* was the first piece he did at Illinois "in which I squared off and said something about policy"—a piece "which I doubt if anybody has read except the people subscribing to it [*POQ*] at the time." Yet he did receive telephone calls from some radio attorneys in Washington who were familiar with it. Two years after the *POQ* piece, Smythe responded in *The University of Chicago Law Review* to an article in a previous issue calling for market forces as a substitute for the public interest standards established by the Communications Act of 1934. Smythe challenged this "ideological neo-conservative initiative" and branded it an "offensive against economic democracy."

Perhaps his final attention to institutional aspects of broadcasting in the United States was a short text he wrote in April 1960, "Outline of a Proposal for Competitive U.S. Broadcast Systems." It was mimeographed and distributed to the few students in his graduate course, Political Economy of Communications. For Smythe, "competitive" did not mean two or more commercial stations in one community but two or more stations under different *forms* of ownership. His plan to have commercial broadcasters bid for licenses is interesting, given recent FCC policy on the cellular telephone lottery and Bush administration plans to auction spectrum space for commercial development. (The status of these plans under President Clinton remains unclear.) Smythe also offered a solution to the perennial problem of funding public broadcasting. That solution has never been acted upon, and as a result public broadcasting has drifted closer and closer to the commercial sector.

Smythe's "Outline" was never published. "I never went back and fleshed it out," he told me. "I didn't have time. I was in a period when I was in a spate of writing all sorts of stuff after coming back from that sabbatical [in Europe]. That was right during the quiz show scandals, too." Smythe recognized some problems with the "Outline," such as what would happen in a community with but one TV channel allocated. "I was trying to protect the noncommercial people, the public service people. [...] But then ... you could never keep the commercial guys from exercising political power to get that frequency assigned to the commercial sector."

Broadcasting has long since been deregulated, of course. The public interest standard seems these days just a faint reminder of a time when there was some slight check on rampant institutionalized greed. The public service responsibility of licensees seems today a very modest rein on the total capture of broadcasting by the naked commercialism of the profit-driven sector. Smythe's proposal "to free commercial broadcasters of legal responsibility under the Communications Act to serve the public interest" has been achieved, unfortunately without the revenue base for public broadcasting.

Outline of a Proposal for Competitive U.S. Broadcast Systems [April 1960]

Premises:

1. Although broadcast channels are public property, they have been used in the past 10 years as if they were private property, i.e., free of substantial control under the "public interest" language of the Communications Act. This is the

context of the scandals and public outcry relating to "rigging," payola, lack of public service programs, advertising abuses, etc. in the past two years.

2. We have had 33 years of trying to make work the policy of licensing private operators to use public frequencies in the public interest under Commission regulation. In broad terms, when broadcasting was less profitable (as in the 1930s), its public service performance tended to satisfy the public interest, and when it was more profitable (as in the period 1941–1960), its public services performance failed to satisfy the public interest fully. This "failure" is relative to the potential inherent in the media of broadcasting, not absolute (e.g., as it is, broadcasting probably satisfies the public interest much more completely than would a general, commercial application of Pay-TV with its patent-control of program and price policy).

3. The ambivalence of the role of the licensed broadcaster, expected to program in the public interest while also expected by his stockholders to maximize income, is at the root of the difficulty with the present system. If means could be found to retain the desirable features of the present system while eliminating the ambiguity and contradictions from within it, we could revise the system to the advantage of all concerned.

4. English experience as well as that of Canada suggest that there may be real advantages in having a broadcast system composed of two parts, supported in different ways: a commercial service and a public service.

5. "Educational Broadcasting" in the United States presently and for the foreseeable future lacks the channel assignments in major centers, the budget, and the staff to provide unaided a public service type yardstick which would offer an effective choice for viewers and listeners as against the commercial system.

Proposal:

To establish competitive broadcast systems in the United States; to free commercial broadcasters of legal responsibility under the Communications Act to serve the public interest (except in those areas where the commercial service continues to enjoy a monopoly); to apply revenue from the rental of frequencies to commercial broadcasters to the support of a public service broadcasting agency.

As to facilities:

Divide all TV, AM and FM commercial frequency assignments into two classes: "C" for commercial and "PS" for public service. The proportion of all channel assignments which should fall into C versus PS should be considered further. The designing of a sensible network of PS stations offers opportunities for greatly improving broadcast service while also presenting some problems. For example, New Jersey as well as New York might be better served if a PS TV station were moved from New York City to New Jersey. The problems are typified by the fact that in the foreseeable future it is unlikely that the PS system would find it sensible to operate its own station in *every* TV and AM community which now has one or more stations. Perhaps the solution of this problem is to provide that every "C" station which serves an area, the population of which lies substantially outside the service areas of all PS stations in the same service (i.e., TV or AM or FM as the case may be), shall continue to operate under the "public interest" obligations of the Communications Act and to enjoy free use of its channel for license terms of the present length.

As to finances:

In return for the freedom from the legal obligation to serve the public interest (see below), "C" stations would be obliged to bid in the open market for their station licenses. Licenses would run for seven-year terms and would be issued to the highest bidder who met FCC minimum qualifications (other than program qualifications, of course). In order to provide minimum financial returns to the public from the commercial use of its radio frequency property, the minimum acceptable bid for any channel assignment should be a percentage of gross revenues from time sales for the seven-year period of the license. It is suggested that this minimum bid should be two percent per annum for the first $100,000, three percent per annum for gross revenues above $100,000 and less than $1,000,000, and four percent per annum for gross revenues of from $1,000,000 up. The application of these percentages to the gross broadcast revenues of commercial broadcasters as reported by the Federal Communications Commission for the calendar year 1958 would yield between $35 and $40 million per year. In order to ensure effective (i.e., non-collusive) bidding, the networks should be required to (a) maintain strict neutrality as to bidding for channels on the part of their affiliates and (b) provide network affiliation to the station using a channel assignment which such station obtained by outbidding the network, in the case of network owned and operated stations. All "C" station channel rental revenues would be earmarked for the use of the PS Agency. Congress should appropriate such supplemental monies as might be required from time to time either for capital or operating budgets of the PS Agency.

As to government control:

For "C" channel assignments, control would be substantially as it is today for all commercial broadcast stations, *except* that no program control would be attempted by the FCC. The "C" channel assignment holders would, of course, be subject to existing types of regulation on monopoly, network affiliation, etc., by the FCC and to other regulation under general laws (such as regulation of advertising by the FTC, etc.).

For "PS" channel assignments, control would lie with a new public agency created to administer a nation-wide system of public service broadcasting stations and networks. This PS Agency would obtain its channel assignments from the Commission under a clear delegation of legislative authority from Congress, spelling out the scope of the facilities which the PS Agency should be given.

As to organization:

There would be no change in organization as far as the "C" channel assignments are concerned.

The PS Agency should be established as a non-profit, public corporation, independent of continuing government control. Supervision of the PS Agency would lie with a Board of Directors composed of men or women representative of education, cultural activities of various kinds, etc., but excluding persons with financial interests in commercial broadcasting and advertising and persons with employment relations to commercial broadcasting and advertising in the two years preceding their appointment to the Board. The Board's composition should be given flexibility through staggering of appointments. The term of its members' appointments should be seven years. Members should be appointed by the President but with statutory protection for appointments of persons belonging to other than the President's political party.

The PS Agency should be authorized to appoint appropriate officers and staff and to exercise wide discretion in planning and operating its networks and stations. It should be authorized to purchase the properties of commercial stations for use on its channel assignments or to build its properties de novo. It should be authorized to make such arrangements with existing and forthcoming educational broadcast stations as might appear mutually desirable, e.g., it might adopt some of them as its own stations or it might enter into networking arrangements with them, etc.

As to policy:

For the "C" stations, the new broadcast program policy would be strictly "laissez faire": they might broadcast as much advertising as they desired and whatever type they desired, etc. Federal Trade Commission-type action would be the only government controls on program and advertising policy.

For the PS Agency: it would operate under a program policy which strictly enjoined it to avoid standardized, mass market program production. The PS Agency would be prohibited from receiving advertiser revenues.

Comment:

We have had plenty of experience to support a change in our broadcast policy.

1. This proposal would eliminate the ambiguity in the position of commercial broadcasters. Presently, they are in a position where they are supposed to try to serve two masters. Under my proposal they would serve only one master: the pursuit of maximum profits. The change should reduce the incidence of ulcers on Madison Avenue.
2. The broadcast channels are public property. This proposal merely acts on this fact. It would require concessionaires to rent their channels, just as does a hotel or restaurant operator in a national park. The proceeds of the rentals would be applied to serving the public service needs of the public which owns the channels, an apparently equitable policy.
3. A practically effective public service broadcasting alternative to commercial broadcasting would be provided. If enough Americans are unhappy about the deficiencies in our broadcast program performance, this is a rather obvious remedy for this unhappiness.

5

"The 'social responsibility theory' of the press in the twentieth century is . . . part of the public relations program of big business"

EDITOR'S NOTE: *Four Theories of the Press,* by Fred S. Siebert, Theodore Peterson, and Wilbur Schramm, was published by the University of Illinois Press in 1956. At the end of 1992, it still was in print. It quickly became a bestseller, used as a text in journalism and media curricula throughout North America and abroad. Indeed, it was a book that spawned courses, rather than merely being assigned in already existing courses. *Four Theories* gave an intellectual patina to teaching and research that long had been dominated by professional, green-eyeshade training. Although it lifted the level of discussion, it also mystified the role of media in society by positing a freedom-control dichotomy that in itself was culture bound and therefore economically bound. Posing as objective, value-free scholarship, the treatise stood out, to some readers, as an example of the precise opposite. Nonetheless, the book has been treated reverentially by most media scholars, and even those who critique it do so from a shared friendly platform.

Four Theories, a work of Cold War scholarship, stands as a demonstration of how academia is subtly influenced by, and in turn influences, dominant domestic and international policy lines. The book staked out a field, defined the terms of discourse, and structured the way the academy—and those who pass through it—understand the communication system. By arguing that "in the last analysis the difference between press systems is one of philosophy," the book ignored the media's roles in a market-driven system based on pervasive commodification of products, services, labor power, and the media themselves. A mere blindspot.

Coincidentally, Dallas Smythe had been studying the relationship between publishing and the burgeoning industrial capitalist system of the seventeenth, eighteenth, and nineteenth centuries. In the mid-1950s he was incorporating this subject into his graduate seminar, Political Economy of Communications. An extensive file, modestly labeled "Freedom of Press," holds reading notes and memoranda that in some cases predate the publication of *Four Theories*. For example, in a handwritten "Note to myself" dated November 1955, Smythe jotted down a few observations about "motivation of production" and "plight of authors dependent on the market."

Pages of notes indicate that Smythe carefully read *Four Theories* as well as Siebert's *Freedom of the Press in England, 1476–1776* (1952) and Schramm's *Responsibility in Mass Communication* (1957). Smythe observed that "Schramm's book distorts history of communication" and "romanticizes the role of theories—e.g. the libertarian theory—and ignores the fact that this theory—to the extent it was consciously articulated at all—was a self-serving rationale used by politicians and businessmen to ornament operations which had other less lofty purposes." The book "de-natures the meaning of technology," Smythe found, because in "reducing it to a disembodied succession of mechanical changes, it ignores the context in which [it] existed. It confuses because it does not deal with historical reality, but rather plays with it."

About Schramm's discussion of the rise of the libertarian press theory, Smythe noted that "political freedom was not a universal right in the eyes of the 18th C. revolutionaries (*vide* the 1789 Constitution on counting slaves for repres. purposes, & the property qualif. for voting). The press freedom he talks about was for men of some substance (entrepreneurs). There was a class structure after the Am. Rev.!" Another of Smythe's notes points out that "WS's astigmatism emerges clearly in speaking of Marxism" and that "'capitalism' is expunged from S's vocabulary, & like 'corporation' & 'monopoly,' doesn't appear in the index of his book."

In Smythe's twenty-one pages of handwritten notes on *Freedom of the Press in England*, we find that "Siebert projects back into the 17th (as also the 16th) C (1) the idea of press freedom, (2) the law of the press. If we look at the practice (policy) of the press we find it monopolistic especially in re Cromwell. The official newspaper of Cromwell & suppression of others is *the* practice in USSR today & for the same reason: to support a revolutionary govt." Smythe's concluding comment on the volume was: "Legal forms, also when unrelated to social class, power &

policy are empty technical devices. This being so, one would expect F. S. to present a confused interpretation of the chronology of (1) expressions of ideas, (2) legal forms. He does."

So when Smythe turned to writing about press freedom and the *Four Theories* phenomenon, he already was convinced that libertarianism "was never an explicit code" but "solely slogans to advance bourgeois interests."

"I got so angry at the *Four Theories* thing," Smythe explained to me, "that I decided to begin writing something which would blast it. And I particularly teed off on Siebert's book and the essay he did for the *Four Theories* about the Puritan revolution period in England. And I began by checking with the library to see how many editions there were of Milton's *Areopagitica* that had been published: one until the nineteenth century. And I believe in the seventeenth century, when he was publishing, it was rare for an edition to be more than, say, 1,500 copies. So it was never republished for over 200 years. What is the tradition of *Areopagitica* that was so important to the press? Nobody heard about it. Then I began looking at Puritan history and I got some left-wing scholarship out on this British historical period and began figuring out what had happened. I never really understood what was involved in that period of rather chaotic behavior. I got something like thirty pages of analysis of context which covered the Cromwellian period to my satisfaction, which made it plain that there was no doctrinal debate about the press involved at all and [that] the principal factors were either motivated by religious dogma or they were motivated by the greed of merchants, headquartered for the most part around London. Those were the polar forces that were engaged. I had a great time of it and I could see that, God, this would be a five- or ten-year operation in order to carry it through and do this carefully for each of these four theories, so I gave it up. I had more important things to do."

The following selection consists of two parts. The first, probably from early 1959, is a brief outline, "Preliminary Statement of the Argument," in which Smythe set down some thoughts on press freedom and its relation to class structure and political economy. The second, "Freedom of the Press Doctrine in Its Class and Politico-Economic Context," most likely written in the first half of 1959, is a short manuscript developing some of the ideas from the outline. It was to be a chapter in a monograph or book that Smythe never completed. He finished another piece, "Libertarian Press Doctrine: The Puritan Revolution Context," which evidently was to be the third chapter. It dealt mainly with historical background and had very little to say about "theory." The chapter entitled "Freedom of the Press Doctrine," Smythe recalled to me, "possibly...was the introduction to the monograph I never completed on my effort to demolish the *Four Theories.* I remember it fondly—and unhappily, because I never published that monograph."

When we were looking through his files, Smythe was surprised to find the text of "Freedom of the Press Doctrine." He said to me, "I didn't remember that I had typed this out—it's not been duplicated. And there are some inserts which will make it difficult to Xerox. It's a draft, introductory, or maybe an overview. It works on the basis of that 'Statement.'"

About the provisional third chapter, "Libertarian Press Doctrine," Smythe told me: "This was supposed to be a part of the foundation of the full argument. If you're going to blow it up to book length, I figured you'd need to go back into the history of these various doctrines, and this is the beginning. It's an attempt to throw light on Fred Siebert's book, not his article in *Four Theories.* I found that book so biased by the idealism with which he was [unintelligible word] I had to do this in order to get my own feet on the ground. [...] I really did a hell of a lot of digging on that stuff in the late fifties."

Smythe never returned to these matters. He was on sabbatical in Europe during the summer and fall of 1959, and that led to his interest in regulation of satellites and satellite broadcasting.

Preliminary Statement of the Argument: Freedom of the Press Doctrine in Light of Social Class Structure, Political Economy, and Power [1959]

1. The general hypothesis: that doctrines (not "theories") of press freedom grow out of the class and power structures of societies and differ in relation to *whose* freedom is protected against restraints from *what sources,* and in the service of *what value patterns or policies.*
2. Libertarian "theory" grew out of the 17th and 18th centuries' situations.
    a. It was an important part of the ideology of the newly ascendant middle class of capitalists.
    b. It was designed to be a shield against threats from government—and feudal government at that—the only source of real threats to press freedom at that time.

c. The "free market place of ideas" was not thought of as being available to the propertyless, disfranchised, illiterate "lower" classes.
d. It existed in a society where no large concentrations of power existed in the business community and where, therefore, restraints from such sources were not possible.
e. With the publishing technology then available, the publishing business was accessible readily to new enterprises with moderate or even modest capital sums. Hence, diversity of political viewpoints on the part of publishers was more probable and deviant ideas could get access to the readers easily.

3. The "social responsibility theory" of the press in the 20th century is blood-brother to the notions of the "trusteeship of business" and "social responsibility of business" which are part of the public relations program of big business.
   a. In general, these notions serve as cloaks of respectability designed to protect big business from public criticism in light of its monopoly characteristics.
   b. These notions are part of the larger business ideology which holds that public government and taxation are malevolent while private government and taxation are benevolent (see Thurman Arnold, *Folklore of Capitalism*).
   c. The fact of huge capital requirements to enter publishing of newspapers, mass circulation magazines, TV, and motion pictures effectively closes off easy access to the ranks of mass media entrepreneurs. Hence, the only way that deviant ideas can get access to the public is by courtesy of the conservatives who operate the mass media. As Merton and Lazarsfeld point out, this bias serves to shield the existing business organization from criticism.
   d. The obvious thrust of the "social responsibility theory" is still to protect the mass media against government, and "freedom" for the mass media is regarded as freedom to penetrate into the affairs of government.
   e. With universal franchise, popular government is not a principal threat to press freedom in the United States, Canada, and similarly organized countries.
   f. Concentration of power in private corporations in these countries give them the autonomy and threatening relation to the mass media which was occupied in the 18th century by monarchial governments.
   g. The "social responsibility theory" is silent with respect to threats to press freedom arising from such concentrations of power in

private corporations. It evinces no interest in penetrating behind the "press handouts" of major corporations comparable to its concern to penetrate behind government "press handouts."

h. In view of the fact that the popular governments in the United States and similarly organized countries conduct their affairs under constant public scrutiny, the public need is for comparable press scrutiny of the affairs of private corporations which so frequently proclaim their trusteeship role.

4. The "social responsibility theory" is formally equivalent in class and politico-economic terms to the press doctrine in the U.S.S.R.
   a. In both cases, the press is effectively dominated by the dominant class.
   b. In both cases, the press "freedom" serves the policies and values of the dominant class.
   c. In both cases, the threats against which the press doctrine protects its freedom come from sources which would jeopardize the class interests of the dominant class.

Freedom of the Press Doctrine in Its Class and Politico-economic Context [1959]

THE OCCASION for the present paper is the growing interest in policies, doctrines and theories related to mass communications. We are not here concerned with theories which develop out of a desire to explain communications from the standpoint of the individual. Rather our interest is in theories which approach the problem from the view of communications as a social process. As a social process the traditional frame of reference is the nation and the major institutions directly concerned in communications: the press (including electronic media and movies). In recent years, this approach has been used by Siebert in *Freedom of the Press in England, 1476–1776*,[1] by Siebert and others in *Four Theories of the Press*,[2] and by Schramm in *Responsibility in Mass Communication*.[3] My present purpose is two-fold: (1) to review and criticize these contributions to our body of knowledge about mass communications, especially from a methodological point of view; and (2) to advance a supplementary or alternative kind of analysis of press freedom.

[1. Class and Power Structures]

In the title essay in *Four Theories of the Press*, Siebert states the methodological stance, which is common to this literature, as follows:

> The thesis of this volume is that the press always takes on the form and coloration of the social and political structures within which it operates. Especially, it reflects the system of social control whereby the relations of individuals and institutions are adjusted. We believe that an understanding of these aspects of society is basic to any systematic understanding of the press.
>
> To see the differences between press systems in full perspective, then, you look to the social systems in which the press functions.[4]

As a general statement, this is unexceptional. However, when it is interpreted, as it is immediately by Siebert, this general formulation is reduced drastically:

> To see the social systems in their true relationship to the press, you have to look at certain basic beliefs and assumptions which the society holds: the nature of man, the nature of society and the state, the relation of man to the state, and the nature of knowledge and truth. Thus, in the last analysis the difference between press systems is one of philosophy, and this book is about the philosophical and political rationales or theories which lie behind the different kinds of press we have in the world today.[5]

Schramm nods even more briefly toward the role of "political structures" and then departs from them never to return with:

> And we start with a look at certain basic assumptions which any society holds—assumptions concerning the nature of man, the nature of society and the state, the relation of man to the state, the nature of knowledge and truth and moral conduct.[6]

Such an approach of necessity is ahistorical, even where, as in Siebert's *Freedom of the Press,* it deals systematically with the regulation of the press in a given time period. What does come out of Siebert's book is a review of historical facts relevant to the 20th century theoretical concerns of a lawyer-philosopher. Thus, in the crucial Civil War period, 1640–66, we find Siebert repeatedly referring to the situation as "chaotic" and essentially meaningless. While it may be granted that there is an element of chaos in war, it is at least susceptible to analysis in terms of the identity, purposes, and policies of the contending parties. It is at least not meaningless. Again, we find him evaluating the significance of periods of English history in terms of the inability of people then living "to grasp those principles which became current only after a century more of experimentation."[7] This sort of study should not be confused with the sort of historical analysis of the social institutions in relation to press policy which he began by talking about and which has yet to appear in any rounded form.

While beliefs and assumptions are, of course, an important part of the social systems within which the press functions, they are by no means an adequate list of the features of a social system for the purpose of theorizing about press freedom. Because of its intimate relation with public opinion since the 17th Century, the policy of the press has been of vital concern to those groups of people who seek to affect the policy of a society. It has been linked with other major institutions (the nature of the chief executive, the legislature, and the courts) in making that policy. But it is essential if we are to have viable theorizing about press freedom to take account in that theory of the functional relationships between the press and other groups of people. Such groups have historically included in prominent roles the churches, the monarch and his feudal dependents in the landed aristocracy, the business organization (meaning historically the capitalist merchants, manufacturers, and bankers), the petit bourgeois (small businessmen, clerks, salespeople, etc.), industrial employees, peasants, serfs, farmers, etc. To use conventional historical and sociological terminology, these *classes* in their relations with each other and with the national state have provided the framework of "the system of social control whereby the relations of individuals and institutions are adjusted," to revert to Siebert's language. Yet they are quite ignored in the analysis of theories of press freedom now current.

The consequences of this omission are serious. Lacking the contextual background against which to appraise and interpret press policy historically, fallacious distinctions are made today. Thus, Siebert and his associates contend that there are essentially two theories of press freedom current today: "The *Soviet Communist* theory is only a development of the much older *Authoritarian* theory, and what we have called the *Social Responsibility* theory is only a modification of the *Libertarian* theory."[8] I contend that this formulation tends to mislead because it ignores the class realities of history after asserting that it would consider them.

The general hypothesis to be tested is that *doctrines* of press freedom grow out of the class and power structures of societies and differ in relation to *whose* freedom is protected in the service of *what value pattern or policies,* against restraints from *what sources.* This hypothesis means, in other words, that the press policy in a society reflects the dominant class interests in that society and that it tends to protect those interests against restraints or intrusions which are inimical to the interests of that class. Corollary No. 1 to this hypothesis is that the press policy of a nation with a newly ascendant class will be consistent with the economic, political, and philosophical point of view of that class and will reflect the formulation of that class point of view as it was in the struggle of that class for power.[9] The remainder of this paper develops these propositions and in doing so reviews the analysis of Siebert *et al.*

2. Tudor-Stuart Press Doctrine

The Tudor period was one of national growth and unification. At its start, central authority was so weak as to make nationality little more than a fiction. England had no national army, no navy, and no central bureaucracy or civil service. The rudiments of these attributes of nationalism were developed by the Tudors. Overseas trade in the hands of the joint-stock trading companies expanded, especially after the crushing of Spanish sea power in 1588. Capital from this trade, from privateering, etc., flowed into the hands of new merchant-capitalists. Coupled with the availability of monastery lands and buildings (confiscated by Henry VIII and sold cheaply to finance his wars), it aided the conversion of feudal land tenure into capitalist agriculture. Thanks to this enclosure movement, the rural areas provided abundant cheap labor. This attracted the merchant-middlemen (who dominated internal trade) to locate the putting-out system of woolen cloth manufacture in the rural areas. The foreign market for English woolens was expanded under the influence of Henry's currency debasement and the resulting decline in the value of the pound in terms of foreign currency. The development of specialization, the application of capital, and the increased dependence on production for the market encouraged the growth of the coal industry, which by 1640 accounted for half of all coal production in Europe. This in turn stimulated iron, tin, glass, soap, and shipbuilding. The development of markets meant that the nation was becoming a single economic unit. Out of all this emerged an increasingly powerful merchant class with a point of view shared by capitalist farmers and non-feudal landowners. Of course, the expansion of capitalism brought the new class into conflict with the feudal system at many points. Resources which came under the control of the new class upset the resource pattern on which feudalism had rested. And the jockeying for power on issues relevant to their self-interest brought capitalists together as against the older, dominant class.

The relative political stability of the Tudor period rested on adroit royal balancing of the feudal lords and the established church as against the capitalist class and their allies among the non-feudal landowners—all in the interest of maintaining the position of the Crown. This balancing was not too difficult as there was considerable looseness of fit in the power situation. The interests of the Crown agreed with those of the capitalist class in important ways, e.g., in respect to the struggle against Spain. And in a limited sense, the interests of the capitalist class and the feudal class were not always in conflict. In the looting of Spanish colonies and trade, they collaborated happily. The Tudor period was, then, a period of dynamic growth and change in which class lines became distinct but did not harden into postures which required forcible reorganization of the power structure of the State.

Against this context, the mechanics of royal control of the press, which are set out in great detail by Siebert,[10] take on added meaning. As he relates, printing was brought under the control of the King not long after it was introduced in England in the 15th Century. From the early 16th Century to the Revolution of 1640, printing and publishing were regulated, licensed, and controlled in detail either by the Crown itself, by the Council, or by officers appointed by the Crown. This feudal press policy was expressed in actions rather than in verbal rationalizations.[11] Such rationalization as there was came implicitly from the logic of feudalism. The Tudors assumed authority which Magna Carta and other feudal limitations on the power of the King had denied the Crown. As Shepard says:

> The great function of absolutism in England as upon the continent was to weld the various dissevered and discordant elements of feudal society into a national unity. During this period parliaments and estates general either disappeared or became subservient instruments of the royal will.[12]

This trend was particularly evident in Tudor press policy. Siebert says that "as the trade in printed books increased and later extended into the field of religious and political controversy, the Tudor statesmen slowly but effectively concentrated the control of the new craft in the hands of the king and Council."[13] As developed by the Tudors, the King's authority over the press was absolute.

> From modest beginnings, such as the appointment of an official printer with special privileges, it had by the end of the century expanded into a complete and complex system of regulation. What Henry VIII began, his daughter Elizabeth completed. In no other country in Europe was the system so delicately balanced or so ingeniously operated. The result was the postponement until the next century of the serious problems arising from political and religious discussion.[14]

It would be a mistake to assume that the strict Tudor press policy succeeded in suppressing near-irrepressible drives toward controversy. The situation did not remotely resemble that of the 18th or 20th centuries. The press of Tudor England was small. There were only a total of 50 or 60 presses in all England in Elizabethan and early Stuart times.[15] One need not feel it "astonishing" that there was so little opposition to the King's absolute control of the press[16] when one considers that reading in Tudor England was restricted to the minuscule portion of the English who were literate. While the best estimates are vague, it seems probable that only one per cent of the population of Elizabeth's England could read. In London, where literacy was the highest in the country, only from one-third to one-half the population was able to read.[17] With poverty and hard work the lot of the bulk of the people, reading was restricted to the clergy, the landed gentry, the town business class, and the children of these classes in schools. Accordingly, the sensitivity of press policy was low, reflecting its limited value in affecting attitudes and opinions.[18]

The pertinent questions by which our thesis may be tested for Tudor press policy are such as these. In its operation, the values of *what* classes were advanced? The values of what classes were restrained? Unfortunately, Siebert's scholarly analysis of the mechanics of press control does not help much with answers to these questions. It does appear clear, however, that Tudor press policy under Henry VIII reflected his strategies in relations with the Reformation, the Roman Catholic Church, and the Church of England at every turn of their torturous course. The press was employed both positively (in encouraging, even surreptitiously, the printing of books and pamphlets favorable to the Crown policy[19]) and negatively (by censoring, burning printed material, and by executions of publishers or authors).[20] After the final break with Rome, executions for circulating Reformation literature stopped and executions for circulating pro-Rome views began.[21] At the same time, continuing censorship and licensing of all kinds of printing was applied to the prohibition of "seditiouse opinions" as well as non-conformance with the established Church of England.[22] This press policy supported the growing strength of the national government just as did Henry's confiscation of the wealth of more than 400 monasteries and the creation of an established church of which he was head.

As is evident from these illustrations, Siebert interprets the press policies of the successive Tudors as personal in motivation.[23] The temptation to personalize the policies and to oversimplify their meaning is obvious. Yet we must anticipate that further research would render these policies meaningful in terms of the political and economic forces operative between the several principal social classes. Some clues in this vein do appear amidst the legalistic analysis which provides the backbone of Siebert's historical study. Thus, under Elizabeth, conflict over press policy in substantial degree related to the drive of the Puritans against the forces which stood for the religious monopoly of the Church of England. In making an issue of pamphlets which attacked the vestments and doctrines of the established church, Field and Wilcocks and their London Puritan group in their *An Admonition to Parliament* in 1572 were clearly expressing the offensive power of the urban capitalist forces as against the defensive power structure composed of the aristocracy, the landed gentry, and the established church. The same is true of the Martin Marprelate tracts. As M. James remarks, under Elizabeth, Puritanism's base in the rising middle classes was already clearly evident.

> It struck its deepest roots among the rising middle classes, who were conscious of their growing importance in the state and eager to remove whatever barriers stood in the way of a full development of their powers.
>
> The course of the civil wars in England made it unmistakably clear that Puritanism was strongest among the middle classes especially in the towns. London supported the parliamentary cause vigorously and became known as "the rebellious city." The clothing towns of Lancashire were Puritan and parliamentarian, despite the existence of a surrounding Roman Catholic countryside. In Yorkshire, Bradford, Leeds, and Halifax; in the midlands, Birmingham and Leicester; in the west, Gloucester, Taunton and Exeter, were all Puritan strongholds. *Puritanism was therefore strongest among those classes which for economic reasons objected to the restrictions imposed by monarchical and Anglican rule.* Thus spiritual conviction and economic interest reacted upon and reenforced each other.[24]

Such an approach makes unified sense not only of the controversies concerning Puritan tracts but also of the drive for freedom of speech in Parliament.

> [T]he most stalwart champions of parliamentary rights were the Puritan members of the House of Commons. This was partly because the Puritans hoped to introduce a reformed religious polity by means of parliamentary legislation.[25]

In this class context, even the otherwise puzzling indifference of the Puritans under Elizabeth to the "principle" of a "free" press finds a reasonable explanation. Siebert, who, as noted above, was puzzled by the absence of opposition to absolute press control, offers no explanation for the fact that:

> No statement of the intellectual principles of freedom is to be found in the writings of the early Puritan authors; in fact their attacks were directed not against the theory underlying the restrictions but against the application of these restrictions to themselves.[26]

Pretty obviously the conflicts which did break out between Puritans and the Crown over press policy were in the nature of limited tactical engagements fought out within the framework of overall class collaboration in the interests of achieving the broader objectives of nationalism and economic growth. Puritans did not attack the "principle" of press control because other manifestations of the same absolutist policy worked to their class interest under the Tudors. Not all of the conflicts over press policy under the Tudors involved even these tactical engagements over class interests. Some related, evidently, merely to the intra-publishing struggle of rivals for markets. Under this heading would come the struggles over the rights of patentees to books under royal patents, rights to unprivileged printing, and other elements in the early history of current copyright law.[27] While membership in the rising middle class doubtless colored the positions taken by printers in these conflicts with Crown instrumentalities, these controversies relate more to the nature of the emerging structure and economic policy of the publishing business than to freedom of the press doctrine as such.

In sum, then, the Tudor-Stuart press policy was that of the dominant alliance of Crown, feudal gentry, national Church, and capitalist class. It generally served to protect the interests of the first three of these groups. In facilitating even in a small way the break with Rome, it also advanced the interests of the capitalist class. While, in general, collaboration between the classes existed in regard to press policy, limited class conflicts are evident in the struggle over Puritan reform efforts in the last quarter of the 16th Century. The absence of principled conflict over and the acquiescence in absolute Crown control of the press by the rising capitalist class reflects its alliance with the waning feudal gentry, the Church, and the Crown in the total situation of England at that time. That situation, in essence, was one in which England was integrating itself into nationhood.

To apply to Tudor-Stuart press doctrine the new journalistic term, *authoritarian*, as does Siebert in his later writing,[28] is more confusing than helpful. A term of recent usage, authoritarian doctrine, as used by Siebert, is broad enough to stretch from Plato to the Nazis and from the Roman Catholic Church to the USSR. Indeed, it seems from his analysis that almost all societies in practice have used it with the principal exception being the brief application of libertarianism.[29] A "theory" as far-reaching as Siebert contends "authoritarianism" to be may escape the charge of explaining too much too simply only by a combination of impeccable conceptualization and unique explanatory power. The "theory" does not meet this test. As he defines it, authoritarianism is:

> a theory under which the press, as an institution, is controlled in its functions and operation by organized society through another institution, government.[30]

As defined, anything *but* an "authoritarian" press policy would seem extraordinary. For in a national state all institutions ultimately come under some sort of state control (via courts, for example), constitutionally prescribed or otherwise. Moreover, the assumption under the definition is that the sole threat to press freedom comes from "government." To demonstrate further the inadequacy of this legalistic "authoritarian" theory, one would only have to show that substantial control over the press could come from a third institution while in legal fact the "government" maintained detachment from interference with the press. This is not too hard to do. Such a society's press doctrine would meet the letter of Siebert's "theory" as *non*-authoritarian, while, in fact, being quite as far from the purpose of libertarian doctrine as those doctrines which Siebert terms authoritarian.

Of course, Siebert's definition of "authoritarian" press policy stems from his own identification with "libertarian" press policy as he has defined it. Such an identification of a scholar with a particular press policy, however permissible it may be, can lead to unfortunate results. For it may itself reflect unconscious acceptance of several fallacies. As Parkinson has pointed out:

> The first lies in the assumption that all history illustrates a story of betterment or progress with ourselves as the final product. The second lies in the assumption that such progress as there has been is a Western [or Anglo-Saxon] achievement in which no oriental can claim the smallest share. History records no such monopoly and no such unbroken progression. What the historian does find, however is a recurrence of the belief that perfection has been reached and that a given constitution (like that of the United States) represents finality. There is, in fact, no historical reason for supposing that our present systems of governance are other than quite temporary expedients. ... The belief that the present or else some other recommended constitution can represent finality is as old or older than Plato. ... It is essentially Pre-Darwinian, however, as a mode of thought.[31]

Notes to "Freedom of the Press Doctrine . . ."

1. Fredrick Seaton Siebert, *Freedom of the Press in England, 1476–1766* (Urbana: University of Illinois Press, 1965).

2. Fred S. Siebert, Theodore Peterson, and Wilbur Schramm, *Four Theories of the Press* (Urbana: University of Illinois Press, 1956).

3. Wilbur Schramm, *Responsibility in Mass Communication* (New York: Harper & Brothers, 1957).

4. Siebert et al., *Four Theories*, pp. 1–2.

5. Siebert et al., *Four Theories*, p. 2.

6. Schramm, *Responsibility*, p. 62.

7. Siebert, *Freedom of the Press*, p. 191.

8. Siebert et al., *Four Theories*, p. 2.

9. This proposition is based on the fact that policies become obsolete as the reality situation in which they arose changes. In a like sense, it is often observed that nations begin fighting the next war with weapons designed in the last war.

10. Siebert, *Freedom of the Press*, Chaps. 1–4.

11. "[T]he Tudors worried not at all about the juristic bases of their powers; it was sufficient that they exercised them *de facto*." Siebert, *Freedom of the Press*, p. 21.

12. W. J. Shepard, "Legislative Assemblies," *Encyclopedia of the Social Sciences*, vol. 9, p. 357.

13. Siebert, *Freedom of the Press*, p. 30.

14. Siebert, *Freedom of the Press*, p. 28.

15. By contrast, in only one establishment in Antwerp, that of Christophe Plantin, there were 25 presses in 1576. Marjorie Plant, *The English Book Trade: An Economic History of the Making and Sale of Books* (London: George Allen & Unwin, 1939), p. 86.

16. Siebert, *Freedom of the Press*, p. 25.

17. R. D. Altick, *The English Common Reader* (Chicago: University of Chicago Press, 1957), p. 17.

18. One cannot use the term public opinion in this context without projecting our current meaning of its political importance into a completely different kind of society.

19. In the 1520s: "While still publicly supporting the church, the king was privately encouraging the distribution of heretical literature. His strategy at this time was to obtain the Pope's permission for his divorce by rendering himself indispensable to the maintenance of the Catholic church in England. He planned to promote surreptitiously the circulation of Reformation books and then become a public hero by wiping out the resulting heresies." Siebert, *Freedom of the Press*, p. 44.

20. Luther's works were burned by the English clergy in 1521. Siebert, *Freedom of the Press*, pp. 42, 44.

21. Siebert, *Freedom of the Press*, p. 45.

22. Siebert, *Freedom of the Press*, p. 48.

23. "Henry controlled the press in the interests of his own supremacy over the ecclesiastical system; the first years of Edward under the Duke of Somerset were honestly devoted to achieving a reformation in religion; Mary, in her turn, sought to re-establish the old order. All three monarchs used the licensing system with only such modifications as were necessary to accord with the changing objectives." Siebert, *Freedom of the Press*, p. 51.

24. M. James, "Puritanism," *Encyclopedia of the Social Sciences,* vol. 13, pp. 3–4. Emphasis added.

25. James, "Puritanism," p. 3.

26. Siebert, *Freedom of the Press,* p. 89.

27. Siebert, *Freedom of the Press,* pp. 64–87.

28. Siebert et al., *Four Theories of the Press,* p. 9. The term does not appear in his earlier scholarly history, *Freedom of the Press in England.*

29. "It [authoritarianism] furnishes the basis for the press systems in many modern societies and even where it has been abandoned, it has continued to influence the practices of a number of governments which theoretically adhere to libertarian principles." Siebert et al., *Four Theories of the Press,* p. 9.

30. Siebert et al., *Four Theories of the Press,* p. 10.

31. C. N. Parkinson, *The Evolution of Political Thought* (Boston: Houghton Mifflin Co., 1958), p. 8.

6

"Cultural industry has gone a long way toward making political candidates into commodities"

EDITOR'S NOTE: In January 1960, Dallas Smythe returned from a sabbatical leave in Europe that ignited his interest in several new areas, such as cultural imperialism, satellite broadcasting, and international regulation of satellites. Before he began extensive development of those subjects, though, he turned his attention to current domestic matters and national policy issues.

John Kennedy and Richard Nixon, the major contenders in the 1960 presidential race, were selected in party conventions that summer. The campaign reflected the ever-growing influence on politics of marketing and advertising techniques, as Madison Avenue was enlisted to create images, sell programs, and merchandise candidates. Although the salesmanship of 1960 might seem quaint compared to that of a generation later, the 1960 campaign went several steps beyond previous ones of the television era.

The 1960 presidential campaign also ushered in the first televised "debates" between candidates. Section 315 of the Communications Act, which guaranteed equal broadcast time for candidates running for the same office, was suspended so that Kennedy and Nixon could go at each other; other parties' candidates were excluded. This maneuver legalized the broadcasting industry's discrimination against selected parties and formalized the blackout on left-wing candidates and platforms.

With the Cold War in full swing, the campaign hinged on which candidate could be the toughest against the Soviet Union, which could best use nuclear weapons to menace the rest of the world, and which could repel most quickly the international communist conspiracy. Two tiny islands off the China coast, Quemoy and Matsu, suddenly became strategic pieces of real estate that the free world might have to defend to preserve Chiang Kai-shek's regime in exile.

Faced with the insanity of the nuclear weapons policy and the lunacy of the political-economic system, Dallas Smythe accelerated his political activity. In the 1950s he often had spoken to religious groups about his TV monitoring studies and his content analysis of religious broadcasting. But in the 1960s he turned to exploring the political process and tried to talk sense to the public about nuclear warfare. He broadened his audience, too.

Dallas was not a polished orator of the old school. He could not bring tears to eyes or hold listeners spellbound with dynamic phrasing, impeccable timing, and dramatic delivery. Smythe's gift was in what he had to say, the power of his evidence, and the flow of his logic. Academics often consider it not their business to speak to audiences of nonspecialists. Smythe felt no such restraint. He eagerly spoke to groups of what some people call ordinary citizens. His talks avoided academic jargon and dealt with subjects in accessible ways. Smythe considered this approach "action," "democracy."

A sample of his work is the talk he delivered to the Adult Education Council in Chattanooga less than two weeks after the election in 1960. "The Modern Media Man and the Political Process" is typical of how he dealt in a popular way with the recent campaign and issues such as the Cold War and international tensions. Some themes in this paper appeared in other talks he was giving around this time, and it was not unusual for him to cut and paste when he developed a new speech. Like many of his talks, this one was never published in the scholarly journals, probably because it did not conform to the standardized format academia requires. It did not meet criteria of "objectivity," new research, and contribution to the field—and the style clearly was too "journalistic" and "popular" to fit comfortably in dense academic publications that typically speak only to themselves. It was good Smythe had tenure, because such output would not have been a plus on his promotion record, and in some circumstances it might have been a minus. Yet the mimeo machine in Smythe's office always was busy meeting public requests for copies of his talks. In a final sense, his speeches had far greater impact on policy and public awareness than did the academic papers published by others in the communications journals at the time.

The Modern Media Man and the Political Process

[An address before the Adult Education Council, Chattanooga, Tennessee, November 17, 1960]

THE SUBJECT TONIGHT deals with TV, radio and the printed media as they relate to the political process of nominating candidates and electing a President. It goes beyond elections to consider the impact of these communication agencies on the formation and administration of national policy. So let me first comment on the nature of the modern media man. Then, let us consider the electoral process itself as it is affected by the modern media man. Third, let us comment on the nature of the modern voter as he relates to the candidates and the issues.

First, the Nature of Modern Media Man

Modern media man is a personable, likeable chap. And he means well. But he cannot be understood unless one recognizes that he lives and works in a corporate environment. He is, if you like the nice name for it, an "organization man," but if you like consistency, we should call him a bureaucrat, for that is the generic name for such people whether they be found in government or business. The modern mass media are typically organized as corporations and they, like their men, are bland and well-meaning too. Above all, they value good public relations for themselves. And so they conduct themselves in such a way as to avoid making unnecessary enemies. If we are critical of them, it must be remembered that there is no imputation of "bad" motives to anyone. The observed results flow from institutional, not personal processes—and from the fact that the ostensible purpose of the business organization is to make and to sell goods and services. It was not designed to run people's lives.

By far the most important corporations which embody the media man in our country today are the broadcasters. Broadcasting (by TV and radio) tends to monopolize over time the sensory attention of the population for materials produced by highly integrated organizations operating over vast spaces. Broadcasting couples a single transmitter with a mass of receivers, where the content is potentially everything and anything which affects people's lives, be it information, entertainment, instruction or education. There are now TV sets in about 90 percent of U.S. households and they are used for more than six hours a day by the average household. Next to work, TV monopolizes more of our time than any other waking activity.

While there are hundreds of TV stations and several thousand radio stations, the sources of program material are few indeed, whether one regards the three or four networks, the three news services, or the number of program producers. That these organizations do indeed monopolize our time is evidenced by the industry terminology. One speaks of the industry existing on the basis of "time sales." The station or network sells the use of its transmitter for clock-hours of time at prices which reflect the probability (derived from audience surveys) that stated numbers of persons will devote the *same* clock-hours to attending their receivers.

The policy of the business organizations which operate the TV-radio industry, the press, comic books, etc., is the same as that of cultural industry in general, of which it is a part. Elaborate technology and heavy capital investment require mass production when applied to entertainment, or when applied to automobile manufacture. Mass production requires the largest possible market—a mass market. Mass production for a mass market means that the product is shaped to offend as few as possible. Because the largest number of potential consumers is to be found in the portion of the population with median or lower incomes, the design of the product or service is especially geared to their taste level. And because adult-educational efforts such as yours are neither universal nor fully developed in our country, the great bulk of the population finds its entertainment, its information, and its education in the products and services of cultural industry.

Standardization of product is a necessary condition to mass production. And standardization of the product of cultural industry as we practice it robs the product of diversity. General Mills tells the writers of its TV and radio dramas:

> In general, the moral code of the characters in our dramas will be more or less synonymous with the moral code of the bulk of the American middle-class, as it is commonly understood. ... There will be no material that may give offense either directly or by inference to any organized minority group, lodge, or other organizations, institutions, residents of any state or section of the country, or a commercial organization of any sort. This will be taken to include political organizations; fraternal organizations; college and school groups; labor groups; industrial, business and professional organizations; religious orders; civic clubs, memorial and patriotic societies; philanthropic and reform societies (Anti-Tobacco League, for example); athletic organizations; women's groups, etc. which are in good standing.

General Mills singles out a few topics:

We will treat mention of the Civil War carefully, mindful of the sensitiveness of the south on this subject. No written material may be used that might give offense to our Canadian neighbors. ...

General Mills' audiences are to see only the best of all possible worlds:

There will be no material for or against sharply drawn national or regional controversial issues. ... Where it seems fitting, the characters should reflect recognition and acceptance of the world situation in their thoughts and actions, although in dealing with war, our writers should minimize the 'horror' aspects. ... Men in uniform shall not be cast as heavy villains or portrayed as engaging in any criminal activity. There will be no material on any of our programs which could in any way further the concept of business as cold, ruthless and lacking all sentiment or spiritual motivation.[1]

This does not caricature; it delineates the policy of cultural industry. It is a policy of providing content which is smoothed out—or homogenized—to offend nobody and to cater to the presumed taste of the largest possible number.

Not only must today's mass media product be standardized; it must be differentiated from yesterday's. For our media men live in a one-day world. Audience loyalties must be evoked in program or magazine "images" which promise that tomorrow's product will be both the same as, *and* better than, today's. To this end superlatives are used to make the insignificant differences which distinguish the two seem real and important. Sensationalism, as it used to be called when it was introduced by "yellow journalism," tends to reduce all experiences to a flat level when linked with the presentation of news in snippets, flanked by commercial announcements. Yesterday's local murder story received the same scare headlines as today's international crisis which actually may extinguish us all—including the mass media men—in a nuclear holocaust. And on TV and radio both are blended with the adjacent announcements for the local power and light company, or some other sponsor.

At this point a frame of reference is needed. What is the function of culture anyway, if not to provide profits from mass-produced psychological pabulum? Wasn't it always this way? The basic social function of culture is

to make available to all members of the species the broadest range of meanings of their own humanity that society makes possible, and, in turn, to help them build such societies as new conceptions of the human potential might require.

> Popular culture can fulfill such functions to the extent that it makes available representations and points of view which enable men to judge a real world, and to change reality in the light of reason, necessity, and human values. To that extent, popular culture also forms the basis for self-government.[2]

The protections for individuals which were written into the Bill of Rights to our Constitution were put there to protect people from the main threat they knew—government. In the 18th century we had no mass media and no cultural industry. To the extent that they were satisfied, people's needs for information, entertainment, and consumer's goods in general were filled in ways which were characterized by heterogeneity rather than standardization. The provision of entertainment, games, medical advice, moral advice, etc., was either entirely non-commercial or came from professionals (in medicine, religion, politics). Even the foodstuffs, clothing, household equipment and utensils, when produced commercially were characterized by custom-manufacturing rather than mass production. Within the past 70 years all this was changed by the entry of mass production industry into these fields. Now we have relatively more of these consumer goods and services. But for this relative plenty we pay a price beyond the cash.

We used to hear about immigrants going through the "melting pot" of assimilation to American ways. Now we understand better, perhaps, that all Americans were going through the melting pot in which ethnic, geographic, and cultural differences were being ironed out by cultural industry.

The mass media men provide us with a superabundance of ephemeral entertainment, snippets of information lacking in context, and virtually no help in structuring our values, or in planning for our long-forgotten Utopias, or in coping with the hard realities of a world torn by cold war and threatened with hot wars. We are reduced to the position of being "consumers" not only of entertainment but of information and of politics. In a mass production society, man seeks to compensate for not knowing his fellow-man by "resonating" to feelings expressed for him by the singers of pop songs. He seeks blindly for his unfulfilled individuality through consumption of mass produced images which lead him nowhere. Alienated and isolated, he takes refuge in privatism. No wonder that he leaps at the opportunity offered by another branch of cultural industry to rediscover nature through buying and using camping equipment and small boats. No wonder that, when such expedients fail his felt needs, he builds up a huge new industry through buying and consuming tranquilizers. As my colleague George Gerbner puts it:

> The change in the experienced quality of life in the mass produced culture of the last fifty years makes an identity harder to achieve and harder to maintain. "The questions of adolescence—'Who am I?' 'Where am I going?' 'What is the meaning of life?'—receive no final answers. Nor can they be laid aside. The uncertainty persists..."[3]

"Not least among the paradoxes confronting 'people of abundance' having 'comfort and fun' in the 'affluent society,'" says Professor Gerbner,

> is the shadow of *want* rather than surfeit in our midst, and around the world. The soothing voice titillates lethargic consumers while muted government reports speak of as many as one out of every five American families living in stubborn pockets of permanent poverty. And before the message is over, somewhere within half a day's jet-range of the voice a spider-bellied child whimpers and lies still forever. The image of the human condition reflected in the selective mirror of mass culture defies full moral comprehension; it can be grasped only in terms of the privileges of the marketplace, of purely private rewards of the moment, dangerously divorced from the world of crying needs with which the present market structure cannot effectively connect.[4]

This, it seems to me, is the predicament to which our nice young mass media men have, unwittingly, brought us. Andrew Fletcher remarked in 1704 that "I believe if a man were permitted to write all the ballads, he need not care who should make the laws of the nation." Our ballad makers are those corporations which operate our mass media, which write our advertisements, which produce and sell our consumer goods and services.

But what of the power of the FCC, you may ask? Can't we somehow regulate these mass media men to get more responsible performance from them? Possibly we can. But we have not begun to cope with the problems in the way of doing this. Consider how responsibility is now diffused. The TV or radio station holds a license and is subject in legal theory to regulation in the public interest (though not in fact because of FCC unwillingness to regulate). Are the stations responsible then? The stations, however, get their program materials usually ready made and centrally produced from networks, syndicates, and news services. These corporations are not regulated (although the networks almost are). Are they, then, responsible? But the programs would not be produced on the air were they not sold to advertising agencies and their advertising clients. It has not yet been seriously suggested that the advertising agencies and the advertisers should be regulated. Are they responsible? To whom? How? As far as the law goes, the advertiser such as General Mills is responsible to its stockholders to make as much profit as possible and to conserve their capital. The advertiser has no *legal* responsibility for the entertainment, the information and the advice he broadcasts (other than the general laws relating to libel and dishonest advertising). Which of these institutions should we hold accountable for the policy of our electronic media when in fact they all share in responsibility for it?

When the FCC is weak and sometimes corrupt in failing to enforce the law, is this not a dereliction of its responsibility? And when the Presidents appoint and the Senate confirms men unable or unwilling to distinguish between the public and the private interest, is this not a dereliction in their responsibility? When we who elect Presidents, Senators and Representatives fail to charge them effectively with the duty to protect our individual and social interests in the cultural area, are we not responsible?

To this last question the answer may be: not entirely. For the mass media men have narcotized us with their homogenized and technically slick products. Paul Lazarsfeld and Robert Merton 12 years ago pointed out that the product of the mass media narcotized us and that the mass media either excluded altogether or softened criticism of themselves and of our social system.[5] In this way, the mass media shelter themselves and private business generally from criticism and from the kinds of corrective action which would require this part of cultural industry to serve the neglected functions of culture. A visitor from Mars, considering us and our rivals in the cold war, would probably say that both capitalism and communism were guilty of authoritarian manipulation of people and of their cultures in the interest of the respective economic systems.

Second, the Electoral Process as It Is Affected by the Mass Media

The simple fact, which is evident in the recent election campaign, is that cultural industry has gone a long way toward making political candidates into commodities with the same characteristics as all other commodities. Richard Nixon, in an unguarded moment in 1957, told the TV and Radio Executives Club of New York that "the public buys names and faces and not platforms and that a candidate for public office has to be merchandized in much the same way as any TV product."[6] No wonder that after the first of the so-called debates, he and his campaign managers were more concerned over the way his face appeared on the TV screen than they were with what was said. It was as if the beer poured into the glass in the TV commercial, shockingly, had no bubbles or foam.

Like any other commodity, the candidates seem to have been homogenized, both in personality and in their speeches. Each of them tried to attract the average voter just as the manufacturer designs his product and its advertising to attract the average income consumer. At the same time, like any businessman, both candidates have tried to differentiate themselves enough to give the "product image" a competitive edge. Nowhere was this clearer than in the discussion of the Quemoy and Matsu islands. Each candidate initially seized on this topic as one for marginal differentiation. Kennedy took what we might call a more liberal view than that of the Eisenhower administration. Nixon took a more conservative view than the administration. Then, as if hypnotized by the fear of losing the brand loyalty of the average voter, both of them hastily retreated to the more central position of the Eisenhower administration.

The TV networks suggested that the recent joint appearances of Nixon and Kennedy were in the tradition of the famous Lincoln-Douglas debates. Of course these TV encounters were not debates. There was no opportunity for systematic presentation of the candidates' views on the range of issues which confronts us all today. The format for these encounters, instead, was directly borrowed from the quiz shows; all that was missing was the isolation booth and the bank officer with the questions. Rather than the $64,000 question, there was a series of questions leading, symbolically, to the power, perquisites and responsibilities of the Presidency. Significantly, the men selected to choose the questions were representatives of the mass media. I understand that this format was suggested by the candidates themselves and that the networks urged a genuine debate format. However that may be, in the event, the mass media intervened—in fact, they literally came between the candidates in the so-called debates. The fact that theatrical concerns over makeup and lighting are most important gives point to Walter Lippmann's fear that

> if the political quiz show becomes the accepted format ... the temptation to rig the show is in many cases almost certain to become too strong to be resisted. As in the quiz shows the prize is too great and the temptation is too strong and corruption is too easy.[7]

The danger is we might have a Charles Van Doren in the White House.

Our assimilation of the political process to the ways of cultural industry—and especially our ways of using TV—supports the tendency to focus election campaigns on the choice of personalities who would, if elected, pursue the same policy. It was remarked by commentators that not since the 1930s have the two parties' policies differed substantially. Inevitably the candidates are speaking in "Me Too" terms. The first of the TV encounters between Nixon and Kennedy made this painfully clear. Kennedy stated a tough foreign policy objective. Nixon made it plain that he and Kennedy agreed as to goals and that their differences lay solely as to means. This, as the Quemoy-Matsu incident revealed, is marginal differentiation and is essentially the same process as is employed in merchandising brands of aspirin or cigarettes on the basis of fictitious or oversimplified distinctions. In politics it tends to degrade the voters and the issues by offering delusively simple slogans in place of answers for complex but understandable problems. In 1952 the problems of the cold war were reduced to the argument that "Ike" could talk to "Joe" (Stalin) more effectively than could "Adlai." And in 1960 we heard it again in the slogan that Nixon, because of his kitchen conversation with Khrushchev, could "stand up" to him better than could Kennedy.

Against the backdrop of the U-2 incident and the collapse of the Paris Summit meeting, it was to be expected that the Get-Tougher-on-Communism line would be played up by both candidates. And so the TV encounters went. Marginal differentiation in this respect led one of the nationally known commentators to remark that Nixon and Kennedy sounded more like poker players than debaters. "You raise me one Down-With-Khrushchev and I'll throw in a Get-Tough-With-Castro." This feature of the marketing contest between the two men caused real concern both in the State Department and among the friendly and the neutral foreign embassies. There was concern that Nixon's bellicose statements about the off-shore islands might provoke the Chinese to military action. There was also a more general concern that the candidates were taking such rigid positions in their rivalry to see who could sound the toughest that future negotiations would be imperilled. Thus, it was pointed out that negotiation is a two-way street, and if one freezes in inflexible positions, future negotiations are jeopardized.

The amount of dispute over the question whether the "image of America abroad" had deteriorated or not is another sign of our tendency to look at all human affairs in terms of the concepts of cultural industry. The very notion of America's "image" is a product of Madison Avenue and of motivation research; in fact, the controversial research reports were the results of studies exactly like those the market researchers make for cultural industry. Joseph Alsop in pointing this out, however, had to reach for another business image in order to affirm the importance of our reputation abroad: "In reality, however," he says, "prestige matters greatly because it is like a quotation on the international political market, and a quotation directly based, furthermore, on the market's shrewd estimate of each nation's power and leadership."[8] If ever there was a sure way to obscure the realities of our difficulties in international affairs it is to treat all motives as if they were reducible to stock market considerations.

There is still another aspect of the so-called TV debates which should be mentioned. They could not have been held, we are told by the TV industry, unless Congress, by passing a Joint Resolution last spring, had not temporarily waived a provision in the Communications Act (section 315). The pertinent part of this section of the law says that "If any licensee shall permit any person who is a legally qualified candidate for any public office to use a broadcasting station, he shall afford equal opportunities to all other such candidates for that office in the use of such broadcasting station. ..." This means that no station is forced to sell time for the broadcast of political candidates' speeches, but that if it broadcasts the speech of one candidate it must also broadcast those of his rivals. The broadcasting industry has tried to get this provision revised repeatedly in recent years in order to free itself of the obligation to broadcast speeches by minority party candidates to an equal extent with those of the candidates for the two big parties. The question of free time is not involved here for in these instances the stations and networks *sell* the time to the parties. Here is a policy issue of some political significance. Are we to freeze in law the conditions which will permit only the Republican and Democratic parties to gain a hearing? While it is easy and cheap to deride the Lars "America-First" Daly, the Prohibitionist, and the Vegetarian parties, what is at stake here is the legal possibility of a Third Party getting a hearing. To change the law, as the networks desire, would leave it entirely to their discretion whether any party may buy time for a candidate's TV and radio programs during a campaign.

The Joint Resolution passed in the last session of Congress suspended this feature of Section 315 with respect to Presidential and Vice-Presidential candidates. The networks, therefore, have been given a chance to show how they might operate if they were given the freedom and responsibility to determine which candidates might be permitted to buy time during a campaign. It would be only natural for them to put their best foot forward. This they have done, even to the extent of donating—not selling—the time for the so-called TV debates to the two principal candidates. And the value of the free time thus donated runs into the millions of dollars. It is not overstating the situation to say that the networks hope to get their way with Section 315 as a permanent matter on the basis of the goodwill engendered by these so-called debates. They have even warned us that it is unrealistic to expect that such debates would be a regular event at presidential elections. Thus the president of one network deserves credit for stating that it is unlikely that if the winner of the recent campaign is again a candidate in 1964 he would be willing to enter into a series of debates with his opponent. Why, it is pointed out, should he give "exposure" to the whole TV audience to a rival less well known than himself?

The conclusion to be reached is that probably such debates would not be repeated often in future campaigns—and that minority parties would have tough sledding in trying to get access to the microphone, if Congress grants the broadcasters the power they seek.

If, now, I can take you back in time to the party conventions of early summer, perhaps you will recall the basis for my saying that the conventions also have been assimilated to the commodity and entertainment aspects of TV. In the first place there is the fact that the conventions are put in the framework of advertising sponsorship—which a study for the Brookings Institution calls a "compromising...relationship. ..."[9] In "producing" the conventions, the implicit policy of the networks appears to be, not the transmission of a maximum of meaningful information, but "a maximum effect of excitement and interest."[10] In a word, politics is to be *consumed* as entertainment, just as is the Game of the Week, the daily Westerns, and the news. The conventions are played as a contest of personalities with the outcome uncertain. In this sense the emphasis on statistics is significant and betrays the kinship of the televised convention and sports events. Electoral votes in the nominating conventions are analogous to runs or points scored. And one may anticipate that convention statistics may some day reach that stage of maturity in which a commentator will remark that Mr. Jones, with 300 electoral votes has broken the record for dark horse candidates for electoral votes tallied in his favor by the delegations from the ten most populous states on the second roll call in a convention with two or more roll calls. And one could expand these statistics indefinitely if we come to keep them in terms of the national extraction of the candidates, their religious affiliations and their states of birth.

When one looks at the conventions in relation to the subsequent campaigns conducted by the image merchants the resemblance changes. From this standpoint, the political convention may resemble the convention of a large automobile manufacturer who is unveiling a new model car. With the background of glamour of a Motorama, with the excitement supplied largely by the off-stage cocktail parties the new candidate is launched into his campaign, replete with slogans and an inspired sales organization covering the whole country.

One other feature of the electoral process has been transformed by TV, and this is the determination of who has won the presidential campaign. Originally the authors of our Constitution thought that the electoral college would elect the President. The coming of the political parties changed that and in effect the election of the electors of a particular party came to determine the winner. For decades, the county courthouse collected and distributed the results of the tallies with increasing speed as telegraph and telephone came to its aid. Election results were not brought to the citizen by courtesy of an advertising sponsor. In the election just completed, 2,900 men and women, and computers of all brands (prominently identified in the programs) were used to conduct this feature of the electoral process. This final stage of the electoral process was also framed with advertising sponsorship. And again, the factors of personality, and of a statistically conceived contest were in the forefront of the explicit meaning of the event.

It would be quite wrong, of course, to assume that things were ideal in politics before TV and the mass media attained their present position. The type of campaigning illustrated by the "Tippecanoe and Tyler Too" campaign was perhaps no more conducive to thoughtful examination of issues of national and world significance than are our campaigns today. The boss system of the 19th century American cities, with its long-continued influence in the selection of presidential candidates, we know to have been characterized by cold-blooded power considerations, unsavory deals, and the like. But in discarding the older way of selecting candidates and campaigning we may have lost more than we realize. For the bosses did represent supplementary government which attended to the needs of people for old age assistance, for juvenile delinquency assistance, and for advice and charity on a local basis. When they lost their influence, local influence tended to drop out of the electoral process. And what took its place was a nationwide machine, available only to the candidate backed by wealthy people or corporations, and depending for its success on the power of publicity, stage-managed by public relations men. Today, given this chrome-plated apparatus, it comes as no surprise to find a large London daily concluding on the eve of our election that one candidate (Nixon) appeared to be a "hollow man," and the other (Kennedy) a "prefabricated man."

To repeat, one should avoid age-tarnished nostalgia for the good old days in politics, for their own sake. But we are dealing here with a transition from local and personal influence in the selection of candidates and the formulation of platforms to organization-men and their manipulation of images via Madison Avenue. If a fundamental feature of our system of government is supposed to be the consent of the governed, it may be a fateful kind of "progress" which replaces local influence with manipulation by the mass media. Mass media marketing of politics may ultimately mean substituting for the consent of the governed, the governing of consent.

Third, the Voter, the Candidates and the Issues

You would probably like to have me analyze the recent election returns and to answer such questions as: Why did Kennedy win? What kept Nixon from winning? How important was the religious issue in the outcome? I wish I could do it but the analysis of voting behavior which would be needed before I could give definite answers to such questions has not yet been completed. To be sure, in political circles and in the mass media people are busy offering explanations of the weight the various factors had in determining the outcome. But these explanations are, as Angus Campbell remarks, usually the "simplest impressionism." It will be at least a year before we can be at all sure of how it worked out the way it did. All that I can do is to suggest certain aspects of this and other recent campaigns.

It is implicit in our constitutional system that, ideally, two things are true in an election. First, that the voters have enough information concerning the available policy alternatives which might be adopted to cope with our foreign and domestic problems so that they can make a rational choice among these policies. And second, that the voters have available to them through the candidates recognizable partisan alternative policies. Angus Campbell and his associates in their recent book, *The American Voter,* conclude after analysis of nationwide interview samples over three national elections that, unfortunately, the first of these assumptions is unfounded.

> The typical voter has only a modest understanding of the specific issues and may be quite ignorant of matters of public policy that more sophisticated individuals might regard as very pressing. ... Neither do we find much evidence of the kind of structured political thinking that we might expect to characterize a well-informed electorate. ... The common tendency to characterize large blocs of the electorate in such terms as 'liberal' or 'conservative' greatly exaggerates the actual amount of consistent patterning one finds. ... It is also apparent from these [studies] that there is a great deal of

> uncertainty and confusion in the public mind as to what specific policies the election of one party over the other would imply. Very few of our respondents have shown a sensitive understanding of the positions of the parties on current policy issues. ... We have, then, the portrait of an electorate almost wholly without detailed information about decision making in government. A substantial portion of the public is able to respond in a discrete manner to issues that *might* be the subject of legislative or administrative action. Yet it knows little about what government has done on these issues or what the parties propose to do. It is almost completely unable to judge the rationality of government actions; knowing little of particular policies and what has led to them, the mass electorate is not able to appraise either its goals or the appropriateness of the means chosen to serve these goals.[11]

We know from other studies that less than a third of the electorate is greatly interested in the election; that less than one fourth think it makes "a good deal" of difference who wins. Even more alarming today as we face the real prospect of the destruction of civilization by atomic, bacterial and chemical warfare, about half of the adult population has no interest in international questions, even in times of crisis. No more than 15 percent of our adults are interested in world affairs to a significant degree. And not more than 10 percent of them typically mention international questions as among those most crucial in determining their votes.[12]

We are accustomed to being told that such massive ignorance and indifference is to be found in totalitarian societies. And it is shocking for us to confront the reality of our own political illiteracy in the light of our relative material affluence and our proclaimed sureness of dedication to the ideals of democracy, especially in speaking to those we still seem to think of as the benighted heathen living in other lands.

Even the audience statistics for the so-called TV debates reveal a shocking alienation from the political process. Making allowance for the fact that the "debates" were perhaps as much to be regarded as entertainment as a discharge of civic duty, still 40 percent of the TV homes in the country were not tuned to the first of them (which had by far the largest audience of the four). About half of the adult population 12 years or older in the East, the South and the Midwest did not watch that first debate; the West was more concerned: only one-fourth of the adults out there did not watch it.

Of course, greater interest and concern with the merits of political issues and parties exists among those with more education, with higher social class, and with higher incomes. Those whose jobs are in the higher echelons of the military, the civil government, the large corporations, and the trade associations are especially interested in these domestic and foreign issues. We therefore come to conclude that these "elite" groups are the only part of our population possessed of adequate information concerning policy matters to meet the presumption of informed voting. And to the extent that these elite groups are the very pressure groups which have axes to grind in policymaking, of course, their knowledge and voting influence tends to identify their self-interest with the national interest. Obviously, the notions of democracy embodied in our Constitution are far from realized in our mass production society insofar as voter knowledge of issues is concerned.

The second assumption for our election process is that there should be available to the voter recognizable partisan policy alternatives. What can we say of policy alternatives available to voters in the domestic field—which was admitted by both parties to be less important than foreign policy? The central domestic issue was probably the question whether or not the national government should use its power to insure prosperity and full-employment in the face of rising unemployment and spreading recession, with Kennedy taking an affirmative position and Nixon preferring to rely on private business to handle this problem. There was a clear alternative here in terms of point of view. But no specific programs or policies were offered or rejected by the two candidates. In choosing between the candidates on this issue, voters were in effect faced with a principle which was vague but important. A second domestic issue, related to the first, was whether or not social legislation—medical care for the aged, and minimum wages, especially—should be extended generously. This issue also distinguished fairly clearly between the candidates. There were two other domestic issues of importance: race relations and the religious qualifications of the candidates. But neither of these issues was openly joined in any clear-cut way by the two candidates. I do not mean that these issues were unimportant; I mean that they were not the subject of full confrontation as between the candidates.

As far as domestic issues are concerned, then, we might conclude that the two bread-and-butter issues of who is responsible for providing jobs, and how social legislation might be extended, offered distinct choices in point of view. It is very important to note that on such issues, as well as on the fringe issues of religion and race relations, American voters act pluralistically. That is to say, they range themselves on various sides of the issues and perceive them in realistic, if vague, terms.

In foreign policy, however, there were no recognizable partisan policy alternatives presented by the candidates. Since 1941 this has been true in every presidential election and for a good reason: we have had a bipartisan foreign policy. Both parties have been agreed on foreign policy and the only question presented to the voters has been which candidate would carry out the policy better. "Better" means for the voter according to his ideas of the goals of foreign policy. And here is where the ignorance and apathy of the voters is most evident. Unequipped by education to understand the dynamics of forces operating within and between foreign nations, and uninformed by cultural industry of these extremely complex matters, voters fall back on primitive psychological mechanisms to articulate their inchoate but very real concern for peace and for the integrity of the individual. The days of isolationism are gone; the great majority of voters recognize that America is inextricably mixed into world affairs. But the aspirations and needs of underdeveloped areas, the dangers of atomic-bacteriological chemical warfare, the goals and tactics of our past foreign policy, the strengths and weaknesses of the United Nations—these factors, to name just a few, are beyond his ken. And so the voter readily accepts stereotypical slogans which over simplify foreign issues and lead him into dangerously jingoistic points of view. An uninformed electorate on foreign policy can easily be led to favor policies which are every bit as totalitarian as those we oppose in foreign countries.

Significantly, the voters' concern with foreign policy is one for peace. And as such, in a remote way, voters seem to have expressed themselves in 1952 and 1956 not on partisan issues but on personalities. For the confidence they felt that Eisenhower—the wise father figure, experienced in military affairs—would end the Korean war was probably a decisive factor in determining the huge Eisenhower majority in 1952. And again in 1956, the promise of reducing world tensions associated with Eisenhower's participation in the Geneva Summit conference seems to have drawn powerful popular support for his claims to preserving the peace. When the visit of Mr. Khrushchev in 1959 ended with indications of lessening of cold-war tensions at Camp David, the public hoped this improved the chances for peace. With the prospect of a Summit conference at Paris in May, the ordinary people hoped that the dangers of war would be further reduced. Eisenhower was known to wish to leave the presidency with the reputation of a man of peace and this Summit conference was the chance to make this a real achievement. I think that had the Paris Summit meeting come off according to expectations, Nixon would have coasted to victory on the Administration's success on the peace issue alone. Sadly, as we know, the U-2 plane violated international law by entering the airspace which all countries (we especially) hold sacrosanct. And when someone (it is said [James] Hagerty, the public relations man at the White House) convinced Eisenhower that he had golfed so much that he had to take responsibility for the incident, the Summit conference was wrecked and the cold war was intensified rather than relaxed. That we tried to blame the crackup of the Summit on the Russians was what the therapists would call displaced guilt, and let us not deceive ourselves on that score.

The Republicans and the mass media, however, launched a campaign which did delude many of us as to the meaning of the Summit crackup. And in the process they appealed to the most jingoistic slogans and forces. Since they could not win on a record of advancing peace, the chosen alternative was to win on a hate-the-Russians theme. I referred earlier to the way both candidates played this theme and will say at this point only that it is a tribute to the real concern of the voters for peace that Kennedy was able to win while still maintaining that the administration should have saved the Summit conference by making the necessary concessions to international law.

Now that the election is over we may hope that our new administration will forget this "masculinity kick" (as David Riesman calls it)—this posture of toughness and realism which is peculiar to us in the United States and is not shared by our allies. Riesman has pointed out in a provocative piece in *Commentary* that this pose often means no more than the opposite of idealism, reasonableness and morality.[13] We might add that a good illustration lay in the U-2 incident. In the name of tough realism we have made liars out of all our teachers and preachers by defending lying as a matter of national policy.

This posture of toughness is especially dangerous in a world which has shrunken, because of our modern missile technology, to the dimensions of a village of 250 people. For, as Dr. Jerome Frank remarks, today no nation can maintain security for its citizens at the expense of the security of other nations.[14] With nuclear missiles ready for delivery to their targets within minutes of launching, mankind faces extermination so long as it places reliance on violence as the basis of settling international disputes. Today we and the Russians both face the immediate necessity of finding ways of living in the same world in peace; the effect of starting a war today will be the destruction of ourselves and our way of life. For something new has happened—new in the history of the human race, that is. For uncounted millennia men settled their disputes by reliance on physical violence. So long as this involved conventional weapons, it was a valid expectation that war could bring victory to one side. But when both sides possess more than enough terror weapons to exterminate us all, war no longer has a victor and a loser. Such survivors as there might be of a nuclear or chemical or bacteriological war would be too busy trying to stay alive, like savages, to pay any attention to the question of who won and who lost.

To survive, we in the world must reduce tensions. We must liquidate the cold war through multi-lateral agreements, through unilateral actions, and through a general lessening of hostility as between nations. Presently we seem blocked by a Thought Barrier from facing up to the real danger of our predicament and from recognizing the paths which are available for our survival.[15] It is in this connection that I return finally to still another aspect of our mass media men and of their relation to the big issues of our time.

Today our foreign policy is made by a relatively small number of men in the administration. And by administration I mean not only the military and civil executive arm of the government, but also the elite of the large corporations, and the trade associations. Within this complex there are sharp rivalries. And the rivals commonly resort to "leaks" to the mass media as a means of advancing their own policy proposals and defeating their rivals. When off-the-record briefings and leaks have been picked up and approved editorially by the news services of our TV, radio and print media, the semblance of public opinion has been created. This may be shocking to us but how could it be otherwise, given the widespread ignorance and apathy of the bulk of the population in relation to foreign policy? By creating a surrogate for public opinion, the mass media thus provide the necessary political basis for forcing Congress to approve the successfully leaked or briefed policy proposals. And this, in short, is the trend in the past 15 years. Given a bi-partisan foreign policy, with no real debate between the parties on genuine alternative policies, how could it be otherwise?

In this situation, the mass media have frighteningly large power to direct the course of our foreign policy. And so I come to a practical suggestion. Add your voices to those heard by the mass media and your Representatives and Senators in Congress concerning foreign policy issues. Approach them assuming, as I do, that they are reasonable men who want to contribute to the survival, not the destruction of men. Recognize that their ways of thinking have been attuned to the needs of cultural industry and politics as these needs used to be. And try to show them how modern media men and modern politicians can meet the new needs of the atomic age. Remind them that, as Albert Einstein said in 1946:

> We can only sound the alarm, again and again; we must never relax our efforts to rouse in the peoples of the world, and especially in their governments, an awareness of the unprecedented disaster which they are absolutely

certain to bring on themselves unless there is a fundamental change in their attitude toward one another as well as in their concept of the future. ... The unleashed power of the atom has changed everything except our ways of thinking.[16]

Notes to "The Modern Media Man . . ."

1. "Madison Ave.'s Program Taboos," *Variety*, October 26, 1960, p. 28.
2. George Gerbner, "The Individual in a Mass Culture," *Saturday Review*, June 18, 1960, p. 11.
3. George Gerbner, "The Individual in a Mass Culture." An address to the Department of Elementary School Principals, National Education Association, March 1960, p. 13.
4. Gerbner, "The Individual in a Mass Culture," NEA address, p. 13.
5. Paul F. Lazarsfeld and Robert K. Merton, "Mass Communication, Popular Taste and Organized Social Action," in Wilbur Schramm (ed.), *Mass Communications* (Urbana: University of Illinois Press, 1949), pp. 459–480.
6. *Variety*, October 1957.
7. Walter Lippmann, *New York Herald Tribune*, October 11, 1960.
8. Joseph Alsop, *New York Herald Tribune*, October 31, 1960.
9. Charles A. Thompson, *Television and Presidential Politics* (Washington, D.C.: The Brookings Institution, 1956), p. 116.
10. Thompson, *Television and Presidential Politics*, p. 54.
11. Angus Campbell et al., *The American Voter* (New York: John Wiley & Sons, 1960), pp. 542–543.
12. Alfred O. Hero, *Americans in World Affairs* (Boston: World Peace Foundation, 1960), pp. 6, 10, 14.
13. David Riesman and Michael Maccoby, "The American Crisis," *Commentary*, June 1960, pp. 461–472.
14. Dr. Jerome D. Frank, *Breaking the Thought Barrier: Psychological Challenges of a Nuclear Age*. Lectures 1 and 2. March 18 and April 1, 1960. Department of Psychiatry, The Johns Hopkins University, Baltimore, Maryland.
15. Frank, *Breaking the Thought Barrier*, and Dallas W. Smythe, "The Spiral of Terror and the Mass Media," Institute of Communications Research, University of Illinois, Urbana, Illinois.
16. Albert Einstein, telegram quoted in *The New York Times*, May 25, 1946, p. 13.

7

"War is like a plague or a disease which all nations should unite to exterminate"

Editor's Note: Probably the most widely known paper Dallas Smythe ever delivered was "The Spiral of Terror and the Mass Media." It was a dramatic, arresting title that caught the sense of how he felt about nuclear policy and where it was leading this country and the rest of the world. Those who remember the 1950s and 1960s know the threat of destruction that hung as a black pall over civilization. They will recall how some citizens built fallout shelters in their cellars or backyards, believing that survival was possible after a nuclear attack. They will recall how public fallout shelters in basements of buildings were stocked with large canisters of water and biscuits so those inside would not starve while they waited for outside radiation to decline. They will recall the cries of "un-American" hurled at those who contested this country's nuclear policy, of "pinko" fixed to those who called for an easing of East-West tensions. Intimidation did not always work. Many voices cried out for sanity, and Dallas Smythe's was one of them.

"The Spiral of Terror and the Mass Media" existed in several slightly modified versions. During my visit with Smythe in December 1991, he exclaimed, "I've discovered that in my file I have copies of two somewhat different versions of this 'Spiral of Terror,' and both of them were apparently used." The talk originally was delivered at the Annenberg School of Communications at the University of Pennsylvania on September 22, 1960. He rewrote parts of it based on "my experience in giving it at these various theological seminaries that I was speaking at—somewhat different in its thrust." He confirmed that "there may be still a third version, sort of like your history of *The Communist Manifesto*"—Smythe's reference to an article I coauthored with Ronald

Bettig ("Translating the *Manifesto* into English; Nineteenth Century Communication, Twentieth Century Confusion," published in *Journal of Communication Inquiry*, Summer 1987). About these versions of "The Spiral of Terror," Smythe said, "You don't have to consider that I feel one is any more authentic than the other."

He fondly remembered the first time he gave the talk, "when Gilbert Seldes was dean of the Annenberg School. That was quite an impressive affair. There were about 300 people in the room. The title had drawn them. And I gave an impassioned presentation. Gilbert Seldes—he was no slouch as a performer, critic, and creative artist—he came down front and said, 'Dallas, you should have been on the stage. That was fantastic.' He said, 'Your title is superb. I couldn't have thought of such a good title.'"

Smythe gave similar "Spiral of Terror" talks in the following months. "Hell, it felt like a former vaudeville circuit. I must have delivered that in ten different places, including theological seminaries, all over the country, even in Texas. And in every place where I delivered it to an audience I got a warm response, especially in the religious establishment. The theologians [...] were delighted to find someone who was willing to talk about the ideological aspects of the Cold War. They were quite openly considering the role of religion as an opponent of oppressive authority, there and here. [...] They were very open-minded about the question. [...] I found genuine freedom of inquiry possible there, when I developed a point of view."

The version of "The Spiral of Terror" presented here was issued in mimeo form by the Institute of Communications Research at the University of Illinois and identified as a lecture presented at the Annenberg School. This is its first publication.

The Spiral of Terror and the Mass Media

**[Annenberg School of Communications,
University of Pennsylvania, September 22, 1960]**

As recently as six months ago I would have offered you under the title, "Mass Communications and Modern Society," an academic survey of the process of communication in the light of what we know of the nature of modern society. It would have been a conventional, non-controversial talk. Since the fateful First of May, however, when the U-2 plane came down in Russia, neither you nor I can afford the luxury of being academic and non-controversial. After all, we can hardly stay in an ivory-tower when the existence of those ivory-towers, and of all life on this planet, is threatened. So today I will talk first about the balance of terror, or as I prefer to call it, the spiral of terror, and then about the way the communications process and especially the mass media play a fateful role of guiding us either to destruction or to continued growth.

Need I convince you that mankind is in a crisis? One super-hydrogen bomb is enough to destroy all life on the earth. In the United States alone, we have 10,000 times this capacity for nuclear destruction. We have even thought of building a Doomsday Bomb, which would cost only between $10 and $100 billion, and which would literally blow the whole earth to bits. In Colorado alone, we have stockpiled enough nerve gas to wipe out all mankind. We have one strain of Botulinus toxin strong enough that a mere glassful, properly distributed, would kill everyone on earth. Not only do we and the Russians have these terror weapons, but we and they threaten to use them. We tell the Russians that if they or their allies make certain moves in relation to Western Europe we will strike with nuclear weapons. The Russians tell us that if we continue to send spy planes over their country they will strike us with nuclear weapons.

It is hopeless to put our faith in defensive measures. Should we feel secure behind our radar screen? We boast that on the offensive we can confuse the Russian defensive radar screen. Certainly, the Russians can do the same thing to ours. Do our Polaris submarines give us safety? Or won't the Russians have an equivalent weapon to use on us? If there are two things certain in this world, one of them is that for every defense there is an offense and vice-versa. The other is that accidents will happen. And if we live long enough with these terror weapons on 24-hour alert, many of them airborne 24-hours a day, one day we will have nuclear war accidentally, even if we don't want it at all. A military man I know, speaking of the world-wide alert called by [Secretary of Defense Thomas] Gates in Paris on May 15, remarked that he was then in West Germany and that in such an alert all men started their weapons or vehicles in motion toward the "enemy." Armed planes took off, tanks started toward the frontiers, missiles were prepared for firing. He said, "Of course, the thing only lasted 8 minutes, and then they called it off. If it had lasted 15 minutes, the planes would have been over some of the targets, and the nuclear bombs would have been dropped."

Let us be reasonable about it. Just maybe, no one will build and use the Doomsday Bomb and blow the world to bits. Just maybe, no psychotics will get control of enough nuclear missiles or bombs, even when the "nth" nation has possession of them, to kill all animal life on earth for 5,000 years. While we can consider these possibilities intellectually, they are emotionally incomprehensible to us. Even so, where do we stand? Even a very small scale nuclear war between ourselves and the Russians would kill at least 6 to 20 million Americans. It is more likely that such a war would kill many more. Thus, Henry Rowen of the RAND Corporation speaks of a study for the Joint Committee on Atomic Energy of the Congress in 1959 of a relatively small attack and says:

> It was estimated that this attack would cause 50 million deaths plus 20 million serious casualties, and the destruction and damage of about one-half of the homes in the United States. This attack, while not the smallest that might occur, is substantially less than the largest that might be experienced in the 1960s.[1]

Even for those who survived the attack itself, our way of life would be gone. As Bertrand Russell says:

> What is quite certain is that the world which would emerge from a nuclear war would not be such as is desired by either Moscow or Washington. ...It would consist of destitute populations, maddened by hunger, debilitated by disease, deprived of the support of modern industry and means of transport, incapable of supporting educational institutions, and rapidly sinking to the level of ignorant savages.[2]

Even Winston Churchill, the man credited with first formulating our policy of cold war in his Fulton, Missouri speech in 1946, spoke of nuclear war in that speech in these terms:

> The dark ages may return, the stone age may return on the gleaming wings of science, and what might now shower immeasurable material blessings upon mankind may even bring about its total destruction. Beware, I say: time is short.[3]

Both victor and loser, if you could ever determine which was which, would be too busy trying to stay alive to bother about the other.

War obviously means that all would lose. And this conclusion is true irrespective of whether we refer to the Democracies or the Communists. It is true whether we be individually Republicans or Democrats. In this view, war is like a plague or a disease which all nations should unite to exterminate.

Why, then, do we nationally regard it otherwise? Why do we say, "Disarmament is necessary but we've learned you can't trust the Russians. The only thing they respect is force. Therefore, only by being stronger than they can we give the Russians an effective reason to disarm. In short, we must first arm more than they in order to disarm." This is the way our foreign policy is justified. This is an absurd and false solution to our crisis for it rests on a false assumption. It rests on the assumption that possession of superior destructive force assures victory. This used to be true. It was true for many thousands of years. It was true in World War II. With old-fashioned weapons one side could overpower the other and impose its will on it. Even the losers in World War II escaped with most of their populations alive, while we in the United States lost hardly more lives in that war than we do in an equal period from accidents of one kind or another. But as we know but have not fully appreciated as yet, superior force no longer means victory: modern war means that everyone loses.

The absurdity of arming to disarm is easy to see in another way. If we try to out-arm them, they will try to out-arm us. Neither side may be ready to discuss limiting the production of the most effective arms because precisely these are what we must keep to be stronger than they are. The race to intensify the "balance of terror" thus spirals until either accidental war or preventive war starts. In these circumstances, disarmament talks are nothing but a screen behind which the arms race continues. C. Wright Mills well calls this "crackpot realism." Permeating our thinking on this, especially today in the presidential campaign, is the idea that the only realistic posture is one of toughness. Riesman and others have pointed out that this "masculinity kick" is peculiar to us in the United States. The English, for instance, do not share it. Riesman has also pointed out in a provocative piece in *Commentary* that this pose of tough realism often means no more than the opposite of idealism, reasonableness, and morality.[4] We might add that a good illustration lay in the U-2 incident. In the name of tough realism, we have made liars out of all our teachers and preachers by defending lying as a matter of national policy.

Our Dulles policy of "massive deterrence" threatened total war if the

Russians made small inroads on what we consider our sphere of influence. It was seen to be ineffective. Would we *really* destroy civilization for the sake of keeping an exiled ruler of China in possession of some islands off the mainland of that country? So the present trend is to build up capacity for fighting "limited wars" (with "small" atomic weapons). While they are intended to be limited, it does not appear that, in fact, they could be kept from spreading to general wars.

A recent paper on "Accidental War" by the Mershon Committee on Education in National Security at Ohio State University concludes that an accidental war is most likely to come about through the spread of a small or limited war. If, they say, in a time of moderate tension a small war occurs, we may have what they call a "self-generating accidental war."

> A major power which considers its interest threatened decides to intervene on a limited scale and does so. Its intervention is met by warnings and threats from the other side. One side, and probably then the other, places its forces on some level of alert. Intelligence-gathering processes are under great strain. National leaders are watching events with anxiety. One side places its forces in a higher state of readiness and the other, predictably, follows suit. The danger at this point is enormously heightened by any pressure to launch a pre-emptive attack. The situation is tense and conspicuously unstable. Any spark—a false radar warning, an accidental overflight, a failure in communications—could trigger an accidental war.
>
> The critical point in this cycle of events is reached not when one side becomes convinced that the other side is about to attack, *but when either side concludes that the situation has deteriorated to a state where war is inevitable.*[5]

No, disarmament negotiations which assume that our real reliance will continue to be on superior destructive power are a trap; our only real hope is the abolition of war. The Pugwash conferences, attended by advisors to leaders in both the West and the East, concluded with a notable absence of qualifying phrases:

> In the end, only the absolute prevention of war will preserve human life and civilization in the face of chemical and bacteriological as well as nuclear weapons. No ban of a single weapon, no agreement that leaves the general threat of war in existence, can protect mankind sufficiently.[6]

Why then do we fail to realize the peril in which we stand? Dr. Jerome Frank of Johns Hopkins University offered an answer to this question in some recent lectures from which I am borrowing liberally in this portion of my remarks.[7] He asks the question: what are the blocks which prevent us, at the individual and group levels, from acting rationally to deal with this crisis? He answers that we respond to this massive danger with a number of psychological mechanisms which lead us to aggravate rather than solve the crisis (somewhat as a mental patient, say an alcoholic, recognizes that "alcohol will kill me," as he takes another bottle to bed with him). Taken all together, these mechanisms are a "thought barrier" to rational alternatives to mutual destruction.

1. The first of these mechanisms is an apathy or fatalism response. The problem is too big to cope with. We're done for. While the person thinks about the crisis, there is a kind of sad pleasure in the extravagant size and inevitability of the apocalyptic disaster. But the person doesn't continue to think about the problem. As Riesman says:

> Although they are willing to countenance arms spending, a large number of Americans cannot bring themselves to contemplate the true horror of war, and so they simply go to sleep when they are asked to "wake up" to the dangers that face them. They have learned that the thing to do with anxiety (whether based on real danger or not) is to rid oneself of it through drink, drugs, or canned fantasies.[8]

To which I would add sex as a common anodyne for nuclear anxiety. To the extent that young people tend to marry younger these days, it may be due in part to the mutually reinforcing tendencies to find relief from anxiety in sex, and to enjoy married life as an adult perquisite today, because they may all be blown away tomorrow.

However that may be, we know that the public is largely apathetic and alienated from concern with the vital issue of survival. *About half of the adult population has no interest in international questions, even in times of crisis. No more than 15 percent of our adults are interested in world affairs to a significant degree. And not more than 10 percent of them typically mention international questions as among those most crucial in determining their votes.* Few Americans believe that they could do much about international affairs even if they knew more about them, other than by voting.[9]

What has been the contribution of the mass media to this apathy? If its attempts—sporadic and unconsidered—to shock the public into awareness of our nuclear crisis have been blunted by a withdrawal maneuver, this is not surprising. For the commodity orientation given everything it touches—even politics—by our commercial popular culture fosters alienation in our citizens. And, as Lazarsfeld and Merton argued more than a decade ago, the escapist nature of most of the content of the mass media has for the citizen a "narcotizing dysfunctional" effect.[10] While the fatalism mechanism is excusable when found in children, it is hard to accept in adults. But there it is.

2. The second mechanism is habituation to the threat. Bernard Baruch expressed this one well: "Time is two-edged. It not only forces us nearer to our doom if we do not save ourselves, but even more horrible, it habituates us to existing conditions which, by familiarity, seem ever less threatening."[11] The disaster hasn't happened yet; perhaps it never will—is the way the mind runs. But on this cushion of self-delusion we get progressively closer to the disaster. Last month, the papers carried a story that the Air Force had established a new organization to select target sites for bombs and missiles in Russia. Twenty years ago, this would have been regarded as almost equal to a declaration of war. In 1939, an "alert" which started all our troops, missiles, and aircraft toward the enemy frontier with live ammunition would have been regarded as even closer to war itself. Today, we hardly notice the fact that we live, every hour and every minute, on the brink of losing our lives, our way of life, and our civilization. *This* is habituation, and it is horrible. Again, our mass media must accept some responsibility. The commercial custom of attracting a daily market for newspapers and a daily audience interest for TV-radio news through the shock-value of violence or the threat of violence—be it the emphasis on accidents and natural catastrophes or the emphasis on wars or warlike developments—tends undiscriminatingly to reduce *all* emergencies to a uniform and meaningless level. Douglass Cater, in speaking of press coverage of Presidential press conferences, says:

> The equating of news with sensationalism distracts attention from grave problems at hand. The press rushes hell-bent after the trivial and the fleeting, ruled more by a compulsion to make headlines than to exercise its more serious calling. Government leaders are capable at times of evasions and even downright deceptions without being clearly exposed.[12]

Quite apart from the debilitating effect of sensationalism is the fact that our mass media typically present all information and especially world-issues in snippets without context. People of limited education (but not necessarily limited intelligence) seldom have the framework in which to place data concerning complex, far-off developments. And our media usually do a very poor job of placing such information in any sort of context except that of the sponsor's product. To this must be added the charge that where an attempt to provide a context is made, it often is distorted by our own propaganda "line." This is more easily detectable with TV than with the other media if you watch it closely. Thus, in broadcasting the full press conference held by Mr. Khrushchev in Paris in May, the context provided by [Richard C.] Hottelet and [Walter] Cronkite described Mr. K. as so irrational that he seemed to be almost chewing the rugs. To be sure, Mr. K. was using harsh words. But while what he said was tough, it was not irrational in the sense in which rug chewing was attributed to Hitler.

3. The third mechanism is denial of the existence of the threat. Sometimes it is deliberate, as when our national leaders talk of our capacity to wipe out Russia while ignoring or minimizing the certainty that we would suffer retaliation. Rare, indeed, is the mass media performance which reports such statements *with the addition of the omitted facts.* Indeed, as Douglass Cater says:

> When the times are really perilous, there is a tendency to abdicate discussion altogether. "One of the remarkable aspects of the Middle East crisis has been the comparative silence of the American people and the almost total lack of debate on the whole thing in Congress," a reporter commented during one tense point in that recurrent crisis (quoting James Reston, *The New York Times*, July 29, 1958). A Congressman who ventured to discuss the issues was told by Speaker Rayburn that it was a good time to avoid public discussion.[13]

4. The fourth mechanism is a fallacious appeal to history. As I pointed out above, the mass media have denatured the feeling of crisis until warnings are not only uncredited, they are effectively unheard by most of our adults. But even for better-educated and thoughtful people, "Wolf" has been cried too often by older men like me. Viewers, with alarm, have built up the feeling that *nothing* can be as bad as we say this crisis is. People think: We've come through other wars, we can survive this one. Death won't come to me this way. Every picked soldier starting on a dangerous mission feels, "it can't happen to me," he will be one of the lucky ones to survive it. But this is a fallacy. From the dawn of history down to the Tokyo firebomb raids, man had increased his life-killing power only by a factor of from 1 to 4,000. But the order of increase in destructive capacity in the past 15 years is between 12,500 to 1 and infinity to 1. Few soldiers would go on a mission if they *knew* all of them would be killed. This is qualitatively a new threat and one which forces us to reconsider our whole policy of reliance on destruction as a means of solving problems.

5. Another mechanism is to argue that nuclear weapons will not be used because they *are* so terrible. For example, poison gas was not used in World War II for this reason. This too is a fallacy, for our whole military power today is based on the use of nuclear weapons, whereas, in 1940, it was based on conventional weapons and not on poison gas. Today, we don't have enough conventional weapons to fight a war.

6. There is a sixth mechanism which is terribly general amongst us. Dr.

Frank calls it the "insensitivity to the remote." A parent who is very upset by a minor accident to a child is quite unmoved by an earthquake which kills 10,000 people in South America. An alcoholic takes a drink, knowing that tomorrow he will feel terrible. We propose to give nuclear weapons to West Germany to deter the Russians today, knowing that today's allies may be tomorrow's enemies and that the Russian problem today may seem as nothing compared to what we may have when Egypt and Israel, China and Cuba have nuclear weapons to back up their aspirations. We have difficulty in foregoing an immediate reward in order to escape later punishment which may be disproportionately severe. While this mechanism may be inherent in the world's culture today, it is not necessarily permanently so.

In fact it has been the historical purpose of education, of most religions, and of the arts to progressively eliminate it through the development of sensitivity to the remote both in time and space. It must be admitted, however, that our mass media today, while encouraging sensitivity in certain ways, also work against it in other important ways. Thus, the whole emphasis on present spending (financed by installment credit) tends to devalue the future. The lack of context in which world news is characteristically presented encourages ethnocentric views and tends to validate whatever opportunistic actions are taken in the names of cherished values like freedom and democracy. Stereotyping, as we shall point out later, has special dangers in our crisis. But it also is used unconsciously by the mass media in ways which perpetuate insensitivity to the remote. For example, see my study of the nationalities of heroes and villains in New York TV drama programs in 1953, where the whole continents of Asia and Africa were virtually unrepresented at all, and villains were disproportionately drawn from European countries while heroes were disproportionately white Americans.[14]

7. A seventh and more easily remediable mechanism is the use of reassuring words to describe our predicament and our actions when these words have lost their meaning in such contexts. For example, we talk of defense against nuclear attack when there is *no* defense. We talk of civilian defense when our experts' studies calmly assume that we can accept 50 million casualties and still keep our civilization going—an assumption which can easily be proved fallacious. Where would *you* get your food, your water, your antibiotics? We talk of national security when, as Dr. Frank says, no nation can maintain security for its citizens at the expense of the security of other nations. We send an airplane that might contain nuclear weapons to spy on Russia and we lie about its purpose. When the

lie is exposed, we say we lied not for some narrow national purpose but to perpetuate morality. We lie to guard our dedication to the truth. When millions of Japanese demonstrate against our President's visit to their country, we dismiss the demonstrations as being the work of Communists. When our national position in the world has deteriorated for 10 years, we hail our "feat of leadership."

For this mechanism our mass media must take a large share of the responsibility. They are the word merchants and the image makers. They are the possessors of "freedom of the press." They it is who have largely abandoned independent evaluation of world affairs and accepted a role of conducting public relations for our national administration. This is what [Douglass] Cater and [James] Reston refer to as "managing the news."[15] And while some of the other mechanisms have been practiced unconsciously by the mass media, that can hardly be said of this one.

8. The eighth and last of the mechanisms is one which we also should be able to do something about. It is the mechanism of stereotyping. Caught in a terribly anxious situation, we stereotype the enemy as all bad, cruel, dangerous, and ourselves as all good, kind, and peaceful. We scapegoat. The circular mechanism is obvious: they are the enemy because they are bad; they are bad because they are the enemy. Underlying this mechanism is a fundamental law of the human mind: people perceive what they expect or assume they will see and hear. For this there is abundant laboratory evidence. In our present situation, we twist communications from the enemy. As Louis Jalle put it, "For Moscow to propose what we can accept seems to us even more sinister and dangerous than for it to propose what we cannot accept."[16] When we meet and like an individual Russian we conclude that it is not the Russian people who are our enemies but their leaders. I must emphasize that it is the same way with the Russians. Their image of us is the mirror-image of the one we have of them. They see us as untrustworthy, war-mongering, and dangerous and themselves as peace-loving and honorable.

What are the dangers of this stereotyping, Dr. Frank asks? There are two, he says: In the first place, the stereotyping tends to disrupt communications between us and the Russians. We are afraid of being called soft-on-Communism if we approach them. We are afraid that we will be poisoned by their propaganda if we listen to them. The effect is to perpetuate the stereotype and to prevent us from correcting its view of them. The second danger is the greater as the stereotyping tends to make itself come true by means of what Robert K. Merton calls the "self-fulfilling prophecy." For example, for some time now the Russians have been making conciliatory proposals and suggestions for disarmament which we consistently reject. How does this affect their image of us and what are the consequences? Since they are undoubtedly convinced of their own sincerity, as we are of ours, our attitude can only serve to exasperate them. Because they distrust us, as we do them, they will naturally conclude from our persistent rejection of their overtures that we are looking for excuses to continue arming and the only possible purpose of this must be to attack them. Their obvious next step might be to conclude that their only hope of survival would be to attack us first. At this point, their conciliatory proposals might indeed become screens for their own arming, heightening our fear that they would attack us, to forestall which we would have to attack them first. Each side now fears that the other side will strike first. As a result, each side frantically builds up its second-strike force so as to be able to retaliate if the other side should strike first. But this is not enough because the side which strikes first has an enormous advantage. Therefore, each side must build up the capacity to strike first so that it can attack if it sees the other side is about to strike first.

The U-2 incident showed the Russians our concern for intelligence about first-strike preparations and confirmed for them this part of the self-fulfilling prophecy. The result is that each country's original policy, that under no condition would it strike first, has begun to shift to the position that it must be prepared to strike first. Despite our President's assurance that we would not start a general nuclear war, we now find the Commander-in-Chief of the Strategic Air Command saying last year, "People must understand that you never must get in the position that you cannot start a war yourself. You always must have a capability to strike first."[17] Finally, the fact that we reach this aggressive posture reinforces the stereotypes.

These are the mechanisms which make up the Thought Barrier behind which we seem, like the lemmings, to be headed for disaster. If I have emphasized the contribution which we in the United States make to the spiraling terror, it is because I know more about our side of the fence; I am sure that analogous mechanisms work on the Russian side of the fence too, but I cannot document them.

These mechanisms the human race has built up over tens of thousands of years. Its survival was not threatened when they were practiced between tribes with primitive technology. But today, thanks to our technology, all the peoples of the world are now effectively living within the limits of a village of about 250 people. And the ways of thinking which formerly served the tribes in a world with room to spare now threaten our total extinction. The issue in our crisis is whether we can change our habits and institutions, whether we can break through the Thought Barrier soon enough to find ways of living together in peaceful competition or whether we are as powerless to save ourselves as are the lemmings. Is there a flaw in the makeup of the human species which is incompatible with its survival? Many of us don't think there is, but if we don't break through the Thought Barrier, we will be wrong. We will not *be.*

What can be done? It is easy to say and difficult to do. In general, it requires two kinds of actions. One is for our nation to enter in good faith in negotiations with the Communists to halt the arms race and to reverse it. The other is for us to reduce tensions through breaking through the Thought Barrier. The two lines of action will reinforce each other. They also have a common base which is simply this: that we must develop non-violent sanctions for settling disagreements between nations. It would indeed be unrealistic to expect that suddenly we should be able to practice Gandhian non-violence on an international scale. Ultimately, however, it is a feasible objective which should not be too surprising to you in a university which bears the name of the great Quaker, William Penn.

You and I in our capacity as students of the mass media of communications, however, have a special opportunity and obligation to ask and answer several questions. What is the role of the mass media in making foreign policy in the United States? What can be done by the mass media to break through the Thought Barrier and thus to reduce tensions and reverse the terror spiral in foreign affairs?

How is foreign policy made in the United States? The forces which make it are shown in the following model [Figure 1]. The strength of the forces is indicated roughly by the heaviness of the lines which surround their names.

You will note that the general public has no appreciable influence in foreign-policy making. This should not be surprising when we recall the small degree of interest it has in this topic and its almost totally passive relation to it. It has more interest and effect on domestic policy matters, but, overall, even in voting for president, we have Angus Campbell and his associates finding:

> Some individuals are sensitive to the full range of contemporary political events; they know what they want their government to do and they use their vote in a very purposeful manner to achieve within their power the policy alternatives that they prefer. Such people do not make up a very large proportion of the electorate. The typical voter has only a modest understanding

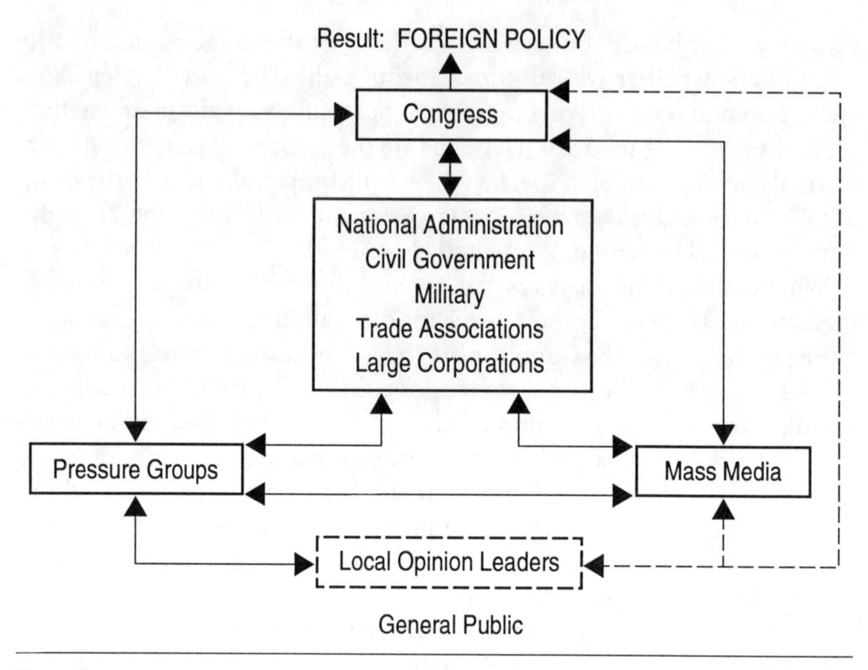

FIGURE 1

> of the specific issues and may be quite ignorant of matters of public policy that more sophisticated individuals might regard as very pressing.[18]

They did not "find much evidence of the kind of structured political thinking that we might expect to characterize a well-informed electorate."

Local opinion leaders, we find, are much more concerned with local problems than national, more with national than international. Those who have the better understanding of foreign affairs tend to be the professionals—the college educated group, including the college faculties themselves. While they talk to each other more than to others in their communities, they do offer the potential for effective pressure on the higher echelons of foreign policy structure. Those local opinion leaders who are in the top business elite and who typically are the decision-making and power wielding leadership for local issues in urban communities are mostly not interested in foreign affairs.[19] They know that their counterparts at the national level speak effectively in this area. Thus, Riesman, in commenting on a recent study which found that community leaders were as much in favor of fighting the Communists in Asia as was the general public, remarks:

> However, we must remember that these are *community* leaders being asked about international matters—matters outside their usual orbits of experience if not of discourse, matters on which it may be that both they and the population at large must accept the dimensions structured for them by national leaders and national media.[20]

Indeed, the evidence is that local opinion leaders' attitudes have come closer to those of the relatively uneducated since the war.

> Paul Sheatsley at the AAPOR [American Association of Public Opinion Research] meetings in 1955 presented the following example: in 1947, 44 percent of grammar school graduates would deny a Communist the right to speak on the radio as compared with 78 percent in 1954, while in 1947, 31 percent of the educated would deny the right as against 71 percent in 1954.[21]

We turn now to the heart of the foreign policy making process: the national administration. The Constitution vests principal authority for foreign policy in the President, hence the Executive branch of the government. But you will note that I am using the term "national administration" in a loose sense to include not only the constitutional administration but also the de facto economic administration consisting of hundreds of trade associations, national business organizations (such as the Chamber of Commerce and the NAM [National Association of Manufacturers]), and the larger business corporations. While loose in a legal sense, this usage has the merit of realism. For the intricate and intimate relations between private business and the civil government, and even more between private business and the military in our government (through contracting for national defense), give the whole complex a unitary character in foreign policy making, in contrast with the other parts of my model.

It is not my purpose here to attempt a refined analysis of the relation of forces within this national administration, nor of their motives. While the influence of the profit motive in relation to war contracts is powerful—H. M. Gray estimates that the cold war has brought some $600 million in war contracts—one should not overestimate economic determinacy. The business elite and their colleagues in the military may, as Riesman says:

> rationalize by putting full blame on the Russians and by parading the horrors of Communism; in effect they want the debate to remain polarized and the proponents of pacifism to seem religious odd-balls.[22]

Yet they are not evil plotters, and their Thought Barrier attitudes are not beyond change.

Apart from the matter of motives, the administration has superior power in policy making because of its command of technology—as in the case of the AEC. Once the technical decisions are taken, Congress and the mass media, and the public are presented with faits accomplis in many aspects of foreign policy making. Even the power to restrict the flow of information, which the administration enjoys, tends to concentrate policy-making power in itself.[23] Structurally, this administration is far from monolithic (as also is that in Russia). The almost innumerable agencies of government with their business clienteles come to represent competitive policies. As Morgenthau says:

> In such departments as State and Defense, the absence of clear lines of authority and of an organization tailored to the functions to be performed *invites* intra-agency war. To win these wars, the belligerents enter into alliances with other belligerents—with factions in Congress and in the White House, with business enterprises, and with the mass media of communications. The deliberate leak to a journalist or member of Congress becomes a standard weapon with which one agency tries to embarrass another, or force the hand of higher authority, or establish an accomplished fact.[24]

In such fashion are policies in foreign affairs advanced by the administration.

But while the administration may *advance* foreign policy in this way, it seldom is able, as it was in the case of U.S. intervention in the Korean war, to be self-sufficient in *making* it. Commonly, the competition of conflicting pressure groups, political groups, and intra-administration factions requires resort to two other theaters of action. One of these theaters of action is the mass media of communications.

Policy trial balloons are "leaked" in the mass media. If they achieve sufficient coverage in the mass media, the illusion of the support of "public opinion" is created. Let leading columnists and the editorial page of *The New York Times* and a dozen or so other newspapers support the trial balloon and for practical purposes public opinion in favor of it has been made. According to Douglass Cater:

> Prior to the announcement of the so-called "Eisenhower Doctrine" for the Middle East, Mr. Dulles engaged in three days of systematic leakage to the reporters on the details. By the third day, when Congressional leaders were finally informed of the new proposal, one news dispatch noted that they "were cautious in their reaction...but the Administration's plan had been so widely publicized before the leaders reached the White House that...they can do little more than adopt the new policy as presented."[25]

It is in this connection that the tendency, observed above, for the mass media to accept uncritically handouts concerning foreign affairs from the White House in the past eight years has strengthened the Thought Barrier immeasurably.[26] The practical abandonment by the mass media of their professed function of serving as a "watchdog on government" in relation to foreign affairs has given the national administration the power to make foreign policy unilaterally subject to no effective check. But the mass media are not merely passive factors in the foreign-policy-making structure. Some chief executives of the mass media have come to hold cold-war points of view which restrict access to the public of other points of view. Thus, we note the commitments of David Sarnoff, Henry Luce, and others to Radio Free Europe and other activities in the cold war. And we note that an NBC commentator who failed to follow the "official" line of excoriating the Russian Ambassador to the UN was promptly punished. Also, we note that Mutual Broadcasting System was recently patted on the back by the House Un-American Activities Committee for its program policy for dealing with the Reds.[27]

Now while communications research has had difficulties in measuring the effects of mass media materials where there is a diversity of points of view represented in them, there has been no doubt about its power when there is a monopoly of one point of view in mass media content. The well-considered judgment of Joseph Klapper on this point is unqualified:

> Research indicates that of the various conditions which make persuasion likely to be successful, one of the most, if not *the* most powerful is a monopoly propaganda position. The term "monopoly propaganda," or "monopolization" is used to refer to propaganda which is for one or another reason unopposed, i.e., which is faced with no competing counter-propaganda.[28]

And Lazarsfeld and Merton remark that monopolization:

> obtains when there is little or no opposition in the mass media to the diffusion of values, policies or public images. That is to say, monopolization of the mass media occurs in the absence of counter propaganda. In this restricted sense, monopolization of the mass media is found in diverse circumstances. It is, of course, indigenous to the political structure of authoritarian society, where access to the media of communication is wholly closed to those who oppose the official ideology. The evidence suggests that this monopoly played some part in enabling the Nazis to maintain their control of the German people.[29]

We seem to have drifted into a situation in which the mass media partly by design and partly unconsciously serve to propagate a cold-war propaganda line which pushes us along the spiral of terror and reinforces the Thought Barrier.

It may sound cynical to hold, as I do, that the mass media *in relation to foreign policy* provide a surrogate for public opinion. But in view of the sedated and apathetic condition of the general public and the slender involvement of the local opinion leaders in foreign policy matters, what other conclusion is possible? It is precisely in connection with the mass media that *in the short run,* the greatest good can be accomplished by people like yourselves in breaking down the Thought Barrier. For I am convinced that many individuals in substantial policy-making positions in the mass media are open to reason on ways and means of breaking through this barrier. The effort should be made to reach them effectively with convincing evidence of the need for change in the ways they handle foreign policy news—ways which I am sure they have grown into unconsciously and unintentionally. Specifically, I mean that they should be told just how stereotyping contributes to their own and everyone's destruction, just how they could counter the "fatalism" mechanism, the "habituation" mechanism, the "denial of the existence of the threat" mechanism, the "fallacious appeal to history," and the "insensitivity to the remote" mechanisms. They ought to be easy to convince that "reassuring but meaningless" words applied to foreign affairs needlessly advance the spiral of terror.

They need to be reminded that their influence in the short run may be decisive in creating the appearance of public opinion and, thus, supporting trial balloons. The conscientious among them will not need to be reminded that in breaking down the Thought Barrier in the short run to help avoid nuclear catastrophe, they will also be slowly educating the bulk of the population which, while ignorant of foreign affairs today, was even more ignorant of them a generation ago. The cultural lag for the bulk of the world's population can be taken care of, given enough time. It is precisely to provide this time free of nuclear war that the mass media should be encouraged to work with our elite groups in the short run to break down the Thought Barrier.

The second and ultimate theater to which the administration takes foreign policy proposals is Congress. The role of Congress tends to be one of providing a court of last resort for the determination of foreign policy. While Congressmen also float foreign policy trial balloons in the mass media, they must choose in official actions between competitive policy proposals, and absorb or otherwise give effect to pressures from pressure groups. They must ultimately pass or refuse to pass policy bills, appropriation bills, confirm or refuse to confirm ambassadors, and the like. In short, they must go through the processes which *validate* the foreign policy proposals which then *become* American foreign policy.

The role of pressure groups on foreign policy is the last to be touched on and that all too briefly. The most effective place for them to work is within the national administration. It has been known for a long time that the Roman Catholic Church affects the policy of the State Department, if only through its role in training foreign service officers through Georgetown University. The pressure groups of the business elite have great influence with the Department of Defense. In this they have been supported by the labor pressure group which has come in recent years to be in substantial agreement with the policy of management in foreign policy. As far as Congress is concerned, the business pressure groups have great influence where their specific interests are concerned.[30] Insofar as Israel enters into policy-making, the Jewish pressure group has specific influence.

There are the intellectuals as a pressure group. Here, indeed, is an opportunity for you to exert influence on foreign policy. Some of the scientists are organized and working for reversal of the spiral of terror. But many of them, under the dynamics of McCarthyism, receded into political apathy if not cynicism. The academic people other than the physical scientists have, for a variety of reasons, overlooked the exciting problems which current international affairs present for their special skills. The Committees of Correspondence, organized by David Riesman and a group of distinguished Boston scholars and social scientists, are stimulating a wide variety of studies on various facets of the problem of working for a peaceful world.[31] In the few short months since the first Committee was organized, there are now at least a dozen on as many campuses. They communicate with each other by circular letters. And, in conjunction with the Liberal Group of Congressmen, they have begun studies on many aspects of our policy problems.[32]

The broad program for groups such as these, and I hope you will organize one here if it has not already been started, is to explore alternative policies to those which now so clearly lead us to destruction. Having explored these policy possibilities, the next task is to spread them within the pressure groups which now effectively make our foreign policy. In this connection, I refer to the elite of the mass media, business, government, and the military. For again, I remind you that there are many in these elites who relish destruction no more than you or I do. Nor should one underestimate the possibility of forming new pressure groups to present the peaceful policy alternatives to the mass media, the national administration, and the Congress.

May I draw to a close with two quotations? Albert Einstein said in 1946:

> We can only sound the alarm, again and again; we must never relax our efforts to rouse in the peoples of the world, and especially in their governments, an awareness of the unprecedented disaster which they are absolutely certain to bring on themselves unless there is a fundamental change in their attitude toward one another as well as in their concept of the future. ... The unleashed power of the atom has changed everything except our ways of thinking.[33]

The other is, if you will pardon the personal note, from my six-year-old son. Several weeks ago a neighbor asked him what he intended to be when he grew up. To this question, children his age since time immemorial have automatically answered something like "a policeman," "a doctor," or some other normal occupation. My son, however, answered, very shyly and quietly, "I won't have time." Puzzled by this seemingly irrelevant answer, the neighbor pressed him for an answer. This time it was, "I won't have time. You know—the atom bomb."

There are some in our country and some in Russia and China who say that it is better to obliterate mankind than to live as Communist or capitalist slaves. These people say that all mankind might justly be destroyed in the name of freedom and democracy. What psychotic nonsense is this? A peasant in India, living at or below the level of subsistence, can see something good and something bad in both capitalism and Communism. If you tell him that he deserves to die for either, he will think you mad. And properly so. Bertrand Russell in *Common Sense and Nuclear Warfare* remarks that it "is an extreme form of religious persecution, going far beyond anything that has been advocated in previous human history" to deny to not only the inhabitants of the Capitalist and Communist nations but the inhabitants of all uncommitted nations, the most elementary freedom, which is the freedom to choose survival—and to deny it in the name of freedom.[34] He points out with a wealth of historical detail that many tyrants, for example, Genghis Khan, have been fully as evil as even the most fanatical anti-Communists believe Stalin to have been. But he adds that none of these tyrannies lasted forever, and we should be glad today that the enemies of these tyrants did not have the power to extinguish human life rather than to submit to them. Today, we need to win again the struggle for tolerance which was won in the 17th and 18th Centuries against religious intolerance. Today, it arises in the name of political tolerance.

Great powers have always been cursed by ethnocentrism. As it is expressed in stereotyping, we have noted its dangers today. Here in its essential form of political intolerance, we confront it again. In one of his unfunny moments, the English political scientist, C. N. Parkinson, refers to one common and fallacious assumption that:

> all history illustrates a story of betterment or progress with ourselves as the final product. The second lies in the assumption that such progress as there has been is a Western achievement in which no oriental can claim the smallest share.

"History," he goes on, "records no such monopoly and no such unbroken progression."

> What the historian does find, however, is a recurrence of the belief that perfection has been reached and that a given constitution (like that of the United States) represents finality.

What we in the United States and those in the Soviet Union should remember daily is that, as Parkinson concludes:

> There is, in fact, no historical reason for supposing that our present systems of governance are other than quite temporary expedients.[35]

This long-view of the problem is valid. But it would be unfortunate to leave the issue at this point. For the assumption underlying the question "Would you rather be a slave or dead?" is wrong. This question assumes that there are only extreme alternatives left to us. And this is not true. There is an enormous range of possibilities in the middle. And the exploration of these possibilities, as well as their implementation, demands of us courageous and exciting efforts. Our value system is today challenged, just as we challenge that of the Russians. We face the virile task of acting to materialize our value system in a peaceful solution of the conflict. In part, this requires bargaining with our antagonists. And in bargaining, we must remember that in international politics as in international radio allocation, to use the words of former FCC Commissioner E. M. Webster, each group "has been forced by circumstances to accept a policy of 'give and take,' realizing that he must give in some instances in order to receive in others."

For the sake of humanity everywhere now living—for the sake of humanity which has striven over uncounted millennia for self-fulfillment, for toleration and for improvement in human life—for the sake of the uncounted generations which can come to this earth in the future to enjoy in mutual respect the fruits of a beautiful life which our technology and our science now offer us—for these reasons, if for none other, we must break through the Thought Barrier and find our way to a peaceful reversal of the spiral of terror.

Notes to "The Spiral of Terror . . ."

1. Henry Rowen, *National Security and the American Economy in the 1960s,* Study Paper No. 18. Joint Economic Committee, Congress of the United States, January 30, 1960. 86th Congress, 2nd Session, p. 24n.
2. Bertrand Russell, *Common Sense and Nuclear Warfare* (New York: Simon and Schuster, 1959), p. 42.
3. *U.S. News,* March 15, 1946, pp. 67–70.
4. David Riesman and Michael Maccoby, "The American Crisis," *Commentary,* June 1960, p. 464.
5. David E. Cummins et al., *Accidental War: Some Dangers in the 1960s.* The Mershon National Security Program. The Ohio State University, June 28, 1960, p. 17.
6. Dr. Jerome D. Frank, *Breaking the Thought Barrier: Psychological Challenges of a Nuclear Age.* Lectures 1 and 2. March 18 and April 1, 1960.
7. Frank, *Breaking the Thought Barrier.*
8. Riesman and Maccoby, "The American Crisis," p. 465.
9. Alfred O. Hero, *Americans in World Affairs* (Boston: World Peace Foundation, 1960), pp. 6, 10, 14.
10. Paul F. Lazarsfeld and Robert K. Merton, "Mass Communication, Popular Taste and Organized Social Action," in Wilbur Schramm (ed.), *Mass Communications* (Urbana: University of Illinois Press, 1949), pp. 459–480.
11. Frank, *Breaking the Thought Barrier.*
12. Douglass Cater, *The Fourth Branch of Government* (Boston: Houghton Mifflin, 1959), p. 154.
13. Cater, *The Fourth Branch of Government,* p. 155.
14. Dallas W. Smythe, *Three Years of New York Television, 1951–1953* (Urbana: National Association of Educational Broadcasters, 1953).
15. Cater, *The Fourth Branch of Government,* pp. 157–169.
16. Louis Jalle, "The Struggle Called Co-Existence," *The New York Times Magazine,* November 15, 1959. Quoted in Frank, *Breaking the Thought Barrier.*
17. General Power, "United States Defense," *Survival,* 1:54–73, p. 57. Quoted in Frank, *Breaking the Thought Barrier.*
18. Angus Campbell et al., *The American Voter* (New York: John Wiley and Sons, 1960), p. 542.
19. Alfred O. Hero, *Opinion Leaders in American Communities* (Boston: World Peace Foundation, 1960), p. 47.
20. David Riesman, "Political Communications and Social Structure in the United States," *Public Opinion Quarterly,* vol. 20, Spring 1956, p. 52.

21. Riesman, "Political Communications," p. 53n.
22. Riesman and Maccoby, "The American Crisis," p. 471n.
23. Hans J. Morgenthau, "Our Thwarted Republic," *Commentary,* June 1960, p. 476.
24. Morgenthau, "Our Thwarted Republic," p. 478.
25. Cater, *The Fourth Branch of Government,* p. 136, quoting *The New York Times,* January 1, 1957.
26. Cater, *The Fourth Branch of Government.*
27. *Broadcasting,* August 29, 1960, p. 68.
28. Joseph T. Klapper, *The Effects of the Mass Media.* Bureau of Applied Social Research, Columbia University, August 1949 (mimeo), p. IV–20.
29. Lazarsfeld and Merton, "Mass Communication, Popular Taste and Organized Social Action," pp. 475–6.
30. Bernard C. Cohen, *The Influence of Non-Governmental Groups on Foreign Policy-Making* (Boston: World Peace Foundation, 1960).
31. Committees of Correspondence, 130 Brattle Street, Cambridge 38, Massachusetts.
32. Marcus Raskin, Secretary, 1725 New House Office Building, Washington, D.C.
33. Albert Einstein, telegram quoted in *The New York Times,* May 25, 1946, p. 13.
34. Russell, *Common Sense and Nuclear Warfare,* p. 88.
35. C. N. Parkinson, *The Evolution of Political Thought* (Boston: Houghton Mifflin, 1958), p. 8.

8

"What is new in weaponry is the development . . . of tactical *nuclear weapons systems . . .* and *the readiness to use them"*

Editor's Note: A little more than twenty years after Dallas Smythe first delivered "The Spiral of Terror and the Mass Media" at the University of Pennsylvania, he returned to the title and to the theme in a paper presented in San Diego at the 1981 Conference on Culture and Communication. The "C and C" conference, as it came to be known, was a series of meetings on communications policy that alternated between sites on the West and East coasts.

By 1981 the Cold War was more than three decades old, and nuclear weapons had not been brought under control. So what was new? Many countries, not just the superpowers, now had nuclear arsenals; tactical weapons had been developed for limited deployment; there was a policy that explained how these pint-sized devices could be used in theatre warfare; and a peace movement in Europe had grown strong enough to challenge this insanity.

In our conversations in December 1991, Smythe explained to me that "The Spiral of Terror (Part 2)" attracted the wrath of a few left-wingers because it "drew a parallel between the military-industrial complex of the Soviet Union and the United States." He said all the evidence in the late 1980s "in the Soviet Union is that the arms race really fed the bureaucratic rigidities" there in much the same way it did in the Western world. The criticism Smythe received from some quarters of the Left was also, I suspect, a playing out of the tensions between those who held pro-China and those who held pro-Soviet views. Smythe had visited China a second time in 1979 and looked approvingly on many aspects of that country's development, whereas he was much less convinced that the Soviet Union was the vanguard nation as an oppositional force to capitalism.

Smythe further developed his position on international nuclear policy in "On Thinking the Unthinkable About Nuclear War and Its Consequences for the Peace Movement" (published in 1984 in *The Critical Communications Review,* volume 2, edited by Vincent Mosco and Janet Wasko). It was a favorite piece; "I like it," he told me. In the article, he said there was a greater danger of global nuclear war in 1984 than in the 1960s because "an accelerating readiness to wage it is evident in the two super powers."

In that 1984 article, he also returned to a position he had stated in "The Spiral of Terror (Part 2)," namely that while we rightly have been critical of U.S. nuclear policy, "we have been blocked from parallel critical analysis of the Soviet Union. ..." To elaborate the point, Smythe said we have "ignored the deforming effects on the Soviet Union's socialist forces of the technocratic-bureaucratic class, just as we closed our eyes to the fact that Soviet foreign policy was building an imperial structure of investments, markets, and exploitation of Third World countries—the mirror image of that of Western imperialism." He warned that Western Marxists fall into "knee-jerk irrationality unless they reject the notion that the Soviet Union knows best and can do no wrong."

When I talked with him in 1991, I asked whether, given the collapse of the Soviet Union, he still would stand by the belief that nuclear war was just as possible now as thirty years ago. "The statement I stand by, as far as the one superpower that remains is concerned, yes. I see nothing in the experience with the Gulf War that would lead me to think anything else. As long as they can control the press as efficiently as they did in the Gulf War—and the pilot study for that was the invasion of Grenada—and the way they handled the intervention in Nicaragua—and the way I think they hope to handle Cuba when they get around to crunching it—it shows a total lack of any scruples about trying to justify the position in any kind of reasonable terms. We're just using terrorism. ..." The threat of nuclear war has not gone away, "except you don't have that rivalry" between the United States and the Soviet Union and there is the Pentagon's worry about "what happens to the Soviets' nuclear weapons."

"Policy on Information and Ideology: The Spiral of Terror (Part 2)" was written by Smythe when he was a visiting professor in the Depart-

ment of Radio-TV-Film at Temple University. He told me the talk was given only once and that it was never published. The text presented here is from Smythe's only copy—a typewritten manuscript that contained several inserts in his own hand.

Policy on Information and Ideology: The Spiral of Terror (Part 2)

[Conference on Culture and Communication, San Diego, February 19–21, 1981]

I AM GOING TO TALK about the madness with which we and the Russians are preparing to launch nuclear holocaust. I speak to you as to experts sharing a critical liberal-left perspective, but also as to human beings who confront the imminence of destruction of civilization and of a large proportion of the world's population. It is timely to do so because we have just gone through a jingoistic mass hysteria concerning the hostages—an ominous foundation for the policies of a new administration apparently dedicated to increasing tensions both domestically and internationally. It is also timely because of the contrary movement for nuclear disarmament gathering momentum in Europe. I refer you to the "Letter to America" by E. P. Thompson, spokesperson for that movement,[1] and to his "Notes on Exterminism."[2] We are at a turning point in the struggle for survival. Conditions call for "controlled pessimism" (in Thompson's words), linked with fast and accurate analysis and the utmost efforts to achieve disarmament. Unless we are successful, the ultimate disaster is no more than two to ten years ahead.

You may well say, "What's new? Haven't we been in the same danger since the Cold War began some 30 years ago?" My answer will be (1) to show what is new in the weapons themselves, (2) to identify and analyze the process of which the weapons are a necessary part from a fresh viewpoint, and (3) to suggest appropriate lines of action for us all.

1. What is new in the weapons themselves? Twenty years ago, when I gave an impassioned talk at the University of Pennsylvania on *The Spiral of Terror and the Mass Media,* the US and the USSR had 6,500 nuclear weapons—more than enough to destroy all life on earth. By 1983 they will have some 24,000 *strategic* nuclear weapons. The mere multiplication of these strategic weapons in a sense does not overwhelmingly increase the danger—after all, people can only die once. What is new in weaponry is the development on both sides of *tactical* nuclear weapons systems suitable for "theater war" (as in Europe or the Persian gulf), *and* readiness to use

them as stated by [Zbigniew] Brzezinski and Vice President George Bush.[3] Plus of course the reduction in delivery time. In 1960 ICBMs took about 30 minutes. Now missiles can hit the US or USSR within about five minutes of launch. Nevertheless, we have lived 30 years in the shadow of MAD (a wonderful acronym meaning Mutual Assured Destruction). In the earlier policy of deterrence, both sides acknowledged that an exchange aimed at the US and the USSR was "unacceptable." In plain words, nuclear war was unthinkable because it would be too destructive. Today what is new is that it is not only thinkable that nuclear war be waged tactically, but official policy provides for just that. Moreover the peace movement in the past, despite brave and persistent efforts, has been inadequate to achieve its aims.

The relative success of deterrence in the sense of ICBMs making nuclear war unthinkable over the past 30 years has masked the fact that all the while the arms industries at both ends of the Exterminist axis have been doing research and development in a ceaseless search for weapons which would assure victory for the nation which made the first strike. And the apparent success in developing tactical nuclear weapons has undermined the precarious stability provided by ICBMs when they were alone. The question arises: in event of a tactical nuclear weapons exchange in a "theatre," would the war be limited to that theatre or would one or both sides escalate into an ICBM exchange into their respective heartlands if it saw itself as losing the tactical war or even in brief stalemate in such a war? The answer would be found in two aspects of the Exterminist axis: technobureaucratic and ideological. The analyses my students and I have made of the nature and reliability of command and control telecommunications networks for "managing" nuclear weaponry in the West (largely from Armed Forces budget hearings in Congress) indicate that under conditions of combat these networks would break down, at least as far as the US is concerned. As Thompson says:

> In such a hair-trigger situation, the very notion of "political" options becomes increasingly incredible. The persons who decide will not be a harassed President or First Secretary...but a small group of military technicians, whose whole training and rationale is that of war, and who can, by no conceivable argument, be said to represent the rational interests of any economic or political formation. Very probably they will act without any "political" mediation.[4]

A further new dangerous factor in the game of nuclear brinkmanship is the insecurity and unpredictability of actions by the ruling groups in both the US and the USSR, as compared with 1960. Then the US dominated the non-socialist world. It was prosperous, profitable, powerful and poised. In the 1980s, its former client states in Western Europe plus Japan are increasingly independent of US control. The collapse of the dollar from 1972 on was a signal of the end of the era that began in 1945. US self-confidence was shaken by its disastrous military defeat in Indochina and by the hostage affair—a foreseeable consequence of its hostility to the Iranian revolution. The aggressive potential of the US will be aggravated by internal tensions associated with inflations, unemployment and repressive internal measures of the Reagan administration. At the other end of the Exterminism axis, the USSR is also subject to destabilizing pressures. Its economic organization has chronically failed to produce sufficient food and other consumer goods. For a variety of reasons (ethnic, religious, economic and political) its aging ruling group faces what Thompson called "all that inflammable human material in Eastern Europe which must be held perpetually under political military and ideological controls."[5]

In short, the danger of nuclear war on a global scale is now very much greater than in 1960 because an accelerating readiness to wage it is evident in the superpowers. Irrationality is reaching epidemic proportions in and between those superpowers: a condition Europeans are now calling "Exterminism."

2. Why call the danger-process Exterminism? Because the superpowers are in a reciprocal death dance in which each cooperates antagonistically with the other. The prospect of each new refinement in nuclear weaponry on one side is the necessary stimulus for the other side to match it or go it one better. It is an irreversible ratchet process, if the relevant populations tolerate it much longer. At one level of analysis the two superpowers are symmetrical, but not equal or in balance. As Thompson says:

> The bomb...is a component in a weapons-*system*; and producing, manning and supporting that system is a correspondent social system—a distinct organization of labour, research and operation, with distinctive hierarchies of command, rules of secrecy, prior access to resources and skills and high levels of policing and discipline; a distinctive organization of production, which, while militarist in character, employs and is supported by greater numbers of civilians (civil servants, scientists, academics) who are subordinated to its discipline and rules.[6]

At this point I must come to terms with my own previous views on this matter—and to some degree most left-liberals in the US and Canada share them. We understand that capitalism has fought communism since 1917 when the Russian revolution took place. We understand that after 1945 capitalism through its leading formation, the United States, undertook to contain, and if possible destroy the Soviet Union by a combination of military threat, economic and cultural offensives. We understand well the dynamics of the Military Sales Effort in the West, as a tax-supported perpetual pump-primer for the economy. We understand how the giant corporations which benefit most from military contracts also dominate the private sector's Civilian Sales Effort. We have observed the "incremental creep" of research and development for the military through think tanks and the cooptation of scientific talents. We understand the way the Military Industrial Complex works to perpetuate itself through the formal state apparatus and through managing news and electoral campaigns via the mass media. Etc.

But we have been blocked from parallel critical analysis of the Soviet Union, for several reasons. One was that until the mid-1960s when Khrushchev fell, the Soviet Union's military preparedness seemed in fact to be defensive and reactive to aggressive initiatives from the United States. Moreover, until then the technobureaucratic structures in the USSR seemed under autonomous political control in pursuit of a non-aggressive foreign policy. And secondly, under the influence of Lenin's theory of imperialism, we saw the superpower confrontation as a holding action by the Soviet Union while capitalism played out its time in the worldwide imperialist struggle. As Thompson puts it, in that view:

> Preoccupation with the horrors of an imaginary nuclear war is diversionary (did not the Viet Cong call that bluff?), and it leads to hideous heresies, such as "neutralism," "pacificism," and to utter confusion in the class struggle. ... Meanwhile, the anti-imperialist struggle prospers in the Third World... and eventually it will be carried thence to the "barbarians" in the capitalist heartlands. The best that these barbarians can do, while they wait, is to engage in frontal class confrontation until the capitalist economies begin to buckle.[7]

Since 1965, however, Soviet military innovation has not simply been reactive and defensive. The SS-20 missiles and Backfire bomber are aggressive. The worldwide deployment of a new and very large navy has aggressive potential. And for years the evidence of the deformed socialism in the Soviet Union has been accumulating: a class struggle (unacknowledged officially) with severe repression of dissent, and the clear ascendancy to power and material privilege of an elite class of technical experts and professionals. Thompson, himself no enemy of socialism or of the USSR, must be quoted again:

> The arms complex is as clearly the leading sector of Soviet industry as it is in the United States, but this is expressed within bureaucratic modes of operation. There is some spin-off from military technology into civilian industry: civil aircraft, nuclear energy. ... The military complex and its successes are upheld as a model of organization and of management techniques, and these are exported to other sectors. Moreover, the needs of the military complex—in particular, the imperatives placed upon centralized planning, priority in access to resources, and direction of scientific skills—affect the structure of the economy as a whole, and colour the decisions of the political managers. ...
>
> At the same time there is a greater direct exposure of the Soviet population to patriotic state propaganda than in most Western democracies: that is, what is (or is attempted to be) accomplished in "The West" by the "free" operation of the media is directly inculcated in Russia by such "voluntary" organizations as DOSAAF: the Voluntary Society for Cooperation with the Army, Aviation and the Navy, with a membership of 80 million, and with clubs, sports facilities, and military-patriotic or civil defence education organized around factories, farms, and schools. And alongside and supporting all this there are the huge, quasi-autonomous operations of the Security Services, inheriting historic traditions of despotism, supporting military-patriotic ideology, and exerting an independent inertia of their own.[8]

The Soviets' thrust toward exterminism is not as aggressive as that of the West, but it has the same kind of autonomous techno-bureaucratic inertial momentum. It has the same kind of incremental growth of weaponry located in the scientific and engineering establishment with the same kind of "lead-time" commitment to innovation in weaponry that we find in the United States. It also supports tendencies in popular culture toward chauvinism, xenophobia, and in relation to China, racism.[9]

What is the role of ideology in the Exterminist axis? On both sides it has the same three functions. It stimulates war preparation. It legitimizes the privileged position of the military-industrial complexes. And it polices internal dissent. And as Thompson says:

> The two camps are united ideologically in only one matter: in mutual hostility to any genuine non-alignment, "neutralism" or "third way." For if such a way were possible, it would strike directly at exterminism's legitimacy.[10]

The picture we now see of Exterminism is of two social systems, reciprocally cooperating with antagonism with each other. While different in important respects there are two over-riding similarities between the superpowers. One is that in both the leading position is held by the technicians and bureaucrats located in institutions with self-perpetuating drives to produce ever more destructive nuclear weapons. The second is that the ideology of each system dominates its culture. Looked at together, the whole US-USSR axis is one enormous military industrial complex.

The irrelevance of classic theory of imperialism lies in the fact that there the exploited population of a colony struggles against the imperial center. There is no such effective struggle yet in either the US or the USSR against the remorseless inertial drift to disaster, unless we make one. Our populations have been entrapped in an autonomous, two-headed monster powered by ideological paranoia and corrupted by worship of instrumental reasoning which confuses abstract war games with human reality. As I turn to my last question it is important to note that because no classical-type class struggle exists in either superpower, the tactics to combat exterminism *exclude* traditional class struggle. Nothing less than ecumenical struggle is required and even so the odds are not good for success.

3. What are the lines of indicated action? The prospect of providing the battleground for a tactical nuclear war has started a European Nuclear Disarmament movement on the part of large masses of people, and some whole nations, to begin detaching themselves from the Exterminism axis—to begin with, by preventing the US from locating the new Cruise missiles on their soil. Imagine: there were 70,000 people demonstrating in Trafalgar Square on October 26, 1980! (And guess what: the American mass media systematically ignore the European Nuclear Disarmament movement.) Norway and Denmark have flatly refused to allow Cruise missiles in their countries. The Dutch and Belgian governments, having originally accepted the NATO decision to accept such missiles, are now reconsidering. Even in West Germany, the issue is still indeterminate. In both Britain and Greece the opposition parties which may win early elections are committed to unilateral disarmament and rejection of theater nuclear weapons. According to Thompson, this international movement has these principles:

a. National and international mobilization "with great rapidity" with a completion date by 1983 when Cruise missiles have been scheduled for deployment.
b. The objective is to strike directly at Exterminism, leading to the dissolution of both the NATO and Warsaw Pact blocs, and "the demystification of exterminism's ideological mythology, and thence permitting nations in both Eastern and Western Europe to resume

autonomy and political mobility." Neutralism and non-alignment everywhere are welcomed as progress against Exterminism's determinist pressures.

c. END strives to ally itself with existing anti-imperialist and national liberation movements everywhere. END has no place for sectarian divisiveness derived from vulgar Marxism. There is, of course, already a growing Non-Aligned Movement based on Third World countries. At its last two summit meetings (at Colombo and Havana) Austria attended as an observer. Why not the Nordic countries at the next summit meeting? The END movement and the Non-Aligned Movement both can be strengthened by cooperating.
d. The most critical and decisive point for END is to "engage in delicate and non-provocative work to form alliances between the peace movement in the West and constructive elements in the Communist world...which confront the exterminist structures and ideologies of their own nations." END sees this as essential to success because it is absolutely necessary that the antiexterminist movement be *non-allied* with either bloc and be seen as such. Otherwise Exterminism with its bases in the weapons-system and support complex will reassert ideological control and resume its thrust. END is very clear that its movement must *not* be mediated by official or unofficial spokespersons for either bloc. It is building a broad front including churches, Eurocommunists, Labourists, trade unionists, ecologists and East European dissidents and citizens unmediated by Party structures. It is regenerated internationalism.

What lines of action are appropriate for us in North America? For us as citizens, the answer seems clear: take stock of your own feelings, your own lives, and then take the collective actions best conceived to combat exterminism at this end of its axis. It seems clear that such group actions should be consistent with the policies of END. Beyond that I would not trespass on your decision-making stance as citizens.

But what about us as critical communications scholars? I hope you will work on that question at this conference and afterwards. For starters, I suggest there are several large problematic issues involved in demolishing Exterminism at its western end which are within the competence of critical communications scholars:

a. Critical attention to the process by which public opinion is made to support and to oppose Exterminism in North America. This calls for a fast critical review of relevant theory and then a close relationship between the theory and practice of antiexterminism.

b. Critical attention to and exposure of the Exterminist logic which underlies most uses of computers, systems analysis, and what commonly passes as social science research. In this connection, please read Joseph Weizenbaum's *Computer Power and Human Reason* with its masterful unmasking of the Eichman quality in most of North America's science and technique. My book, *Dependency Road*, tries to do the same thing from a different perspective in its chapters 10 through 12. The struggle for historical materialist method and against logical positivist philosophy is one against the ideological roots of Exterminism.

I do not pretend to have an over-arching command of theory or of the range of information about the realistic process by which popular consciousness, ideology and policy are produced under exterminist pressures in the US and Canada. To pursue that will require a collective commitment and effort by as many of us as possible. It is a daunting challenge. Yet the possibility to see our children live out their lives, or even to live out our own, depends in large measure upon how we meet this challenge. Your critical comments on this critical analysis would be very much in order.

Notes to "Policy on Information and Ideology . . ."

1. *The Nation*, January 24, 1981, pp. 67–93.
2. *New Left Review (NLR)*, May–June, 1980.
3. *The New York Times*, March 30, 1980; *Time*, January 12, 1981, p. 22.
4. *NLR* 10.
5. *NLR* 6.
6. *NLR* 7.
7. *NLR* 5.
8. *NLR* 20.
9. *NLR* 21.
10. *NLR* 24.

9

"It is necessary to recognize that the American people are constantly brain-rinsed with this rigid ideology"

EDITOR'S NOTE: In the early 1960s, Dallas Smythe was busy on numerous fronts: writing on space communication, urging international regulation of satellites, and challenging private ownership of U.S. satellites; speaking to religious groups about churches and mass media; saying his last on the *Four Theories* phenomenon; conducting (with my assistance) an inventory of public issues programs on radio and television; and working (with my assistance, again) on a submission to the FCC on behalf of UHF television interests favoring deintermixture of UHF and VHF stations in central Illinois. No doubt his greatest passion was reserved for his peace activities, which are described in some detail in the selections from his autobiography presented earlier in this volume.

Smythe's speech "Peace in a Shrinking World," which has remained unpublished, was given in Chicago to the Voters for Peace on February 5, 1963. On the copy he gave me in 1991, Smythe wrote that the talk was "possibly my best." Of section II, he said, "This has some fire." But about his statement that it would be "unrealistic" to think of "restoring capitalism in Russia," he noted in the margin, "Here I blew it!"

The Cuban missile crisis in October 1962 had brought the world to the brink of nuclear war and had demonstrated just how far the major powers would go to force each other's hand. It was a showdown on a dusty street in a Hollywood Western. The bipartisan foreign policy in the United States left precious little room in government for disagreement over the official nuclear line. Even if U.S.-Soviet tensions could be reduced somehow, there was the imminent danger that a mistake on one side could unleash an accidental war that would be just as devastating as if the assaults and counterassaults had been part of an intended policy of mutual annihilation. Nuclear arsenals were poised on both sides of the Iron Curtain.

The U-2 incident in May 1960, the Bay of Pigs fiasco in April 1961, the Cuban missile crisis the next year, the continued atmospheric testing of nuclear devices, and escalating sabre-rattling around the world all contributed to the decision of Dallas Smythe and his family to leave the United States. They felt that if they had to perish in a nuclear war, they did not want to die as Americans. Thanks to a friend in Canada, Smythe was able to make contact with several universities there. He visited them in January 1963 to explore appointment possibilities. The following month he delivered "Peace in a Shrinking World" in Chicago. He told me "This was my last public comment on peace as a U.S. citizen." In the summer of 1963, Smythe and his family left the United States.

Peace in a Shrinking World

[Address before the Voters for Peace, McCormick Place, Chicago, February 5, 1963]

My purpose tonight is to raise two questions. First, what is the political situation which faces us—and by us I mean all who give more than lip-service to a desire for peace? Second, what are the implications of this situation for peace groups? But first let me state the assumptions I am making:

1. Nuclear war is totally unacceptable. I reject in this connection the idiotic choice between being "red" or "dead." There are a host of alternative ways to be neither "red" nor "dead."
2. Nuclear deterrence inevitably will lead to nuclear war if it is continued long enough. The one sure meaning of technology, especially military technology, is that it is made to be used. The probability of accidental or unintentional nuclear war is not great in any given month; but as things now go it rises to a virtual certainty over a period of 10 or 15 years. The probability that repeated trips to the brink, such as we recently witnessed over Cuba, will produce a deliberate nuclear war is much higher.
3. The aspirations of former colonial peoples, seeking the benefits of industrialization and of political freedom, guarantee that for the

immediate future there will be a succession of popular revolutions—of which the Congo and Cuba are examples—and these revolutions would continue if all Communists were suddenly transported to Mars.

4. While this revolutionary process may be accelerated or slowed, may be assisted in peaceful ways or repressed with violence, it is irreversible. It is quite unrealistic to think of restoring colonial control to the Congo, or of restoring capitalism in Russia.
5. The miserable state of chronic tension between states which we call the Cold War must quickly be organized on a more stable, enduring and peaceful basis. In a world shrunken by the development of technology to the relative size of a single village, not only peaceful but mutually respectful relations between states are essential. The capacity for making war must be eliminated.
6. In re-making our policies to produce these realistic results we have available to us the tradition of aspiring to a democratic form of government. If in fact we have departed largely from practicing democracy, it remains, I believe, the best way out of the mess in which we find ourselves. If the American people were adequately informed about the real situation and if their governmental institutions represented them, I am confident we could develop and conduct a sound foreign policy.

* * *

What then is the political situation which faces us? In approaching this question, it is of the utmost importance to realize that as the sociologist W. I. Thomas once said (and I paraphrase him): whatever people define as real in a situation is real in its consequences. Putting this in other words: by expecting certain things to happen we think and act in ways which tend to make them happen.

The power structure in our country defines the world situation as one in which we are in a state of inevitable quasi-war between two bi-polarized power centers. And this quasi-war will continue for "a long twilight struggle"—to use a favorite phrase of our President's. Twilight, let us remember, is followed by night. I submit that this is an unrealistic view of the world situation, except as our thinking it makes it so. Moreover, it seems to concede the inevitability of nuclear war. We are fond of saying that the Russians are prisoners of an unrealistic ideology. But we are prisoners of an ideology which is rigid and blind to the reality of what is happening in the rest of the world. This ideology of ours is expressed in cliches, half-truths and assumptions, all of which are debatable, and many of which are demonstrably false. I put these cliches in clusters.

The first cluster is: We are good and they are bad. We are humane; they are not; we are honest; they are liars. Being honest, we tend to be naive and to expect others to be honest too; but if we deal with them, they will do us in by underhand methods. This is the Black-and-White syndrome, sometimes called the Lone Ranger theory of history.

The second cluster centers on the proposition that Communism is an international conspiracy. (How glad our John Birchers must have been to hear our President say this when he announced the Cuban blockade.) The Communist parties in the world all take orders from Moscow. Communists never tell the truth. To understand them you must invert whatever they say. If they ask for peace they want war. And so on. In reality, depending on where one lives—America, Russia, China, Africa, South America—either Communism or Capitalism looks like a conspiracy—if one defines the real situation as one which requires war—hot or cold. If an American looks on Communism in a setting defined as warlike, then surely Communism is a conspiracy. If a Russian looks on Capitalism in a setting defined as warlike, then to be sure Capitalism is a conspiracy. But both Communism and Capitalism are more than conspiracies in reality. Depending on who is looking at them, both of them are economic systems, both are political systems. Depending on who looks at them, both are symbols of hope for the future or symbols of catastrophe.

The third cluster holds that most—if not all—of our foreign relations problems are caused by the Communists. If it were not for them, foreigners would admire us for our democratic values, our generosity, and our technological progress. The reason they don't is basically the fault of the Communists. This being so, anyone who resists Communism in foreign countries automatically deserves our support. And no one else does. Therefore, counter-revolution (or roll back) anywhere in the world is good.

The fourth cluster centers on the proposition that the only appropriate response to foreign problems is military. The Communist hordes are held back from military aggression all over the world only by their fear of our military might. The only way to deal with them is by the Big Stick, thermonuclear prevailance or deterrence, military and paramilitary intervention, and, in general, toughness. Toughness is the only way to defend free enterprise. Armaments give us security. Civil Defense will protect us. Billions for defense but not a cent for socialism. It is not socialism to have the government spend $50 billion for weapons; it would be socialism if the government spent the same amount for education or for public works. Negotiations with the enemy lead to appeasement unless the enemy accepts our terms completely. You can't trust the Russians. And you shouldn't even think about the Chinese—maybe they'll go away, all 650 million of them. Peace is impracticable and utopian. Better dead than red. We will threaten to start a thermonuclear war to get our way over Cuba and Berlin, but we won't actually start it unless we subjectively feel provoked enough to do so.

The fifth cluster is closely related. It centers on the proposition that our policy on foreign problems must be authoritatively determined by the "judgment" of our Commander in Chief. Only he has access to the essential scientific secrets. Because foreign problems are only soluble in military terms, the military knows best. Experts, if employed by the military, are always right—otherwise they are regarded not as "hard-nosed," but as "soft-headed." Discussion of foreign problems is likely to breach security or at least to help the Reds by showing that we are not united behind our leader. Bipartisanship in foreign policy is necessary to defend democracy. When we approach a crisis in foreign affairs the press and broadcasters should discourage public debate. Don't rock the boat. Congress should avoid debate on sensitive foreign policy issues. Trust our leaders. They know best and will take care of us if anyone can. This is, of course, a totalitarian doctrine. We try to conceal this fact by assuring ourselves that a major difference between us and them is that we are pluralistic whereas they are monolithic; for us the individual is sacred, for them only the system.

The sixth cluster reflects the fact that for us, technique, know-how, and winning are the all-important values. Technology, as in the case of nuclear weapons, controls policy. Computers give us answers. We must win the race. To defend freedom and liberty abroad, we must curtail civil liberties and freedom of the press at home. In the name of freedom we violate the rule of law internationally, as in the U-2 incident, as in the Cuban invasion attempt at the Bay of Pigs, and as in the naval blockade and violation of Cuban airspace by our reconnaissance flights which apparently still continue. This boils down to saying: we are peace-loving and will fight for peace anywhere; our U-2 and Cuban lies were justified by our dedication to the truth. Peace requires war. War means peace. We have high moral purpose and therefore our good ends justify our sometimes immoral means. (Note that one of our favorite criticisms of the Communists is that for them we say the ends justify the means.) What matters is the preservation of our economic system. Sooner than change our Madison-Avenue-led privatized system of mass producing and mass distributing consumer goods, we will take *any* risks—and of course subject the rest of the world to these risks too. If NATO members or SEATO members are so short-sighted as not to see the necessity for ever more powerful military machines, we will make this "judgment" on their behalf, unasked. We are the self-appointed defenders of the "free world."

These are some of the elements of our ideology in regard to the outside world. They mutually reinforce each other. And as we act them out they are also reinforced. For example, having mistakenly identified the Cuban problem as a military problem—sometime in 1959 when the "judgment" was taken to give it "the Guatemalan treatment"—we interpret the subsequent real events so as to justify the original, mistaken interpretation. These ideological cliches have a nasty way of being self-fulfilling prophecies.

To understand our situation as far as peace is concerned, it is necessary to recognize that the American people are constantly brain-rinsed with this rigid ideology. (I do not use the term brain-washed because that is apparently a communist invention and I prefer to recognize our own inventions for what they are.) But there is more to the situation than simply an ideology. There is its inseparable Siamese twin: the actual foreign policy in deeds and words which, as I have suggested, interacts with the ideology in mutually supportive ways. It is therefore necessary to push the inquiry a bit further and to ask: how does foreign policy get made? How does ideology get made? A full answer to these questions would take longer than my available time, but let me summarize an answer.

On matters of domestic policy we have a democratic, pluralistic system. On important issues, Republicans usually can be distinguished from Democrats. Voters are often, perhaps usually, presented with genuinely alternative solutions to many problems: such for example as hospital insurance. There is a domestic counterpart to the ideological cliches that we employ in dealing with the foreign world, but it is porous and generally not decisive in forming people's attitudes on issues. Voters can more easily verify the accuracy of the press in presenting facts on domestic issues. And while there have been notorious biases operating in parts of our mass communications media on domestic affairs, there is relative freedom of information there, as compared with foreign affairs.

On matters of foreign policy, however, we have essentially a totalitarian system. Since 1941 we have had a bipartisan foreign policy, which means that there is no substantial difference between the two parties in the main objectives of our foreign policy: since 1946 these have been cold-war objectives stated in the terms of the brain-rinsing cliches. Because both parties agree in the essentials of our foreign policy, the only choice available to voters has been which candidate would execute them better. And here the efforts to differentiate the candidates have been ludicrous. Would Dick be better equipped to "stand up" to Khrushchev than Jack because he had sparred briefly with Khrushchev in the kitchen of the American exhibition home in Moscow? Or take the involuted pattern in the "Great Debates" in which Nixon, who had been a secret planner of the Bay of Pigs invasion, was chagrined to find that Kennedy was taking a "tough" line on Cuba, and therefore Nixon argued that any sponsorship by the U.S. of an emigré invasion of Cuba would be bad because it would be immoral; it would violate our neutrality laws and our pledges to the charters of the O.A.S. and the United Nations.

We have lately been treated to the fiction that politics must stop at the water's edge. If the fact of being in a near-warlike situation be urged in justification for it, you are entitled to ask: how did we fight World War I without it? Why during even the terrible times of the Civil War was bipartisanship not observed? Why was it unnecessary in the Mexican War period? In the War of 1812? Why was it not written into the Constitution? The fact is that our Constitution plainly assumed that voters would be presented with alternative courses of foreign policy when national elections took place. The powers of Congress were written in such a way that there should be the check of independent and free consideration of treaties which were required to have the advice and consent of the Senate.

Our foreign policy starts from the Administration. And this term should be thought of in this connection as including much more than the President and the State Department. It includes those huge empires of bureaucratic and business-affiliated executives known as the Department of Defense with its various service arms. And it includes the relatively small number of huge corporations whose contracts account for the bulk of our armed forces procurement. Senator [Hubert] Humphrey put into the *Congressional Record* on October 5, 1962, findings from a report which the bipartisan coalition tried to suppress on the economic impact of disarmament. I quote him briefly:

> The defense effort of the U.S. is highly concentrated in a few industries and a few companies. The military-industrial complex that former President Eisenhower warned the country against is one which appears to be centered in a few hands and in a few key places. ...
>
> 24 companies accounted for 70 percent of the entire defense expenditures represented by the study. In other words, of almost $22 billion in defense

> spending about $16 billion went to 24 companies. There were four companies each receiving over $1 billion in defense sales. Another four companies received from $500 million to $750 million and 12 received from $250 to $500 million. ... And today, when weapons systems have become so complex, we have transferred to some of these industrial and technological giants great power and influence over the development of these weapons systems. The continued concentration of economic power and the loss of the government's decision-making power over aspects of defense policy are trends in the defense effort which should worry us. (Quoted in I. F. Stone's *Weekly*, October 15, 1962)

Whether we are thinking of minor elements in foreign policy (such as the decision on the Skybolt weapon system) or of major ventures in brinkmanship (such as the Cuban policy in October), the proposals stem from within the Administration. In either case, some sort of sanction called "public opinion" is needed to validate the proposals. What do we mean by public opinion here? Public opinion of the little people as registered by polls is *not* what we mean; it is remote from the actual decision-making process. By resorting to public opinion we mean that the product of the press itself is taken as a substitute for public opinion. Crises may be manufactured by "managing the news," by "using news as a weapon," by playing propaganda devices with the cooperation of the mass media. Prime Minister [Harold] Macmillan in his famous "golf links" interview in August 1961—an interview never fully reported by the American mass media—indeed said that the 1961 Berlin crisis was "all got up by the press." As a publisher himself, he is an expert on such matters. In the more recent Cuba crisis, we had a clearer demonstration. Over a weekend, leaks to the press, ominous rumours echoed by columnists and commentators on TV and radio played on our anxieties and frustrations. When the President presented his fait accompli over TV on that Monday night the press was ready to go all-out. The editorial opinion, the commentators, and the columnists, not to mention the "managed" stories in the news columns in the following days, *were* the public opinion needed to support the policy.

To sum up this process: The Administration (including the military-industrial complex) makes foreign policy by its power over the Congress and the mass media. This is a bi-partisan affair on essential policy, as for example was our Cuban blockade and brink crisis. The mass media—the huge industrial producers of information—are closely linked with the Administration in many ways, and on foreign policy they cooperate closely with it. The mass media brain-rinse us into accepting or condoning the policy which is made. The mass media *are* a substitute for public opinion in foreign policy making. And the rhetoric which is used by the Administration and the mass media to justify the policy is the ideological grammar which I outlined earlier.

What name should we give this process? The "Warfare State"? Too general. "Ike's military-industrial-complex-at-work"? Perhaps. For myself I go back to Franklin D. Roosevelt's "Economic Royalist" speech in Philadelphia in 1936. He referred to the "industrial dictatorship" which exercised control over the conditions of men's work. The dictatorship to which he referred was a simpler and less concentrated one than the one we now face. Thoughtful and sympathetic students of big business like T. N. Levitt[1] and Richard Eells[2] do not shrink from using uglier words for the kind of corporate fusion with government to which I am referring: the words *feudal* and *fascist*. For myself I prefer to call it a foreign policy dictatorship in which a self-perpetuating oligarchy controls not only the very fact of our lives but also through the brain-rinsing of our attitudes, our minds.

Is this too strong? Can anyone name one Senator, one Congressman, one public figure of any national reputation who dared publicly oppose the Administration's Cuban trip to the brink? In England you can find a loyal opposition capable of this. But our constitutional system, once it is degraded by bi-partisan foreign policy, is incapable of distinguishing between criticism of administration policy and disloyalty. On foreign policy we have substituted the "governing of consent" for "consent by the governed."

Choose whatever name you like for it. The fact is that our foreign policy uses a rigid and monolithic ideology. It is perpetuated—not out of personal malice or evil intent but out of bureaucratic inertia and the faulty allocation of power—as between private and public governments. This is the realistic situation which recently prompted Harold Taylor to say that our capacity to destroy the world is now credible to all; but how credible is our capacity to help the world solve its problems? Our credibility in this capacity is low and dropping lower every month that we stay prisoners of our rigid ideology. Every month that we follow its inexorable mandate to dig ourselves into one untenable foreign policy position after another. Walter Lippmann put it well when in 1961 he said:

> The root of the error is to equate, instead of to differentiate between the Communist movement...and the world-wide movements of social reform and social revolution, which almost everywhere seek national independence

> and non-alignment with the great powers. ... The wave of the future is social reform and social revolution driving towards the goal of national independence and equality of personal status. In this historical tendency, Mr. Khrushchev will be, as Mr. Alsop tells us he is supposed to have described himself, "the locomotive of history" only if we set ourselves up to be the road blocks of history. (New York *Herald Tribune,* June 13, 1961)

* * *

What are the implications of this grim situation for the peace groups? The threshold implication is that some institutional changes must be made. It is quite hopeless to expect that foreign policy—and hence the chances for peace—will change merely because new faces appear in Washington—even friendly faces. For as we have noted surely in the past two years, the new faces, operating within the old institutions, will continue the old monolithic cold-war policy.

The institutional changes needed if we are to revitalize the democratic process are three: (1) Restore a free marketplace of ideas in our mass media in regard to foreign affairs, i.e., break up the rigid cold-war ideological view of the world. (2) Restore partisanship to foreign policy; i.e., make available at election time fundamentally alternative choices in foreign policy. (3) Reduce and control the decision-making power of the military-industrial complex; i.e., make Congress and the Executive responsible to the electorate again.

It is easier to say than to do. Peace groups' tactics, such as working within the two big parties for the selection of good candidates, encouraging expression of opinion by citizens to their elected representatives, conducting educational political campaigns for independent or write-in candidates, would be a sound plan if we had 20 years in which to work. But if, as I believe, we will be lucky to have five years, I submit that hard grass-roots political work of this kind alone cannot bring about the necessary institutional changes in time. Something more is needed. We are trying to move a mountain with pick and shovel. Our native ingenuity is challenged. Can we improvise a steam shovel from spare parts lying around?

If my analysis is correct, we might as a first step try to restore the free marketplace of ideas. We have to open some holes in the paper and air-wave curtain so that people can begin to see the real world outside. There seem to be two feasible ways of doing this. One is to use fully every opening available in the existing mass media. This means massive and universal use of Letters to the Editor columns. It means asking for time on public service programs constantly and generally. It means pressing for time to reply on controversial issues. It means encouraging the sponsors and networks and stations responsible for the few TV and radio programs which do permit discussions or treatments of controversial issues. And increasingly the purpose of this use of the mass media should shift from mere publicity about the peace movement to presentation of our point of view.

The other road back to a free marketplace of ideas is the development of new media enterprises under our own control. Suppose, for instance, that a national newspaper devoted to world news developments and with the quality of *The New York Times* were published and distributed by the peace movement as a whole. Or suppose that the kind of radio station operated by the Pacifica Foundation in Berkeley, New York and Los Angeles were expanded into a nation-wide FM radio network with its own news staff. (And incidentally the Pacifica stations right now need your support against the efforts of the bipartisan coalition to close them down.) The general frustration and irritability of the American people in regard to the Communist menace, I think, is a joint product of two facts. The mass media fail to represent the dynamic developments outside our borders so that foreign problems perennially take us by surprise. And despite our ever mounting arms budget and our superabundance of overkill capacity, we never reach the promised "security." Would not the very fact that a "peace" press prepared its readers for the rapid developments which in fact occur put pressures on the older press to improve its performance? And wouldn't a growing public begin to think our view of the world made more sense? I think it possible that the frustration which threatened to explode into madness in October might, with better information available to it, turn into a force for major institutional change rather rapidly. I wish I felt sure that there is in the peace movement the readiness for a sustained, united effort of this kind. The immediate response to the Cuban crisis, when cleavages were forgotten, and to the recent House Committee hearings on Women for Peace give some reason for optimism.

At the same time that we try to restore the free market place of ideas, we should move to restore the pluralism of foreign policy alternatives contemplated by the Constitution. This means direct action on the political front. Here I would like to propose what might be called "civic disobedience" as a new approach. Civic disobedience would mean massive refusal to vote in national elections *unless* there is a candidate who publicly stands for an alternative to our monolithic bipartisan foreign policy. This would be a public declaration that the duty of a good citizen to register his choice between alternatives requires him to withhold his vote when no choice is available. It would say in effect: "If we can't vote for peace, we won't vote for war." It would attack directly the tradition of "voting for the lesser evil." This tradition had a basis when foreign policy alternatives were debated in national elections. With a bipartisan foreign policy there is only one policy—and therefore no possible lesser evil. Our political candidates, as Mr. Nixon once remarked, are merchandised like soap or cigarettes. If the "image" of Mr. A in the campaign somehow appeals to your psyche more than the image of Mr. B, you may under present conditions think you are voting for the lesser evil in choosing Mr. A. In the same fashion you may buy brand X cigarettes because they are toasted and this appeals to you more than brand Y, which offers its thinking-man's filter. In reality there are no real differences between the cigarettes; and they both cause cancer. There is no lesser evil in bipartisan foreign policy election campaigns either.

There are those who say that if there is no difference between the parties on foreign policy, we still should vote for the one with the best position on domestic issues. To this I would reply that the issue of war and peace is of such overriding significance that we must be prepared to pay the price domestically which may be required to force the parties to break their foreign policy coalition. There will be no civil rights at all if we cease to be.

Suppose that peace-concerned voters are able to play a key role in selecting, financing and electing a handful of Senators and Representatives. And suppose that in other election districts where bipartisan candidates are running in 1964, we were able to persuade even a substantial minority of voters to vote "NO" by withholding their vote for national office. The successful bipartisan candidate in the latter districts, with only minority support, would feel powerful pressure to strengthen his position. And the political parties too would feel the ground slipping beneath them. If such an approach could work, it could work quickly. And a "no-party party" would require far less in organization and money than a third party. To carry it off would require concern and conviction, but a far lower order of heroic dedication than the nonviolent approach calling for civil disobedience. It might well lay a broad base for subsequent more vigorous "noncooperation" such as refusing to submit to "taxation without representation"—itself an honorable tradition in this country—if the needed institutional reforms come too slowly. I am not sure whether this proposal makes sense. Let others make better ones.

The most difficult of the three institutional reforms will be the third: bringing under control the military-industrial complex. It can only be solved by solving the first two. It can only be accomplished through reform of foreign policy making: by breaking up the bipartisan coalition, by restoring its constitutional power to Congress and to the electorate, by populating Congress with representatives responsible to the voters instead of to Big Business and by restoration of a free marketplace of ideas regarding foreign affairs. As these steps are taken the overweening power of the military-industrial complex will be curbed and the paramountcy of popular control of our policy through government re-established by restricting the power of Big Business.

The final implication of my analysis is that we face a tall order of work which challenges the resources of peace groups. Have we got what it will take to do the job? The peace groups have a fund of valuable experience in developing novel ways of bringing their views to the public. One thinks of vigils, marches, petitions, the women's flight to Geneva, the embryonic general strikes, Polaris actions, Everyman voyages, walks to Moscow. As a result of these and the nonviolent civil rights struggles in the South, jail-going is regaining the honorable status it had in the days of the Abolition and women suffrage crusades. Another great asset is the tradition of ingenuity for which Americans are justly famous. Technique is our forte. Our students today find politically irrelevant outlets for their ingenuity—they see how many bodies can be packed in a bus or they race elephants, or conduct marathon telephone conversations. We may hope that this institutional inventiveness will be turned to serve the substantive objectives of the peace movement. And most important of all our assets is the deep concern of most people for the dimly seen dangers of nuclear war. This concern is presently stifled by the brain-rinsing with the ideology of the Warfare State. Our problem is to restore it in the spirit of the motto of the Center for the Study of Democratic Institutions: feel free.

As I see it, our task is to help organize the creative capacities of millions of Americans toward a foreign policy which is based on realistic considerations of human, and therefore of national interest.

Notes to "Peace in a Shrinking World"

1. T. N. Levitt, "The Dangers of Social Responsibility," *Harvard Business Review*, September–October 1958.

2. Richard Eells, *The Meaning of Modern Business* (New York: Columbia University Press, 1960) p. 271.

10

"Is . . . the real role of the FCC . . . one of advocate and agent for the private companies?"

EDITOR'S NOTE: Dallas Smythe wrote "The Space Giveaway," a two-part series in *The Nation,* during the historic moment when satellite communication in the United States was taken from public hands and put into the private sector. The decision was a significant triumph for private interests, but it was a victory that did not come easily. Some background will put these articles into perspective.

World War II spurred the development of electronics and scientific knowledge about propagation characteristics in the VHF and higher portions of the spectrum. In the postwar period, the global dominance of U.S. military power and business interests provided incentives for development of sophisticated systems of global communication that would not depend on cable or high frequency radio links.

In England, Royal Air Force electronics officer Arthur Clarke, who later became a leading science fiction writer, proposed in October 1945 using three earth satellites at a height of about 22,000 miles as relay stations for international telephone and television communication. Three months later, the U.S. Army Signal Corps successfully bounced radar signals off the moon, proving that transmission outside the earth's atmosphere was possible. A reporter for *The New York Times* wrote that applications "almost beyond immediate comprehension" were being forecast. Speculation immediately followed that an artificial satellite, if one somehow could be put into orbit, might become the hub of a new kind of international communication system.

Western Electric and Bell Laboratories, subsidiaries of AT&T and among the prime defense contractors during World War II, remained deeply involved in the military effort in the postwar period. AT&T also recognized that demand for trans-Atlantic telephone service would soon far outstrip the capacity of high frequency radio links, and in the late 1940s it began working on problems of space satellite communication. Western Electric became the main defense contractor on certain missile programs, such as the Nike Zeus, in the late 1950s. It also was involved in developing the network of computer-assisted air defense direction centers and the ballistic missile early-warning system. In addition, AT&T provided much of the guidance and communication systems for the space exploration program.

The Soviet Union launched Sputnik I, the first artificial earth satellite, in October 1957. The response from the United States was an all-out commitment of resources to the space race. Explorer I, the first U.S. satellite, was launched in January 1958. Neither of these instruments was designed for communication, however. More powerful rockets on the drawing boards assured that future generations of satellites would be larger than the devices launched so far and that military applications would become important considerations.

Meanwhile, a team of scientists at Bell Laboratories pursued the communications component and built three prototype communication satellites. (Another division of AT&T had installed the first trans-Atlantic telephone cable, which began commercial operation in September 1956.) In December 1959, AT&T asked NASA to grant it authority over the entire satellite communication field, with the exclusive right to build and operate a system at its own expense. It was clear, though, that much of the necessary scientific knowledge had been developed under contract with the government. Other communications companies and defense contractors vigorously objected. NASA turned down AT&T's proposal.

At about the same time, a team at Bell Laboratories and the Jet Propulsion Laboratory persuaded NASA to fund a project that led to the launching in August 1960 of Echo, a plastic-skinned balloon 100 feet in diameter. Because it contained no electronic gear, Echo was a passive satellite that merely reflected back to earth radio waves directed to it, much as the moon had done in 1946. With Echo, the contractors successfully demonstrated transcontinental voice connections, using transmitting and receiving terminals designed and built by Bell Laboratories. Echo also bounced messages from the United States to England and France. The next step was construction and testing of an active satellite—Telstar I.

In January 1961, AT&T finally received authorization to begin planning for the launch of Telstar for *experimental* communication. Two months later, President Kennedy asked Congress for additional funds to speed up development of communication satellites. In July he issued a statement outlining his administration's policy on satellite ownership and operation, which Dallas Smythe refers to in his two-part series. AT&T maintained that any communication satellite system was but an extension of the existing telephone network and that it should be privately owned, preferably exclusively by AT&T. Not surprisingly, other aerospace contractors and communications companies wanted to share that ownership. However, many senators, representatives, and government officials believed satellite communication was part of the space program and should be publicly owned.

The battle raged throughout 1961 and early 1962. Smythe spoke to professional groups and wrote several articles on the subject, arguing for public ownership, perhaps under the sponsorship of the United Nations. In August 1961 he testified before the Senate Subcommittee on Monopoly, and the following year he challenged the FCC's ability to regulate a private company effectively in testimony to the Senate Subcommittee on Antitrust and Monopoly. As Smythe points out in his autobiography, he also prepared material that Senator Russell Long used in the fourteen-day filibuster against the administration's bill. The anti–public interest forces were too strong, though. The Communications Satellite Act, which created the privately owned Communications Satellite Corporation, was approved August 31, 1962. Just seven weeks earlier, AT&T had launched the first active communication satellite, Telstar I, which Smythe considered a "publicity gimmick." Telstar later was used in successful experimental transmissions of telephone and television signals across the Atlantic and was immortalized in a popular song and a display at Disneyland.

In his conversations with me, Dallas Smythe said "The Space Giveaway" was a natural piece to include in this collection because it "can serve to blanket a whole bunch of these special studies and testimonies I gave before committees." It was "a very compact and meaty piece," he felt, one he liked very much.

The Space Giveaway, Part 1: Who Will Own Communications Satellites? [1961]

In our communications activities, as in many other areas of our culture, the debate between the forces working for public benefit and those devoted to private privilege has never been resolved. This ambivalence in our "national purpose" is thrown into sharp relief by the development of communications satellites. The issues are not fully and fairly presented to the private citizen by our mass media of communications, long bemused by the slogan-fallout of the public relations campaigns of industry. In government, the debate is waged in terms of power pressures as well as logic and argumentation.

Our frantic race for space since the first sputnik went up has been mostly concerned with technical questions: how soon, how big, how successful. But now we are possessed of a technology which permits us to make practical use of satellites for communications. We are committed by both the Eisenhower and Kennedy administrations to emphasizing these peaceful uses of outer space as our counter to the Russians in the cold-war race for prestige from space.

The communications satellites are problematic precisely because they offer an embarrassingly wide array of tantalizing practical—and peaceful—benefits. For example, we face the need to enlarge drastically our transoceanic facilities for telephone and telegraph messages during this decade to care for booming intercontinental traffic. Communications satellites can handle this expanded traffic at much lower costs than conventional ground facilities. (Dr. Lloyd Berkner has been quoted as estimating that the cost of telephoning by communications satellites to any point in the world should not exceed 10 cents!) But there is much more involved than this.

Brig. Gen. David Sarnoff of RCA recently said that, because of communications satellites:

> Ten years hence, it is conceivable that a billion people in virtually every nation on earth will be watching the same program, at the same time and in color, with simultaneous translation techniques making it understandable to all.

Initially there is the objective of transmitting TV programs across the

---

This article, "The Space Giveaway, Parts 1 and 2," by Dallas W. Smythe, *The Nation*, October 14 (pp. 242–245), and October 21, 1961 (pp. 264–268), is reprinted with permission from *The Nation*.

Atlantic. The satellites have such capacity that still other practical applications are now visible. They can be used for the facsimile transmission of mail, newspapers and magazines; business data of all kinds can be transmitted world-wide. All of these practical uses have been suggested by "hard-nosed" businessmen. It is reasonable to conclude, however, that any present appreciation of the ultimate usefulness of the communications satellites is limited. New uses will develop in the future. Conservative estimates by the Bell System indicate that by 1970 the annual revenues earned by a communication-satellite system could easily reach several billion dollars.

Despite our frequent announcements that we intend to use space technology for peaceful purposes, the highest priority for communications-satellite development has been for a world-wide system for exclusive military use to provide:

> an integrated, secure system of military communication which will operate under any anticipated conditions against any interference, either man-made or natural, and providing three essential types of service—first, communication between any points on the surface of the earth, including the polar regions; second, communication between any point on the earth's surface and aircraft or ships; and third, broadcast service whereby military information or orders could be transmitted to all military elements throughout the world. Each of these three services is required to be available on an instantaneous basis.

Several points are notable here: (1) the military specifications are a comprehensive, world-wide system with an absolute maximum of reliability—a much higher standard than civilian communications facilities demand; (2) while the traffic in this system will be military, it includes precisely the same *kinds* of services and facilities as would be needed for a civilian system, although the latter could be built to less exacting standards; (3) where the greatest possible speed in attaining an operating system is desired, *it is assumed that the Armed Forces could "own" and operate the orbited system* which is being built under contracts by a number of private corporations, with Bendix Corporation the prime contractor.

The code name for this military-satellite system is ADVENT. ADVENT will use three satellites, approximately evenly spaced around the earth at an elevation of 22,300 miles above the equator. Moving at the same relative speed as the earth rotates, the satellites will remain fixed in relation to positions on the surface of the earth, and thus are "synchronous." They are "active" (i.e., equipped with receiving and transmitting equipment).

Because of their fixed position, they can work with simple, fixed, ground antennas; no complex and extensive tracking equipment is necessary. Also because of their fixed position, they provide the flexibility of permitting the interconnection of any two or more points on the globe. (The USSR is also said to be concentrating on developing a system of synchronous satellites capable of world-wide transmission of color TV.) A synchronous system, known as SYNCOM, is also being built under NASA with Hughes Aircraft Corporation as prime contractor, evidently for civilian purposes. Test launchings for both of these systems are expected in 1962.

Active-satellite systems (RELAY for NASA with RCA as prime contractor, and an unnamed system designed, built and launched for the Bell System under a contract with NASA, with direct costs being borne by the Bell System) which will orbit at "low" altitude (between 4,000 and 8,000 miles) are also under development. Because of their low altitude and motion relative to the earth's surface, these satellites can provide only an inflexible and limited coverage of the globe. Between forty and fifty of them would be needed to link, *by pairs,* the major communications centers of the world. It is this non-global system which the Bell System seeks to stake out for civilian communications. As General Telephone has pointed out, if each of ten surface points were to be equipped to communicate directly with the remaining nine by means of low-altitude satellites, it would require more than 400 satellites and at least 180 large moving antennas and associated tracking equipment. While this system would serve the immediate Bell System purpose of enlarging facilities between a few points, it would provide limited service, far removed from a world-wide system. Research-and-development launchings of both low-altitude systems are expected in 1962.

The much publicized ECHO satellite now appears to be receiving little encouragement. This is a "passive" (i.e., reflecting, as it has no receiving or transmitting equipment) system, which suffers from all of the disadvantages in coverage and flexibility that relate to the low-altitude active satellites. It has the further disadvantages of requiring (1) extremely sensitive receiving equipment to pick up and amplify the weak signals diffracted from the satellite and high-power transmitters to beam signals to it; and (2) tight discipline on an international scale in the use of the satellite because, having no orbited receiving equipment, it will "accept" any signals beamed to it.[1]

The electronic and communications equipment in space and on the ground for all three types of satellites are within the present state of the art, i.e., the time and effort to perfect the "hardware" are all that stand between us and realization of the advantages of communications satellites as a technical matter. And a long list of major corporations in the aerospace and electronics industries are already involved in one or another of the military and NASA projects. With the technology of communications satellites thus well advanced, we face head-on the issue already stated—whether they will be developed primarily for public benefit or private gain.

Today the Federal Communications Commission lends its official prestige to creating the myth that, in the words of Commissioner Craven before a Senate committee, "Telecommunications facilities for public use in this country have *always* been privately owned and financed, subject to Government regulations..." (emphasis supplied). This goes even further than the company for which the FCC is running interference; the Bell System characteristically speaks of a "tradition" of private ownership with public regulation. The industry's attempt to rewrite our history is shockingly crude. For until a generation ago, the choice of private or public ownership for our communications facilities was still being hotly debated.

Acting under the unqualified authority conferred by the Constitution (Article 1, Section 8), the Post Office Department nurtured Morse's telegraph invention, paying for the research and development on it. Unlike all other major countries, we permitted the telegraph to fall into private hands, with the result that it was exploited for private privilege and failed of development here such as occurred elsewhere. By the end of the century, more than seventy bills had been introduced in Congress to authorize public ownership of the telegraph. Nineteen times committees of the House and Senate reported on such bills, seventeen times favorably. Yet never were the bills passed.

Radio repeated the pattern between 1900 and 1920. The Armed Forces, particularly the Navy, developed radio telegraphy and telephony into a comprehensive system and absorbed all existing commercial radio common carriers in 1917. Even the wire-telephone and telegraph companies were taken over in 1918. While this government ownership took place during World War I, it was intended by the Wilson administration to be more than a wartime expedient. Thus, Josephus Daniels, Secretary of the Navy, testified on the resolution for seizure that the government "should control and own telegraph, telephone and all means of communication permanently," as also did Postmaster General A. S. Burleson. The Wilson administration, in 1914, had announced a communications policy which called for government ownership and operation of radio, telegraph and telephone. And by the end of World War I, the government in its own right had a patent position in radio sufficient to dominate the field. All of this is conveniently forgotten today by the beneficiaries of private privilege and their agents.

At the end of World War I, the private communications industry suffered from a mutually blocking patent stalemate which impeded its further development, as well as from the threat of continued public ownership. By a massive public relations and lobbying program between 1918 and 1920, private industry had its way on ownership. Private ownership of the telephone and telegraph facilities was restored under regulatory and financial terms arranged by the industry. From this time on the telephone and telegraph companies have firmly supported the concept of their regulation as "public utilities." As the Celler Antitrust Subcommittee has demonstrated, the Bell System, biggest of these companies, has the capacity to use for its own purposes the Federal Communications Commission as well as other government agencies—and did so during the 1950s. The public-utility regulatory procedure in telephone and telegraph has effectively protected the "regulated" companies against public criticism in a neat inversion of the original purpose of the reformers who had initiated public-utility regulation.

Also between 1918 and 1920, the government was forced to give up its position in the provision of radio service, and the communications market was parceled out as part of a national and international arrangement among the Bell System, General Electric, Westinghouse and the British Marconi Company, covering cross-licensing of patents and division of markets along both product and geographical lines. These patent pool agreements, although attacked under antitrust laws, remained the de facto basis for dividing the market until, in the 1940s, they lost their force through the expiration of the basic patents. The present scramble for positions in communications satellites thus is a new struggle for markets by giant corporations.

The communications satellites also offer an opportunity to private industry to accomplish by indirection what it has been prevented by Congress from doing directly; merging the international communications activities of the telephone, cable and radio-telegraph and radio-telephone companies. In this little-understood sector of our communications system, the Bell System has enjoyed a monopoly of overseas telephone service, Western Union Telegraph Company and the International Telephone and Telegraph Company have parceled out the undersea telegraph-cable business, and RCA Communications, Inc., and International Telephone and Telegraph have divided the great bulk of the overseas radio-telegraph traffic. These are the principal international common carriers operating under a policy of competition, of whose interests the FCC is so solicitous in regard to communications satellites. Over the past thirty years, perhaps a dozen attempts have been made by the companies to frame legislation which would permit some kind of permissive or mandatory merger of these cable and radio carriers. But all of these attempts have failed when they confronted the traditional policy of the Congress of insisting that the anti-trust laws and certain sections of the Communications Act express a firm national policy against merger and monopoly in international common-carrier communications.

Before considering the proposals for the organization of communications-satellite systems, what are the organizational implications of the technology? The synchronous satellites, which are obviously the best system, imply a new and unprecedented organization. They have unique functions. They are in no sense extensions of previous methods of conducting communications by ocean cable or conventional radio-telegraphy or radio telephony. As General Electric puts it:

> The communications satellite system would perform a service for the common carriers all over the world; they will be its customers. ... It will not solicit or receive traffic directly from the public. It will, in a sense, represent an extension of the facilities of not one, but of all carriers. It will be a different kind of business than has heretofore existed—i.e. a common carriers' common carrier for the handling of traffic on a global basis.

While the satellites would have to interconnect with ground stations to transmit traffic, the problems of managing them are different from those of running existing means of communication. There is, therefore, no technical reason why they should be under the same organization as the older means of communication. In fact, the opposite is true: the political, economic and technical characteristics of the satellites require that they be organized and controlled *separately* from the ground stations with which they should work.

Whereas the conventional cable and radio facilities may be readily duplicated and competition may exist between them, the satellite system is analogous to a world-wide telephone exchange. It is flexible and multilateral in its traffic capabilities, whereas conventional facilities are fixed and bilateral. It has enormous capacity, and duplication of rival facilities (e.g., by the Russians and ourselves) is as destructive of efficiency and economy as is the operation of rival telephone exchanges in the same city.

A high degree of centralization of authority over the switching of channels is necessary, hour-to-hour, for communications satellites to use the scarce radio frequencies on a globally shared basis.

The political and foreign-relations significance of the communications satellites distinguishes them sharply from conventional facilities. There are many profound political implications. Other countries concededly should share in the ownership as well as the use of the satellites: how much, when and how are delicate matters for international relations. The non-commercial significance of the satellites is enormous: broadcasting by television and radio and other non-point-to-point uses gives them an inescapable international and national political importance. They are intimately associated with the international control of the use of the radio spectrum. In this connection, the changing needs of the less-developed countries require sensitive adjustment from time to time in the character of both frequency assignments and facilities provided through the satellites.

The legal status of objects in outer space is, of course, as yet undefined. But it is clear that private property in such objects, as we have previously known the institution, is impossible.

Whether it be in terms of the relation to space law, radio-frequency use or international negotiations, the communications satellites imply so much about sovereignty (internationally as well as nationally) that new national and international organization is clearly called for in their use. And it is absurd and arrogant to support that one country's private enterprise should own an operable communications-satellite system and preside over the international relations which it will require. What is called for is a nonprofit public authority to operate the communications satellites as a service to all existing communications agencies—private in the case of the United States, and public in virtually all other countries. Such a public authority might in time be placed under the U.N., as the president of Philco Corporation has proposed. If this mode of organization is adopted, the traditional policy of competition among U.S. common carriers could be continued and private monopoly avoided.

A final organizational implication of satellite technology comes from the fact that the research-and-development work on them has been nurtured by government, not private business. No private company could launch communications satellites at its own expense, if the enormous development costs of the rockets and associated gear were taken into account. While ocean cables can be installed by private companies, communications satellites have to be "installed" by government, and the cost of this installation inescapably rests, for the most part, on the taxpayer.

This is the factual backdrop against which the issue of ownership and control of civilian-use satellites is projected.

Notes to "The Space Giveaway, Part 1 . . ."

1. After publication of the first part of "The Space Giveaway," Smythe sent a note to *The Nation* clarifying his description of passive satellites:

"In referring to ECHO-type satellites, I noted that, having no orbited receiving equipment, they will 'accept' any signals beamed to them. The inference might be that such a disadvantage does not inhere in the 'active' satellites. I am advised that the low-altitude 'active' satellites, as presently planned, also may accept any signals beamed to them on the correct frequency. While the same might be true of synchronous satellites like ADVENT, the latter may be equipped with anti-jamming devices, etc., which will permit them to accept only signals intended for them.

"Generally speaking, the conclusion I drew remains correct: tight discipline on an international scale in the use of communications satellites seems inevitable."

The Space Giveaway, Part 2: Public Benefit Versus Private Privilege [1961]

THE FIRST INDICATIONS of possible government policy on ownership and control of communications satellites were ex parte and ex cathedra statements which repeated the public-relations "line" of the Bell System.

In October, 1960, the Administrator of NASA in a speech said: "Traditionally, communications services in this country have been provided by privately financed carriers competing with one another to serve the public interest under federal controls and regulations. There seems to be no reason to change that policy with the advent of communications satellites."

The Bell System had originally proposed that it be given exclusive advantage during the winter of 1960–61 by asking the FCC for permission to start commercial service trials of space communications linking this country, the United Kingdom and Western Europe—including telephone, TV and data-transmission service. This proposal, which was a request for the assignment of non-common-carrier frequencies in an allocation proceeding, was denied on the ground that it would interfere with the disposition of other issues, but the FCC obligingly suggested "experimentation" on common-carrier frequencies which it provided Bell for this purpose.

In the spring of 1961, communications-satellite systems of different types were in research-and-development stages. Just which system would be most efficient and economical was not known. The relation in *operation* of the military-owned systems to others which might be devoted to civilian uses was not defined. Given the fact that the satellites would have vast political and foreign-policy significance, it was premature to freeze them in the mold of organization which had grown up around ocean cables. The advent of the new Administration provided an opening for new points of view as to how communications satellites should be organized for operational purposes. This opening was seized by some of the companies which were active in space research and development, but which were not presently communications common carriers. Lockheed Aircraft Corporation suggested that the proper organizational form was a "common carriers" carrier—i.e., a new company to own and operate the communications satellites, the company to be jointly owned in turn by manufacturers of satellite hardware and the major communications common carriers. General Electric created a subsidiary, Communications Satellites, Inc., with the same end in view. Meanwhile, small-business interests became vocal on the subject. Antitrust concern was aroused in the Department of Justice and in Congress. And the issue of private ownership was caught up in the pressure process which is our national government.

The initiative, tactically, was retained by the Bell System and the common carriers. And it focused on the Federal Communications Commission. The FCC, under its new chairman, Newton Minow, has espoused the public rather than the private interest in its policy on broadcasting. But with regard to communications satellites, it is shocking to find that Minow has been at one with his industry-minded colleagues. In the words of Commissioner Craven, FCC spokesman before the Senate Committee on Small Business in August:

> The Commission's efforts...are based upon the conviction that satellite communications will and should take its place within the framework of our private-enterprise system, under which public communication facilities are owned and operated by private companies subject to government regulations. This conviction is consistent with Congressional policy expressed in the Communications Act of 1934, as amended.

This appeal to the Communication Act of 1934 approaches the frivolous, for while the Act *permits* private operation of communications carriers, it does not *prescribe* it. It would be equally valid to argue the opposite: by remaining silent on the ownership of the then-known means of communications, Congress reserved a free hand for itself with respect to new techniques such as the satellites.

Regarding communications satellites "primarily as another means of relaying long-distance communication" (the point of view urged by the Bell System), Commissioner Craven testified that the FCC, on March 29, had instituted a formal inquiry, soliciting views from the industry as to the best method for international common carriers to participate in the ownership of a satellite system. General Electric and General Telephone and Electronics tried in vain to get the ownership base of what the commission quickly came to call the "consortium" broadened to include space industries like themselves. In its "first report" in Docket 14024, the FCC held that participation should be limited to the common carriers (which effectively means the Bell System, RCA, International Telephone and Telegraph and Western Union).

The commission's bias toward serving the carriers' rather than the public interest was openly displayed in this report. Referring to the "interested carriers" as "acting under the aegis (aegis—n. a shield of protection: *Webster's Abbreviated Dictionary*) of the Commission"—a term also used by A.T.T. spokesmen—it announced meetings for the perfection of a plan for this consortium in a report which held that "the international carriers themselves are logically the ones best qualified to determine the nature and extent of the facilities best suited to their needs." The report also stated that the FCC sought to avoid "disrupting operational patterns that have been established in the international common carrier industry." The commission was aware that the carriers ran the danger of violating the antitrust laws and tried to protect them with its "aegis." On July 21, in announcing that it had held a meeting of the "Ad Hoc Carrier Committee" some time earlier, the commission gave this explanation:

> The Commission recognized that additional information with respect to the organization and operation of any such joint venture was required before its feasibility and efficacy could be properly assessed, and that such information could best be afforded by the submission into the record of this proceeding of a concrete plan formulated by the interested common carriers. We also recognized that such a concrete proposal could not be formulated without those carriers engaging in discussions among themselves; but that such discussions would possibly engender charges of antitrust violations. Accordingly, we called the meeting of June 5 to consider plans and procedures whereunder such discussions and planning could go forward with propriety.

In a second notice of July 21, the commission announced its procedure for the creation of the consortium. It would provide an officer to preside at all discussions of the Ad Hoc Carrier Committee. Such discussions would be conducted in strict adherence by the commission; the agenda, however, would be initially formulated by the committee. Participation in discussion by other government agencies would be at the discretion of the committee.

Responding to steadily mounting protest against the prospect of monopoly emerging from the servile role of the FCC, the National Aeronautics and Space Council considered communications-satellite policy, at the request of the President. The report of the space council then emerged as a statement of Presidential policy on July 24. Private ownership and operation of the U.S. portion of communications-satellite systems was "favored" (note that the term was not "mandatory"), provided that it could meet eight "requirements":

1. New and expanded international communications services be made available at the earliest practicable date;
2. Make the system global in coverage so as to provide efficient communication service throughout the whole world as soon as technically feasible, including service where individual portions of the coverage are not profitable;
3. Provide opportunities for foreign participation through ownership or otherwise, in the communications-satellite system;
4. Non-discriminatory use of, and equitable access to, the system by present and future authorized communications carriers;
5. Effective competition, such as competitive bidding, in the acquisition of equipment used in the system;
6. Structure of ownership or control which will assure maximum possible competition;
7. Full compliance with antitrust legislation and with the regulatory controls of the Government;
8. Development of an economical system, the benefits of which will be reflected in overseas communications rates.

In his statement, the President wisely emphasized that the present status of the program, both civil and military, is that of research and development and that to date, no arrangements between government and private industry contain any commitments as to an operations system. The statement concluded with the expression of a desire that "development of this new technology to bring the farthest corner of the globe within reach by voice and visual communication, fairly and equitably available for use, proceed with all possible promptness."

While the Presidential statement of July 24 imposed responsibility for compliance with its terms on the space council, the FCC has continued to stage-manage the creation of a monopoly which in effect is the merger Congress has repeatedly refused to sanction. In its supplemental notice of inquiry of July 21, the commission stated conditions which, it contends, implement the Presidential policy statement, but which, on their face, substantially erode the plain meaning of the President's words. Thus the crucial second condition, calling for global service as soon as *technically* possible—even to areas where service would be unprofitable—is reduced in the FCC "conditions" to "A commercially operable communications-satellite system will be expected to provide the *potential* means for global coverage" (emphasis added). "Potential" is a weasel word which would fit perfectly the typical private monopoly's preferred policy of skimming the cream from the most profitable markets while deferring indefinitely service to the unprofitable. A second obvious reduction is the transformation of the fourth Presidential condition, which calls for non-discriminatory use and equitable access to the system for present and future common carriers. In the FCC version, this condition is limited by the language "...for the purpose of obtaining communications facilities in the system *to serve overseas points* with the types of service which they may be licensed or authorized by the Commission" (emphasis added). The limitation to overseas service is clearly intended to protect the Bell System monopoly of domestic telephone service from the threatened inroads by the General Telephone and Electronics Corporation and others.

Unanswered are a number of important questions, many of which have not been sternly put as yet. Many of these questions never were satisfactorily answered in previous Senate consideration of the property merger of the international common carriers. Who is to set the terms on which proprietorship of the consortium is to be allocated? The present carriers? With other industrial groups added? Or ultimately, the government? If securities are to be sold to the public by the consortium (as some carriers and others have advocated), is the government in effect guaranteeing the capital and a return thereon through its role in creating the consortium?

Who is to protect against wrong decisions on technology (e.g., if a superior technique existing outside the consortium is rejected in favor of an inferior technique owned inside the consortium)? Who is going to insure that newcomers to the business of conducting communications will have open access to the consortium?

Who is to have the authority to make decisions for the consortium—the corporate participants or, ultimately, the government? Chairman Minow, testifying before the House Judiciary Antitrust Subcommittee on

June 14, said that the FCC would be in a "constant supervisory position," as also would be NASA and the Department of Justice. Are these agencies equipped to discharge this kind of administrative responsibility in a specialized technical area such as communications satellites? But in the same testimony, Chairman Minow *also* said that decisions ultimately would be made by the private companies. Who will make the decisions?

As the supervisory role to which the FCC aspires is a management function, how can the FCC serve both in this role and as regulator? Is there not a hopeless confusion of roles involved in the consortium? Is, in fact, the real role of the FCC in the consortium one of advocate and agent for the private companies rather than representation of an independent public concern? Finally, in view of the intimate intermixture of private and government influence in the creation and prospective operation of the consortium, in just what respect is this scheme "private enterprise" of a "traditional" sort, as the Bell System propaganda characterizes it? Is the whole thing not simply a device by which private interests may obtain profits from the use of public agencies and public money in the operation of a technology which itself is impossible of reduction to private property? Is it not a new and much more offensive Dixon-Yates?

Argumentation by the proponents of private ownership runs in familiar terms and may be summarized quickly from recent testimony by the Bell System. Satellites offer Bell another way to render service. The responsibility for establishment, ownership and operation of these "additional common carrier facilities" should be placed where it belongs—with the carriers responsible to the public for service. This is consistent with long-standing U.S. policy which places responsibility for efficient public communications on privately owned common carriers under public regulation. No government subsidy would be required under this system (ignoring the billions of dollars which make the communications satellites possible through space research and development). Competition would be preserved, as the communications satellites would be available to all. Private ownership will take advantage of the carriers' experience in working with communications agencies in foreign countries. No carrier would dominate the system, and ownership of the satellite should be based on the volume of traffic (Chairman Minow estimated that 90 percent of the volume would be Bell System traffic). The Federal Communications Commission will protect the public interest through regulation. (How a *national* regulatory agency can regulate an *international* operation partly owned and conducted by foreign *entities* is not explained: even in conventional cable and radio communication, it has never been effective.) Chairman [Overton] Brooks of the House Committee on Sciences and Astronautics urges speed in getting the system into operation and says: "I think it would be a serious mistake to squabble about the niceties of legal ownership."

For the opponents of private privilege, the arguments are more varied. Thirty-five members of Congress, including Senators Humphrey, Kefauver and Morse, in a joint letter to the President on August 24, urged that we do not at present know which system can be put into use first, nor which system will be most efficient once in orbit. Given this technological uncertainty, the complicated question of ownership and control is even more uncertain. Prudence, they argue, requires a further investigation of the broadest aspects of the ownership question, unimpeded by premature decision as to ownership. During the development period, all possible speed should be made while careful study is given to the question of ultimate control. It is pointed out by others that, as far as speed being related to ownership is concerned, our military ranks communications satellites as of high urgency, yet the military system being built under contract by private industry will be publicly owned. If speed for defense use of communications satellites is best served by public ownership, the same must also be true of the less urgent civilian uses.

The thirty-five Congressmen support the eight conditions set forth in the Presidential policy statement and condemn the FCC's efforts to create the consortium as "contrary to the policy established by you; they [also] are contrary to the principles of the antitrust laws." The consortium, they say, would be intolerable from the standpoint of the public interest, quoting the Department of Justice as considering the opportunity to favor purchases of equipment produced by the Bell System's subsidiary, Western Electric, to be irresistible. They also quote the head of the Antitrust Division of the Department of Justice as testifying that "the degree of concentration in this field may very well be one of the reasons why America is not further advanced in the field today than it is. ... Our system has not produced as it should, and the public interest has suffered because there has been undue concentration in this field." If private ownership is preferred to public, the communications-satellite system must afford all interested U.S. communications common carriers, *domestic as well as international*, opportunity to participate in the system, and must afford all interested communications and aerospace manufacturers a parallel opportunity. Otherwise, they warn the President, the plan would be in direct violation of the antitrust laws and would require special legislation from Congress. They add that no Executive order or decree of any agency can override the antitrust laws.

The thirty-five Congressmen see the ramifications of this remarkable system as likely to be truly revolutionary. An awareness that our understanding of the implications of the new technology is likely to lag behind developments themselves leads them to urge that no decisions concerning ultimate control be made until the entire system becomes fully operational.

No contracts, decisions or acts which may prejudice the ultimate decision should be permitted in the interim. During this period the Congress should be allowed to exercise its Constitutional responsibility to supervise activities of federal agencies regulating foreign and domestic commerce. Also during this period, all possible questions of international agreements, cooperation, control and ownership related to other nations and the U.N. should be thoroughly explored.

A drum-fire of critical statements supports these attacks on the monopolistic drive of the Bell System. That redoubtable organization currently says little publicly, relying on its immense political influence on Capitol Hill as well as in the administrative agencies. Of the latter, the Bell System clings closest to *its* chosen instrument, the FCC, to work its will with communications satellites. A prognosis of the outcome of the debate is now premature. What is certain, however, is that the consequences of the ultimate decision will be far-reaching, not only on our national communications policy and our giant corporations, but on foreign relations and—ultimately—on the possibility of a peaceful world.

The large issue is whether the trademark of our hugest monopoly and its policies is to represent the people of the United States in the first practical use of our space effort—in the sensitive area of communicating information, attitudes and feelings among the peoples of the world. In traditional terms, will the forces working for public benefit or those self-confessedly "dedicated" to private privilege prevail?

11

"Require the corporate dissolution of the Bell System empire in order to create a system of independent viable entities"

EDITOR'S NOTE: Looking through Dallas Smythe's record, I was struck by the considerable consulting work he did for a variety of organizations: the National Council of the Churches of Christ, the National Association of Educational Broadcasters, the Canadian Royal Commission on Broadcasting, the UHF Committee for Competitive Television, the All-Industry Local TV Music License Committee, the Canadian government's Department of Communications, motion picture theatre interests, several broadcasting companies, and others. He also conducted studies for, and testified on behalf of, the American Communications Association. The ACA was a CIO union that represented all employees of Postal Telegraph Company (absorbed by Western Union in the early 1940s) and employees in New York and Detroit of Western Union Telegraph Company.

Smythe's relationship with the ACA began in 1938 when he was working for the federal government in Washington. He organized a local of the radical United Federal Workers Union (CIO) and taught an elementary economics course under its auspices. Two ACA officials were students in the course, and one (Daniel Driesen) was the ACA's legislative representative. Driesen helped immensely when Smythe, as part of his government work, studied whether telegraph messengers should be covered under wage and hour laws. In the early 1940s, Driesen also provided the contacts that eventually brought Smythe to the Federal Communications Commission as chief economist. During his years on the FCC, Smythe maintained friendly ties with the ACA.

Smythe's lengthy testimony, portions of which are published here for the first time, was written in the last half of 1963, during his first semester at the University of Saskatchewan, and presented the following year in Washington. In May 1962, the FCC had opened Docket 14650 to study problems facing the domestic telegraph industry (i.e., Western Union). Revenue from public message service had been declining as the public shifted to long-distance telephone communication. Business and private line use seemed to be the future base for Western Union but, as Smythe points out in his study, AT&T had been moving beyond voice communication into record communication, thereby threatening the telegraph company's core.

The significance of this 1964 testimony is that Smythe proposed breaking up AT&T into several smaller, competitive companies. This break-up actually was achieved in 1984 in the Modification of Final Judgment that terminated the Justice Department's 1974 antitrust suit against AT&T. A previous federal antitrust case, filed in 1949, had been settled in 1956 by a consent decree that left AT&T intact.

In this study of AT&T's "offensive use of its enormous size and power," Smythe finds that "over a period of almost 75 years it has gravely violated the antitrust laws; that on occasion it has coerced and imposed its will on both the federal and state levels of government; [and] that it has employed its vast power ruthlessly. ..." He concludes that AT&T's "size, power and inherent monopolistic aggressiveness constitute a violation of the antitrust laws which can only be laid to rest by a permanent and drastic dissolution of the power structure which has made these offenses possible, and indeed inevitable."

In our conversations in December 1991, Smythe told me that Western Union was losing business because of "AT&T's cut-price, really predatory pricing of tariff services, for example, TELPAK. You know what TELPAK was like—they [AT&T] sold broadband capacity, and the customer could use it any way he liked. So if he used it to connect his branch offices together, he didn't need to send telegrams, he could just use this low-cost channel capacity. And AT&T just took customers away from Western Union like mad." Why were hearings not held earlier than the 1960s? Smythe said, "We had tried to get the commission to act on this issue and proposed a hearing in the late 1940s, and the commission had finally halfheartedly approved one but quickly acquiesced when the Budget Bureau, under AT&T influence, said 'no.' So this was a delayed hearing, and it was part of what you might call the late progressive spring in the FCC, when Newton Minow [March 1961 to June 1963] was there and they had two or three commissioners who were, as Harold Ickes would have put it, not inclined to automatically put the private interest before the public interest."

Smythe said that "Western Union's submission to the hearing had made the same factual base that I was using—that they were losing their market to AT&T through unfair competition. It was in violation—they didn't really stress this—it was in violation of the antitrust law. Western Union wasn't about to call me as a witness, for reasons that I'm not quite sure of—anyway, ACA did."

At the time of the hearings, Smythe explained, ACA "had the New York metropolitan area and precious little else at that point in telegraph. It had a substantial membership in broadcasting and then in international communications with RCA and [...] Commercial Cable. It had its strength there. It had lost control totally of any members in the land-line telegraph service in the United States after the merger" because Western Union had set up company unions that had been welcomed into the AFL. When elections were held, ACA "was just overwhelmed by the pressures of the company and the company union in every place except New York City, which they retained. They withstood about eight or ten raiding operations by Western Union [...] and then finally they were worn down. It was a cumulative effect of the whole right-wing movement in the Cold War period, plus the fact that they were always vulnerable to being red-baited. Now the officers had all severed any possible connections with the Communist Party in compliance with the Taft-Hartley Act, but the company still used that label on them."

The day before Smythe was to leave Regina for Washington, he received a call from a liaison man whom he knew at Sasktel, the local telephone company. "He was a nice Joe, and we had gotten acquainted and discovered we could talk to each other. And he told me, he said, 'Say Dallas, didn't you mention you were going down to the FCC?' I said, 'Yeah, I'm leaving tonight—going down to testify in the special telegraph investigation. Why are you asking?' 'Well, I was just curious. Are you—how would you characterize yourself? Democrat? Republican?' He was obviously wanting to know if I was radical or not. And I said, 'I'm perfectly willing to answer your question, but let me ask you a question first. Is AT&T asking you for this information?' He chuckled and he said, 'You guessed it.' And so this guy asked me this innocent question. I gave him a snow job. [...] 'I believe in conserving the valuable things from the past. [...] And where change is indicated, I'm in favor of change, aren't you?' That's what I said to him—he couldn't quarrel with that. [...] Guys are innocent up here."

Smythe described the hearing as a "dramatic setting." "For this occasion with me appearing, since I had been chief economist for six years, the whole Telegraph Committee [of the FCC] appeared—the commissioners, two of whom I knew personally from the days when I was working there. And when they called for me to take the stand, the AT&T lawyer stood up and made a speech about ten minutes long listing all the reasons why my testimony should not be admitted. He was prepared and had seen that report [Smythe's prepared testimony]. And it was everything from libelous to hearsay to speculative to biased. Every adjective you could think of, he threw in there." Still, the FCC allowed Smythe's testimony.

Smythe told me: "I had one thing going for me which surprised the commission—I'm not sure AT&T was surprised by it. It goes back to the consent decree which was entered into by AT&T in 1913, the Kingsbury Commitment. And my God, when I said this, and I summarized the impact of it—it limited AT&T's imperialist expansion within the communications carrier field—and the three members of the commission were all looking at each other and blinking their eyes. They'd forgotten about it entirely."

"In the corridors, in the intermissions," Smythe said, "there were not only ACA officers and lawyers—and incidentally, they had Vic Rabinowitz who was their counsel, one of the famous civil libertarian lawyers—it was not just those guys that would come up and speak to me privately, but the Western Union officers would. They were old friends of mine. I had known them from when I was at the FCC, and they were in my corner in this hearing completely. I was fighting their fight for them."

Of Docket 14650, Smythe said that "nothing came of it except the ventilation of the gripes that Western Union had against AT&T, with cause, and I used those gripes as the basis to argue that AT&T was oppressive and should be disintegrated."

Looking back on those events, Smythe declared to me: "I'm sort of embarrassed by that testimony now. You might say in your introductory note about it something like: 'This was an instance of trying to use the reigning doctrine about market forces against the system.'"

Testimony on Behalf of American Communications Association: FCC Docket No. 14650 (Domestic Telegraph Operations and Services) [1964]

My statement falls into four parts. In the first, I will comment generally on the available policy alternatives for a national telecommunications system. In the second, the present situation is analyzed. In the third, some antitrust aspects are considered, and, in the fourth, a concrete proposal is set forth for what I would regard as the best national policy.

It is impossible to give intelligent consideration to any aspects of the communications industry in the United States without a full appreciation of the size and power of the mammoth Bell System. Any consideration of a communications policy can be seen in proper focus only against such a backdrop of the dominant position which the Bell System occupies in the market for telecommunications service. This dominance ranges from virtually 100 percent for all overseas telephone service to 97 percent for all public voice telephone service, 89 percent of the TWX-teleprinter service, and zero for public message telegraph service. If the total telecommunications market—domestic and international—served by U.S. common carriers be looked at in terms of the types of entities which serve it, and if we measure participation by operating revenues in the same year, then the Bell System occupied 93 percent of the field, other telephone companies 3 percent, Western Union domestic service 3 percent, and international telegraph and cable carriers 1 percent. (Computed from Federal Communications Commission, *Statistics of Communications Common Carriers*, year ended December 31, 1960.)

In any terms, the Bell System is a quasi-political state of a magnitude ranking it with the world's great powers. Bell System revenues in 1959 were larger than the combined national public revenues of Canada and Sweden. They were $2 billion larger than the combined national public revenues of Denmark, Norway, Sweden and Finland. They were $2 billion larger than the public revenues of Italy. The stature of Bell power within the United States is equally impressive. To equal Bell revenues in 1959 it would have been necessary to aggregate the total public revenues (including grants in aid) of the 32 poorest states of the Union, or those of the five states with the most public revenues. To equal the total assets of the Bell System at the end of 1959, it would be necessary to add together the total assets of Standard Oil of New Jersey, General Motors and the United States Steel Corporation. And the same kind of result occurs when one thinks of the Bell System in terms of people. If each of the 728,978 employees of the Bell System at the end of 1962 be assumed to represent a family, it would require the entire family population of the seven smallest mainland States of the Union to equal the Bell population. Or if each of the 2,210,671 shareholders of Bell System stock at the end of 1962 be assumed to represent a family, it would require the entire family population of the 13 smallest mainland States of the Union to equal that measure of the Bell population. If individual States be compared with the Bell System, Oregon (with 716,000 families) comes closest to equalling the Bell System employee-family population, and Texas (with 2,368,000 families) comes closest to equalling the Bell System stockholder-family population. (Population data from *Statistical Abstract*, 1962, p. 44; Bell System data from A.T.&T. *Annual Report*, 1962.)

I: The Available National Policy Alternatives

As is implicit in the terms of the order establishing the present proceeding, there are in general three choices available to the United States as policies for governing the organization of the telephone and telegraph industries and for determining the possibility of maintaining an adequate public message telegraph service. These choices are:

1. To permit the establishment of a single monopoly to handle all telecommunications in the United States.
2. To provide government operation or subsidy for the telecommunications system.
3. To encourage and foster two or more viable communications companies, one of which shall be AT&T and another Western Union.

The first of these choices involves determining in a conscious fashion that we want one company to take over all or substantially all the telephone-telegraph business of the country, or by permitting the same result to come about by inaction. It seems quite clear that if nature is allowed to take its course, with the rules of the game remaining as they have been in recent years, the Bell System will destroy Western Union by preempting those markets where Western Union can earn the profits necessary to support the essentially unmechanizable and therefore unprofitable core of the public message telegraph service. Despite its denials that it has selectively raided Western Union's markets, the Bell System cannot obscure the fact. Indeed, the Bell representative, Vice President George L. Best, stated in this proceeding that Bell selected for its markets everything *but* the public message telegraph service when he said:

> While AT&T is ready and willing to consider any sound proposal as to how the Bell companies can be of any further help in providing to the public efficient communications service in this country, we have no *desire to furnish public message telegram service and see no need for doing so*." (Transcript, pp. 184–185; emphasis added)

There are compelling reasons why our national telecommunications policy should not sanction one entity as provider for all or substantially all service. [...] There can be little doubt that the anti-trust policies of the United States apply to this industry as well as to any other. The United States Supreme Court has held frequently that the mere fact that an industry is regulated does not result in a repeal of the anti-trust laws and, indeed, both the Court and the Commission have applied anti-trust considerations in many cases arising under the Communications Act. I shall leave detailed discussion of this point to counsel and shall proceed on the assumption that the national policy, as is set forth in the Sherman and Clayton Acts, is equally applicable to the communications industry.

A structure such as that presented by the dominant position of the Bell System in the telecommunications industry is so heavily monopolistic in character that it violates both the affirmative conditions for expecting efficiency and the negative condition of avoiding excessive private power which [... are ...] the twin principles underlying our free enterprise policy in this country.

At a later point I will comment in some detail on the ways in which the Bell System has been and is in violation of the anti-trust laws. Thus far the Bell System has escaped effective prosecution for these violations. To continue to sweep these violations under the rug is to say, in effect, that we have two anti-trust policies in the country: one for the Bell System and one for the rest of us. This result could come about only through the massive and frightening power which we have permitted it to acquire. In view of its size and power it is not surprising to find that it thinks and acts in political terms in ways which confuse it with our government and distinguish it sharply from free competitive enterprise. Driven by dynamic forces within its huge expanse, the Bell System's incursions into markets previously or presently served by Western Union on terms inimical to Western Union's continued profitable participation in such markets clearly will end up in extinguishing Western Union as a significant part of the American telecommunications system.

If one closes one's eyes to the present and future political implications of the economic power which the Bell System now has and may in this way increase, there still remains the haunting question: how can such a huge monopoly have the incentives to perform service at reasonable prices and to innovate service improvements as fast as possible? This is the unique characteristic of competitive conditions [...] which our national pro-competitive policy expresses through the anti-trust laws as the essential ground rules for all of our free enterprise. Since all the historical evidence confirms the conclusion that competition serves the public interest by encouraging technological innovation, improving and expanding services and lower[ing] rates, and conversely that monopoly inhibits these developments, the "one big company" national policy on telecommunications cannot be squared with the Commission's injunction from Congress "to make available, so far as possible to all the people of the United States a rapid, efficient, nationwide, and world-wide wire and radio communications service with adequate facilities at reasonable charges." (Title I, Section 1, Communications Act of 1934, as amended)

A second course of policy which is theoretically available today is to place the responsibility for providing telegraph service on the federal government, either through outright operation or through some sort of subsidy from that source. This alternative is not supported today. However, it must be added that to the extent that the Bell System acts *like* a government, its espoused policies may be pushing us to this ultimate conclusion in fact.

The third available policy alternative—which I think of as the "viable entity" policy—is to find some basis for establishing and maintaining a substantial degree of autonomy for more than one entity in our domestic telecommunications industry. This policy alternative has two justifications. The first of these is the national antitrust policy. As indicated above, there is a firm pro-competitive policy which permeates the Communications Act. This pro-competitive policy rests on, among other considerations, the presumption that under it incentives to provide telecommunications service of sufficient extent and quality and with innovations in service as frequent[ly] as possible—all at the lowest possible prices—are more likely to be forthcoming than where a monopoly exists. The second justification for the viable entity policy is that if Western Union be used as a basis for one of the viable entities, the public interest in a continued nationwide public message telegraph service may be protected in the long run. Remember in this connection the fact that the Bell System would not be interested in providing such a service under any conditions. And remember that, as Mr. McMains said:

> No country in the world has found the public message service to be dispensable. In every country, as I stated before, some means of support has been found so that the public message service can continue to serve the general public need for a service of this kind. Although the public message segment of the telegraph business will probably continue to decline in volume, I do not forsee any point in time when it will be possible to consider it to be non-essential or of negligible volume. (W.U. Exhibit 13, p. 45)

What might be the ground rules for applying a "viable entity" policy? Historically, we have had the doctrine of record versus voice communications as a basis for this implicit policy ever since the Kingsbury Commitment in 1913. The legislative history of the 1943 merger amendments to the Communications Act makes it clear that the division of record from voice communications was relied on to produce healthy economic conditions as between the telephone and telegraph industries. It was reiterated in the "Communications Study," Senate Document No. 53, June 22, 1953, and in the report of the President's Communications Policy Board, in 1951.

Today, however, you are told by Mr. Best of the Bell System that "a separation between voice and non-voice services would be impractical, uneconomical, and not in the public interest" (transcript, p. 181). And Mr. McMains stated his company's belief that:

> a separation of voice and record services could have been achieved and, indeed, could still be achieved in large measure, if the Bell System were willing or could be compelled to bring it about. (W.U. Exhibit 13, p. 5)

What is the significance of these statements?

In 1913 when the voice-record doctrine was first adopted, technology tended to divide along organizational and functional lines. That is to say that the technology of telegraphy was functionally and organizationally separate from telephony to a high degree. But in the interim the situation has changed. Mr. Best says the separation is impractical "because of the way the technology has developed and because of the way customers want to use communications facilities" (transcript, p. 181). And as Mr. McMains says:

> What may not be so generally understood, however, is that service offerings and rate structures have gone far beyond the changes in technology in speeding and extending this obliteration of the historic differences that once existed between record and voice communication. (W.U. Exhibit 13, p. 6)

The WADS, WATS, TELPAK, and analogous services initiated by the Bell System, in other words, have functionally merged large segments of record and voice services and have combined them in rate packages available solely from that System. In one way or another the advocates of monopoly seek to justify it on the ground that modern technological developments have rendered obsolete the distinction between voice and record communications—and even Mr. McMains, whose company is suffering the depredations of the Bell monopoly, falls into the trap of accepting the slogan at least in part.

There is a great deal to be said against the slogan that there is now no distinction between the technologies of voice and record. A voice is still a voice. And a record communication is still a record communication, today, as it has been since man began making use of the most primitive forms of communication—carving on stone or bending saplings, etc. What is relatively new is the development of the technology of broad band circuits and switching which permit the alternate or simultaneous use of the same facilities for voice and record. The technology of telecommunications today thus *permits* operational arrangements for the alternate or simultaneous use of the same facilities for voice and record. But the technology does not *require* that all such operational arrangements be housed in the same organizational structure. There are familiar examples where organizational separateness is maintained while there is operational integration. In international telephony, the Bell System operates one end while foreign PTT administrations operate the other. In our own country, there is operational integration of the Bell System and Western Union to the extent that the latter leases circuits from the former while their organizational identities are preserved. Now obviously telecommunications technology requires the operational interconnection of telephone or telegraph services *end-to-end,* as in the international example, if any such service is to be provided. The same is true of interconnection within a country, as between the Bell System and independent telephone companies, and the same should be true of interconnection between the Bell System and Western Union. But there is no technical requirement that voice and record communications operations be merged under one corporate roof. Indeed, the distinction between them is one of our historic ground rules which is still valid as part of the basis for determining the scope of viable entities in our telecommunications industry. The Commission, I submit, should never permit itself to become confused on this essential point, that while technological progress may *permit* operational and organizational integration and centralization, it does not *require* it. And before determining what *will* be required, the Commission will want to take account of our procompetitive antitrust policy and the public need for a public message telegraph service.

The argument which the Bell System employs to gloss its drive for hegemony should be recalled here. Competitive duplication of local exchange services is not at issue here, so we may dispense with straw men; I am not proposing duplicate local telephone exchanges. However, when the argument shifts to the alleged disadvantages to the public of having competition in long distance private wire or interconnecting telephone service, we may join the issue. In this area, the Bell System's position is that competition is guilty unless proven innocent. I submit that the burden of proof is on the monopolist, and that it cannot sustain it against our national procompetitive policy. It is no answer at all for the Bell [System] to say that the public does not want competition in this field; after half a century of public relations indoctrination, the public opinion polls, measuring surface cliches, can only reflect the propaganda to which the public has been subjected. I also reject the Bell doctrine handed down from Theodore N. Vail that:

> Competition can only exist where there are abuses, either in the way of unreasonable profits or of excessive capitalization; and where control and regulation are effective, these abuses cannot exist or continue. Consequently competition and control and regulation do not go together, and if a mistaken public opinion demands competition in established fields of "sufficient" and "efficient" service given under control and regulation, the result will be duplication of plant, for which the general public must sooner or later pay either in the loss of capital invested, or in higher charges necessary to pay returns on the capital invested in the duplicated plant. (T. N. Vail, "Public Utilities and Public Policy," *Atlantic Monthly,* vol. 111, pp. 307–19, March 1913.)

This doctrine, which appears even in FCC opinions in the not distant past, collapses (1) when the advantages of competition are taken into account, and (2) if its built-in assumption that the universal monopoly is perfectly efficient is exposed.

There is certainly a powerful tendency for the aggregation of private power represented by the Bell System to press for universal monopoly. But there is no assurance that the integration of organization which the technology permits will be maximally or even optimally efficient, even for the existing scope of that monopoly. One thinks, in that connection, of the lack of external examination of the efficiency of the Bell monopoly;

history suggests that there never has been an organization of such huge size, immune to external critical review of its administrative efficiency, which avoided gross inefficiencies. One thinks of the wastes in its procurement and maintenance procedures where the cozy relationship with Western Electric provides an incentive for wasteful procurement, stockpiling, and maintenance procedures. And one thinks of the uneconomic expenditures it makes from ratepayers' money for advertising and public relations designed to mold and to control public opinion and our governmental processes. We are certainly entitled to assume that such a massive public relations program is undertaken for what the Bell System regards as essential corporate purposes. Whether these corporate purposes are compatible with the public interest could only be determined by that searching, critical examination by disinterested persons which has thus far been avoided.

No human organization is perfect—not even the Bell System—and I am suggesting that the "viable entities" policy should start with this fact. It should determine the best mix of markets and organizations to achieve a structure which would yield the best result in terms of incentives and resources. It should proceed by empirically balancing the advantages and disadvantages of different possible combinations of market structures and organizations. The result of this "trading off" process may correspond in part to the record-voice dichotomy; in part, it may not. In this respect, my position may be similar in principle to that stated by Mr. McMains when he abandoned exclusive reliance on the separation of voice and record services and said:

> Instead, we advocate the establishment of policies which will provide the economic basis for broader competition in the public interest so that Western Union may provide this competition and, at the same time, continue to furnish an adequate public message telegraph service. (W. U. Exhibit 13, p. 6)

The difference between Mr. McMains' position and my own seems to be that I would hope that the viable entities policy would encompass exclusive provision of record communications by the telegraph industry and even go beyond this to provide a long range solution to the problem of imbalance in corporate power in the American telecommunications system.

The conclusions to be drawn from this analysis of the voice-record matter are: (1) As a technological matter, monopoly of telecommunications is not necessary or "natural"; conversely, the advantages of maintaining interconnected service between viable entities are those inherent in our procompetitive national policy; (2) The traditional national policy which favored a division of the telecommunications market between firms engaged primarily in voice and those in record communications still has validity. However, the gross imbalance in power between the Bell System and Western Union today makes this record-voice distinction inadequate as the basis of market division; (3) Hence, viable entities based on, but going beyond, the traditional record-voice criterion are required today. As a first approximation to this solution, I will suggest in my fourth section some considerations entering into a possible viable entities policy.

[Sections II and III omitted]

IV: Proposal

It is respectfully submitted that the Federal Communications Commission should now espouse a national policy on telecommunications which would include important structural and policy changes if the public interest in telecommunications service at reasonable prices is to be served, consonant with the spirit and letter of the Communications Act of 1934, as amended. The effect of these changes would be to create viable entities in our domestic telecommunications system. This proposal is consistent with the application of our national procompetitive policy in a number of analogous areas where ground rules divide industry along functional lines, producing what may be called a functional separation. This has been a fairly standard technique used by Congress to preserve competition between alternative or close substitute services and to prevent undue concentration of power. Examples are the separation of rail, water, air and truck transportation, electric and gas distribution, investment and commercial banking, and life and casualty insurance.

These proposals would assure the continuation of a public message telegraph service by associating in the same company with such service all telegraph service and all mixed voice and record services. It would go beyond this to create competitive conditions between telephone entities on the one hand and the telegraph entity in providing circuitry, etc. It would leave the enormous message telephone business to the specialized telephone companies. Lastly, to protect the foregoing changes from being reversed by the present massive power of the Bell System, and to establish conditions in which competitive incentives might operate within the voice telephone markets, it will be necessary to dissolve the Bell System by creating from it some thirty to thirty-five independent operating entities. In logical sequence, these changes are as follows:

1. Immediately cancel and prohibit the type of tariffs represented by WADS, WATS, DATAPHONE, and TELPAK which have the effect of giving away telegraph service as a bonus if the customer buys stated quantities of telephone service from the Bell System. This proposal would seem clearly within the Commission's authority to accomplish forthwith.
2. Immediately adopt and take steps to effectuate a policy which would (a) deny the Bell System all private combined voice and record telecommunications services, and (b) invite Western Union to provide all private combined voice and record telecommunications services.
3. Immediately adopt and take steps to effectuate a policy which would deny the Bell System monopolies in the provision of private wire telephone and TV and radio program transmission services, and which would encourage Western Union to enter these fields and to compete with the Bell System in them.
4. Immediately adopt and take steps to effectuate a policy which would deny the Bell System monopolies in the provision of long distance telephone circuitry for interconnecting purposes and which would encourage Western Union to enter this field and to compete in it with the Bell System.
5. Immediately order the liberalization of the ATT-Western Union leases for circuit capacity which presently prevent Western Union from employing these facilities to offer mixed voice and record business. Mr. Best, of the Bell System, objects that to do this would "not constitute competition but rather a subsidy" (transcript, p. 181). The fact is, however, that the Bell System public message telephone service presently is being used to provide a subsidy to that part of the Bell System which is invading telegraph markets with monopolistic practices. For the Commission to order the Bell System to follow practices which, when combined with the other changes proposed, would provide a reasonable basis for expecting the public to benefit from competitive incentives within the industry is a perfectly proper step. The Commission presently has the authority to accomplish this step either under its powers to attach conditions to radio licenses (of which the Bell System is a principal beneficiary) or otherwise under the Communications Act of 1934 as amended.

6. Immediately move effectively to require the Bell System to divest itself (on reasonable terms as to price) of its telegraph business, to wit:
   a. The entire TWX plant, equipment, and business.
   b. Its Private Line Teletypewriter Service and any other private wire telegraph leased circuits and associated equipment and plant. If the Commission's own authority to accomplish this result is inadequate (and it should first be fully explored before concluding that it is inadequate), the Commission should urge anti-trust action to this end by the Department of Justice.
7. Immediately adopt and take steps to effectuate a policy on facility interconnection and tariffs which would:
   a. Require the Bell System to provide full interconnection of the telegraph company's facilities with the network and terminal facilities controlled by the Bell System.
   b. Permit and encourage Western Union to provide long distance voice circuitry within the United States using land lines, microwaves, or communication satellites connecting independent telephone companies and Bell System exchange facilities.
   c. Permit and encourage international telegraph carriers to offer international voice service via communications satellites, submarine cables, and other means in conjunction with the new domestic arrangements described in (a) and (b) above. The present authority of the Commission would seem ample to support these actions.
8. Immediately move effectively to require the corporate dissolution of the Bell System empire in order to create a set of independent viable entities for the conduct of the telephone operations, research and equipment manufacturing and supply operations of that System. A precise plan for the operational and organizational outcome of this proposal obviously would require careful study by the Commission. The time, the opportunity, and the resources for such a careful study have not been available to me. However, it may prove interesting to consider a rough illustrative model of how this might be done.

Some considerations entering into such a model are offered in Appendix A. It is of interest to note that even with Bell operations distributed among some 35 companies rather evenly, some of the resulting entities would be very large: Illinois Bell, if left as one entity, would have some $1,509 million in assets and net income of $96 million as of 1962. By contrast, Western Union had $277 million in operating revenues and $7 million in net income in 1962 while the largest entity in the ranks of the independent telephone companies, the General Telephone System, had $2,564 million in total assets, $579 million in total operating income, and $75 million in net income in 1962.

How viable would Western Union be if the recommendations made above were all adopted? Obviously the engineering studies which would be needed if one were to estimate Western Union's assets under those conditions have not been made. It should be possible, however, to approximate the effect on Western Union's revenues of these recommendations. Western Union Exhibit 12, submitted in response to the Commission's letter of July 30, 1963, provides some informed estimates. A total of eight assumptions were there stated, of which one is:

> that the WATS, TELPAK, and any WADS tariffs, including developmental WADS, are found unlawful by the Commission, that no new tariffs are filed for these services, and that the current rates for Western Union's services do not change

coupled with the assumption that "full interconnection, as proposed by Western Union, is permitted by the telephone companies." Appendix B [not reproduced here] sets forth the portions of Western Union Ex. 12 which are relevant to estimates of Western Union's revenues in 1965, assuming my recommendations are implemented, and makes certain changes in them to bring them into closer accord with these recommendations. The Exhibit 12 estimates for Message Telegraph are accepted intact. Western Union is assigned the full estimate of market revenue for Telex and TWX. Western Union's estimate of Tel(T)ex revenues are accepted with the comment that they are understated because they were determined by multiplying the estimate of per-station revenues by the number of Telex stations. The acquisition of TWX would increase this factor. Western Union is assigned the full estimate of market revenue for Private Wire Telegraph and Alternate Record Voice services. Western Union's Exhibit 12 assumed that it would receive 3.1 per cent of the market revenue for Private Wire Voice service. I have assumed that by virtue of its enhanced competitive position, Western Union would receive 6 per cent of this market revenue in 1965. Western Union's Exhibit 12 estimates for Autodin, Telemeter, and Broadband Switching are accepted intact. Western Union is assigned the full market estimate for Facsimile-Telephoto. There remain to be estimated Western Union's probable revenues from providing Long Distance Telephone interconnecting service and from competing in the market for TV and radio program transmission. Western Union makes no estimate for these services, nor do I find in Bell System submissions any basis for making estimates. I accordingly show these items with a question mark in lieu of a revenue estimate.

The total Western Union revenue for 1965, estimated in this way, is $662,126,000. This sum is somewhat less than twice the total shown for 1965 under the assumptions given by the Commission (see last page of Western Union Ex. 12). It is also about two and one half times the total revenues of Western Union in 1962. If we are concerned to provide a sufficient economic base for Western Union to become a viable entity in our telecommunications system, however, the inadequacy of Western Union's proposals is evident. The effect on Western Union's revenue position of giving effect to Assumption E plus full interconnection is to increase its revenue from $264.1 million in 1962 to $347.6 million, an increase of only $83.5 million, or a mere one per cent of the Bell System's 1962 total revenues of $8,980 million. My own proposal seems a modest one in light of the same objective when one realizes that it would increase Western Union revenues from $264.1 million in 1962 to about $662.1 million in 1965, an increase of $398.0 million, or only four per cent of the Bell System's 1962 total revenues of $8,980 million. With the firmer base provided by $662.1 million in revenues in 1965, however, it is only reasonable to anticipate that Western Union might pursue its long-frustrated goal of plant improvement and initiate a program of improving the quality and availability of public message telegraph service and of stimulating the demand therefor by rate reductions. And the users of all telecommunications services might rest easier in the knowledge that to the extent practicable, given the technology of communications, they would receive the benefits of service improvement and rate reduction from the rivalry of viable competitive entities, and the protection against the excessive concentration of private power which are the objectives of our procompetitive national economic policy.

While Western Union can be viable in rivalry with the Bell System companies individually after dissolution of the Bell monopoly, it cannot hope to be viable when subject to the universal pressures exerted by the combination of these companies in the aggregate power of the Bell System, as it now stands. The means for effecting this kind of dissolution of the Bell System are, of course, available to the Commission. A firm determination to accomplish this objective is an obvious first step, and a strong recommendation to this effect to the Antitrust Division of the Department of Justice is an obvious second step.

APPENDIX A Rough Model of Results of Dissolving the Bell System: Corporate Entities, Total Assets, Current Assets, Operating Revenues, and Net Income, 1962 Basis

New Company	Old Company	Total Assets 12/31/62	Current Assets 12/31/62	Operating Revenue 1960[a]	Net Income 1962
		millions of $			
1	Bell Telephone Company of Pennsylvania	1,160	62	419[a]	65
2	Illinois Bell Telephone Company	1,509	81	541[a]	96
3	Michigan Bell Telephone Company	848	47	317[a]	45
4	Mountain States Telephone and Telegraph Company	1,033	52	317[a]	56
5	New England Telephone and Telegraph Company	1,122	78	405[a]	61
6	New Jersey Bell Telephone Company	972	56	347[a]	59
7	Northwestern Bell Telephone Company	859	41	286[a]	49
8	Southern New England Telephone Company	397[a]	22[a]	136[a]	20[a]
9	Wisconsin Telephone Company	386	18	129[a]	21
10	Pacific Northwest Bell Telephone Company	675	39		33
11, 12	Long Lines Department	1,503[a]	81[a]	524[a]	103[b]
13, 14, 15	Pacific Telephone and Telegraph Company	3,156	159	1,120[a]	153
16, 17, 18	Chesapeake and Potomac Telephone Company	176	15	68[a]	9
	Chesapeake and Potomac Telephone Company of Virginia	389	21	128[a]	25
	Chesapeake and Potomac Telephone Company of Maryland	455	21	144[a]	24
	Chesapeake and Potomac Telephone Company of West Virginia	168	8	57[a]	8
	Diamond State Telephone Company	70	3	24[a]	4

19 20	Ohio Bell Telephone Company	771	51	296[a]	51
	Cincinnati and Suburban Bell Telephone Company	135[a]	12[a]	54[a]	8[a]
	Indiana Bell Telephone Company	311	17	113[a]	21
21 22 23	New York Telephone Company	2,830	196	1,062[a]	150
24 25 26	Southern Bell Telephone and Telegraph Company	2,623	130	833[a]	142
27 28 29	Southwestern Bell Telephone Company	2,465	129	787[a]	154
30- 33	Western Electric Company, Inc.	2,308	967	2,762[c]	135
34	Bell Telephone Laboratories, Inc.	105	21		

[a]1960 data because 1962 data not available
[b]"Balance transferred to General Department"
[c]Net sales

SOURCES OF DATA: 1962 data for operating companies from AT&T Co.; 1962 data for Western Electric and Bell Labs from *Standard & Poors;* 1960 data from F. C. C., *Statistics of Communications Common Carriers,* Year ended December 31, 1960.

[NOTE: In Appendix A, Smythe showed the configuration of a new telephone industry after the proposed dissolution of the Bell System (AT&T) and its restructuring into thirty-four separately owned companies. Some of the former Bell companies were to be spun off in their entirety. For example, Bell Telephone Company of Pennsylvania (in the "Old Company" column) was to be spun off without being split up into smaller companies. That is, "New Company" number 1 was to consist of the former Bell Telephone Company of Pennsylvania. However, several of the former Bell companies, because of their large size, were to be split up further into smaller entities. As an example, Pacific Telephone and Telegraph Company, with total assets over $3.1 billion at the end of 1962, was to be broken up into three smaller firms, numbered as 13, 14, and 15 in the "New Company" column in Smythe's chart. Several of the other companies were to undergo a different realignment. The four Chesapeake and Potomac companies and the Diamond State Telephone Company were to be reconfigured into three new firms, numbered 16, 17, and 18 in the "New Company" column. The Bell System's Long Lines Department, which provided long distance telephone service, was to be dissolved into two new companies, although it is not clear from Smythe's discussion whether each would have a separate territory in the United States, or whether the two would compete with each other throughout the country. Smythe did envision Western Union getting into the long distance voice transmission business and offering interconnection for radio and television networks. Both of those activities would compete with services offered by the two new companies carved out of Bell's former Long Lines Department. Finally, Smythe also proposed breaking Western Electric, the manufacturing subsidiary of the Bell System, into two competitive firms, although Bell Laboratories would be allowed to remain intact after the dissolution of the Bell System. Smythe's plan was ambitious, and it is interesting to compare it to the new configuration of the telephone industry following the antitrust dissolution of the Bell System in the early 1980s.]

12

"Technology . . . is highly political in character and imbued with the ideological point of view of the originating system"

EDITOR'S NOTE: Dallas Smythe's contribution to international communication studies hardly can be overestimated. However, his involvement with the United Nations Educational, Scientific, and Cultural Organization (UNESCO) came to a screeching halt in 1972 after he presented "Reflections on Proposals for an International Programme of Communications Research" at the International Association for Mass Communication Research (IAMCR) meeting in Buenos Aires. The genesis of this paper, published here for the first time, reveals much about the politics of international organizations.

Smythe's relatively brief association with UNESCO began, he told me, with his activities in IAMCR. He attended the association's 1968 meeting in Ljubljana "at which I met [James] Halloran, and I'd known [Herb] Schiller, and he was there. I met [Kaarle] Nordenstreng, and I met the Yugoslav people, particularly Breda [Pavlic], who was the secretary of the thing and the organizer. [...] Halloran, Nordenstreng, Schiller, and I formed a natural little group and implicitly agreed to a common policy. We were all in favor of autonomy for Third World nations and we all had a nonpartisan position on the Cold War, and we weren't going to be apologists for either side. But we were going to be realists. [...] We were ripe for a program such as UNESCO was later going to develop on the international information order."

Smythe explained to me that through contacts Halloran and Nordenstreng made with the staff of UNESCO, a meeting was called "of representatives from the First World and the Soviet Union, the East block, and from the Third World." The meeting was held in Montreal in June 1969 and produced *Mass Media in Society: The Need of Research* (UNESCO: Reports and Papers on Mass Communications, No. 59). The conference raised the notion that UNESCO should take a position on what Third World countries and others, faced with the so-called free flow of communication, might do to protect themselves and preserve their autonomy. Halloran and Nordenstreng were there as British and Finnish representatives, respectively. Smythe attended the conference as a Canadian representative and was on the drafting committee. "I worked hard on that to support our position," he told me. "I won most of those little tactical battles about the language. So the language of that document [...] contains the germ of the whole anti–free flow position of UNESCO [...] as an international program in communication and information." In the words of the official report, "The meeting strongly recommended that Unesco consider a major international study of the present and future effect of communication on the relations between changing societies and social groups and on the individuals comprising them." As well, the meeting felt that the free flow of information, the one-way flow, and the need for "cultural privacy" were concepts "worthy of deeper inquiry." The report's recommendations were approved by the 16th General Conference of UNESCO in November 1970, which authorized the director-general "to promote research within the framework of an international programme on the effects of mass communication in society."

As a follow-up, UNESCO sponsored a consultants' conference in Paris in April 1971, which Smythe, Halloran, and Nordenstreng attended. "The same actors were really there as in Montreal," Smythe told me, "and we did design a program, which was published, which fleshed out in terms of communications policy—to some extent theory—how this thing should work that was determined in principle in Montreal." That report was *Proposals for an International Programme of Communication Research* (UNESCO: COM/MD/20, September 10, 1971). A number of UNESCO-sponsored studies flowed from that report, including *Television Traffic—A One-Way Street?* (UNESCO: Reports and Papers on Mass Communication, No. 70) by Kaarle Nordenstreng and Tapio Varis, for whom I surveyed television programming in the United States.

The 1972 IAMCR meeting was held in Buenos Aires, and the consultants who wrote the UNESCO *Proposals* the year before attended. In Smythe's words, "Since the personnel of the experts' panel were also all at IAMCR, we said, 'Why don't we have a second look at the panel's report and see if we have any modifications or qualifications or additions or subtractions?' [...] That was the position that was taken. I think I voiced it, and some people said, 'We agree.'"

Indeed, a fresh look was important, because between the Paris meeting of 1971 and the Buenos Aires meeting of 1972 Smythe had spent a month in China, at a time when few Western visitors were permitted. "Out of it," Smythe told me, "had come a stronger conviction on my part of the strength of the position the Third World should have. Out of it had come a feeling I had sharpened up in China because [...] I agreed with all of the points of view that I'd heard expressed on media policy. [...] I liked the Cultural Revolution attitude towards ideology and communication. [...] " Smythe's visit to China eventually led him to write a memorandum-like piece that he called "After Bicycles, What?" At the time of the Buenos Aires meeting, though, it had not yet been put on paper.

What was on paper was "Reflections on Proposals for an International Programme of Communications Research," written especially for the Buenos Aires meeting, in which he developed some ideas prompted by his visit to China. Smythe distributed the paper, which, he said, "did upset the applecart." He proposed that "commodities had ideological content" and that "cultural screening" was necessary. The presentation was so offensive to the West, particularly the United States, Smythe contended, that he was dropped from further UNESCO participation. He admitted, though, that "if I had distributed 'After Bicycles,' it would have had that effect, too."

In his talks with me, Smythe referred to "the damage I did to myself" with this 1972 paper. "That's the one that got me terminated in UNESCO."

Reflections on Proposals for an International Programme of Communications Research

[IAMCR General Assembly and Congress, "Communication and Development," Buenos Aires, Argentina, September 1972]

THIS BRIEF PAPER is aimed to help in the development of the work flowing from "Proposals for an International Programme of Communications Research" (Unesco COM/MD/20—hereafter referred to as the proposals). I served on the panel which prepared the report on which those proposals were based and I support them. However, most of my time in the last 16 months since those proposals were formulated has been spent in studying the relation of communications policies and research to development in a sample of countries drawn to represent the range of development problems in a world divided ideologically (China, Chile, Hungary, Japan, United Kingdom and Yugoslavia). The proposals speak often of critical analysis; now I want to make some critical analysis of our work in the light of later experience. Perhaps it may help to put the proposals in realistic terms as they might be understood by people in the developing nations. I want to consider what seems to me to be the central problem which we did not analyze sufficiently in the proposals: The meaning of development and technology and the scope of communications. But first a few words about the general theme and line of the proposals.

I can just hear some people in developing countries reacting to those proposals in such terms as these. "It is all very well to 'logically' outline the necessary sequence of communications policy planning, as the proposals do, but the real world is political, not logical. And in no single country in the world is it possible to go through the logical steps proposed in sequence and perfect efficiency." To which my answer is that, of course, the comment is both correct and irrelevant. The authors of the Unesco proposal knew that they were setting up an abstract model. They knew that no single developing nation could or would follow it *seriatim* and without deviation. They knew, however, that it is essential for developing nations to realize that there can be a coherent, general plan for the development of a nation's communications policy and institutions. Such a realization of the centrality of communications policy to the development process can be productive of nothing but good to the extent that it raises issues concerning the meaning of communications and community. A planning model such as that of the proposals makes it possible for each nation to make use of particular features of the plan which are politically possible and desirable at any given time. Moreover, the interpretations placed on the plan will vary according to the political processes and values in different countries. Thus, for example, the concept of "communications research" which to the Chinese implies elitism and alienation may, nevertheless, be applied there in fact by peasants applying critically the knowledge in the *Thoughts of Mao Tse-Tung* to commune communications problems. In any event, Unesco proposals at this point in historical development must emphasize "logic" rather than "politics" of any particular kind in dealing with politically sensitive areas such as communications policy. This is not to say, however, that in discussing Unesco policy we cannot or should not give full rein to consideration of the philosophical and ideological problems which exist in the real world. Only by a candid dialogue within as well as between the nations can the human race develop its potential to live in a humane world. All not only can, but must, learn from all.

I remarked that critical attention should be directed to the meaning of development and of technology and to the scope of our concern with communications. What are some of the dimensions of this cluster of problems?

In April, 1972, Mahbub ul Haq, senior adviser of the World Bank, speaking to an international development conference in Washington, referred to the well-known fact that the gap between rich and poor nations has widened to more than 2,200 dollars in per capita income and that by 1980 it would widen by half as much again. He went on:

> The developing countries have no choice but to turn inwards, and to adopt a different style of life, seeking a consumption pattern more consistent with their own poverty—pots and pans and bicycles and simple consumption habits—without being seduced by the life styles of the rich.
>
> This requires a redefinition of economic and social objectives which is of truly staggering proportions, a liquidation of the privileged groups and vested interests which may well be impossible in many societies.[1]

The notion of technology is central to this trenchant statement. Let us pause to examine what technology means. It is a word which is generally used but seldom examined, and, because it figures importantly in the proposals, we must consider it carefully. Does "technology" include science? Clearly, it is closely related to science. And as so related it bears the inevitable political character of science. Is "technology" equivalent to *applied* science or "research and development" as western culture puts it? Clearly, it implies and includes research and development. The agenda as to *what* shall be researched and developed, and the decisions as to which items are to be carried thereafter to actual innovation (implementation in general practice), are conditioned by the power structures of the societies which are doing the research and development. Therefore, technology so identified is highly political in character and imbued with the ideological point of view of the originating system. Most often, however, "technology" is also taken to include the innovation and operation of the fruits of research and development. It is in this ultimate and broad sense that E. G. Mesthene of the Harvard University's Program on Technology defines technology: "the organization of knowledge for practical purposes. ..."[2] It is also in this broad sense that W. Leiss defines as "technological rationality"—"the purposeful organization and combination of productive techniques, directed either by public or private authorities."[3] And the writings of H. Marcuse largely revolve around the notion of the repressive character of technological rationality.

When technology is defined this broadly it is co-extensive with society, at least with modern western society. However, and this cannot be overemphasized, there is a tendency in western societies to reify "technology" as if it were an independent universal variable. There is a tendency to regard it as something that is happening to societies without their awareness and consent and beyond their control. The fact is that technology in the broad sense is nothing but what a society does to itself. Both popular and serious critics of contemporary western society concerned with the evident imminent ecological disaster resulting from environmental pollution blame it on "technology." And when they do this they are scapegoating. The real responsibility lies in the organization and policy of society—the ideology of western capitalism. And, similarly, the hopes of using "technology" to cure western society's ills are illusory pie in the sky. As McDermott says:

> If religion was formerly the opiate of the masses, then surely technology is the opiate of the educated public today, or at least of its favorite authors. No other single subject is so universally invested with high hopes for the improvement of mankind generally and of Americans in particular. The content of these millennial hopes varies somewhat from author to author, though with considerable overlap. A representative but by no means complete list of these promises and their prophets would include: An end to poverty and the inauguration of permanent prosperity (Leon Keyserling), universal equality of opportunity (Zbigniew Brzezinski), a radical increase in individual freedom (Edward Shils), the replacement of work by leisure for most of mankind (Robert Theobald), fresh water for desert dwellers (Lyndon Baines Johnson), permanent but harmless social revolution (Walt

> Rostow), the final comeuppance of Mao Tse-tung and all his ilk (same prophet), the triumph of wisdom over power (John Kenneth Galbraith), and, lest we forget, the end of ideology (Daniel Bell).[4]

The proposals correctly state:

> Every society has an indigenous culture the values of which should be given prime consideration in planning for national development. But culture is not static or simply a remnant of the traditional past. Present patterns must be studied in relationship both to the historical past and the technological future. (p. 10)

The desire of developing nations for *some* kind of advanced technology—to develop some kind of efficient mass production of consumer goods—is very understandable. The question, "What's wrong with us getting washing machines (or small automobiles, or carpets for the living room, etc.) is difficult to deal with when one runs into it in Eastern Europe or South America. For someone from the heart of the U.S. empire to deny this desire is to seem to want to deny a share in what one enjoys to those who have not. But if the developing nation accepts the consumer goods which it wants from the western imperialist system, it inevitably accepts the values of that system.

An example is the need for washing machines. I assume that everyone agrees people should have efficient machines to clean clothes and household linen. There appear to be two ways to build a technology to meet this need of a developing nation. The western imperial way is to provide washing machines small enough to do the washing for a nuclear family. Western supra-national corporations will supply this need, either through exporting such machines to a developing nation or by providing the know-how and capital to build a factory to manufacture such machines in the developing nation if market considerations warrant it. The developing nation thus will get washing machines suitable to the western lifestyle of alienated individual nuclear family housing. They will also find themselves paying for fictitious "values" built into the machines (e.g., streamlined designs, as if aerodynamic qualities were relevant to a washing machine, a spectrum of colors to match the kitchen decor, etc.). They will also find that the parts and materials used in making the machines are engineered for a relatively short useful life—i.e., that planned obsolescence has been built into them. In short, that their resource allocation and consumption patterns have been forced into the wasteful model of North American capitalism. The other way to provide washing machines would be to engineer them to fit the extended family structure generally found in developing nations. In this mode, the washing machines *and* housing development would provide for multiples of extended families. The washing machines would have larger capacity and longer useful life because they would take advantage of the economies of scale and the economies of designing for long useful life (rather than planned short-life obsolescence). Why should a family need to own its small washing machine if it could have ready access to a large machine used by the community? The political/ideological implications of the choice of models should be obvious.

The same alternative implications exist for solving the problem of personal transportation. The choice of the private automobile as the solution to this problem inevitably leads to traffic congestion (if indeed the masses are to be served rather than a managerial class). It leads to pollution of the air with exhaust fumes. It leads to the allocation of scarce capital to building highways, bridges, etc. to alleviate the traffic congestion. It leads to building an expensive infra-structure of gasoline stations, garages, replacement parts, skilled mechanics, and a delivery system of heavy trucks to distribute them. While thus engaged, the developing nation restricts the development of its health and educational facilities because of the prior decision to favour the private automobile in resource allocation. I emphasize the less obvious structural effects but must at least mention the obvious ideological fact that private ownership of automobiles educates individuals to be selfish, aggressive, hedonist individuals. It is antithetical to the values aspired to in socialism.

Of course, there is also an alternative technology possible to meet the need for quick, safe, personal transportation. Mass transportation by vehicles is a well-known technology. And there are unexamined possibilities of using for the same purpose horizontal escalators in network layouts for urban transportation. Such a system would simultaneously enjoy the economies of scale, pollution-free electrical power, and the flexibility for individuals to enter and leave the mechanism, which is impossible with regimented mass transport by vehicles. The alternative transport technology would have obvious ideological effects consonant with autonomous development for a nation.

Many other important illustrations of the ideological consequences of modes of meeting people's laudable desire for improved living conditions could be given—some from mass media services. And, indeed, at a later point I propose this as a priority area for communications research. But now I offer these examples to show the consequences if a developing nation uncritically accepts the consumer goods and services offered by the western imperial system, either directly or as mediated through certain socialist nations. If the developing nation takes this course, it accepts and adopts the repressive implications of the social organization which western technical rationality requires. It accepts the trend toward environmental pollution which western technical rationality carries as its corollary. It ignores the wisdom of the advice quoted above from Mahbub ul Haq.

We must emphasize, then, the correctness of two statements from the proposals (p. 13):

> Moral values, social and traditional considerations must not be slighted in the *process* of decision-making for development. ...
>
> The role of the suggested institutionalized communication policy council will, therefore, have to be a continuing one as watchdog, as adviser, and as coordinator within the broader framework of national development policy, undertaking to continue the constant critical analysis of the meaning of *communication in society.*

Increasingly, it becomes evident that popular culture—the services and "software" and other consumer goods—is both a result of and a cause of humanity's awareness of its own predicament and its own potential. Today's popular culture embodies—carries—views as to the meaning of life and the means of living as well as the possibilities for all of life's values to be realized. And as a carrier of these views, it instructs and guides humanity in regard to present and future actions.

In this broad sense, politics are always everywhere in command of social life. What men and women have to decide is which kind of politics they will live with in the future. The cult of the individual is the central theme of western (capitalist) culture since the Renaissance. It manifests itself in popular culture through assumptions that individuals should be given freedom to be serious or frivolous, industrious or lazy, concerned with building a better society or cultivating private thoughts, feelings and pleasures, and so forth. The popular culture created to cater to these many purposes educates people to conform to the easy path for individuals, but for developing nations it results in the toleration of neocolonialism. Alternatively, popular culture *could* help people to build the new forms of social organization which socialism will develop. These new forms of social organization will develop out of the pre-existing culture and the unique institutional requirements to create socialist man, for whom social concern will balance individual considerations. In the immediate future, it is probable that in order for developing nations to begin on the latter path it will be necessary to regard the two alternative cultural policies as mutually exclusive. A developing nation can, as the Chinese say, go the capitalist road. *Or,* it can go the socialist road. It cannot go both at the same time. Not only is this one of the lessons learned by the Chinese in the Cultural Revolution, but it also is indicated by the stern warning given by Mahbub ul Haq.

In this context, we may consider the question which the proposals pose and leave unresolved:

> What should be national policy regarding "cultural privacy" to protect the fragile pattern of autochthonous cultures against the massive intrusion of foreign mass media contents? Where is the demarcation line between a "protective screening" and a harmful "isolationist" policy which would deprive the nation of the cultural achievements of the "universal" world? (p. 19)

I hope that this conference will debate this question and reach some firm conclusion on it. For my part, I suggest that it is necessary to recognize that the "universal" world is one in which the great mass of the population does not enjoy "high culture" because it is too hungry, too ill-clothed, too sick, and too ill-housed to do so. Moreover, the "old order" of neocolonialism in the developing world is so stratified by social class, political and economic considerations that in the absence of cultural screening, the great masses of the population will not benefit from the cultural achievements of the "'universal'" world in any real or proximate sense. If this be true, then the question as posed is insubstantial and merely rhetorical. The force of the political axiom that "politics are basically local" rests on the primacy of the case for self-government and the competence of people at and below the nation level to judge best their collective interest. When to these observations is added the case which can be made for cultural screening there seems little ground for doubt that the burden of proof rests with those who would introduce foreign technology to justify its intrusion. To those who make development plans for a nation, the first and the ultimate question to be asked and answered is "What kind of development, for whom, when, and how?" And when offered the "know-how" of engineers from any outside source, the development planners should insist on answers to the question, "Know-how to produce what, for whom, and why?"

If these thoughts correctly reflect the spirit of the proposals, then several critical points must be made: (1) At certain vital passages of the proposals, the permissibility of uncritical acceptance of imported technology seems to be granted; in my opinion, this is not defensible. (2) The relation of communication policy planning to development planning should be clarified and expanded in the proposals.

At several key points the proposals endorse the introduction into developing nations of new communications technology in an uncritical fashion. At page 19, it is said:

> At this time, the whole prospect for international communication is being decisively influenced by what is in effect a revolution in technology. On the one hand, for example, direct broadcasting through satellites opens immense possibilities for wider propagation of media far beyond geographical, political, ideological and cultural boundaries. On the other hand through such things as cassettes, discs, facsimile, CATV, individuals in many countries could have their range of choice tremendously increased through an international marketing system which would operate almost independently of national production capacities. The implications and effects (social, political, legal, cultural, commercial, educational) of such technological possibilities are of enormous importance in the formulation of national communication policies.

To endorse the "international marketing system" function of selling western imperialist technology in the communications area and to invite developing nations to accept such technology *without the caveat of prior cultural screening* is to do the gravest disservice to the need of developing nations to determine their own future technology. Moreover, to assume that all developing nations must want to increase the "range of choice" for individuals is to be very partisan in the world conflict of ideologies. In some developing nations, the dispersion of energies and attention and resources attendant to a mid-Atlantic style of range-of-choice life is productive only of the perpetuation of neo-colonialism and counterproductive to autonomous development.

And at p. 10, it is said:

> In order that the new communication technologies can "fit into society," can be functional within it, and that policy making and planning can reflect the needs of people, much more multidisciplinary research is required. New models for communication patterns must be produced in which the operation of inter-personal communication systems are combined with modern media structures to give a much more complete picture of how communication and diffusion of different types of information really take place.

The same essential criticism runs to this advice. To tell communications researchers that they must accept the alleged reality of uncritical acceptance by developing nations of new communication technologies which should "'fit into society'" is to endorse the continuation of western imperial cultural imperialism.

The relation of communications policy planning to development planning clearly has two levels: One advisory/participatory and the other instrumental or derivative. It may be that the case for each is not sufficiently clear in the proposals. Both are legitimate. And of the two, the former requires the greater force in presentation because resistances to it will be greater.

Clearly, the realization of communications policy research as a participant in national development planning is dependent on evident competence and relevance on the part of communications policy researchers. It would seem obvious also that IAMCR is an organization which ought to foster such development-related communications policy research. It, therefore, is necessary for IAMCR to create a process and the conditions in which research designs and researchable propositions related to national development will be generated and developed. I, therefore, propose that our work in this Congress be directed to the consideration of such models for research. And I suggest that the core area where such models for research should be located is the ideological/political consequences of popular culture. You will note that I am using "communications" in the broad sense which the proposals properly recommend at page 7. To launch a trial balloon in this arena and to illustrate the issues involved, let me sketch very roughly such a research model. Let us suppose that on a continuum there were arrayed all of the artifacts which comprise a developing nation's culture. Thus, at the one end (the left for me because my culture reads from left to right) would be the least value loaded and most concrete artifacts: unprocessed products of agriculture, extractive industry, and fisheries. At the other end would be the most abstract and value-laden means of communications—perhaps poetry, painting and music. Obviously, the cinema, TV-radio, and press would be at or close to that end. As my earlier discussion suggested, such items as washing machines and personal transportation are loaded with ideological consequences. The position on this continuum occupied by an artifact would denote the ideological/political potential effects and consequences of the artifact. Let us suppose, moreover, that it is possible to have several different levels of such continua with the different levels representing, for example, (1) traditional pre-capitalist culture, (2) modern capitalist culture, and (3) socialist culture. The research design would have to accomplish the analysis of the meaning, effects, and consequences of each artifact in politico-ideological terms, i.e., it would have to answer questions such as these: How does this artifact predispose or educate people to a particular ideological/political view of life? From what sort of social relations does this artifact arise? Is there a social as distinct from individual need for this artifact? What sort of artifact is appropriate to a particular ideological/political view of life? What changes in social relations would be necessary in order, e.g., to produce the artifacts most appropriate to socialist culture? And so on.

The fact that communications research *until now* has not given such a design serious consideration and that communications research tools may be inadequate *now* to cope with this design may be admitted. But at that point the challenge stands clearest: Let us develop the necessary tools and use them. If it be suggested that the task I am suggesting has never been done and is beyond man's capacities at this point in time, I must remind you that in principle the task has been done (even if in the absence of communications researchers) as far as regards the first two levels of continua. The famous Querelle des Anciens et Moderns which went on intensively in France for more than a fourth of the 17th Century was just such an analysis and sorting-out of the arts and handicrafts under the impact of the Renaissance on the previous medieval culture. From that controversy emerged the seven Fine Arts as known in modern capitalist culture. From that controversy—which engaged people in Italy, England, Germany, the Low Countries—came the *Encyclopedia* in the late 18th Century which literally defined all knowledge in terms of modern capitalist culture. Indeed, the Renaissance as a whole amounted to a cultural screening of medieval culture which was necessary if modern capitalist culture were to have coherence and identity, ideologically/politically speaking.[5]

Notes to "Reflections on Proposals . . ."

1. *Daily News*, Budapest, April 25, 1972.
2. Harvard University Program on Technology, *Fourth Annual Report*, 1968. Quoted in John McDermott, "Technology: The Opiate of the Intellectuals," in A. H. Teich (ed.), *Technology and Man's Future* (New York: St. Martin's Press, 1972), p. 152.
3. William Leiss, *The Domination of Nature* (New York: George Braziller, 1972), p. 199.
4. McDermott, "Technology," p. 151.
5. Dallas W. Smythe, "Cultural Realism and Cultural Screens," *Lo Spettacolo*, 1972 (in press).

13

"The power of capitalism today rests on its success in developing capitalist consumption *relations"*

Editor's Note: "After Bicycles, What?" (along with "Blindspot") is certainly Dallas Smythe's most well-known piece. This renown is amazing, because the work has never been published until now. It has gotten around by word of mouth and in some cases has been circulated in third- and fourth-generation photocopies. "Bicycles," as it has come to be known, has attained legendary status. I recall being at conferences where some participants were asking each other, "Have you read 'Bicycles'?" and "Do you have a copy of 'Bicycles' I can borrow?" I have no recollection of the first time I heard about or read "Bicycles." It seems always to have been part of my professional life, as I am sure it has been of the lives of some other communication scholars.

"Bicycles" resulted from Smythe's visit to the People's Republic of China in December 1971 and January 1972, thanks to a grant he received from Canada Council allowing him to study ideology and technology in several countries. A memorandum written in the third person served as the springboard for the piece, which Smythe developed during discussions with his wife, Jennie.

Reflecting on this visit to China, Smythe told me, "I agreed with all of the points of view that I'd heard expressed on media policy when I talked to the people in the cinema industry—production, exhibition, and distribution—and to the people in the newspapers, people in the radio—they didn't have television at that point—and the people I talked to in book publishing—in fact, people I talked to everywhere, in communes. I liked the Cultural Revolution attitude toward ideology and communication, with one exception." As Smythe explains in "Bicycles," that exception was what he heard at the university in Beijing. "I asked to be taken to the university to meet with political economists, philosophers, political scientists who would be interested in the same kinds of questions I was. It was a total disaster."

As Smythe recalled the incident, he said, "The head of the group I met was, I think, the previous president of the university, who had a Ph.D., I think from either Yale or Harvard, [...] who had been kept on as a vice-chairman of—they then called them—revolutionary committees, [...] but the chairman was a PLA [People's Liberation Army] man who didn't know what the hell was going on and he was just nominally there, symbolically, as the chair." Smythe first raised the question of ideology and technology "because I had a gut feeling [...] that this could be a problem for China. In fact, in reading Chairman Mao's writings, I hadn't seen that he had avoided the problem. He hadn't brazenly stated it in the way in which Lenin did. [...] You know, Lenin took the position, 'We need Henry Ford over here and electricity and then we'll have socialism.' Well, anybody who could say that had written himself out of the ballpark as far as I was concerned as a political economist."

In discussing this matter with the vice chairman, Smythe said, "'I happen to think that technology is loaded with ideology.' So he said, 'It's not ideological. Don't you understand if the workers controlled the means of production then the technology will serve the interests of the workers?'" Smythe then paused and remarked to me, "I heard it!" Then he took up the story again, "'I don't believe it. I don't think it works that way.' And they said, 'Oh yes, Marx said it.' And I said, 'Well, let me give you a couple of illustrations. You've got railroads in China. Why are they where they've been built? [...] Were they built to serve the interests of China, or were they built to serve the interests of *compradors* who came and wanted to penetrate China [...] to exploit your resources, labor, minerals, and everything else? [...] When you took over, you didn't have a north-south railway system at all—you couldn't travel or send freight from the north of China to the south of China. There were no means to do it. Everything was penetrated from the coast.' I said, 'Don't you see that the way in which your railroad, quote, technology was designed and implemented was to serve the interests of the people who designed it? And you inherited this. Now you say that you're going to use it for the interests of the public. So what? You still don't have a north-south railroad. So, don't you see the political, economic, ideological significance of this question?' He replied, 'No, we don't. It's totally nonideological.'"

Smythe told me the second example he used was television. "'Are you aware that in the West television was designed and innovated for two associated reasons? One, to make possible an immediate market for motion pictures in the people's homes, because there's a limited number of theatres and an enormously greater number of homes, and it was as an extension of Hollywood—one of the reasons it was designed and innovated to have small screens appropriate to a living room in a home. [...] And the other reason was to have a vehicle for producing labor power, which would serve as a marketing agent for consciousness industry.' Well, they didn't understand what that meant. That was totally over their heads. [...] " At this point, Smythe recalled to me, he suggested that because China did not then have a TV system, one could be innovated that was two-way (with a built-in public feedback mechanism) and that was based on large screens (for use in communes, assembly halls, cafeterias, etc.). "People could make statements, which would then be open for relay to everybody. [...] You'd have everybody speaking to everybody. It would not be a one-way system to sell you motion picture entertainment or commodities."

Smythe said the university people were not taken by this idea but that it was of interest to "the people concerned with ideology." In particular, Smythe remembered, there was a three-star general, "and he knew what I was talking about. [...] He said, 'The word has gotten to me that you have made a very interesting suggestion, something we should consider, about a two-way TV system.'"

Smythe drafted "Bicycles" and a memo on cultural exchange a little more than a year after his visit. Both pieces were sent to the first secretary of the Chinese embassy in Ottawa and then forwarded to Beijing. Smythe heard through a well-informed Chinese colleague in Canada that they were being considered in government circles and, as he wrote in one of his last letters to me in mid-1992, "that means Party, too." It was because of this government consideration that Smythe allowed "Bicycles" to remain unpublished. He wrote to me: "It justifies my non-publication of the piece, i.e. that I intended it for internal use by the Party and govt. and did not want it to be used in any distorted way by the Teng faction which even then was obstructing the Maoists." Smythe said that during his interview with the three-star general, "I felt that in a sense he was treating me as a comrade, and there was an implied obligation to keep my criticisms within the family." Smythe never did hear what became of "Bicycles," and because of political changes he lost some contacts in China. "But meanwhile I delayed [publishing it]

because I had many other things to do and [...] maybe they were going to get back to me in six months, and maybe not. And Mao died [in 1976] and I concluded that what's the point of it now? Might as well go public with it. But then it had lost its timeliness, and so I didn't. I circulated it [but] I didn't even do that until after I failed to get a response from China. [...] They never did release me from my obligations, so I just concluded eventually that it disappeared."

Some features of "Bicycles" have appeared in other things Smythe wrote. He said, for example, that it "is absorbed and muddied up" in a few chapters of his book, *Dependency Road.* "But I think it has a cogency taken as it is," he told me, and he was eager to see it published, even twenty years after it was written.

After Bicycles, What? [March 1973]

1. [Introduction]

CHINA IN THE PAST thirteen years has established the basis for a new socialist process of living and working; this is the lasting contribution of the Cultural Revolution to the reorganization of thinking and working in China. It has also demonstrated to its people's satisfaction that the process works. Food, clothing, housing, [and] health services are available equitably and adequately to the whole population. But at this time (1973) it is evident that a new generation of politico-economic problems is appearing, even as the Little Red Guards and their older brothers and sisters near their maturity. The new generation of problems are created by the Chinese socialist successes to date. And like the generation of problems solved in the Cultural Revolution, the presently appearing problems arise from the common cultural womb from which socialism is emerging: capitalism. The new generation of problems focus on the imminent need to consider how China will apply its new socialist decision-making process to the determination of what consumer goods China will produce for its people when they reach the point of saying: we now produce enough food, enough simple warm clothing, enough housing, enough health care for everyone's welfare; after bicycles, what will we produce next? It is to the analysis of the ideological problems which that question will raise that this article is addressed. Once the physiologically "necessary" goods and services are available in adequate supply for everyone, the choice of less physiologically mandatory goods and services to be produced will be found to raise grave ideological issues. To adopt capitalist luxury goods such as private automobiles, family-sized washing machines, family-sized refrigerators, one-way TV, etc. for Chinese production would be to equip Chinese families with that many educational instruments leading to the capitalist cultural road. This proposition, later to be considered in more detail, raises other and deeper questions. Is technology autonomous, i.e. everywhere in the world necessarily the same in its essential form and consequences? During the Cultural Revolution the "capitalist roaders" were properly charged with policies which would have had the Chinese tail behind the West for centuries. And the "socialist roaders" wanted a process to be built by which China could leapfrog ahead of capitalism. In the production of what kind of goods and services? Those essentially similar to what capitalism provides, or a different set of goods and services appropriate to socialist men and women? How different, and why different, when it comes down to practical choices? And how will the Chinese decision-making processes proceed to cope with this set of problems? Chairman Mao clearly understands the point we raise. The question remains whether the higher, middle and lower echelons of the Communist Party do—and what the masses of peasants, workers and PLA people think and are ready to do about the problem. Is it possible that over this issue the struggle might take the proportions of a second Proletarian Cultural Revolution?

2. Smythe's Experience on This in China

When Smythe visited China in December–January, 1971–1972 he was concerned to raise the issue of the ideological implications of technology in conversations with responsible persons in TV-radio, electronic research and development, and departments of Economics at universities. In talking with people in TV-radio he raised it as the problem of the innovation of colour TV on a mass basis throughout China. Presently the total investment in equipment for TV is very small, and he was told that China was planning a truly nationwide TV system. He asked whether the plan was to adopt the western technique which presently is embodied in the limited TV system now used in China. The answer was affirmative and his Chinese hosts asked him what alternative there was. He replied that the existing TV technique had been developed under capitalism to make possible the sale of motion pictures and other commodities to people in their homes. At the time when TV was developed in capitalist countries it would have been quite possible to design it as a two-way system in which each receiver would have the capability to provide either a voice or voice-and-picture response to the broadcasting station, which might then store and rebroadcast these responses or samples of them. But for its purposes, capitalism needed only a one-way system and this is what was developed. In other words, the TV station speaks to the people but the system does not permit the people to speak back to the TV station. It is essentially and intentionally an authoritarian system. The Chinese responsible persons then asked Smythe why he thought it would be desirable in China for the TV system to be a two-way system (i.e. one which would permit the people to talk back to the TV station). He replied that during the Cultural Revolution the Chinese people had made much use of *tatzupao* [posters pasted on walls or signboards] and that a two-way TV system would be like an electronic *tatzupao* system. Now when China was still not handicapped by possessing a fully developed western style TV system, it would be possible for China to design a TV technology which would serve its ideological purposes, rather than to adopt uncritically a capitalistic technology for TV which embodied capitalist ideology. The TV-radio people in Shanghai, Nanking, Peking, Wuhan and Kwanchow responded with interest and indicated they would think about the suggestion.

When Smythe was in Peking the same idea was discussed with responsible persons at Tsinghua University, including professors Chien Wei Chiang, and Tung Shi-pai, and their response was to the effect that it was a good idea and would be presented to higher authority for consideration. There was ready understanding of the class and ideological nature of technology on the part of the physical scientists at Tsinghua University and on the part of the responsible persons in the broadcasting institutions.

At Peking University, however, the contrary was true. In a meeting on 27 December, 1971 with Professors Chou Pei-Yuan, Weng Yu-Tang, Lao and others—all teachers of economics or philosophy, Smythe raised the issue of the class character of technology, the ideological character of consumer goods and services, and the ideological character of innovation/investment. He illustrated the problem by discussing one-way as against two-way TV. Initially he was told that it seemed he was raising a question suitable to engineers rather than philosophers and social scientists. When he persisted however, the issue was joined. And the Peking University professors all took the position that "technology itself has no class nature but it will be used to serve the interests of a certain class." For example, they said:

> In capitalism, TV serves the capitalist class and plays a political role by its content. In socialist countries TV will serve socialism. The relation between the superstructure and the economic base is a dialectical one. The super-

> structure must fill the needs of the economic base. The socialist economic base requires a socialist superstructure. If it does not fit, then innovation in it is necessary. So the Cultural Revolution is a kind of political revolution resulting in change in the superstructure. ...
>
> In the field of communications, in old China, they used broadcasting as a means of advertising and also as a means to consolidate their reactionary rule. It has been completely changed since Liberation. In broadcasting we now have a broadcasting station in each village and a telephone also. ... So the technology serves the class which has political control. ...
>
> We use the mass movement in adopting new technology. We also take good points from foreign technology. Take black and white TV for example. When we develop it, we should develop it gradually. It is not correct to say we should adopt nothing from capitalist countries. Due to the leadership of the Communist Party and Chairman Mao Tse Tung, our speed will be much greater than in capitalist countries and we also rely on the masses and the mass line. ...

To this Smythe replied:

> I make no criticism at all of the process by which the Chinese produce new technical developments in China. I have seen the advantages of your three-in-one principle in operation on technical innovation. But to say that in importing foreign technology you get ideologically neutral technique is incorrect in my opinion. You say that technique comes from workers and intellectuals and that it is therefore not ideologically loaded in favour of capitalism. As far as your development of Chinese technique in China is concerned, I accept that. But the development of technique in capitalist countries comes from huge corporate laboratories such as Bell Telephone Laboratories, where many thousand of physicists, chemists, other scientists and engineers are assembled to do research and development work. The capitalist corporate managers pick and choose only those ideas for development which offer the probability of developing new and profitable markets or reducing costs in their operations in old markets. So the innovations which do take place in capitalism do embody in different ways—one of which I illustrated with the one-way TV example—the ideology of capitalism. In my opinion China should filter all foreign technological developments which it considers adopting very, very carefully for their more or less hidden ideological consequences.

To which the Chinese professors responded through their most senior comrade:

> Science and technology come from the masses which also include the technical personnel. Science and technology in capitalist countries serve the capitalist class. In China communications serve the masses. We are now beginning TV. TV serves the people, to educate them, to tell them how China is fighting imperialism and supporting People's Liberation movements. ...

The Peking University interview ended on this note. Smythe's last contact with the issue while in China took place at his concluding interview in China, with Li Shu-Fu, Responsible Member, Department of Political Work, Kwantung Provincial Revolutionary Committee. In greeting Smythe prior to a conversation on other topics, Comrade Li remarked that he understood Smythe had made an interesting suggestion regarding two-way TV in his conversations in China.

3. Some Remarks on "Technology"

What do we mean by technology? I suggest that it has three kinds of meanings. (1) The first is closely related to science. In this sense technology has the same political character as does science: it involves the decision (or perhaps merely awareness of the possibility) to apply knowledge in some practical way—and both the knowledge in question and the practical use to which it is put arise out of the political process. But at its border with science, technology is an abstract thing: the *possibility* of testing out some part of knowledge in such a way that practical uses might emerge. When one refers to the pollution of the atmosphere in a city as being caused by modern technology, one clearly refers to something other than this narrow conception of technology. (2) The second kind of meaning of technology is broader than the first because it extends the first to include also what is called "research and development." Broadly speaking R & D involves work which proceeds in two logically opposite directions: (a) experimental work which embodies the results of new scientific knowledge and proceeds to answer the question: if we put this new knowledge to work, what practical results will it have? (b) experimental work which proceeds from known practical problems towards new solutions based on new knowledge and which answers the question: can we now find a practical solution to a certain practical problem, given that we can now apply some new scientific discoveries? In this meaning of technology we can speak of it properly as the search for an optimum *technique* of doing something. The terminology of capitalism has now for about a century obscured the act that the R & D applications of knowledge are forms of *art.* Indeed until near the end of the 19th century, economists customarily referred to the "industrial arts" to mean what we here call "technique." And patent law under capitalism still retains this relic of the Greek approach to life when it relates patent rights to improvements "in the state of the art." So the term which became the generic description of the products of R & D work was "invention." The fact that politics controls arts and inventions and that the choice of art form and content and of inventions should be made deliberately according to which political road is to be followed is of course obvious concerning R & D work. But R & D work is still not broad enough to match the scope of meaning which is often given to technology. The inventions which it has created have not yet been applied or popularized. Nor have their probable consequences when applied necessarily been evaluated. (3) The most common meaning of technology in western capitalism is based on the second but extends it to include the full implementation—or "innovation"—of the results of the R & D work. E. G. Mesthene of Harvard University's Program on Technology defines technology as "the organization of knowledge for practical purposes. ..."[1] When so defined, technology is co-extensive with modern western society. For the applied "organization of knowledge" covers all of the aspects of practical living under capitalism—from the design of the "hardware" of industrial and military applications of knowledge, to the regimented alienation of recreational activity in capitalism's national parks.

Is "technology" autonomous? Jacques Ellul[2] and others maintain that the answer is affirmative. Autonomous in this connection means universal and beyond the scope of politics. In our opinion technology is not autonomous in any of the three kinds of meaning which we have identified. Just as what constitutes science at any given time and place reflects the world view and the political structure of society of the particular culture at that time and place, so the first kind of meaning of technology is culturally (i.e., politically) determined. The possibilities of applying knowledge at a given time and place inevitably reflect the political structure of that society. In the sense of R & D technique (meaning #2), technology even more evidently reflects the purposes of resource allocation by a particular cultural complex—a highly politically determinative state at a particular place and time. For example, Smythe was told by the economists and philosophers at Peking University that railroads were neutral, ideologically; that they served the imperialists before Liberation but equally well served the People's Republic afterwards. This is a dangerous half-truth, because by assuming the existence of railroads the purpose and ideological effects of the *innovation* of railroads is excluded from analysis and implicitly regarded as autonomous. The fact is that in the 19th century railroads were built by the imperialists in China and elsewhere in Asia, Latin America and Africa to serve exploitation of those areas as colonies. So the routes on which railroads were innovated did have obvious ideological consequences when they were innovated and subsequently.

The third kind of meaning of technology in which it is understood as coextensive with the rules, work discipline, etc. of technique as employed in practice after its innovation is still more obviously a matter of political behaviour. In all three senses of the term, then, the reification of "technology" as an autonomous force must be ruled out.

Is the *idea* that technology is autonomous, i.e., politically neutral and universal, itself a political concept? Yes, it is a political concept and reactionary as well. The reification of technology as a universal tendency (an autonomous factor) inevitably leads people to regard technology as something that is happening to them without their consent, awareness or the possibility of their controlling it. To blame environmental pollution on "technology," as commonly happens in advanced capitalist countries, is to scapegoat. The real responsibility for environmental pollution rests with the system which creates the pollution. In capitalist nations it rests in the policy and organization of capitalist society, i.e., ultimately on the ideology of modern capitalism. In the United States, criticism by people of technological unemployment has been diverted from the capitalist system to the support of utopian schemes for replacing work by leisure for most of mankind. And "technology" has been used as a slogan to rationalize and disguise imperialist policies. In short, "technology" has been held out to the people as a cure for all of capitalism's ills. This is illusory pie in the sky. As McDermott says:

> If religion was formerly the opiate of the masses, then surely technology is the opiate of the educated public today, or at least of its favorite authors. No other single subject is so universally invested with high hopes for the improvement of mankind generally and of Americans in particular. The content of these millennial hopes varies somewhat from author to author, though with considerable overlap. A representative but by no means complete list of these promises and their prophets would include: An end to poverty and the inauguration of permanent prosperity (Leon Keyserling), universal equality of opportunity (Zbigniew Brzezinski), a radical increase in individual freedom (Edward Shils), the replacement of work by leisure for most of mankind (Robert Theobald), fresh water for desert dwellers (Lyndon Baines Johnson), permanent but harmless social revolution (Walt Rostow), the final come-uppance of Mao Tse-tung and all his ilk (same

prophet), the triumph of wisdom over power (John Kenneth Galbraith), and lest we forget, the end of ideology (Daniel Bell).[3]

But quite apart from its reactionary implications in advanced capitalist countries, the idea of the autonomy of technology carries with it hidden implications which are at best problematic, and at worst supportive of feudal and capitalist cultural features. The uses of technique (in the sense of machines of ever-growing sophistication) in capitalism have been linked with alienation of people, with specialization of functions of people, and with hierarchical arrangements of people in bureaucratic structures. Moreover, the uses of technique in that sense have for the past four centuries in the West been wedded to the notion that man must dominate nature. The consequences of the defilement of nature which this entails are now becoming evident, even to the capitalist power structure. But the notion that there is a technical solution for every problem merely leads the western nations into still further attempts to dominate nature, with still further distorting effects on development. And when western technical experts come to a developing nation to demonstrate the "know-how" with which to use their technical gadgets, the awe with which the alleged autonomy of technology is carried by them tends to transplant all of these consequences of capitalism into the consciousness and practice in the developing nation. In every sense of the word, "technology" is a reactionary political fact in the present state of the peoples of the world. With a different world view socialism can embody in the counterpart term which it will develop over the next few centuries a quite different and constructive set of values.

In dealing with their own problems of organizational structure and policy, the Chinese, as proved by the Proletarian Cultural Revolution, are fully capable of dealing with the problems generated by the development of *Chinese* technique. But we question whether the Chinese are adequately aware of the consequences to their system of importing technique and the products of technique from the capitalist world. The common acknowledgement by the Chinese that they lag behind the West in many respects in their technical development but that they hope to catch up quickly because of their socialist system suggests as much. In what way will it be possible for the Chinese to catch up with Western technical development if the latter is to be the yardstick against which Chinese development will be measured without patterning Chinese development on Western criteria? Surely the Chinese perspective should be to leave the West behind by developing socialist culture which will be quite different from and incommensurable with Western technological development. There is no *socialist* road in Western capitalist technological development. And just as there has been no Western precedent for the change in human nature from selfish to unselfish which the Cultural Revolution portends, so there need be no constraint in Chinese development to measure its material accomplishments by western standards. To try to develop in that way would be to implicitly forecast a return to the capitalist road.

4. Invention, Investment and Obsolescence: The Same Process in Art and in Economic Activity

Chairman Mao in *Talks at the Yenan Forum on Literature and Art* stated clearly the process by which something new is created and popularized in the arts. The process is a dialectical one. The something new is created out of the experience of the masses. And the masses in using the something new transform it and themselves. In the transformation process the masses change it and themselves to some degree. In changing their cultural life and themselves, the masses outgrow old ways of life—ways of talking, singing, thinking, doing. In outgrowing old ways of life (and developing new ways), the masses discard some parts of their former ways of talking, singing, thinking and doing.

The Proletarian Cultural Revolution established that proletarian politics will be in command of all cultural life. It was also *said* that proletarian politics would henceforth be in command of all economic life. But while it is evident that performing and literary artists have been transformed in the process of proletarian politics being in command of all cultural life, it is not evident that economists and philosophers have been transformed in respect to proletarian politics being in command of economic life. As Smythe's interview at Peking University suggests, perhaps economists and philosophers continue to use mechanically and dogmatically certain cliches derived indirectly from our common cultural heritage of capitalist thinking. We refer to their views concerning the political character of technique and technology. For the Peking interview revealed that they seem to regard technique and technology as autonomous and non-political. And quite unlike the responsible persons who actually operate the TV-radio stations, and quite unlike the technical experts at Tsinghua University, they exhibited a rigidity which even resisted completely the possibility of a dialogue on the subject.

Economic theory, in its essentials, in dealing with technique should not be different than Chairman Mao's theory concerning art and literature.

The creative act in the case of economic life may be termed invention. The process of generating the creative act, in economic life as in other cultural life, must grow out of the practice of the masses of people as well as out of knowledge about non-human nature. The process of popularizing the invention which economists often call "innovation" involves spreading the use of the invention by the masses of the people. Because invention in economic life usually involves tools, machines or physical products of some kind, the possibility of their being changed, or even of their uses being changed from those which were predicted, is perhaps much less than in the case of the literature and art, although this statement may need critical scrutiny. In any event, inventions used in economic life, whether they be producers' or consumers' goods, certainly change and transform the users. And in changing their lives as a result of using new inventions in economic life, the masses of the people outgrow old ways and discard some parts of those old ways. In economic terms, obsolescence—the recognition of the functional replacement of the old by the new economic goods—is the name given to the old which is displaced by the new. In practical terms, investment by the masses of the people in new consumer goods, e.g. bicycles, makes obsolete older means of transportation (trains, buses or even walking to some extent).

As far as concerns innovation in *production* equipment, there is no particular reason to doubt the care and thoroughness with which proletarian politics are in command of economics in China. Sufficient evidence of the care with which the alienating effects of technique is considered prior to innovation in that area does exist. But as regards consumer goods there is a real question as to the adequacy with which proletarian politics will command the decision to innovate. And for this concern there are two kinds of reasons.

In the first place, Marxism has not paid the attention to this problem which the problem deserves. Marx and Marxism have concentrated on man's production relations. There are many reasons why this was correct at any time but especially at a time in man's history when man's potential productive capacity was still inadequate to provide sufficient basic food, clothing, housing, health and other cultural services to the whole population. But the power of capitalism in the late 20th century world does *not* rest on capitalism's success in providing its populations sufficient of such basic goods and services; on the contrary it is notorious that a major part of the population under capitalism does not enjoy sufficient of such basic goods and services but rather lives in pockets of poverty.

The power of capitalism today rests on its success in developing capitalist *consumption* relations. These consumption relations motivate the population to buy consumer goods on the basis of style changes, imitation of happy, wealthy people, fear of loneliness, sexual appeals, etc. The means by which the population is motivated are two-fold: (1) The attractive nature of the product itself. This is the chief purpose of the design and materials from which the product is made, the design of the packages in which the product is sold, and a debatable but evidently tolerable level of quality control in the manufacture of the product. (2) The skill and effectiveness with which the product is advertised and marketed to the consumer.

In order for the capitalist system to survive (i.e. to keep its profits at stable and rising levels), consumption relations dictate that the products be designed with definite built-in obsolescence and self-destruct qualities. They are made so that they will become obsolete or worn-out within a definite and short period of time so that they will have to be replaced. The quality of materials and construction is therefore controlled so that vital parts of the consumer goods will wear out or break within short periods of time. For example a family-sized washing machine is expected to require such expensive parts replacement within seven years that the consumer will trade it in on a new model. So generally is all this understood now that it is becoming common to refer to the "consciousness industry" as that grouping of industries which produces consumer goods and services and which operates the communications institutions, vocational education, marketing and advertising. It is important to emphasize that the consumer goods and services to be mass produced under capitalism are *designed,* made and sold not primarily to serve the people, but to keep the people in a "rat race" in which they work as hard as they can to buy as many consumer goods as they can so that they generate the necessary profits to satisfy the system and retain their jobs so that they can work as hard as they can. In short, capitalism's raison d'être today rests on the success of its "cultural industry," which includes all consumption goods, and in which capitalist politics are always in command. And the followers of Marx in economics and philosophy have not yet caught up with the capitalists in understanding this aspect of how monopoly capitalism works.

The second reason for concern that proletarian politics in China will command decisions to innovate consumer goods is that in this as in other major problems of socialist construction, China has no relevant experience from elsewhere to guide it onto the socialist road. The Soviet Union and other socialist countries have conspicuously failed to establish a cultural screening process which would filter out inventions and product and service innovations with respect to ideological consequences. The innovation of private automobiles and the imitation of the tradition of "style" in clothes and cosmetics are illustrations. It is not necessary to argue these specific cases in detail, but merely to mention the fact that in regard to private automobiles the consequences are that a substantial share of the social surplus is diverted from the area of public consumption to the investment in factories to produce the automobiles, in elaborate highway systems of roads, in a distribution system for petroleum products, tires and other replacement parts for automobiles, for parking lots and garages to house the automobiles. And this is not the end of the road for such capital investment, for once the private automobile industry gets established it will produce a demand for another industry to manufacture camping trailers, another to make small boat trailers, and others to manufacture outboard motors and small boats for leisure use of individuals, not to mention tents, camp equipment, etc. The immediate economic effect of popularizing the automobile for private ownership is thus to divert a substantial share of the society's productive effort from other public purposes (education, health, etc.) to the gratification of individuals' desires for automobiles. Politically, the privately owned automobile educates people to be selfish, aggressive, hedonist individuals.

Similarly with style in clothes and cosmetics, which currently are features of capitalist economies and arise out of and reinforce class distinctions in bourgeois society.

The point of the preceding argument is that consumer goods, which embody capitalist values such as style and planned obsolescence, are a trap which capitalism presents to new socialist systems—a trap of which the masses of Chinese peasants, workers and PLA soldiers should beware.

5. Cultural Screening: A Necessity for Developing and Socialist Societies

Huang Chen, Head of the Delegation of the People's Republic of China, in speaking to the 17th Session of the UNESCO General Conference, said on October 25, 1972:

> We stand for the normal growth of cultural, scientific and educational exchanges and co-operation among the peoples of all countries so as to increase their mutual understanding and friendship. We hold that progressive cultures of all nations, regardless of the length of their history, have their respective characteristics and merits, which should be the cultural nourishment of

> other peoples and serve as examples in their cultural development. There can be mutual assimilation and overcoming of one's own shortcomings by learning from the strong points of others. Of course, this assimilation is by no means uncritical eclecticism. *An analysis should be made of foreign cultures. Even their progressive elements should be appropriately adapted to the specific domestic conditions according to the needs of the people and conveyed through national forms before they can answer the purpose of serving the people at home.* It is inadvisable to the development of national cultures to have blind faith in foreign things and transplant them in toto. (Emphasis supplied)

In this statement the Chinese are both stating a general goal for intercultural exchanges and stating an intention to use a screening process to insure that intercultural exchanges to which they are a party will be helpful to them on the socialist road. The general goal is "mutual assimilation" and "learning from the strong points of others." In principle the general goal might be restated in terms of the proposition: international exchange of cultural materials should result in coexistence of cultures so that each culture's universal meaning may be appreciated in the unique cultural context of its origin, with mutual comprehensibility and non-displacement of the receiving culture. But mankind is still a long way from developing to a condition where this utopian goal can be reached in practice. Meanwhile there are grave problems attaching to the screening process which is necessary to protect the seedlings of socialist culture from being overwhelmed by the individualist-ethic which permeates capitalist culture.

At the risk of seeming to be impertinent, we wish to warn the Chinese people of the importance and the hazards of the "analysis...adaptation" process which is emphasized in the preceding quotation.

It is not clear that the Chinese people have properly identified the political aspects of technique which in the next ten to twenty years will be crucial to the development of the "socialist road" as distinct from the "capitalist road." Chairman Mao clearly understands well the general nature of these political aspects of technique. But there are indications that Chairman Mao's understanding of them has not yet adequately informed the administrative processes and the universities.

The 20-year embargo which the United States imposed on exchange of knowledge and commodities with China was probably a great favour to China. An impermeable cultural shield protected China from the influence of United States ideology as incorporated in all manner of cultural artifacts and services. It, together with the later withdrawal of Soviet technical assistance, meant that the Chinese would have to depend on themselves for technical development. As a result the Chinese Revolution firmly established the mass line process for socialist decision-making. Now China is entering the period when it will already have solved the pressing problems of producing enough food, clothing, housing, medical care for everyone. At this point a gigantic step into Communism is possible. That step would be taken by the decision that the question "after bicycles, what?" should be answered in favour of public goods and services and against goods and services for individual, private use. The policy of "serve the people" can be pursued directly and most effectively by allocating creative talents of the people and resources into the production of things and services which all may enjoy and learn from—parks, museums, science, education, libraries, wild-life refuges, architecture, and other arts (including two-way TV) of all kinds. Let food, clothing, housing be maintained at a utilitarian level (that is, no "style" element), and innovation in such matters be directed toward ultimately free distribution according to need.

This is a dialectical process, like everything else in life. The struggle against the capitalist road will increasingly be in terms of a struggle to screen out and avoid the insidious appeals to private, individual considerations of personal vanity and sex as they are embodied in capitalist consumer goods and services (for example, private automobiles, stylish clothing, cosmetics). In principle the question to ask is: will such-and-such an innovation in consumer goods and services serve the masses collectively, or as individuals? The statement that China will "catch up with" or "leap-frog" ahead of capitalist technology is a dangerous one for it implies that socialist technique can be measured against the accomplishments of capitalist technique. While this comparison is possible in terms of the physical processes involved in science and research and development of producers' goods, it is not possible in terms of consumer goods. For consumers' goods, the capitalist and socialist roads fork and go in different directions. And the process which Huang Chen refers to for screening the products of foreign cultures should be popularized amongst the Chinese people as a necessary protection of the socialist road.

In principle the sort of cultural screening called for has been practiced by mankind for many millennia. The perpetuation of languages is a cultural screening device, for languages embody the cultural view of a people. Traditional cultural artifacts, services and institutions embody a particular world view held by a people and serve to transmit and protect it against foreign ideological intrusions. In their own development, western capitalist states through practicing the policies called "mercantilism" erected legal screens which protected their developing systems from rivals. Friedrich List, the bourgeois German-American economist, when writing *Das Nationale System der Politischen Oikonomie* during the period of the early Marx, advocated a systematic protectionism for developing capitalist states. The notion of a "free flow of information" arose in practice in the 1850s at the time when Great Britain was repealing the taxes on newspapers and the Corn Laws and adopting its imperial system of free trade. It did this not because of devotion to the principles of freedom of trade and information but because it served the purposes of the British Empire at that time to have such policies. And the United States' communications and cultural diplomacy since 1945 in favour of the "free flow of information" is blood brother to its world-wide imperial policy of economic expansion. Any "open door" culturally in terms of consumer goods and services on the part of China in the 1970s would seem to be unthinkable.

Notes to "After Bicycles, What?"

1. Harvard University Program on Technology, *Fourth Annual Report, 1968*. Quoted in John McDermott, "Technology: The Opiate of the Intellectuals," in A. H. Teich (ed.), *Technology and Man's Future* (New York: St. Martin's Press, 1972), p. 152.
2. In his *The Technological Society* (New York: Knopf, 1964) and other works.
3. McDermott, p. 151.

14

"There can be no Marxist theory of the media until there is a general Marxist theory of communications"

EDITOR'S NOTE: At the 1972 IAMCR meeting in Buenos Aires, Dallas Smythe presented a paper that eventually led to the end of his working relationship with UNESCO. At the 1974 IAMCR meeting in Leipzig, he presented a paper that began to sum up several major themes in his work and foreshadowed the "Blindspot" article he was to write three years later. "The Role of Mass Media and Popular Culture in Defining Development," published here for the first time, also elaborated theoretical lines of analysis that stemmed from his visit to the People's Republic of China a few years earlier.

The title of the paper may be somewhat misleading because of the term "development." To some readers, the term conjures up images of Third World nations at the opposite end of the spectrum from industrialized countries. Such nations often are described as "underdeveloped," "developing," or "industrializing." They are said to be mainly non-urban, largely dependent on agriculture, and sparsely served by mass media systems. It is clear from Smythe's paper that he understands the term in another way. He believes all countries are in some process of evolution, that all are "developing" in some way, but that such change is not necessarily beneficial for the human condition. He refers to what the Chinese call the "socialist road" and the "capitalist road" as an example of two paths of development that are diametrically different. A society does not stand still; its course of change is a function of its economic system.

The paper's purpose is deceptively innocent—"to state and briefly develop the practical and theoretical significance of the role of massively institutionalized communications media and the related arts and popular culture as the agenda-setters for populations," in Smythe's words. From that topic sentence, he moves quickly to pointing out that the media in capitalism are far more important than other institutions in "reproducing a particular kind of human nature." The "main function of the mass media in this system is to produce audiences prepared to be dutiful consumers," motivated to pay taxes to keep the defense establishment going and brainwashed to be faithful adherents to the dominant ideology. "The real end-product is the commodity to be sold, and the audience produced by the mass media is but part of the means to that end." Smythe argues that the "portion of mass media content which is not explicitly advertising in form," such as TV programming, "functions as a lure or bait to catch and keep people paying attention. ..." As a result, a "particular kind of audience" is constructed to receive an advertising message. This audience is really a product, an "intermediate good" that is necessary "to complete the marketing process" for an advertiser. In sum, according to Smythe, the media in monopoly capitalism function to set the agenda that "best services the interests of the capitalist system."

In his view, then, in order for industrial capitalism to continue "developing" it had to develop a media system to serve its own ends of commodity production and allegiance production. Inevitably, this process also involved a "power struggle between class interests" over who could control development and for what purposes.

In this paper, Smythe attends as well to the concept of "technology" and its political character. "The very hardware of technique itself," he points out, "embodies and requires reproduction of the basic elements of capitalism." This especially is true of "communications hardware," which is "a carrier of the ideology and the class structure of capitalism." Therefore, technology's relationship to development needs to be understood more clearly. Smythe suggests how we can situate this inquiry and explains the differences between "administrative" and "critical" research and theory. He argues that a general Marxist theory of communication needs to consider the human being a "message system- and symbol-using animal," not just a working animal. Although the latter concept may have sufficed when Marx was describing the industrial capitalism of the nineteenth century, it no longer is a complete description. "The commodity/cash nexus must be looked on as a communication/information nexus and vice versa."

Smythe concludes the paper by asking: "When will Marxism pay attention to perhaps its major blind spot: The need to develop a Marxist theory of communications?" He spent the next eighteen years working on an answer to that question.

The Role of Mass Media and Popular Culture in Defining Development

[International Association for Mass Communication Research, Conference on Mass Communication and Social Consciousness in a Changing World, Leipzig, September 17–21, 1974]

THE PURPOSE OF THIS PAPER is to state and briefly develop the practical and theoretical significance of the role of massively institutionalized communications media and the related arts and popular culture as the agenda-setters for populations. The policy which effectively governs what appears on the agenda produced by these institutions has a special role in defining the terms in which "development" of individuals and societies take place.

Human beings are human by means of the relationships which *are* the process that links them together. The social habits known as institutions are systematic relationships of people. They have specialized agendas for their own actions (the family for the nurture of children, "work" organizations with "production" activities, military and other security institutions for the use of force to perpetuate a certain class structure's control of people and other resources, the formal educational system for systematic instruction in the techniques and values of the dominant social system, medical for the treatment of illness and accident, etc.), but they also embody in their actions and incidentally propagate the ideological theory and practice of the whole social system. Dependent on the application of mass production techniques, the specialized institutions for communications were late arrivals (printing since the 16th and electronic since only the 19th century). While other institutions have as *incidental* to their specialized functions the general function of legitimizing and directing the development of the social system, the communications institutions have this as their specialized function.

It is misleading to define the communications institutions bureaucratically as only the press, radio-TV, book industry, cinema, or even with the addition of telecommunications (meaning users of the electromagnetic spectrum). The industrialization through mass production of the arts and handicrafts has grafted into the communications institutional complex music (through the recording industry), photography, the commercial application of art to product and container design for the full range of consumer goods and services, the fine arts, and through teaching machines and related software, an increasing fraction of formal educational practice. The function of "information" transfer, which in the 18th century was the province of the press and the post office, is now diffused through this broad complex of institutions. And the flowering of computers and information processing has added a new level of meaning to the "informational" function of the "communications" complex—a function of serving as the means of production, exchange, and consumption of "information" in the sense of Norbert Wiener's definition, "a name for the content of what is exchanged with the outer world as we adjust to it, and make our adjustment felt upon it."[1] Through its penetration of the work institutions, the military, and all other major institutions, the integration of computer-type information into the "communications" institutional complex seems fully to justify christening the whole sprawling communications institutional complex *consciousness industry.*

The capitalist system, like other social systems, has its coherent agenda which claims the attention of its constituent institutions and population. And through their words and actions, its peoples spend their daily lives according to how their real conditions, with all of the contradictions and conflicts which such real conditions produce, are affected by the demands on that agenda. For most people, much of the time, the substance of the capitalist daily agenda is painfully manifested by the wage/price squeeze, the unmet needs for medical attention, etc. For most people, much of the time, they are instructed in the meaning of the daily agenda through their contacts with work, religious, police, school, etc. organizations. But for virtually all of the people, all of the time, the agenda which directs their attention is that which, perhaps mostly in their so-called leisure time, comes to them from the mass media segment of the consciousness industry. Priorities in their agenda tend to be set by the priorities assigned to topics or themes in the mass media. The informal daily education of the population is conducted by the mass media, which tend to select some topics and ignore others, give precedence to some and not others, and frame contexts and select content all according to standards which perhaps owe more to custom than to malevolent design, and more to unconscious synchronization of decisions than to conspiracy. Because it is the special institutional function of the mass media to produce their hourly/daily/weekly quota of what, for lack of better words, we still refer to as "news," "entertainment," and "information," the unique function of the mass media of communication stands first among equals amidst other institutions in the business of reproducing a particular kind of human nature. And it is probable that the political tendencies which saturate all of the organs of capitalism will continue to perpetuate the capitalist system even after socialist revolutions and into the transitional stage to socialism.[2]

For my part, identification of the structure of the capitalist mass media agenda-setting process grows out of an analysis of the politico-economic dynamics of the system which is briefly as follows. The United States empire has been strategically on the defensive but tactically on the offensive following the conversion of about one-third of the world's population to socialist systems. Economically, the successes of United States monopoly capitalism in developing markets and investments in western Europe, Africa, Asia, and Latin America have been very great. Militarily, the United States empire is protected by massive destructive power, supplemented now as a result of intensive research and development in areas such as Indochina, Indonesia, Brazil, and Chile by substantial competence to deny indigenous liberation movements the effective ability to control their own future development.

The basis of sustained growth in United States capitalism since 1945 is the spontaneous cooperation of the relatively few giant monopoly corporations (there are few in each major industry and they aggregate about 500 for the whole system), each of which accumulates and cherishes the surplus derived from its managed markets for the relative autonomy and security that surplus provides the corporation. The deliberate collusive avoidance of price competition between giant monopoly corporations engaged in consumer goods production provides stability to the system. The continued growth of the system's surplus depends on the innovation of "new" models of familiar products and of "new" products and services. Replacement markets are generated by designed obsolescence: by style changes and by deliberate standards of quality in manufacture which produce tolerably short product lives and predictable "junking" of familiar products (because it would cost more to repair them than to replace them). And the stylistic features of all consumer goods and services are based on calculated manipulation of public taste so that consumers increasingly pay for images rather than use-values. There are two broad classes of markets in which the "Sales Effort" works to generate the surplus which powers the monopoly capitalist system. The first and most easily recognizable of these broad classes of markets is the Civilian Sales sector, where ordinary civilians buy their consumer goods and services. But if left to depend on this sector alone for its growth, the monopoly capitalist system would be plunged into ruinous depression. To compensate for the "leakiness" of the system (the accumulation of surplus by corporations and their direct beneficiaries in lieu of the distribution of surplus to workers so that they in turn could buy the products produced), the Military Sales sector must be maintained as a giant and increasingly generous "pump primer," as well as for its real function in protecting the security of the capitalist system against dissidents and criminals at home and liberation movements in American economic colonies.[3]

It is in this context that we identify the agenda-setting role of the mass media and consciousness industry in the broader sense (as including related cultural industry). The prime item on the agenda of consciousness industry in monopoly capitalism is to produce *people* in markets motivated to buy the "new models" of consumer goods and services and motivated to pay the taxes which support the swelling budgets for the Military Sales. The task of consciousness industry is to market these goods and services. In performing this role, the mass media under monopoly capitalism are the cutting edge of a team of cooperating institutions, together properly called consciousness industry. The mass media institutions are typically large monopolies linking regional markets and linking TV, AM-FM broadcasting, newspapers, magazines, books, and cinema. They also intersect the ownership of giant monopoly corporations in manufacturing and banking.

Typically, when a "new" model of a consumer good or service is designed, the process begins where it ends in market considerations. It begins with market research into the characteristic features of a hypothetical product or service which will "sell." Then the product/service is designed, drawing on engineering research and development to incorporate into it controlled obsolescence and optimum appearance features. The actual product's potential salability considerations are matched by equal concern with the design of the container and the anticipated level of the shelves and location in the supermarket where, according to market research, the prospective "customer" will be most likely to transfer semi-consciously the container to the shopping cart as a result of subliminal clues. Following this, the final marketing plan (test markets, promotional plans, selection of type of media for advertising to reach the target market described in terms of age, sex, ethnic composition, income level, geographic location) is perfected. Finally, the production process is itself activated and the whole "campaign" put into operation.

It is evident that in economic terms the main function of the mass media in this system is to produce audiences prepared to be dutiful consumers (beneath the specific brain-washing which "sells" the audience member on the product is the frequent reminder: If you don't buy, buy, buy, the GNP will fall and you may be unemployed, so in your own self-interest, buy *something*). And in economic terms, the audiences produced are themselves "intermediate" products—i.e., their production *is* a marketing cost, not an end in itself. The real end-product is the commodity to be sold, and the audience produced by the mass media is but part of the means to that end. Which is to say that the system exists and functions to preserve itself—and the mass media are its cutting edge.

The portion of mass media content which is not explicitly advertising in form, in this system, functions as a lure or bait to catch and keep people paying attention to the output of the mass media enterprise.[4] As such, the luring "program" content of TV is designed to attract the particular kind of audience the advertiser plans to produce as the intermediate good to complete the marketing process for his product.

The media function of producing audiences is not limited to audiences designed as intermediate products essential to the marketing of consumer goods. It also includes the production of audiences designed for the end-product: Public opinion. For example, the long conflict between Nixon and the press recently focussed on "Watergate" *is* a struggle to produce public opinion on one side or the other. Indeed, Nixon's elective campaigns in 1968 and 1972 were designed and administered by the same methods employed in the production of consumer goods markets.[5] Nixon had been a pioneer in manufacturing public opinion for anti-communism and treating election candidates as commodities.[6] "Managing the News" is the name given by public relations specialists to the deliberate manipulation of mass media news by factions in government and business to produce public opinion supportive of one or another government policy or as a sufficient, short-term surrogate for public opinion, the news, or opinion in the press supportive of one or another policy. Public relations specialists and the public opinion polling industry, analyzed by Professor Herbert Schiller,[7] are a vital segment of consciousness industry.

There is a second type of item on the agenda set by the mass media under monopolistic capitalism. This is an "hegemonic filter" (to use Nordenstreng's phrase) and includes the following practices (some of them systemic in iteration, others directly applied to specific advertising and "non-advertising" mass media content).

1. Pervasive reinforcement of the ideological basis of the capitalist system: Human nature is necessarily selfish and possessive. It has always been this way: You can't change human nature. Therefore, look out for number

one; let the other fellow take care of himself. Private business is clean and efficient; public government is inherently bad, and politics are dirty; therefore, public taxation is bad, private prices (they may be thought of also as private taxes) are good. Private property is virtually sacred; public planning which would interfere with it is inherently bad. In fact, that government is best which governs least. We should be objective, pluralistic (within the limits acceptable to the system). Communism is an international conspiracy. The difficulties which capitalism experiences in developing countries (Vietnam, Chile, etc.) are caused by Communists, and, therefore, counter-revolution anywhere is good and should be supported by capitalism. The only response appropriate in developing countries is military; force is the only thing Communists respect. Foreign policy is too complex for citizens to understand; therefore, decisions should be made by the head of state and his military advisers. Technology and winning are the most important values and our high moral ends justify our means. We are the defenders of the "free world," and we will take any nuclear risks to preserve our system (President Kennedy).

2. The flexibility of the capitalist system permits the mass media to air and coopt structural conflicts which deeply threaten the system. Thus, the cold-war anti-communist inquisition inaugurated by Representative Richard M. Nixon and associates in 1946 in the United States was facilitated by the mass media. So later were the Black civil rights movement, the anti-Vietnamese war movement of the late 1960s, and the exposure of the runaway authoritarianism of President Richard M. Nixon known as "Watergate." In this way and in token respects through media content, individual and ethnic alienation is kept within limits tolerable to the system. Cultural industry supports such cooptative response to contradictions within the system: The distinctive clothing, jewelry, hair styling, and music of the "counter-culture" of the 1960s was quickly adopted and profitably mass produced and mass marketed by consciousness industry. A safety razor manufacturer in 1974 advertises its "track 2" razor with the slogan: "It's a Revolution; Enjoy the Revolution."

3. While unplanned by any single organization, the combined effect of the enormous mass of advertisements and standardized non-advertising content which bombard the individual without cessation from the totality of mass media have the systemic effect of placing high on the agenda a barrage of noise which effectively deters consideration of structural possibilities of alternative systems of social relationships. As Robert Merton and Paul Lazarsfeld wrote in 1948, the net effect is to "dysfunctionally narcotize" the population.

For these media not only continue to affirm the *status quo,* but, in the same measure, they fail to raise essential questions about the structure of society.[8]

The relation of the mass media to the "real" world of food, clothing, housing, people living and people dying is dialectical. The mass media are concerned with images. They specialize in producing "the society of the spectacle." Because consciousness industry produces consumable, saleable spectacles, its product treats both past and future like the present—as blended in the eternal present of a system which was never created and will never end. The society of the spectacle, however, cannot be abstractly contrasted with the "real" world of actual people. The two interact. The spectacle inverts the real and is itself produced and is real. Hence, as de Bord says, objective reality is present on both sides. But because the society of the spectacle is a system which stands the world really on its head, the truth in it is a moment of the false. Because the spectacle monopolizes the power to make mass appearance, it demands and gets passive acceptance of the "real" world. And because it is undeniably real (as well as false), it has the persuasive power of the most effective propaganda.[9] Because the commodities produced under the guidance of consciousness industry appeal to people's real needs, albeit deceitfully for the most part, the synthesized impact of the spectacle and the reality smashes traditional institutions and values wherever it encounters them.

The function of the mass media in the monopoly capitalist context, to summarize, is to set the agenda which best serves the interests of the capitalist system. And in principle, this agenda is dominated by the process of selling commodities and producing audiences (out of people) to be used by capitalist industry to enhance its profitability and political security. This is the face of the capitalist mass media which is presented to ex-colonial countries, to socialist countries, and to the developed market areas of Europe.

This analysis has emphasized the broad, dominating features of the monopoly capitalist system and overlooked the dimension of contradictions which riddle it, intersecting it in innumerable parameters. One of these contradictions must, however, be identified because it provides the entrée to the problems of "development" globally, individually, and at intervening levels of organization. I refer to the ecological crisis, world-wide in potential scope, which manifests itself most sharply in the heartland of monopoly capitalism in the form of environmental pollution. Biologist Barry Commoner[10] finds that the options are rapidly narrowing and force the choice on humanity of barbarism or a fundamental social reorganization which eliminates the capitalist system.

For the greater part of the world's population as yet, "development" is defined by the monopoly capitalist system through the agenda set by its consciousness industry. What is involved in the concept of "development"? Nothing less than the totality of life for human beings is involved. The total process of social interaction of individuals through institutions. The process character of development is evident when we ask: Who will determine the kind of development to be pursued? Through what process is the determination to be made? What kind of development is to be pursued? How? When? Why? And most fundamentally, for the benefit of what class of people? The answers given to these questions will describe the "development" any people will experience. In the total power struggle between class interests which is involved in "development," the peculiar technical forms of power embodied in the mass media where they themselves are developed will play the agenda-setting role in all ideological systems. The mass media, as the specialized institutions created for this purpose, will guide but not decide in any deterministic fashion the evolving struggle between contradictory power concentrations within the system. Or, putting it negatively, what is *omitted* will hardly shape the strategic level of policy determination for that society, e.g., can hardly enter into mass consciousness. At the tactical level, e.g., the eve of forcible revolution, the revolutionary forces must overcome by other means the technical advantages which the control of the mass media confer on the defenders of the status quo. In a fundamental sense, control over the means of informing people is the basis of political power—whether those means be the barrel of a gun, informal political education, or the mass media of communication, but, in the nations with "advanced" technique, the media's role is likely to be a major factor.

In the present state of affairs, "development" is customarily closely linked with "technology." In the past 20 years, the ex-colonial countries have been given aid and advice to adopt advanced "technology" in order to "develop." As Joan Robinson suggests, the purpose and effect of such aid, whether given through the UN family of organizations or unilaterally, is to perpetuate the systematic underdevelopment of the ex-colonial countries.[11] "Technology" as the term is generally used uncritically in socialist no less than capitalist countries means not only the hardware of machines, chemical and physical processes, but the software, the "know-how," the instructions for performing the operations associated with the hardware. The software, know-how, and instructions come out of the capitalist system, even if by imitation and by example as in the case of the Soviet Union. As such, they reflect, embody, and require reproduction of the class structure and possessive individualism of their capitalist womb, if they are to be used "efficiently" (as defined by their capitalist parents). But this is not the full extent of the political character of technology as exported from the "advanced" to the ex-colonial countries. The very hardware of technique itself embodies and requires reproduction of the basic elements of capitalism. The "take-off" for the flowering of capitalist industry was identified by Rostow a few years ago with the construction of heavy industry (steel, chemicals, energy) based on the mobilization of population in urban areas where massive capital investment yielded "efficient" (i.e., profitable) development. The Soviet Union, reaching the same conclusion from history, followed that pattern of development with similar results in terms of productivity, forced removal of rural population to large cities, hierarchical subordination, material incentives, and personal selfishness. The extreme example of this view of technology is Yugoslavia.[12] The Chinese in the past 15 years referring to this as the capitalist road opted instead for decentralization of heavy and light industry and simultaneously attacked hierarchical bureaucracy, the capitalist myth of the universal efficiency of specialization and division of labour, material incentives, the alleged immutability of human nature, and selfishness in the first of what they expect to be a process of Cultural Revolutions.

The private automobile is another eloquent example of the hardware of "development." For an ex-colonial country to innovate the technology of the private automobile is to commit a substantial proportion of its human and natural resources to the construction not only of automobiles, but highways, parking facilities, a business system for the distribution of fuel, and the repair and servicing of cars. Nor is this the extent of the commitment, for with the automobile go trailers, campers, towed boats, etc.—a host of fringe industries. Such a commitment of resources must be at the expense of other private and public services, including health and education.

Communications hardware, of course, is a carrier of the ideology and the class structure of capitalism. In China, when I studied their communications institutions in 1971–72, the nature of their future TV broadcast system was not yet determined. They had assumed that they would adopt some variant on the system employed elsewhere in the world—a system developed by capitalism for its own purposes which involves a one-way flow from central transmitters to distributed receivers. But they were considering the possibility of designing a two-way system, so that from the receiving stations, signals might be transmitted back to the broadcast station—an electronic *Tatzupao* system for mutual rather than centrally directed communication.

It should by now be evident that the political relationship of technology to "development" should be recognized. At the threshold it must be understood that the alleged autonomous or "apolitical" nature of "technology" is a myth. Technology is the fruit of social systems, embodies their consciousness, values and policies, and tends to reproduce them wherever it is carried regardless of juridical issues as to private versus worker legal title to property. To cast problems such as environmental pollution in terms of "technology" is to scapegoat. The cause of environmental pollution is the capitalist order. To identify the cause as "technology" is to misdirect attention to the teleological forces imputed to nature or to supernatural forces and to exculpate the real culprit. Technology itself is a political thing. So also is the notion that technology is apolitical. Even the Chinese slogans betray the fact that while they have successfully established a decentralized process by which the masses of peasants, workers, and PLA people can define the "socialist road" which they have chosen over the "capitalist road," they have not yet dealt systematically with the problem of filtering out the capitalist elements in technology. Having opted for the socialist road, it is inconsistent to also say, as they sometimes do, "we are behind the capitalists in development. But we will catch up." How can one travelling one road catch up with another on a different road?

The foregoing analysis may clear the way for consideration of the problem of communications theory from the standpoint of critical (i.e., Marxist) theory. At the risk of over-simplifying, let us visualize a two-by-two matrix. One dimension is labeled "theory," the other side "researchable problems." On both sides now visualize two categories: "administrative" and "critical." By administrative theory, I refer to the applications of neopositivistic, behavioral theory. By critical theory, I refer to applications of critical (Marxist or quasi-Marxist) theory. By administrative researchable problems, I mean how to market goods, how to improve the efficiency of media operations, etc. By critical problems, I mean research addressed to macro institutional structure and policies. Now let me fill in the boxes with some names of scholars and researchers.

In the application of administrative theory to administrative problems, market research is an obvious example. Such studies, so abundant in monopoly capitalism, in my opinion, yield results which are usually trivial from a general theoretical point of view because they are not susceptible of yielding results which may be combined to get even capitalist system-wide empirical evidence. And while the sponsors of such research may be satisfied with the results, such studies are usually shot through with dubious concepts and procedures.

The box dealing with "critical researchable problems" from the standpoint of "administrative" theory is of more interest. Here, for example, we are dealing with studies of what policy and structure should be proposed to handle problems created by direct broadcast satellites or problems of national policy in dealing with public opinion. But the methods will be neopositivist and uncritical of the ideological status quo. Professor Ithiel de Sola Pool has recently reported on the rapid increase in social science research addressed in the United States to telecommunications organizational and policy problems.[13] This type of research is not exactly new, even in the United States. Under government auspices (RAND Corporation and various "think tanks"), such policy research throve as long as two decades ago, although Pool is correct in noting its recent extension (usually under government subsidy) to universities. Professor Schiller has analyzed the respects in which such research, because of the point of view of the sponsor and the scholar concerned with it, suffers from the endemic disadvantages of the positivist theoretical approach.[14] From a different ideological context but with similar methodological commitment to the status quo, one recalls some early work of Elisabeth Noelle which studied the process of public opinion formation about 1940 and found it acceptable that the population should receive its orders from the head in the interest of achieving "transcendent political and cultural values."[15] Of course, these two examples span a variegated range of policy research within the capitalist system. This category of research is extremely valuable from a Marxist point of view because not only does it provide necessary insights into the policy and structure of capitalist communications institutions, but much should be learned from close Marxist analysis of the theoretical processes of bourgeois communications science by analogy to the way Marx used the theories of Smith, Ricardo, and other bourgeois philosophers to sharpen his own theoretical tools.

The box where administrative problems are dealt with from the standpoint of critical theory, likewise, now has a rich, if heterogeneous, content. Here we begin by noting that much bourgeois, liberal research is to a large extent *implicitly* (but not explicitly) Marxist in its critical approach to communications behavior within its uncriticized institutional framework. Much of the research inspired or directed by Paul Lazarsfeld in the 1940s falls in this category. And the same may be said of Hadley Cantril, James Halloran, and others. From my admittedly inadequate familiarity with the work of communications researchers in the European socialist nations, it seems to me that their work also is focussed on administrative problems within their given social systems.[16] But as they bring to these problems Marxist tools, they are able to deal usefully with, for example, problems such as consciousness as it is related to the operation of the mass media and public opinion in ways which may provide valuable bases for later general theoretical investigations.[17] Because such work seems to stop short of examining critically the process by which communications policies and structures are determined by the power processes and class struggle within their own countries, and in capitalist countries, it hardly seems possible for them or their "opposite numbers" in the capitalist countries to develop a general theory of the mass media or, more importantly, of communications.

This brings me to the fourth box where macro problems are addressed from the standpoint of critical theory. Enzensberger correctly says that the media are "an empty category in Marxist theory" and argues persuasively the case for a Marxist theory of the Media.[18] One applauds his arguments as to the extent to which Marxists in the capitalist world have failed to come to terms with the problems posed by the nature of the media (at pp. 18–19, 27–29), while finding him guilty of McLuhanesque technocratic errors in regarding new electronic media as universally accessible and (through his ignorance of the political economy of the radio spectrum) unlimitedly possible (pp. 18, 20–21). Nevertheless, his analysis is provocative when he notes the decentralizing tendency which inheres in current electronic-information processing technique and the mobilizing potential of multilateral communications hardware (pp. 14–16), the fact that the mass media have made obsolete the 18th Century conception of Art as the autonomous product of an autonomous artist and with it the bourgeois aesthetic system of Kant (p. 30), and the new mass production of ambiguity (which he calls "dirtiness") by which consciousness industry has produced the society of the spectacle (pp. 18, 24–25).

But by fixing his attention on the *media,* Enzensberger reduces drastically the significance of the "empty category." My thesis is that there can be no general Marxist theory of the media until there is a general Marxist theory of communication from which it will flow inevitably. And there will be no general Marxist theory of communication until Marxism comes to comprehend man as a message system– and symbol-using animal as well as a working animal. My analysis of the agenda-setting function of the consciousness industry and within it the media suggests that such a Marxist communications theory is a necessary tool for understanding capitalism's consumption relations. Marx's environment was dominated by the Industrial Revolution and his thrust was properly toward man's work relationships. But since his time capitalism has extended man's alienation from work relationships to include alienation from leisure relationships. It is especially in this sense that the Chinese slogan that politics are always in command and that culture is perhaps the strategically decisive theatre of political command is correct.

The starting point for a general Marxist theory of communications is probably at the theory of commodity exchange. Money and communications are closely intermeshed. Mirabeau said, "The two greatest inventions of the human mind are writing and money—the common language of intelligence and the common language of self-interest."[19] Both are media of exchange, both are storehouses of value, and both provide standards of deferred settlement of accounts. Perhaps most importantly, in light of information theory and cybernetics, both are concerned with the exchange of information and confer power through the political control of information. The dialectical paradigm with which Marx described exchange in the *Grundrisse* applies both to the exchange of money and communications:

> Exchange...implies a universal interdependence between the producers, but at the same time the complete isolation of their private interests and a division of social labour, whose unity and mutual fulfillment exists as an external, natural relationship, independent of the individuals.[20]

Not to be ignored here is the fact that just as capitalism has developed sophisticated and decentralized mechanisms for the use of credit (always defined as money), so too its recent development of decentralized mechanisms for producing information (and storing and retrieving it through computers and electronic exchanges) has extended the nexus of market relationships on both levels (i.e., money and information), linked to each other. The commodity/cash nexus must be looked on as a communication/information nexus and vice versa. And, obviously, in developing a general communications theory, the linear theory of communications, embodied in Lasswell's formulation and in Shannon and Weaver, should be transcended and disregarded. Such capitalist administrative theories encapsulate the authoritarianism of hierarchical capitalist organizational modes and are at bottom unsound, deriving as they do from a misleading analogy of communication to transportation rather than to exchange.[21] The required general theory, by approaching capitalist society from this point of view, may provide strategic and tactical understanding of the obstacles to systemic change which capitalism has created. When will Marxism pay attention to perhaps its major blind spot: The need to develop a Marxist theory of communications?

To my knowledge, very few efforts have been made in this direction. I know of the promising beginnings made by Nordenstreng and other Finnish scholars. In their 1973 study, Nordenstreng and Varis preliminarily explore the historical process of communications development from a critical point of view, identifying the agenda-setting role of the mass media as well.[22] And in a 1974 paper, Nordenstreng reports theoretical work in Scandinavia bearing on the relation of the mass media to consciousness which explicitly introduces general Marxist theory.[23] The qualifying phrase "to my knowledge" may be important. For language barriers bar me from literature in many countries. And lack of a systematic network for even exchanging bibliographical aids is a severe handicap. The new series of bibliographies, *Marxism and the Mass Media: Towards a Basic Bibliography,* produced by Seth Siegelaub[24] is an invaluable step toward filling this gap.

Notes to "The Role of the Mass Media . . ."

1. Norbert Wiener, *The Human Use of Human Beings* (New York: Doubleday, 1960), Anchor Books edition, 1954, p. 17.

2. Pannekoek, the Dutch Marxist, pointed out in 1920 that in November, 1918, the German state was powerless and workers for the moment were masters; yet they did not take control. "That proves that still another secret source of power of the bourgeoisie existed which was untouched and which permitted them...to newly construct their domination. This secret power is the geistige power of the bourgeoisie over the proletariat. Because the proletariat masses were still wholly ruled by a bourgeois mode of thought, after the collapse they rebuilt with their own hands bourgeois domination." A. Pannekoek, "Weltrevolution und kommunistishen Taktik," in Pannekoek and Gorter, *Organization und Taktik, der proletarisischen Revolution,* p. 131, quoted in Russell Jacoby, "Towards a Critique of Automatic Marxism: The Politics of Philosophy from Lukacs to the Frankfurt School," *Telos,* no. 10, Winter, 1971, p. 125.

3. This over-simple summary necessarily ignores massive contradictions within the monopoly capitalist system. While seeking stability, that system generates stability because of the endemic price inflation which its oligopolistic practice produces. The cost of maintaining its world-wide gendarme apparatus from 1945 to the 1970s forced the U.S.A. to devalue the dollar beginning in 1971 and destroyed international monetary stability. In turn, this coincided with capitalist hegemonic tendencies in Japan and the European Common Market leading to a more polycentric capitalist system less dominated by the U.S.A. than in the preceding generation. The multinational corporations—about two-thirds of which are dominated by U.S.A. capital—produce most of their profits outside the U.S.A. and thus are essential parts of U.S. monopoly capitalism and at the same time create destabilizing frictions within the U.S. domestic market as well as in other countries.

4. The illusion that the "editorial" side of the press or the electronic media is devoted to disinterested, "objective" reportage of events in the real world and that the advertising

side is irrelevant to this end but necessary to provide the enterprise with the "freedom" to be "socially responsible" persists partly out of institutional inertia and journalistic mores nostalgically reified by conscience-bothered journalists, but mostly out of a systemic inhibition on admitting the facts. See Upton Sinclair, *The Brass Check* (Pasadena, 1919); Fred Friendly, *Due to Circumstances Beyond Our Control* (New York: Random House, 1967); A. J. Liebling, *The Press* (New York: Ballantine Books, 1961).

5. Joe McGinniss, *The Selling of the President, 1968* (New York: Trident Press, 1969).

6. In 1957, he said that the public buys names and faces and not platforms and that a candidate for public office has to be merchandized in much the same way as any TV product. *Variety,* October 1957.

7. Herbert I. Schiller, *The Mind Managers* (Boston: Beacon Press, 1973). James Aronson, *Packaging the News* (New York: International Publishers, 1971).

8. Paul F. Lazarsfeld and Robert K. Merton, "Mass Communication, Popular Taste and Organized Social Action," in Wilbur Schramm (ed.), *Mass Communications* (Urbana: University of Illinois Press, 1949), p. 459.

9. Guy de Bord, *The Society of the Spectacle* (Detroit: Black and Red, Box 9546, 1970), pp. 6–9.

10. Barry Commoner, *The Closing Circle* (New York: Knopf, 1971), especially chapter 13.

11. "In short, the aim of aid is to perpetuate the system that makes aid necessary." Joan Robinson, *The New Mercantilism* (London: Cambridge University Press, 1966), p. 25.

12. Dallas W. Smythe, *Yugoslavian Communications: Through the Ideological Looking Glass* (provisional title, in process of publication). [This manuscript was never published. TG]

13. Ithiel deSola Pool, *The Rise of Communication Policy Research,* paper for the annual meeting of the International Broadcast Institute, Nicosia, Cyprus, 14–18 September 1973.

14. Herbert I. Schiller, "Waiting for Orders—Some Current Trends in Mass Communications Research in the United States," *Gazette,* vol. 20, no. 1, 1974, pp. 11–21.

15. "The role that public opinion plays in America and Germany is very different. In the great 'democracy' on the other side of the ocean it has the function of a corporation whose millions of stockholders dictate the policy of the enterprise. In National Socialist Germany, it seems to us rather as the body of the people (Volkskorper) which receives its orders from the head and guarantees their accomplishment, so that through the working together of head and limbs transcendent political and cultural values can be achieved. In the one case public opinion rules; in the other it is led." Elisabeth Noelle, *Meinung und Massenforschung in U.S.A.* (Frankfurt/Main: Verlag Moritz Diesterweg, 1940), p. 1. The same author also quotes approvingly from Reichminister Goebbels: "The people shall begin to think as a unit, to react as a unit and to place itself at the disposal of government with complete sympathy." p. 134. The original text is not available to me. These quotes are from Leo Bogart, "Is There a World Public Opinion?" *Polls,* vol. 1, no. 3, Spring 1966, pp. 1–9.

16. See, for example, Y. A. Sherkovin, "The Mass Media and Their Role in Social Life," *Soviet Psychology,* Fall 1972, vol. 11, no. 1, pp. 65–84.

17. Scholars concerned with mass communications research in those countries held a conference in Budapest at the invitation of the Mass Communications Research Centre

of the Hungarian Radio and Television in 1971 which provided exciting materials. Andras Szekfu et al. (eds.), *Public Opinion and Mass Communication* (Budapest: Hungarian Radio and Television, Mass Communication Research Centre, 1972).

18. Hans Magnus Enzensberger, "Constituents of a Theory of the Media," *New Left Review,* no. 64, November–December 1970, pp. 13–36.

19. Quoted in H. A. Innis, *The Bias of Communications* (Toronto: University of Toronto Press, 1951), p. 8.

20. Karl Marx, *The Grundrisse* (David McLellan, ed.), (New York: Harper and Row, 1971), p. 67.

21. When the message is produced, delivered, received and produces its effects, it is still at the source. It has not been displaced as with goods transported.

22. Kaarle Nordenstreng and Tapio Varis, "The Nonhomogeneity of the National State and the International Flow of Communications." George Gerbner et al. (eds.), *Communications Technology and Social Policy* (New York: John Wiley & Sons, 1973), pp. 393–412.

23. Kaarle Nordenstreng, "From Mass Media to Mass Consciousness: Current Thinking in Scandinavia," in the process of publication.

24. Seth Siegelaub[...]. [NOTE: Seth Siegelaub is associated with International General, a publisher of books on communication, culture, and ideology.]

15

"The material reality under monopoly capitalism is that all non-sleeping time of most of the population is work time"

EDITOR'S NOTE: "Communications: Blindspot of Western Marxism" is undoubtedly Dallas Smythe's most widely discussed published article. Although it appeared more than fifteen years ago, "Blindspot"—as it has come to be known—continues to provoke thought and debate. It raised a subject and, indeed, a way of conceptualizing the audience-media relationship that still is heuristic.

One question I cannot answer with certainty is why Smythe waited until 1977 to publish his ideas—I recall him talking about them as early as 1960. Indeed, the history of "Blindspot" goes back even further than that. He told me during our lengthy interview in December 1991 that "the first vague formulation of the 'Blindspot' proposition" was in a talk he had given to the Consumer's Union Conference in 1951: "I think I formulated it as early as that, though I didn't pursue it and write it up in any fashion." That speech, with the vague suggestion of what later would become "Blindspot," was published the same year in *The Quarterly Review of Film, Radio and Television.* In the printed version of the speech, Smythe pointed out that "Radio and television offer a complex of 'products,'" one of which is "known as station time, and sometimes as audience loyalty (measured by ratings) which stations sell to advertisers." He wrote that although the "industry refers to this as a market for time, [...] it is not that simple." What is really sold, Smythe explained, is "*the probability of developing audience loyalty to the advertiser*" (original emphasis).

This observation certainly hints at, but is hardly the same as, his

"Blindspot" declaration: "I submit that the materialist answer to the question—What is the commodity form of mass-produced, advertiser-supported communications under monopoly capitalism?—is audiences and readerships." The "Blindspot" article reveals a sophistication and a reliance on Marx that are absent completely in the earlier paper. I suspect that Smythe waited to publish his views until he felt they were thoroughly developed and theoretically grounded. Still, it is interesting to compare elements in the 1951 article to those he incorporated in the 1977 piece.

It seems that Smythe was prompted to write "Blindspot" after reading Hans Magnus Enzensberger's *The Consciousness Industry,* published in 1974. "One of the reasons I wrote the 'Blindspot' was that West German writer who's written on consciousness," Smythe said to me. "You see, I had originally written a paper which included the 'Blindspot' argument," and "its introduction was a takeoff, a critical takeoff from Enzensberger. I didn't let the 'Blindspot' stand on its own feet originally. Gerbner refused to publish it" in *Journal of Communication,* "but he did take [...] my critique of Enzensberger. I sent the whole thing to Enzensberger, but it was combined. And I had a very nice letter back from him saying, 'Very interesting argument, but why in hell are you being so academic about it and keeping yourself out of the story—why [...] don't you make more positive statements? You want to get people to listen. You'd better do that'. And I began doing it more, and the fact is that you get more force."

Smythe's critique of Enzensberger appeared in the Winter 1977 issue of *Journal of Communication.* In the book, Enzensberger argued that "there is no Marxist theory of the media" and that, with the exception of Walter Benjamin, "Marxists have not understood the consciousness industry and have been aware only of its bourgeois-capitalist dark side and not of its socialist possibilities." Enzensberger claimed that the "inadequate understanding which Marxists have shown of the media and the questionable use they have made of them has produced a vacuum in Western industrialized countries into which a stream of non-Marxist hypotheses and practices have consequently flowed." Smythe responded to this challenge in the "Blindspot" piece: "The argument presented here—that western Marxist analyses have neglected the economic and political significance of mass communications systems—is an attempt to start a debate, not to conclude one."

"Blindspot" had precursors, but it also had *post*cursors. As Smythe described it to me: "I rotated the thesis slightly and expanded a somewhat different version of it" that was published in 1981 as "Communications: Blindspot of Economics" in *Culture, Communication, and Dependency: The Tradition of H. A. Innis,* edited by Melody, Salter, and Heyer. "Harold Innis [...] was what that whole book was about," Smythe told me, "and I am not much interested in anything that takes off in that direction. I think he was a vastly overrated character."

Smythe told me as well that "at the suggestion of a Canadian book publisher, I blew it [the 'Blindspot' article] up to book dimensions, called *Dependency Road.* [...] I didn't send him [the manager of college book sales] any drafts until I had the thing completely finished. [...] By the time I'd finished it, [...] he'd gotten fired, because they had to economize in order to meet the U.S. competition." After that, "I first went to the University of Toronto Press, and they looked at the manuscript and said, "Well, if you reduce it from 300 pages to maybe 125, cutting out all the nontheoretical material, we might be interested in it, if you could get a Canada Council grant to subsidize it.' I said 'Thank you very much.' [...] I couldn't get it published in Canada [...] so I went down south" to get it published by Ablex.

Smythe's work on the "Blindspot" thesis was never finished. In our interview, he told me, "I'm now considering a piece on what amounts to a 'Blindspot' update." He said he wanted to respond to criticisms that "I do violence" to Marx's views of the process of circulation by "not taking Marx's assumptions correctly. [...] And I want to review that issue, but I want to put it in a slightly different context. If you think of the argument of the 'Blindspot,' you're dealing here with a triangle. You've got the advertisers who are the operators of consciousness industry for all consumer goods in one corner. You've got the media in another corner. The audience is in the third corner. The controversy in the academic journals about the 'Blindspot' is all related to the axis between media and audience. None of it is related to the axis between audience and advertisers. And very little of it is related to the axis between advertisers and the media. And they revolve like puppets, going back to textual analysis of the damned messages, between media and audiences. It's this idealist fixation. [...]

"I want to put a new perspective on that axis between audiences and so forth. I want to argue that it is the market, in total caps, which is the purpose and result, and social profitability which keeps the capitalist system functioning. [...] And I want to link this model to another triangle, namely the iron triangle [...] which involves the whole market for military goods and military security [...] and which is the place where the R&D funds are advanced, which then filter down to make profitable innovations. [...] So, the two models overlap," and "I want to see if I can't integrate the two triangles, the iron triangle and the invisible triangle." Smythe said critics of his work "have systematically avoided addressing the fact that the triangle exists; they just talk about the 'Blindspot' as if it were between the media and the audience."

One early criticism of "Blindspot" was written by Graham Murdock and published, along with Smythe's rejoinder, in the Spring–Summer 1978 issue of *Canadian Journal of Political and Social Theory.* Murdock pointed out that for Smythe "the value and relevance of the western Marxist tradition [...] is an obstacle to be cleared away [...] rather than a resource to be drawn upon," and that "a critical engagement with western Marxism is still indispensable to the development of a comprehensive and convincing Marxist analysis of mass communications." Smythe's "wholesale rejection [of European Marxism] seems to me to be rooted in an over-simplified view both of the tradition itself and of the historical experience to which it speaks. This is Smythe's own blindspot." Murdock's substantial critique, which still deserves careful reading, offered Smythe the chance to defend his thesis and explain it in more detail. One of Smythe's Canadian colleagues, Bill Livant, also leaped into the fray. When the *Journal* called a halt to the printed debate in its pages, the discussion continued in conference papers, letters, and private talks among an ever broader group of participants. Even as this book goes to press, the "Blindspot" debate still goes on.

Communications: Blindspot of Western Marxism [1977]

THE ARGUMENT presented here—that western Marxist analyses have neglected the economic and political significance of mass communications systems—is an attempt to start a debate, not to conclude one. Frequently, Marxists and those radical social critics who use Marxist terminology locate the significance of mass communications systems in their capacity to produce "ideology," which is held to act as a sort of invisible glue that

---

This article was originally published in *Canadian Journal of Political and Social Theory,* volume 1, number 3, Fall 1977, pp. 1–27, and is reprinted here with the permission of that journal. Selections from *Monopoly Capitalism,* copyright © 1966 by Paul M. Sweezy, are reprinted here with the permission of Monthly Review Foundation.

holds together the capitalist system. This subjective substance, divorced from historical materiality, is similar to such previous concepts as "ether"; that is to say, the proof of its existence is found by such writers to be the necessity for it to exist so that certain other phenomena may be explained. It is thus an idealist, *pre*-scientific rather than a *non*-scientific explanation.

But for Marxists, such an explanatory notion should be unsatisfactory. The first question that historical materialists should ask about mass communications systems is *what economic function for capital do they serve,* attempting to understand their role in the reproduction of capitalist relations of production. This article, then, poses this question and attempts to frame some answers to it. Much of what follows is contentious because it raises questions not only about changes in capitalism since Marx's death but also, in some instances, about the adequacy of certain generally accepted Marxist categories to account properly for these developments. However, as Lenin remarked in a different context, one cannot make an omelette without breaking the eggs.

The mass media of communications and related institutions concerned with advertising, market research, public relations and product and package design represent a blindspot in Marxist theory in the European and Atlantic basin cultures. The activities of these institutions are intimately connected with consumer consciousness, needs, leisure time use, commodity fetishism, work and alienation. As we will see, when these institutions are examined from a materialist point of view, the labour theory of value, the expenses of circulation, the value of the "peculiar commodity" (labour power), the form of the proletariat and the class struggle under monopoly capitalist conditions are also deeply involved. The literature of Marxism is conspicuously lacking in materialist analysis of the functions of the complex of institutions called the "consciousness industry."[1]

The blockage in recognizing the role of the consciousness industry traces back to a failure to take a materialist approach to communications. Both economic goods in general and communications goods in particular existed long before capitalism and monopoly capitalism. While *specialized* institutions for the mass production of communications (i.e., newspapers and magazines) appeared in capitalism in the eighteenth century, these institutions did not reach their mature form until monopoly capitalism shifted their principal economic base to advertising in the late nineteenth century. By a grave cultural lag, Marxist theory has not taken account of mass communications. This lag in considering the product of the mass media is more understandable in European (including Eastern European) countries than in North America. There the rise to ascendancy of advertising in dominating the policy of newspapers and periodicals was delayed by custom and by law. Even in the radio-TV broadcast media, the role of the state (through ORTF, BBC, ITV, East European state monopolies, etc.) has been resistant to the inroads of monopoly capitalism—as compared with the United States and Canada. But the evidence accumulates (recent developments in British, French, West German and Italian mass media, for example) that such traditional resistance is giving way under the onslaught of pressures from the centre of the monopoly capitalist system. Europeans reading this essay should try to perceive it reflecting the North American scene today, and perhaps theirs soon.

At the root of a Marxist view of capitalism is the necessity to seek an objective reality, which means in this case an objective definition of the *commodity* produced by capitalism. What is the commodity form of mass-produced, advertiser-supported communications? This is the threshold question. The bourgeois idealist view of the reality of the communication commodity is "messages," "information," "images," "meaning," "entertainment," "orientation," "education," and "manipulation." All of these concepts are subjective mental entities and all deal with *superficial* appearances. Nowhere do the theorists who adopt this worldview deal with the commodity form of mass communications under monopoly capitalism on which exist parasitically a host of sub-markets dealing with cultural industry, e.g., the markets for "news" and "entertainment." Tacitly, this idealist theory of the communications commodity appears to have been held by most western Marxists after Marx as well as by bourgeois theorists: Lenin,[2] Veblen, Marcuse, Adorno, Baran and Sweezy, for example, as well as Galbraith and orthodox economists. So too for those who take a more or less Marxist view of communications (Nordenstreng, Enzensberger, Hamelink, Schiller,[3] Murdock and Golding,[4] and me until now) as well as the conventional writers exemplified in the Sage *Annual Review of Communications Research*.[5] Also included in the idealist camp are those apologists who dissolve the reality of communications under the *appearance* of the "medium," such as Marshall McLuhan.[6] No wonder, as Livant says, that "the field of communications is a jungle of idealism."[7]

I submit that the materialist answer to the question—What is the commodity form of mass-produced, advertiser-supported communications under monopoly capitalism?—is audiences and readerships (hereafter referred to for simplicity as audiences). The material reality under monopoly capitalism is that all non-sleeping time of most of the population is work time. This work time is devoted to the production of commodities-in-general (both where people get paid for their work and as members of audiences) and in the production and reproduction of labour power (the pay for which is subsumed in their income). Of the off-the-job work time, the largest single block is time of the audiences which is sold to advertisers. It is not sold by workers but by the mass media of communications. Who produces this commodity? The mass media of communications do by the mix of explicit and hidden advertising and "programme" material, the markets for which preoccupy the bourgeois communication theorists.[8] But although the mass media play the leading role on the production side of the consciousness industry, the people in the audiences pay directly much more for the privilege of being in those audiences than do the mass media. In Canada in 1975 audience members bore directly about three times as large a cost as did the broadcasters and cable TV operators, combined.[9]

In "their" time which is sold to advertisers workers (a) perform essential marketing functions for the producers of consumers' goods, and (b) work at the production and reproduction of labour power. This joint process, as shall be noted, embodies a principal contradiction. If this analytical sketch is valid, serious problems for Marxist theory emerge. Among them is the apparent fact that while the superstructure is not ordinarily thought of as being itself engaged in infrastructural productive activity, the mass media of communications are *simultaneously* in the superstructure *and* engaged indispensably in the last stage of infrastructural production where demand is produced and satisfied by purchases of consumer goods. Chairman Mao Tse-Tung provided the Marxist theoretical basis for such a development as that which created the contemporary capitalist mass media when he said:

> When the superstructure (politics, culture, etc.) obstructs the development of the economic base, political and cultural changes become *principal and decisive.*[10]

The basic entry to the analysis of the commodity form of communications is acceptance of the significance of the concept of monopoly in monopoly capitalism. Baran and Sweezy's *Monopoly Capitalism*[11] demonstrated how monopoly rather than competition rules contemporary capitalism, and it may be taken as the reference point from which to address this issue. Like J. K. Galbraith,[12] Baran and Sweezy emphasize the role of management of demand by the oligopolies which dominate monopoly capitalism. Both civilian and military demand are managed to provide the consumption and investment outlets required for the realization of a rising surplus. The process of demand management begins and ends with the market for the commodity—first as "test markets," and, when product and package production have been suitably designed and executed, as mass advertising-marketing. But Baran and Sweezy fail to pursue in an historical materialist way the obvious issues which are raised by demand-management-via-advertising under monopoly capitalism.

What happens when a monopoly capitalist system advertises? Baran and Sweezy answer, as does Galbraith, *psychological* manipulation. They cite Chamberlin as providing in 1931 the authoritative definition of contemporary advertising.[13] Moreover, they somewhat prematurely foreclose further investigation by stating flatly: "The immediate commercial purposes and effects of advertising have been thoroughly analyzed in economic literature and are readily grasped."[14] The mass media of communications possess no black box from which the magic of psychological manipulation is dispensed. Neither bourgeois nor Marxist economists have considered it worthwhile to ask the following questions which an historical materialist approach would seem to indicate:

a. What do advertisers buy with their advertising expenditures? As hardnosed businessmen they are not paying for advertising for nothing, nor from altruism. I suggest that what they buy are the services of audiences with predictable specifications who will pay attention in predictable numbers and at particular times to particular means of communication (TV, radio, newspapers, magazines, billboards, and third-class mail).[15] As collectivities these audiences are commodities. As commodities they are dealt with in markets by producers and buyers (the latter being advertisers). Such markets establish prices in the familiar mode of monopoly capitalism. Both these markets and the audience commodities traded in are specialized. The audience commodities bear specifications known in the business as "the demographics." The specifications for the audience commodities include age, sex, income level, family composition, urban or rural location, ethnic character, ownership of home, automobile, credit card status, social class and, in the case of hobby and fan magazines, a dedication to photography, model electric trains, sports cars, philately, do-it-yourself crafts, foreign travel, kinky sex, etc.

b. How are advertisers assured that they are getting what they pay for when they buy audiences? A sub-industry sector of the consciousness industry checks to determine. The socio-economic characteristics of the delivered audience/readership *and* its size are the business of A. C. Nielsen and a host of competitors who specialize in rapid assessment of the delivered audience commodity. The behaviour of the members of the audience product under the impact of advertising and the "editorial" content is the object of market research by a large number of independent market research agencies as well as by similar staffs located in advertising agencies, the advertising corporation and in media enterprises.[16]

c. What institutions produce the commodity which advertisers buy with their advertising expenditures? The owners of TV and radio stations and networks, newspapers, magazines and enterprises which specialize in providing billboard and third class advertising are the principal producers. This array of producers is interlocked in many ways with advertising agencies, talent agencies, package programme producers, film producers, news "services" (e.g., AP, UPI, Reuters), "syndicators" of news "columns," writers' agents, book publishers, motion picture producers and distributors. Last but by no means least in the array of institutions which produce the audience commodity is the family. The most important *resource* employed in producing the audience commodity are the individuals and families in the nations which permit advertising.

d. What is the nature of the content of the mass media in economic terms under monopoly capitalism? The information, entertainment and "educational" material transmitted to the audience is an inducement (gift, bribe or "free lunch") to recruit potential members of the audience and to maintain their loyal attention. The appropriateness of the analogy to the free lunch in the old-time saloon or cocktail bar is manifest: the free lunch consists of materials which whet the prospective audience members' appetites and thus (1) attract and keep them attending to the programme, newspaper or magazine, and (2) cultivate a mood conducive to favourable reaction to the explicit and implicit advertisers' messages.[17] To say this is not to obscure the agenda-setting function of the "editorial" content and advertising for the populations which depend on the mass media to find out what is happening in the world, nor is it to denigrate the technical virtuosity with which the free lunch is prepared and served. Great skill, talent and much expense go into such production, though less per unit of content than in the production of overt advertisements. Only a monstrous misdirection of attention obscures the real nature of the commodities involved. Thus with no reference to the "Sales Effort," Baran and Sweezy can say:

> There is not only serious question as to the value of artistic offerings carried by the mass communications media and serving directly or indirectly as vehicles of advertising; it is beyond dispute that all of them could be provided at a cost to consumers incomparably lower than they are forced to pay through commercial advertising.[18]

Under monopoly capitalism TV-radio programmes are provided "free" and the newspapers and magazines are provided at prices which cover delivery (but not production) costs to the media enterprise. In the case of newspapers and some magazines, some readers characteristically buy the media product *because* they want the advertisements. This is especially the practice with classified advertisements and display advertising of products and prices by local merchants in newspapers and with product information in advertisements in certain magazines (e.g. hobby magazines). Regardless of these variations, the central purpose of the information, entertainment and "educational" material (including that in the advertisements themselves) transmitted to the audience is to ensure attention to the products and services being advertised. Competition among media enterprises produces intricate strategies governing the placement of programmes in terms of types of products advertised and types of "free lunch" provided in different time segments of the week (e.g. children's hours, daytime housewives' hours, etc.): all this in order to optimize the "flow" of particular types of audiences to one programme from its immediate predecessors and to its immediate successors with regard to the strategies of rival networks.[19]

e. What is the nature of the service performed for the advertiser by the members of the purchased audiences? In economic terms, the audience commodity is a non-durable producers' good which is bought and used in the marketing of the advertiser's product. The work which audience members perform for the advertiser to whom they have been sold is to learn to buy particular "brands" of consumer goods, and to spend their income accordingly. In short, they work to create the demand for advertised goods which is the purpose of the monopoly capitalist advertisers. While doing this, audience members are simultaneously reproducing their own labour power. In this regard, it is appropriate to avoid the trap of a manipulation-explanation by noting that if such labour power is, in fact, loyally attached to the monopoly capitalist system, this would be welcome to the advertisers whose existence depends on the maintenance of that system. But in reproducing their labour power workers respond to other realistic conditions which may on occasion surprise and disappoint the advertisers. It seems, however, that when workers under monopoly capitalist conditions serve advertisers to complete the production process of consumer goods by performing the ultimate marketing service for them, these workers are making decisive material decisions which will affect how they will produce and reproduce their labour power. As the Chinese emphasized during the Cultural Revolution, if people are spending their time catering to their individual interests and sensitivities, they cannot be using the *same* time also to overthrow capitalist influence and to build socialism.

f. How does demand-management by monopoly capitalism, by means of advertising, relate to the labour theory of value, to "leisure" and to "free time"? As William Livant puts it, the power of the concept of surplus value "rests wholly on the way Marx solved the great value problem of classical political economy, by *splitting the notion of labour in two,* into labour in productive use and labour power (the capacity to labour)."[20] Labour in productive use in the production of commodities-in-general was Marx's concern in the three volumes of *Capital,* except for volume 1, chapter 6 and scattered passages in the *Grundrisse.* It is clear from these passages that Marx assumed that labour power is produced by the labourer and by his or her immediate family, i.e., under the conditions of handicraft production. In a word, labour power was "home-made" in the absence of dominant brand-name commodities, mass advertising, and the mass media (which had not yet been invented by monopoly capitalism). In Marx's period and in his analysis, the principal aspect of capitalist production was the alienation of workers from the means of producing commodities-in-general. Now the principal aspect of capitalist production has become the alienation of workers from the means of producing and reproducing themselves. The prevailing western Marxist view today still holds the incorrect assumption that the labourer is an independent commodity producer of labour power which is his to sell. Livant says it well:

> What often escapes attention is that just because the labourer sells it (his or her labour power) does not mean that he or she produces it. We are misled by fixating on the true fact that a human must eat and sleep into thinking that therefore the seller of labour power must also be the producer. Again the error of two combines into one.[21]

We need a dialectical materialist description of the production of labour power, of the capacity and incapacity to labour and of the relationship of the production of labour power to our ability to live as human beings.[22]

Am I correct in assuming that all non-sleeping time under capitalism is work time?[23] William Livant, in commenting on a draft of this article, points out that the assumption should be plainly stated. As he puts it, a Marxist view

> sees leisure time correctly as time of production, reproduction and repair of labour power. This production, reproduction and repair are activities. They are things people must do. As such, they also require labour power. To be sure, this latter labour power you do not have to sell directly to capital. But you do have to use it to produce labour power in the form you do have to sell.

> Why was this hard to see? I think we can find the answer if we look at 'non-work' time. Marx points out many times (e.g. *Capital,* Vol. 1, Ch. 6) that wage labour only becomes possible if your labour power becomes a *personal possession,* which it is possible for you to sell. You can do what you 'want' with it. ... Non-work time is labour power which is *yours not-to-sell.* Hence it seems to be doubly your personal possession. ...
>
> When we see this, we can fit it within what Marx called the 'false appearance' of wage labour (citing *Wages, Prices and Profit,* Peking, 1973, pp. 50–1)...I think this false appearance has its other side. Just as it appears, at work, that you *are* paid for all the labour time you *do* sell, so it appears, off-work, that the labour time *you are not paid for is not sold.* ...
>
> Work and non-work time bear interesting relations that need examination, to see beneath the false appearances. They in fact *divide* the whole world of commodities in *two.* For at work it is principally commodities-in-general that are made and distributed. Those who make and distribute these commodities do not sell them. But off-work, we find something else. What is being produced there is primarily the peculiar commodity, labour power. And off-work, those who make this commodity, also do not sell it. But it is sold, as surely as commodities-in-general made at the workplace.[24]

It should be clear that for at least several generations labour power in advanced monopoly capitalist countries has been produced primarily by institutions other than the individual and his/her family. The mass media of communications and advertising play a large and probably dominant role through the process of consumption (by guiding the making of the shopping list) as well as through the ideological teaching which permeates both the advertising and ostensibly non-advertising material with which they produce the audience commodity.[25] When cosmetic counters in department stores display "Boxed Ego" (Vancouver, December, 1975), the dialectical relation of the material and consciousness aspects of the production of labour power should be evident.

What has happened to the time available to workers and the way it is used in the past century? In 1850 under conditions of cottage industry, i.e. unbranded consumer goods, the average work week was about 70 hours per week (and the work force was predominantly male).[26] At about the time when Marx was writing the *Grundrisse,* workers' savings, under the most favourable conditions of exploitation, could make possible

> the worker's participation in the higher, even cultural satisfactions, the agitation of his own interests, newspaper subscriptions, attending lectures,

> educating his children, developing his taste, etc., his only share of civilization which distinguishes him from the slave. ...[27]

In that simple stage of capitalist development, Marx could see that the relentless accumulative process would proliferate commodities:

> Capital's ceaseless striving towards the general form of wealth drives labour beyond the limits of its natural paltriness (*Naturbedurftigkeit*), and thus creates the material elements for the development of the rich individuality which is as all-sided in its production as in its consumption. ...[28]

Many other references may be cited from the *Grundrisse* to similar effect. But all this assumed that consumer goods were not monopolized by brand names and that workers could dispose of their non-work time subject only to class and customary (i.e. traditional) considerations. In 1850, the average American worker could devote about 42 hours per week (168 hours minus 70 hours on the job and 56 hours of sleep) to such "cottage industry" type of production of labour power.

By 1960, the average time spent on the job was about 39.5 hours per week—an apparent reduction in work time of almost 30 hours per week (to which should be added 2.5 hours as a generous estimate of the weekly equivalent of annual vacations). Capitalist apologists equated this ostensible reduction in work time with a corresponding increase in "free" or "leisure" time. The reality was quite different. Two transformations were being effected by monopoly capitalism in the nature of work, leisure and consumer behaviour. On the one hand, huge chunks of workers' time were being removed from their discretion by the phenomenon of metropolitan sprawl and by the nature of unpaid work which workers were obligated to perform. For example, in the contemporary period travel time to and from the job can be estimated at 8.5 hours per week; "moonlighting" employment at a minimum of one hour per week; repair work around the home, at another five hours per week; and men's work on household chores and shopping at another 2.3 hours per week. A total of 16.8 hours per week of the roughly 32 hours of time supposedly "freed" as a result of capitalist industrialization is thus anything but "free." A further seven hours of the 32 hours of "freed" time disappears when the correction for part-time female employment is made in the reported hours-per-week.[29] Three-fourths of the so-called "freed" time has thus vanished.

The second transformation involves the pressure placed by the system on the remaining hours of the week. If sleeping is estimated at eight hours a day, the remainder of the 168 hours in the week after subtracting sleeping and the unfree work time thus far identified was 42 hours in 1850 and 49 hours in 1960. We lack systematic information about the use of this "free time" for both dates. We do know that certain types of activities were common to both dates: personal care, making love, visiting with relatives and friends, preparing and eating meals, attending union, church and other associative institutions, including saloons. We also know that in 1960 (but not in 1850) there was a vast array of *branded* consumer goods and services pressed on the workers through advertising, point-of-sale displays, and peer group influence. Attendance at spectator sports and participation in such activities as bowling, camping, and "pleasure driving" of the automobile or snowmobile—all promoted for the sake of equipment sales by the consciousness industry—now take time that was devoted to non-commercial activities in 1850. In-house time must now be devoted to deciding whether or not to buy and then to use (by whom, where, under what conditions, and why) an endless proliferation of goods for personal care, household furnishing, clothing, music reproduction equipment, etc. Guiding the worker today in all income and time expenditures are the mass media—through the blend of advertisements and programme content.

How do Baran and Sweezy deal with the use made of this illusory increase in free time? Deploying Veblen's concept of conspicuous consumption and thereby emphasizing the status-seeking character of workers' consumption decisions, they treat leisure time (without quotation marks) in psychoanalytic terms as time spent willfully in passivity and idleness:

> This propensity to do nothing has had a decisive part in determining the kinds of entertainment which are supplied to fill the leisure hours—in the evening, on weekends and holidays, during vacations. The basic principle is that whatever is presented—reading matter, movies, radio and TV programs—must not make undue demands on the intellectual and emotional resources of the recipients: the purpose is to provide 'fun', 'relaxation', a 'good time'—in short, passively absorbable amusement.[30]

What is wrong with this partial truth is: (1) it ignores the relationship of monopoly capitalism's Sales Effort, particularly advertising, to the problem; and (2) it substitutes casual bourgeois observations[31] for an historical materialist attack on the problem.

As against the seven hours per week of apparent "non-work" time gained by the average worker between 1850 and 1960, how much time does he now spend as part of the audience product of the mass media—time sold to the advertisers? Here the audience-measurement sub-industry gives us some information. David Blank, economist for the Columbia Broadcasting System, in 1970 found that the average person watched TV for 3.3 hours per day (23 hours *per week*) on an annual basis, listened to radio for 2.5 hours per day (18 hours *per week*), and read newspapers and magazines one hour per day (7 hours *per week*).[32] If we look at the audience product in terms of families rather than individuals, we find that in 1973, advertisers in the U.S. purchased TV audiences for an average of a little more than 43 hours per home per week.[33] By industry usage, this lumps together specialized audience commodities sold independently as "housewives," "children" and "families." In the "prime time" evening hours (7:00 to 11:00 p.m.), the TV audience commodity consisted of a daily average of 83.8 million people, with an average of two persons viewing per home. Women were a significantly larger proportion of this prime time audience than men (42 percent as against 32 percent, while children were 16 percent and teenagers, 10 percent).

We do not know even approximately how the worker's exposure to the mass media articulates with the other components in his/her use of "free time." It is relatively easy to determine how much radio listening and newspaper and magazine reading takes place while travelling to and from work. But much TV and radio programming is attended to incidentally while engaged in other activities such as performing household chores, visiting with friends, reading, and now even while attending spectator sports.[34] This is the context in which we may pursue the question, how demand management by means of advertising in monopoly capitalism relates to the labour theory of value, to "leisure" and to "free time." It should now be possible to obtain some clues to the nature of work which workers perform in relation to advertising. If freedom is the act of resisting necessity, what is the nature of the process by which workers react to advertising, and why is it profitable for advertisers to advertise? An advertising theorist, Professor T. N. Levitt, says, "Customers don't buy things. They buy tools to solve problems."[35] It appears that the purpose of advertising, from the perspective of the advertising corporation, is to establish in the worker's consciousness (1) the existence of a "problem" facing the worker (acne, security from burglars, sleeplessness), (2) the existence of a class of commodities which will solve that problem, and (3) the motivation to give top priority to purchasing brand X of that class of commodities in order to "solve" that "problem." Given this situation, the realistic process of audience-members' work can be best understood in terms of the ever-increasing number of decisions forced on him/her by "new" commodities and by their related advertising. Unfortunately, while workers are faced with millions of possible comparative choices among thousands of "new" commodities, they lack scientifically objective bases on which to evaluate either the "problem" to be solved by buying the proffered "tool" or the efficacy of the "tool" as a solution to the "problem." In this situation, they constantly struggle to develop a rational shopping list out of an irrational situation.[36] As Linder puts it, the most important way by which consumers can cope with commodities and advertising is to limit the time spent in thinking about what to buy.

> Reduced time for reflection previous to a decision would apparently entail a growing irrationality. However, since it is extremely rational to consider less and less per decision there exists a rationale of irrationality.[37]

Monopoly capitalist marketing practice has a sort of seismic, systemic drift towards "impulse purchasing." Increasingly, the work done by audience members is cued towards impulse purchasing. Again, Linder is insightful:

> To begin with advertising is a means of making factual knowledge more accessible than otherwise. Second, it serves to provide quasi-information for people who lack time to acquire the genuine insights. They get the surrogate information they want to have, in order to feel that they are making the right decisions. ... The advertiser helps to close the information gap, at the same time exploiting the information gap that is bound to remain.[38]
>
> As the scarcity of time increases, the emphasis in advertising will be displaced in the direction of ersatz information. The object will be to provide a motive for an action for which no solid grounds exist. ... Brand loyalty must be built up among people who have no possibility of deciding how to act on objective grounds. As routine purchasing procedures gain in importance as a means of reducing decision-making time, it will become increasingly important to capture those who have not yet developed their routines.[39]

In this connection, the new and sophisticated interest of market researchers in the relationship of advertising to children is very significant. According to the publisher of one recent study:

> As the authors see it, consumption is a perfectly legitimate and unavoidable activity for children. Consequently they reject a strategy directed at protecting kids from marketing stimuli. What is necessary, then, is to acknowledge that children are going to watch television commercials and to prepare them to be selective consumers.
>
> *How Children Learn to Buy* provides evidence to confront existing theories in the emerging field of consumer socialization. The work is essential to

everyone concerned with the effects of advertising: sponsors, ad agencies, the television industry, educators, governmental regulators, consumer researchers, and parents.[40]

Constrained by the ideology of monopoly capitalism, the bourgeois notion of free time and leisure is only available to those who have no disposable income (and for whom it is, of course, a bitter mockery) and to those who are so rich that, as Linder says, for them, "the ultimate luxury is to be liberated from the hardships of having to do one's own buying."[41] For everyone else, "free time" and "leisure" belong only in the monopoly capitalist lexicon alongside "free world," "free enterprise," "free elections," "free speech," and "free flow" of information.

What has happened to the time workers spend off-the-job while not sleeping is that enormous pressures on this time have been imposed by all consumer goods and service branches of monopoly capitalism. Individual, familial and other associative needs must be dealt with, but in a real context of products and advertising which, taken together, make the task of the individual and family basically one of *coping* while being constantly on the verge of being overwhelmed by these pressures. In this context, the work of the audience members which advertisers find productive for them is one of learning cues which are used when the audience member makes up his/her mental shopping list and spends his/her income.

g. Does the audience commodity perform an essential economic function? Baran and Sweezy state that "advertising constitutes as much an integral part of the system as the giant corporation itself"[42] and that "advertising has turned into an indispensable tool for a large sector of corporate business."[43] In this they go as far as Galbraith who said "the marginal utility of present aggregate output, ex-advertising and salesmanship is zero."[44]

But is the production and consumption of the audience commodity for advertisers a "productive" activity in Marxian terms? Baran and Sweezy are contradictory in answering this question. They tell us that advertising expenses, "since they are manifestly unrelated to necessary costs of production and distribution—however broadly defined—they can only be counted as a part of aggregate surplus."[45] But after some agonizing over whether finance, insurance and real estate (which account for about twice the volume of national income as represented by advertising) are productive, they abandon their theoretical footing for rejecting expenses of circulation as unproductive of surplus:

Just as advertising, product differentiation, artificial obsolescence, model changing, and all the other devices of the sales effort do in fact promote and

> increase sales, and thus act as indispensable props to the level of income and employment, so the entire apparatus of 'finance, insurance, and real estate' is essential to the normal functioning of the corporate system and another no less indispensable prop to the level of income and employment. The prodigious volume of resources absorbed in all these activities does in fact constitute necessary costs of capitalist production. What should be crystal clear is that an economic system in which *such* costs are socially necessary has long ceased to be a socially necessary system.[46]

I am aware that *Capital* can be and has been read frequently as denying the productivity of the expenses of middlemen in general. As I read the work, however, it seems to me that in *Capital* Marx was concerned to analyze the operation of capitalism under the then realistic conditions of competition and the organization of industry as being generally *unintegrated* from raw material processing through exchange to the consumption process.[47] Marx also clearly did not assume the predominance of branded commodities or the prevalence of advertising. If one turns to Marx's "Introduction to the Critique of Political Economy," however, it seems probable that his analysis of monopoly capitalism, had such been possible in his time, would have answered the question of the productivity of advertising differently. Indeed the following passage accommodates the phenomena of advertising, branded merchandise and monopoly capitalism in managing demands.

> Consumption produces production in a double way...because consumption creates the need for *new* production, that is it creates the ideal, internally impelling cause for production, which is its presupposition. Consumption creates the motive for production; it also creates the object which is active in production as its determinant aim. ... No production without a need. But consumption reproduces the need. ... Production not only supplies a material for the need, but it also supplies a need for the material. As soon as consumption emerges from its initial state of natural crudity and immediacy—and, if it remained at that stage, this would be because production itself had been arrested there—it becomes itself mediated as a drive by the object. The need which consumption feels for the object is created by the perception of it. The object of art—like every other product—creates a public which is sensitive to art and enjoys beauty. Production thus not only creates an object for the subject, but also a subject for the object. *Thus production produces consumption (1) by creating the material for it; (2) by determining the manner of consumption; and (3) by creating the products initially posited by it as objects, in the form of a need felt by the consumer. It thus produces the object of*

> *consumption, the manner of consumption and the motive of consumption. Consumption likewise produces the producer's inclination by beckoning to him as an aim-determining need.*[48] It is clear, firstly, that the exchange of activities and abilities which takes place within production itself belongs directly to production and essentially constitutes it. The same holds, secondly, for the exchange of products, in so far as that exchange is the means of finishing the product and making it fit for direct consumption. To that extent, exchange is an act comprised within production itself. Thirdly, the so-called exchange between dealers and dealers is by its very organization entirely determined by production, as being itself a producing activity. Exchange appears as independent and indifferent to production only in the final phase where the product is exchanged directly for consumption.[49]

On such a footing it is possible to develop a Marxist theory of advertising and of branded commodities under monopoly capitalist conditions. When the president of the Revlon corporation says: "We manufacture lipsticks. But we sell hope," he is referring to the creation of products initially posited by it as objects in the form of a need felt by the consumer—similarly with Contac-C, the proprietary cold remedy which so disturbed Baran and Sweezy.[50] The denial of the productivity of advertising is unnecessary and diversionary: a cul de sac derived from the pre-monopoly-capitalist stage of development, a dutiful but unsuccessful and inappropriate attempt at reconciliation with *Capital.*

h. Why have Marxist economists been indifferent to the historical process by which advertising, brand-name merchandise, and the mass media of communications have developed in monopoly capitalism over the past century? Why do they continue to regard the press, TV and radio media as having the prime function of producing news, entertainment and editorial opinion and not audiences for sale to advertisers? The evidence for the latter is all around us.

Baran and Sweezy do indeed indicate how much advertising has grown and when, i.e., by a factor of ten between 1890 and 1929.[51] *But not why, how and with what connections.*

In the first three quarters of the nineteenth century, newspapers and magazines in the countries going through the Industrial Revolution were characterized by: (a) diversity of support as between readers' payments, subsidies from political parties, and advertising (most of the latter being information about commodity availability and prices and not about branded merchandise); and (b) a cyclical process of technological improvement with consequent larger printing capacity, lower unit costs, lower unit prices of publications, larger profits, capital accumulation and reinvestment in new and more productive plants, etc.[52] In that period, marketing of consumer goods was characterized by: (a) predominance of unbranded merchandise; (b) unintegrated distribution of commodities with the middleman being the most powerful link in the production-to-consumer chain; and (c) consequently, lack of massive advertising as a means of managing demand.

In the second half of the nineteenth century, capitalism faced a crisis. The first stage of the development of the factory system under conditions of competition between relatively small capitalists had succeeded in mobilizing labour supply and exploiting it crudely under conditions documented so ably by Marx in *Capital*. The very success of the system bred grave threats to it. Politically conscious labour unions posed revolutionary threats to capitalism.[53] Moreover, capitalist manufacturers were vulnerable to the power of the workers because the highly skilled workers possessed more knowledge about the production process than did their employers.[54] Manufacturers were thus blocked from ready control of their work force and from innovating the new and increasingly sophisticated machine processes of mass production which the rapid progress in physical sciences and engineering made possible. When they looked at their marketing methods, manufacturers were also beset by chronic insecurities. The periodic business cycles in their crisis and liquidation phases forced manufacturers into cut-throat pricing (of unbranded merchandise, typically) because of the pressure of overhead costs. The result was a short life expectancy for competitive industrialists.

In sum, a watershed in the development of capitalism had been reached. As M. M. Knight said, "Down to the last quarter of the nineteenth century, commerce dominated industry; after it industry dominated commerce."[55]

Capitalism's systemic solution to the contradiction between its enormous potential for expanding production of consumer goods (and the profits to be thus realized) and the systemic insecurities posed by people as workers and people as consumers was to move to large scale rationalization of industrial organization (through vertical, horizontal and conglomerate integration).[56] This conferred control over supplies and prices in the factor markets, and in the marketing of end-products. But to make such giant integrated corporations viable, their operations had to address directly the problem of people (1) as workers at the job where they were paid, and (2) as buyers of the end product of industry. The systemic solution was a textbook example of the transformation of a contradiction on the principle "one goes into two." This was an ideological task and it was solved by capitalizing on the deeply held ideological reverence for scientific rationality in the pursuit of possessive individualistic material goals.

After militant unions had been crushed by force between 1890 and 1910, scientific management was applied to people as workers. Knowledge about the work process was expropriated from skilled workers to management. The work process was reduced to "ladders" of dead-end "tasks" to complement whichever more sophisticated generations of mass production machines were innovated. And through varieties of "incentive" wage plans, linked with promotion-from-within on the basis of seniority, supported by company welfare plans (and later social insurance through government), the workplace where people got paid was transformed ideologically.[57] People learned there that work under monopoly capitalism involves competition between individuals whose possessive needs necessarily set them in conflict with each other rather than with the owners of the means of their (concealed) cooperative production. The carrot which systemically motivated them was the pursuit of commodities, which joined this half of the ideological exercise with the next.

Simultaneously the system dealt with its problem of people as buyers of end products. As on the job front, science was invoked. The objective was personal satisfaction, and the rationale was efficiency. The term "consumer" was invented to describe the desired object. Advertising and the creation of mass produced communications (press, radio and TV principally) were developed as the specialized means to this systemic end. Even if a seeming "overproduction" of consumer goods threatened the profitability of an industry, the ability of a company to distinguish its products from unbranded similar products allowed its sales and profits to grow in security. If studies are done—I have been able to locate none—of the history of brand names, it will be found that this was how brand name loyalty became an essential weapon in industry when the trusts which produced the present oligopolistic empires of monopoly capitalist industry became dominant features of the industrial landscape. Certainly the Baran and Sweezy thesis that monopoly capitalism manages demand through market controls and advertising would seem to carry as its corollary the hypothesis that something like the *suction* of commodities from the material production line to the oligopolistic end-product markets has replaced the atomistic *circulation* of commodities typical of Marx's time as the model of monopoly capitalist marketing. While historical scholarship in marketing seems conspicuously undeveloped, fragmentary evidence from studies of marketing history tend to confirm the outline of the process here sketched.[58]

For example, Joseph Palamountain says, "Great increases in the size of manufacturers or retailers have changed much of the distribution from a flow through a series of largely autonomous markets to a single movement dominated by either manufacturer or retailer."[59] Simultaneously, the newspaper and magazine industries found themselves in a position to vastly increase the productivity of the printing trades in the last quarter of the nineteenth century. Technical advances in typesetting, printing (including colour), photographic reproduction, etc., could be financed if someone would foot the bill. The newspaper and magazine entrepreneurs (the William Randolph Hearsts and their rivals) invented the "yellow journalism" which took advantage of this situation. The cycle of capital expansion ensued in accelerated speed and scope. Production and circulation were multiplied, while prices paid by the readers were held constant or decreased. And the "mass media" characteristic of monopoly capitalism were created in the 1890s. It was these mass media, increasingly financed by advertising, that drew together the "melting pot" working class from diverse ethnic groups which were flooding in as migrants to the United States into saleable audiences for the advertisers.[60]

The advent of radio-telephony in the first two decades of this century made possible the use of the same principle which had been proven in the print media. And so commercial radio broadcasting became a systemic innovation of, by, and for monopoly capitalism. When the pent-up civilian demand at the end of World War II, and the generous capital subventions of a government intent on winning that war, had provided electronics manufacturers with shell-loading and other war plants easily convertible into TV set manufacturing, and when a complaisant FCC could be manipulated into favouring TV over FM broadcasting,[61] TV was approved and largely financed out of capital accumulated from commercial radio broadcasting's profits.[62]

Why was this media complex rather than some other mode of marketing developed by monopoly capitalism to create and control "consumers"? Because it offered a cheaper and more efficient mode of demand management than the alternatives which could be devised. What alternatives? The obvious alternative was "more of the same" methods previously used in marketing: heavier reliance on travelling salesmen to push goods to retailers, heavier use of door-to-door salesmen. To calculate the opportunity cost with a hypothetical elaboration of a marketing system designed to sell branded commodities without advertising was and is a horrendous prospect. Moreover, it would be pointless because mass production of (branded) consumer goods and services under capitalism would not have happened, absent advertising. An indication of the efficiency of the audience commodity as a producers' good used in the production of consumer goods (and a clue to a possible measure of surplus value created by people working in audiences) is provided when we compare advertising expenditures with "value added" by retailing of consumer goods and services. In 1973 in the U.S. some $25 billion was spent in advertising while personal consumption expenditures were about $800 billion. Three percent of the sales price as the cost of creating and managing demand seems very cheap—and profitable. The system also accrued valuable side-benefits. Institutional advertising and the merchandising of political candidates and ideological points of view in the guise of the free lunch and advertising messages were only appreciated and exploited systematically after World War I when propaganda and its associated public opinion polling were developed for war promotion purposes.

To summarize: the mass media institutions in monopoly capitalism developed the equipment, workers and organization to produce audiences for the purposes of the system between about 1875 and 1950. The prime purpose of the mass media complex is to produce people in audiences who work at learning the theory and practice of consumership for civilian goods and who support (with taxes and votes) the military demand management system. The second principal purpose is to produce audiences whose theory and practice confirms the ideology of monopoly capitalism (possessive individualism in an authoritarian political system). The third principal purpose is to produce public opinion supportive of the strategic and tactical policies of the state (e.g., presidential candidates, support of Indochinese military adventures, space race, détente with the Soviet Union, rapprochement with China and ethnic and youth dissent). Necessarily in the monopoly capitalist system, the fourth purpose of the mass media complex is to operate itself so profitably as to ensure unrivalled respect for its economic importance in the system. It has been quite successful in achieving all four purposes.

If we recognize the reality of monopoly capitalism buying audiences to complete the mass marketing of mass produced consumer goods and services, much further analysis is needed of the implications of this "principal and decisive" integration of superstructure and base which reality presents. First, the contradictions produced within the audience commodity should be understood more clearly. I refer to the contradiction as between audience members serving as producers' goods in the marketing of mass produced consumer goods and their work in producing and reproducing labour power. I think that the consciousness industry through advertising-supported mass media produces three kinds of alienation for the members of the audience commodity: (1) alienation from the result of their work "on the job," (2) alienation from the commodities-in-general which they participate in marketing to themselves; and (3) alienation from the labour power they produce and reproduce in themselves and their children. It would seem that the theory of work needs reconsideration.

Then connections to other areas need to be examined. Among such connections there come to mind those to Marxist theory about social consciousness (and false consciousness), to theory about the nature of the class struggle, the nature of the proletariat under monopoly capitalism and sex chauvinism, and to theories of the state. The last of these seems obvious if this analysis is considered in connection with the recent articles by Gold, Lo, and Wright.[63] The role of the mass media and the consciousness industry in producing the audience commodity both as commodity-in-general and peculiar commodity might provide the real sinews to the structural-Marxist model of the state of Poulantzas and to the theoretical initiatives of Claus Offe in seeking the processes within the state which "guarantee" its class character. The connection to the work of de Bord[64] regarding consciousness is proximate. The relation of industrially produced images to the "real" world of nutrition, clothing, housing, birth and death is dialectical. The mass media are the focus of production of images of popular culture under monopoly capitalism, both through the explicit advertising and the "free lunch" which hook and hold people in audiences. Because the consciousness industry produces consumable, saleable spectacles, its product treats both past and future like the present—as blended in the eternal present of a system which was never created and will never end. The society of the spectacle, however, cannot be abstractly contrasted with the "real" world of actual people and things. The two interact. The spectacle inverts the real and is itself produced and is real. Hence, as de Bord says, objective reality is present on both sides. But because the society of the spectacle is a system which stands the world really on its head, the truth in it is a moment of the false. Because the spectacle monopolizes the power to make mass appearance, it demands and gets passive acceptance by the "real" world. And because it is undeniably real (as well as false) it has the persuasive power of the most effective propaganda.[65]

Finally, another example of necessary connections is that to the theory of imperialism and socialism in the present stage of monopoly capitalism. There are many ways by which a theory of commodity production through mass communications would strengthen the analysis, for example, of Samir Amin.[66] The cocacolonisation of the dependent and peripheral countries cannot be grounded in Marxist theory without attention to the production of audience commodities in the interest of multinational corporations. It would link Amin's theory to Herbert Schiller's work on the relation of the mass media to the American empire.[67] And, when linked with analysis of the ideological aspects of science and "technology," it could strengthen the development of a non-economistic, non-positive, non-Eurocentered Marxism. Analysis of such connections is inviting but beyond the scope of the present essay.

Notes to "Communications: Blindspot . . ."

1. To demonstrate this in detail would require a lengthy analysis which would deflect the present article from its affirmative purpose. Gramsci, the Frankfurt School writers (Adorno, Horkheimer, Marcuse, Lowenthal), Raymond Williams, Poulantzas, Althusser, and Marxists concerned with the problems of developing nations (e.g. Samir Amin, Clive Y. Thomas)—none of them address the consciousness industry from the standpoint of its historical materialist role in making monopoly capitalist imperialism function through demand management (concretely through the economic processes of advertising and mass communications). This is precisely the blindspot of recent Western Marxism. In the developing debate it would be useful to have studies bearing on whether and why such writers have or have not dealt with this aspect of monopoly capitalism. Reality imposes a burden of proof on them as well as on me.

2. Lenin held a manipulative theory of the mass media and admitted naivete in this respect. "What was the fate of the decree establishing a state monopoly of private advertising issues in the first weeks of the Soviet government? ... It is amusing to think how naive we were. ... The enemy, i.e., the capitalist class, retaliated to this decree of the state power by completely repudiating that state power." "Report on the New Economic Policy," Seventh Moscow Gubernia Conference of the Russian Communist Party, October 21, 1921, in *Lenin About the Press* (Prague: International Organization of Journalists, 1972), p. 203. Lenin's *Imperialism* is devoid of recognition of the relation of advertising to monopoly capitalism and imperialism.

3. *The Mind Managers* (Boston: Beacon Press, 1973).

4. "For a Political Economy of Mass Communications," *The Socialist Register*, 1973.

5. Sage Publications, Beverly Hills.

6. Cf. Sidney Finkelstein, *Sense and Nonsense of McLuhan* (New York: International Publishers, 1968); Donald Theall, *The Medium Is the Rear View Mirror* (Montreal: McGill/Queen's University Press, 1971); and my review of the latter in *Queen's Quarterly*, Summer, 1971.

7. I am indebted to Professor William Livant, University of Regina, for much hard criticism which he formulated in a critique of a draft of this paper in December 1975.

8. The objective reality is that the ostensible advertisements and the material which comes between them, whether in the print or electronic media, have a common purpose of producing the audience. It is an interesting consequence of the idealist perspective that in most liberal analysis the "advertising" is considered to be separate from

the "news," "entertainment," "educational material" which is interlarded *between* the advertisements.

9. The annual cost to audience members of providing their own broadcast receivers (and paying for Cable TV), consisting of depreciation, interest on investment, maintenance and electric power, amounted to slightly more than $1.8 billion, while the over-the-air broadcasters' (Canadian Broadcasting Corporation plus private broadcasters) and Cable TV operators' costs were about $631 million.

10. "On Contradictions," *Selected Works of Mao Tse-Tung,* vol. 1 (Peking: Foreign Languages Press, 1967), p. 336. Emphasis added.

11. Paul A. Baran and Paul M. Sweezy, *Monopoly Capitalism* (New York: Monthly Review Press, 1966).

12. *The New Industrial State* (Boston: Houghton Mifflin, 1967).

13. E. H. Chamberlin, *The Theory of Monopolistic Competition* (Cambridge, Mass.: 1931).

14. *Monopoly Capitalism,* p. 116.

15. It is argued by one of my critics that a better term for what advertisers buy would be "attention." At our present naive stage concerning the matter, it does *seem* as if attention is indeed what is bought. But where people are paid for working on the job, should Marxists say that what the employer buys is "labour power" or "the manual dexterity and attention necessary for tending machines?" Where I refer to audiences as being produced, purchased and used, let it be understood that I mean "audience-power"; however it may turn out upon further realistic analysis to be exercised.

16. The pages of *Variety* report on cases where the ostensibly non-advertising matter in the media, which I call the "free lunch," attracted an audience which has propensities incongruous with the particular product or service being advertised; in such cases the program is cancelled and the audience discarded.

17. The "free lunch" concept of the mass media was first stated by A. J. Liebling, *The Press* (New York: Ballantine Books, 1961).

18. *Monopoly Capitalism,* p. 121. Or for elaborate obfuscation, see Fritz Machlup, *The Production and Distribution of Knowledge in the United States* (Princeton: Princeton University Press, 1962).

19. See Les Brown, *Television: The Business Behind the Box* (New York: Harcourt Brace Jovanovich, 1971).

20. William Livant, "Notes on the Development of the Production of Labour Power," 22 March, 1975. (dittoed)

21. William Livant, "More on the Production of Damaged Labour Power," 1 April, 1975, p. 2. (dittoed)

22. In arguing that all non-sleeping time under capitalism is work time, I go beyond Samir Amin who says: "Social time is split into non-working time and working time. But here too the former exists only to serve the latter. It is not leisure time, as it is called in the false consciousness of alienated men, but recuperation time. It is functional recuperation that is socially organized and not left up to the individual despite certain appearances." ("In Praise of Socialism," *Monthly Review,* September, 1974, p. 8). Amin also has the blindspot which does not recognize the audience commodity which mass media have produced.

23. I am perhaps wrong to exclude sleeping time from work. The dividing line between recreation of the ability to work while awake and sleeping may be illusory. It may

be that the head coach of the Washington, D.C. "Redskin" professional football team, George Allen, is closer to the mark than most economists when he tells his players, "Nobody should work all the time. Leisure time is the five or six hours you sleep at night. You can combine two good things at once, sleep and leisure." Quoted in Louis Terkel, *Working* (New York: Pantheon, 1974), p. 389.

24. William Livant, "The Communications Commodity," University of Regina, 25 December, 1975, p. 7. (photocopy)

25. For present purposes I ignore the ancillary and interactive processes which contribute to the production of labour power involving also the educational institutions, the churches, labour unions, and a host of voluntary associations (e.g. YMCA, Girl Scouts).

26. The following analysis draws on Sebastian de Grazia, *Of Time, Work and Leisure* (New York: Anchor, 1964).

27. Karl Marx, *Grundrisse* (London: Pelican, 1973), p. 287.

28. Marx, *Grundrisse*, p. 325.

29. Part-time workers (probably more female than male) amounted in 1960 to nineteen percent of the employed labour force in the United States and worked an average of 19 hours weekly. If we exclude such workers in order to get a figure comparable to the 70 hours in 1850, we consider the weekly hours worked by the average American male, who worked at least 35 hours per week, and find that they averaged 46.4 (as against 39.5 for all workers). For the sake of brevity, I omit the counterpart calculation of "free time" for women. No sexist implications are intended.

30. *Monopoly Capitalism*, p. 346.

31. "...the manufacturers of paper and ink and TV sets whose products are used to control and poison the minds of the people. ..." (*Monopoly Capitalism*, p. 344)

32. David M. Blank, "Pleasurable Pursuits—The Changing Structure of Leisure-Time Spectator Activities," National Association of Business Economists, Annual Meeting, September, 1970. (ditto)

33. *Broadcasting Yearbook*, 1974, p. 69.

34. For many years patrons at professional baseball and football games have been listening to portable radios broadcasting the same game. In 1975 I observed that patrons at professional football games are beginning to watch the same game on portable TV sets for the "instant replays."

35. T. N. Levitt, "The Industrialization of Service," *Harvard Business Review*, September, 1976, p. 73.

36. I use the term "rational" here in the common sense usage, that the result should be one which can be "lived with," is "the right decision," which "makes sense." I imply no Benthamist calculus of utilities or pleasure or pain.

37. Staffen B. Linder, *The Harried Leisure Class* (New York: Columbia University Press, 1970), p. 59.

38. Linder, *The Harried Leisure Class*, pp. 70–71.

39. Linder, *The Harried Leisure Class*, p. 71.

40. Publisher's blurb for Scott Ward, Daniel B. Wackman, and Ellen Wartella, *How Children Learn to Buy: The Development of Consumer Information Processing Skills* (Beverly Hills: Sage Publications, 1977).

41. Linder, *The Harried Leisure Class*, p. 123.

42. *Monopoly Capitalism*, p. 122.

43. *Monopoly Capitalism*, p. 119.

44. John K. Galbraith, *The Affluent Society* (Boston: Houghton Mifflin, 1958), p. 160.
45. *Monopoly Capitalism,* p. 125.
46. *Monopoly Capitalism,* p. 141.
47. At the outset of volume II, *Capital,* Marx says: "It is therefore taken for granted here not only that the commodities are sold at their values but also that this takes place under the same conditions throughout. Likewise disregarded therefore are any changes of value which might occur during the movement in circuits." Karl Marx, *Capital,* vol. II, box II (Moscow: Progress Publishers, 1967), p. 26.
48. Marx, *Grundrisse,* pp. 91–92. Emphasis added.
49. Marx, *Grundrisse,* p. 99.
50. Referring to a reported $13 million advertising budget which produced $16 million in drug store sales, expressed in wholesale prices, they say: "Allowing for a handsome profit margin, which of course is added to selling as well as production cost, it seems clear that the cost of production can hardly be more than a minute proportion of even the wholesale price." *Monopoly Capitalism,* p. 119.
51. *Monopoly Capitalism,* p. 118.
52. Cf. A. Aspinall, *Politics and the Press* (London: Home and Van Thal, 1949).
53. The young and conservative Richard T. Ely, writing in 1886, presented a sympathetic and respectful account of the radicalism of the existing union movement in the United States. Richard T. Ely, *The Labour Movement in America* (New York: T. Y. Crowell & Co., 1886).
54. Catherine Stone, "The Origins of Job Structures in the Steel Industry," *Review of Radical Political Economy,* Summer, 1974, pp. 113–173.
55. M. M. Knight, H. E. Barnes, and F. Flugel, *Economic History of Europe* (New York: Houghton Mifflin, 1928).
56. Robert A. Brady, *The Rationalization Movement in German Industry* (Berkeley: University of California Press, 1933) and his *Business as a System of Power* (New York: Columbia University Press, 1943). Also T. Veblen, *The Theory of Business Enterprise* (New York: Viking Press, 1964).
57. Jeremy Bentham and Charles Babbage had publicized the ideas; Taylor and his successors were the experts who applied them. See Harry Braverman, *Labour and Monopoly Capital* (New York: Monthly Review Press, 1974); Catherine Stone, "The Origins of Job Structures in the Steel Industry," and Bryan Palmer, "Class, Conception and Conflict: The Thrust for Efficiency, Managerial Views of Labour and the Working Class Rebellion, 1903–1922," *Review of Radical Political Economy,* Summer, 1974, pp. 31–49.
58. Edwin H. Lewis argues that: "Prior to [the] Civil War, in the United States, the wholesaler was typically the dominant factor in the channel. Small retailers and frequently small manufacturers as well, depended on the wholesaler to carry stocks and to give credit or financial support. Following the Civil War, large scale retailers became the dominant element in the distribution of convenience goods and certain shopping goods. As manufacturers have grown larger and as oligopolistic conditions have prevailed in many industries, the manufacturer has held a position of strength in the channel." Edwin H. Lewis, *Marketing Channels* (New York: McGraw Hill, 1968), p. 163. According to Philip Kotler: "A change began in the 1890's with the growth of national firms and national advertising media. The growth of brand names has been so dramatic that today, in the United States, hardly anything is sold unbranded. Salt is packaged in distinctive manufacturers' containers, oranges are stamped, common nuts and bolts are packaged in cel-

lophane with a distributor's label, and various parts of an automobile—spark plugs, tires, filters—bear visible brand names different from that of the automobile." Philip Kotler, *Marketing Management,* 2nd ed. (Englewood Cliffs, NJ: Prentice Hall, 1972), p. 446.

59. Joseph C. Palamountain, Jr., "Vertical Conflict" in Louis W. Stern, *Distribution Channels: Behavioral Dimensions* (Boston: Houghton Mifflin, 1969), p. 138.

60. Stuart Ewen, in *Captains of Consciousness* (New York: McGraw-Hill, 1976) provides abundant documentation of the purposiveness with which monopoly capitalism used advertising and the infant mass media for this purpose in the period around and following World War I.

61. L. P. Lessing, *Man of High Fidelity: E. H. Armstrong* (Philadelphia: J. B. Lippincott Company, 1956).

62. Why did the cinema, generally conceded to be part of the mass media, not become producers of audience products as part of the systemic bulge of the consciousness industry after 1875? To this, there are several obvious answers. The cinema requires an audience assembled outside the home. It is in the ancient traditional mode of the theatre, arena, assembly, etc. As such it had its own momentum and defined its prime product as the sale of a seat at a particular location and time in relation to the exhibited film. What the advertisers needed—and what capitalism developed as a specialized part of the process of mass producing and mass marketing consumer goods—was a method of mobilizing people to work at being consumers *in their alienated separate homes.* This advertising supported media made possible. The motion picture industry is not so isolated from the marketing process as this explanation might suggest. "Tie-ins" for consumer goods are a normal part of the planning and receipts (often unreported for tax purposes) of the producers, directors, writers, and star performers in theatrical films.

63. David A. Gold, Clarence Y. H. Lo and Erik Olin Wright, "Recent Developments in Marxist Theories of the Capitalist State," *Monthly Review,* October 1975, pp. 29–43, November 1975, pp. 36–52.

64. Guy de Bord, *The Society of the Spectacle* (Detroit: Black and Red, Box 9546, 1970).

65. de Bord, *The Society of the Spectacle,* pp. 6–9.

66. Samir Amin, *Accumulation on a World Scale* (New York: Monthly Review Press, 1974) and "Toward a Structural Crisis of World Capitalism," *Socialist Revolution,* April 1975, pp. 9–44.

67. Herbert I. Schiller, *Mass Communications and American Empire* (New York: Augustus Kelley, 1971), *Communication and Cultural Domination* (White Plains: International Arts and Sciences Press, 1976).

Rejoinder to Graham Murdock [1978]

THE ASSERTION is made that I propose a choice between a theory of economic process and a theory of ideology; that by a "serious oversight" I have "abolished the problem of ideological reproduction entirely"; that I failed "to come to grips with the European/Marxist tradition"; that I don't "settle accounts" with that tradition, but "simply refuse to pay." If these assertions were well-founded, then indeed my paper would have been misconceived and mischievous. I refute these charges but I welcome the opportunity to clarify and to some degree extend my thesis.

Murdock's criticisms reflect the very Eurocentered, class-biased, reductionist tendencies which warranted my paper in the first place. He has a curious inclination to reduce the real and the theoretical frame of [the] paper which hinges on the meaning of "Western Marxism" in its title. I had elaborated this frame as "a blindspot in Marxist theory in the European and Atlantic basin cultures," and "This lag in considering the product of the mass media is more understandable in European (including Eastern European) countries than in North America." By implication the antithesis of "Western Marxism" in this context is Eastern Marxism, specifically Chinese. Neither praise nor blame for Chinese Marxism is implied by my exclusion of it from the object of my attack. Chinese Marxists have not had to deal with the full impact on their population of the Consciousness Industry, powered by that advertising vehicle of Western Capitalism, the commercial mass media of communication. But to expand on this rationale in my article would have been to extend its scope unduly. Chinese communications theory deserves its own analysis. Is it not reductionist and Eurocentered to restrict the grounds for evaluating my paper's argument, as Murdock does, to Europe and within Europe to that part which lies between the Berlin Wall and the Azores? Marxist writings from the Americas are totally ignored, those from the Soviet bloc dealt with separately in Murdock's reply and the implications for the world capitalist order of my frame of reference are denied.

Do I propose a choice between a theory of the economic process and a theory of ideology and opt for the former? Do I reduce the function of the mass media in "relaying" the ideologies which legitimate capitalist relations of production to their function in "completing the economic circuit on which these relations rest," as Murdock charges? If this is how the argu-

---

This article was originally published in *Canadian Journal of Political and Social Theory*, volume 2, number 2, Spring–Summer 1978, pp. 120–127, and is reprinted here with the permission of that journal.

ment of the blindspot paper is perceived, I failed to express myself clearly enough in writing it. The part which advertising, political candidates, institutions and ideological points of view in the guise of the free lunch and advertising messages play in the work set for the audience commodities to do is recognized. It is provisionally concluded that the work which audience members do for advertisers takes place in a household context where familial, individual and other associative needs must be dealt with. I explained how the twin of the household matrix was that at the job, where the ideological lessons are built into the job descriptions, promotions possibilities, and incentive wage arrangements. What I was trying to say regarding the production of ideology boils down to these propositions; that commodities as well as ideas carry ideological meaning, that at the job matrix there is ideological instruction, and [that] at the household matrix, where income-spending decisions are made, the commercial messages or mass media output are to be considered in relation to the role of the audience as a do-it-yourself marketing agent and reproducer of labour power. In the interaction within and between these matrices, consciousness is produced and ideology cultivated—just how we do not yet know. These propositions are intended as a beginning toward understanding how ideology and consciousness are produced, not as disembodied abstract processes in the realm of psychology divorced from the nitty-gritty of daily life, but as part of the latter. We North Americans have had half a century to observe how the monopoly capitalist corporations through demand management via advertising and mass communications dominate culture and produce *mind slavery* (a tendency toward ideological tunnel vision). It would indeed be useful now to see some studies bearing on whether or not the writers in the Western Marxist tradition have dealt with this aspect of monopoly capitalism and, if so, how. The proximate reality imposes this burden of proof on them, not on me alone. When a mythical little boy shouted that the king wore no clothes, it was time for his elders to verify the proposition, and they did.

Is the North American situation a genuine paradigm for monopoly in relation to culture, or is it, as Murdock seems to suggest, that Western Europe is a special case, somehow fixated in nineteenth century production relations and isolated from the effects of monopoly capitalist transnational corporations, advertising, and mass-marketing, mass-communications processes? Murdock concedes a "measure of truth" in my assertion that the North American situation is paradigmatic, but says that I "oversell" it. His argument is curiously like that of Jeremy Tunstall's *The Media are American.*[1] North American media do hold a pivotal place in the world media system, as source of ownership and investment, as exporter of products, technologies and organizational styles, and as exporters of English-language media material. He then argues that "the European situation displays important differences which are reflected in the emphases and preoccupations of Marxist theorising" and that my "failure to acknowledge and come to terms with these departures has produced (my) own blindspots about western Marxism." He does not indicate what these important differences are, but cites "three particularly important omissions" on my part; but first my answer to the immediate question.

I had not considered it necessary to demonstrate that transnational corporations, linked oligopolistically with major domestic monopoly corporations in capitalist countries, form a web of production and merchandising activity for consumer goods and services which spans the capitalist countries and even penetrates the "socialist" economies of Eastern Europe. Their rapid penetration of markets previously less rationalized is the result of strategies involving advertising, advertising agencies, takeovers, influence, aggressive merchandising of consumer goods and services and skillful propaganda for the "free flow of information." This has been analytically described by Schiller, Nordenstreng, Mattelart, and others[2] and it did not occur to me that Marxist readers of my blindspot article would need to be reminded of these facts. Murdock toward the end of his reply confirms what he had tried to deny in charging me with "overselling" my central thesis. "The expansion of consumerism was accompanied by a dampening down of industrial conflict and class struggle. ..." Welcome to the club. The ignominious defeat of the Henry A. Wallace Progressive Party in the 1948 election carried a similar message for North American Marxists who paid attention. Western Europe is not a special case, even if the implicit bourgeois assumptions of its Marxists seem to make it one.

The first of my alleged omissions is that I "drastically underestimate the importance and centrality of the state in contemporary capitalism." Of course I am aware of the lively interests by Marxists in Europe and North America in recent work on the theory of the state. This debate may indeed be central to the elaboration of an overarching theory of the superstructure. But theories of the state are at a level of abstraction remote from the nitty-gritty level where daily the institutions of monopoly capitalism use commodity marketing and the mass media to push capitalist ideology, to absorb the energies of the population in such a way that the old-style class struggle withers away, and conflict takes on the "demographic" character that Murdock uses to describe it (which happens curiously enough to be the specifications advertisers use to identify the audiences which they buy from the media). Is it necessary to regard work on the theory of the state and work on the theory of the audience commodity as mutually exclusive? I had thought each could benefit by work on the other.

True, I was silent as to how my theoretical analysis applied to the peripheral or third world economies. This silence was due, not to my analysis applying only to advanced capitalist economies, as Murdock would have it, but again because I thought the connection to be obvious. Wherever the transnational corporations and their allied advertising agencies, mass media programme and technique peddlers go in the third world or into socialist countries, there the practice of producing audiences as commodities designed to market goods and ideas to themselves goes also. Chile is a good example, and I'm glad Murdock raised it. Schiller and I published an article which pointedly drew the contradiction between the uninterrupted activity of consciousness industry in the interest of capitalist transnational corporations in the daily lives of Chileans and the unrealistic assumption on the part of the Allende government that once basic industry had been nationalized, popular support would carry the Unidad Popular over into the transitional stage to socialism—and we did it before the putsch, not *post-mortem.*[3] I see the world capitalist system as having systemic integrity, albeit of a kind full of contradictions; I do not see it as a series of discrete structures and problems, as Murdock's reply seems to do.

In dealing with the issue of the state, Murdock raises a very important issue, that of class struggle. He says I gave no indication of how it might be accommodated within my framework. He is correct, I did not. The reason was that I didn't know how to do so, not that I considered it irrelevant. So I left the class struggle at the point of the reproduction of labour power—a very unsatisfactory position in which to leave it. Murdock observed, as noted, that the "dampening down of industrial conflict and class struggle . . . accompanied the expansion of consumerism" and this had a lot to do with misperception by the left of the counterculture's potential for revolution. In North America since 1945 there has been an abundance of strikes and lockouts, and a dearth of class struggle. Coincidentally the ideology of workers and their unions has been predominantly economistic—the conflict is over sharing capitalism's goodies. To discern class struggle in North America one must look at minority ethnic groups (Blacks, Chicanos, Puerto Ricans, Native People) in class terms, and in that limited context it has been visible at times. Now that in the post–1968 period, European Marxists must face the same phenomenon, let us pursue the analysis of how ideology is produced in the daily round of life of workers, prominent in which is their experience as unpaid "workers" for advertisers. Perhaps through such analysis the dampened class struggle may be reactivated.

His second charge of "omission" is that I portray the mass media under monopoly capitalism as a smooth and unproblematic process. Of course, if you examine the media and advertising at close range, a dog-eat-dog competition for power and profit is evident. Monopoly corporations continuously struggle to create "new" services (cable TV originated in [the] western United States in the late 1940s), and the struggles between terrestrial common carriers, cable companies and aerospace giant corporations pushing satellites displayed a tug-of-war for favour from the state to give just one example. In the area of software, a daily and weekly struggle characterizes the actual audience production scene. I have analyzed and written about these struggles for 30 years. More recently others (William Melody, Herbert Schiller, Manley Irwin, et al.) have joined in this work. But my blindspot article was intended to focus on theory, not industry structure and policy; and the *systemic* characteristics were what I emphasized, at a sacrifice of detailed authenticity which would have blown the paper to the dimensions of a book. I contend that the enterprise "trees" do constitute a smoothly functioning monopoly capitalist "forest" because of and despite their intra-mural conflicts.

Have I underplayed the "independent role" of content in reproducing dominant ideologies? Is it to underplay the secondary role of the mass media to emphasize the primary role, neglected in the literature of the past century? Nevertheless I was and am dissatisfied with my treatment of the dialectical relation of media "content" to "advertising." I use quotes around the words to emphasize that they have no existence separate from each other. Humphrey McQueen, quite independently, came to the same conclusion:

> To make sense of Australia's media monopolies, it is essential to get the relationship between the media and advertising the right way round: commercial mass media are not news and features backed up by advertising; on the contrary, *the commercial mass media are advertisements which carry news, features and entertainment in order to capture audiences for the advertisers.* ... It is a complete mistake to analyse the relationship between media and advertising by supposing that the media's prime function is to sell advertised products to audiences. On the contrary, the media's job is to sell audiences to advertisers.[4] (Emphasis in original)

Within a given programme or newspaper or magazine, there is an integration of style and content between the ostensibly "advertising" and "non-advertising" content. Both must meet the advertisers' standards of what is entertaining, informative, and provocative. Murdock emphasizes that I ignored cinema, popular music, comic books and popular fiction. Superficially, as Murdock says, it seems that selling audiences to advertisers is not the primary raison d'être of these media. But, as he must know, their "content" is cross-marketed between themselves, and between themselves and the mass media: stories, stars, songs, and films are passed from one to another medium and there cross-blended with the dictates of advertisers. For an axiom of the trade is that if it will sell as a paperback or song it will work as [a] lure for the commercial mass media. So their apparent independence is illusory within the monopoly capitalist system.

I am accused of abolishing the problem of ideological reproduction entirely. In reality what I have abolished is the simplistic model of *direct* manipulation by the state or the government propaganda ministry. This I have done in the pursuit of a more realistic if more complex and presently obscure process by which consciousness industry produces ideology. In this connection, further consideration of the characteristics of the audience as commodity produces a provocative and possibly fruitful question, which I will put in the form of a conundrum: What mode of work is it which has the following characteristics: One is born into it and stays in it from infancy to the old folks' home; one is not consulted as to the precise work to be done tomorrow; work tasks are presented and done; and lastly, one is unpaid? Answer? Slavery? Yes, and the audience too? Is it not correct, as a matter of political economy, to refer to a category of work (not to all individual audience members any more than to all slaves) as "mind slaves"? Even before television, bourgeois sociologists Paul F. Lazarsfeld and Robert Merton concluded that the mass media audiences were systemically subject to "dysfunctional narcotization."[5]

In support of the charge that I have underplayed the independent role of the content in reproducing relations of production, Murdock says that I have committed a serious oversight. "Materialist analysis needs to begin by recognizing that although integrated into the economic base, mass communications are also part of the superstructure, and that they therefore play a double role in reproducing capitalist relations of production." I refer him to my paper:

> If this analytical sketch is valid, serious problems for Marxist theory emerge. Among them is the apparent fact that while the superstructure is not ordinarily thought of as being itself engaged in infrastructural productive activity, the mass media of communications are simultaneously in the superstructure *and* engaged indispensably in the last stage of infrastructural production where demand is produced and satisfied by purchases of consumer goods. (Emphasis in original)

And I later refer to "the implications of this 'principal and decisive' integration of superstructure and base which reality presents."

It was beyond the scope of my paper to try to explain *why* there has been a Western Marxist blindspot, to which question Murdock devotes the last five pages of his reply. No doubt this question should be raised and answered. But the purpose of my paper was to establish a *prima facie* case that such a blindspot does exist. Readers of his reply and my rejoinder, and possibly other replies and further rejoinders, will determine whether I have succeeded or not. Because Murdock has raised the why question, I will close this rejoinder by volunteering what might be some clues to the answer. Doubtless the factors which he mentions played a part in producing the blindspot—superstructural domination via propaganda management by the fascist states; and the "ossification" of Soviet Marxism. But I suggest that the persistence of usually implicit bourgeois class conceptions of "Culture," "Science," "Technology," and hierarchical bureaucratic organizational structures are to be found endemic amongst Western Marxists, and that these preconceptions have produced the blindspot regarding consciousness industry and ideology. Hence the need to challenge and re-examine the European tradition through a perspective which owes much to the Chinese experience.[6] My view is that Marxism at bottom arises from historical dialectical materialism and class struggle through political economy. It is what Murdock calls the "culturalist" legacy of Western Marxism which stands suspect of being deficient in regard to such terms. I suggest that the way to a Marxist theory of how ideology is produced by monopoly capitalism is to use an historical, materialist, dialectical method always seeking the reality of class struggle, and the terms will reflect political, economic and psychological aspects of the process. Finally, I do not believe the first obligation of Western Marxism to be to speak "to the real theoretical silences within classical Marxism." It smacks of static abstractions. I believe the first obligation of Marxist theorists is to use the obvious and trusted tools to analyze and predict the development of modern monopoly capitalism.

Notes to "Rejoinder to Graham Murdock"

1. Jeremy Tunstall, *The Media Are American* (New York: Columbia University Press, 1977).

2. Herbert I. Schiller, *Mass Communication and American Empire* (Boston: Beacon Press, 1971); *The Mind Managers* (Boston: Beacon Press, 1972); *Communication and Cultural Domination* (New York: International Arts and Sciences Press, 1976); Kaarle Nordenstreng and Tapio Varis, *Television Traffic: A One Way Street?* (Paris: UNESCO, 1974); Richard J. Barnett and Ronald E. Muller, *Global Reach* (New York: Simon and

Schuster, 1974); A. Mattelart and A. Dorfman, *How to Read Donald Duck: Imperialist Ideology in the Disney Comic* (New York: International General, 1975).

3. Herbert I. Schiller and Dallas W. Smythe, "Chile: An End to Cultural Colonialism?" *Society*, 1972, vol. 9, no. 5, pp. 35–39, 61.

4. Humphrey McQueen, *Australia's Media Monopolies* (Camberwell: Victoria, Australia, 3124; Widescope, P.O. Box 339) 1977, pp. 10–11.

5. Paul F. Lazarsfeld and Robert K. Merton, "Mass Communications, Popular Taste and Organized Social Action," in L. Bryson (ed.), *The Communication of Ideas* (New York: Cooper Square Publishers, 1948, 1964).

6. Charles Bettelheim, *Class Struggle in the USSR. First Period: 1917–1923* (New York: Monthly Review Press, 1976).

16

"Canada has not taken the necessary steps to achieve cultural autonomy because we lack the political will to do so"

EDITOR'S NOTE: In "Culture, Communication 'Technology,' and Canadian Policy," Dallas Smythe applies many of his ideas to the specific case of Canada. Because it is an *industrialized Western* country dominated for the most part by United States capital and policy, Canada stands in an unusual position among the world's nations. Yet it shares with many undeveloped dependent colonies an absence of autonomy that renders it impotent in the face of global politics and currents of change.

With roots in Canada, Smythe never let his vision stray too far from that country, whatever his interests happened to be at any point in time. A few examples from his vast body of work demonstrate this focus. In the late 1950s, he worked closely with the Royal Commission on Broadcasting to survey programming on Canadian radio and television stations. This research followed his pioneering studies of television content in the United States. In the mid-1960s, Smythe prepared a monograph, *The Citizen and the Mass Media of Communications,* for the Canadian Citizenship Council. Five years later, he carried out the first of many studies for the Department of Communications in Ottawa; he called it *The Relevance of United States Telecommunications Experience to the Canadian Situation.* In the mid-1970s, he also authored *A Study of Saskatchewan Telecommunications.* With William Melody in 1985, Smythe wrote another comparative study for the Department of Communications, *Factors Affecting the Canadian and U.S. Spectrum Management Processes.* The list would be incomplete without *Dependency*

Road: Communications, Capitalism, Consciousness, and Canada, Smythe's book, published in 1981. In its introduction, he described it as "a study of the process by which people organized in the capitalist system produced a country called Canada as a dependency of the United States, the center of the core of the capitalist system. [...] Canada is effectively part of the United States core of monopoly capitalism."

In the paper, published here for the first time in English, Smythe picks up on several themes introduced in *Dependency Road.* "[W]e are simultaneously the most dependent on the United States of all capitalistically advanced countries, and an American neocolony among many Third World neocolonies," he writes. Smythe responds to critics who faulted his book for amounting to economic determinism because (they said) it gave the impression that consciousness industry (CI) is irresistible. "On the contrary," Smythe replies, "it is analysis of a dialectical struggle in which CI is resisted by people and their older institutions," although he concedes that "in reality CI now is clearly the stronger side."

Smythe points out that in Canada, "frequent royal commissions and government policy statements keep telling us that we need to do certain things in order to establish our elusive identity." But "Canada has not taken the necessary steps to achieve cultural autonomy because we lack the political will to do so, with the costs it would entail." As Smythe analyzes the problem, "The split between our Canadian need for cultural autonomy and our policy and actions which move us to greater dependence on foreign TNCs is currently bound up with the illusion that 'high technology' and the law of comparative advantage will magically confer autonomy on us. In fact they will have the opposite effect."

For Smythe, there are only two possible courses that respond to Canada's schizophrenia. One leads Canada into complete integration with the United States—"a realistic if unattractive option." The other entails a social policy working toward Canada's disassociation and withdrawal from the United States—"in principle realistic" but "immensely difficult." Smythe sees no third option because "the record of the past century shows that piecemeal reform doesn't achieve its professed objectives." Although Smythe recognizes that it may be "too late for the autonomy course to succeed," he argues that it is not too late to *try* to make it happen.

"Culture, Communication 'Technology,' and Canadian Policy" was delivered as the Southam Lecture at the 1986 meeting of the Canadian

Communication Association. Smythe told me that "the Southams own this big chain of newspapers in Canada, and they endowed a lecture, and by a nice irony I was invited to give it. [...] I didn't get any fee out of it, but at least they paid my expenses." Smythe explained to me that he wrote and delivered the paper "in white heat." There was a "large French Canadian component to the meeting in Winnipeg where I delivered it, and, boy, did it get an enthusiastic response." The paper was subsequently published in a French-language journal. Smythe felt that this paper succinctly tied together what he had to say about Canada.

Culture, Communication "Technology," and Canadian Policy

[The Southam Lecture, Canadian Communication Association, Winnipeg, June 6, 1986]

BECAUSE LIFE AND CHANGE are processes of contradictions in every thing and person, it is necessary, if we want to have any identity, to be aware of what are the principal contradictions in each set of relationships. In Canada our principal contradiction in relation to our identity is that of the interests of the Canadian people vs. transnational capital. In the global society, the principal contradiction is between people, especially in the Third World, and transnational capital. In both, transnational capital is now the dominant aspect of the contradictions. For Canada the two are linked by the fact that we are simultaneously the most dependent on the United States of all capitalistically advanced countries, and an American neocolony among many Third World neocolonies.

My argument is that we serve our struggle for autonomy best by cultivating our own values. But we should recognize that our politico-economic structures and policies will either weaken or strengthen us in that struggle for autonomy. These structures and policies include the laws and practices of our governments, our private sector, the arts, and our personal and informal associational activities. Obviously, in this paper, it is impossible to analyze all the relevant relationships. But I will try to sharpen a few analytical tools, and single out some salient policy directions and alternatives.

"Culture" is one of a cluster of related concepts including: "art," "ideology" and "consciousness." Most basic of these is consciousness. It is "awareness of the realities of existence. Without it there can be no knowledge," as the Buddhists tell us. And consciousness is not only individual, it is collective, where consensual validation creates group consciousness and confirms a view of reality for a people.

One dimension of consciousness is ideology, which as Tran Van Dinh says, "is a concentrated, dynamic, directional manifestation of consciousness." For our indigenous people, ideology is the "Great Spirit." And since civilization brought us social classes, ideology is the system of values with which people either support or attack a particular class-dominated social system. Here is an example of an ideology:

1. Personal possessiveness is essential to human beings. Private property is essential in a political system.
2. The main goal of life is to consume commodities and services.
3. Freedom and conflict are individual, not collective matters.
4. Commodities and services do not educate us or form our values; they just contribute to our comfort and pleasure.
5. A conflict of ideas need not be resolved. Every person to his/her own taste.
6. It is possible and desirable to be neutral or objective while working in the mass media, educational institutions, government and business. It is not, as Mark Twain put it, a question of "Who are you neutral against?"
7. And most important, "You can't change human nature." The status quo is timeless.

To what politico-economic system does this ideology belong? Or, reverse those seven propositions and you have most of the elements of another ideology. This one is survival-oriented in ecological terms for us, human animals, on a planet which we are now in imminent danger of destroying through nuclear war and through the economic systems which make nuclear war probable and preparation for it profitable.

Where does ideology come from? Not from outer space, or great men or great ideas—but from human experience in trying to solve human problems. It can be a powerful material force, as Marcos, Duvalier, and the Shah of Iran learned.

The usual definition of "culture" in civilized societies is those arts which the ruling classes have favoured. By art, I mean as the *Encyclopedia Britannica* puts it: "the general principles of any branch of learning or any developed craft." Art then spans every craft from poetry to plumbing. Validating this broad span of crafts is the fact that under Western patent law, a patent is granted for improvement in the "state of the art," whatever it may deal with. But "culture" is often synonymous with "high culture." In the past four centuries in Europe, "high culture" became the "fine arts" (painting, sculpture, music, poetry, and architecture, with dance, theatre, opera and prose literature sometimes added). These were the survivors in a process of debates and state-sponsorship of schools in which all the arts of ancient and modern times were contenders. Thus, fencing, alchemy, astronomy, astrology, transportation and agricultural arts were winnowed out in the process. Three ideological propositions came to permeate our fine arts and later other arts (e.g., sports): (1) People and every thing were defined as natural systems which worked by analogy to machines; hence technique became central, and, being defined as natural, technique was value-free. (2) The arts, being focussed on technique, should be apolitical; hence art-for-art's sake. Technique, reduced to its rudimentary structures, provided a boundless vista for projecting feeling and "sensibilities" by art "consumers." (3) Individualism, private property, competition and market organization became essential to the arts. Competition bred "geniuses" and the monopoly power of the "star system." The commodification of the product of artists separated them from their consumers by markets. Aesthetics became less (if ever) a set of principles used by creative artists and more a buyers' guide by which elite patrons rationalized their tastes. The illusion that the values of the high culture were timeless and universal make them what national governments consider "a potent propaganda weapon of the Cold War."[1] Whatever the motives of the creative artists, high culture is loaded with ideological, that is, political consequences.

Down to the last quarter of the 19th century, "high culture" co-existed with the arts (in the general sense of that term) of the lower classes. Lower class arts have several names: "folk," "ethnic," "indigenous," "traditional," etc. There was direct borrowing between artists working in "high culture" and "lower class" art. And, in contrast with the present, the arts—fine and all the rest—had not been incorporated into mass production of culture.

From the advent of Renaissance-based "high culture" the various arts have been regarded by the ascending ruling classes as areas separate from each other, even to be treated as discrete spatially. Some European scholars have recently suggested that culture does not define a subject area of art as we have been accustomed to believe, but rather is an *aspect* of *all* areas. Culture, they say, is the aspect of enjoying the effort to meet needs. Moreover, they insist this creative effort to meet needs must be the immediate end itself. That is to say that the end to be pursued must be defined by the groups and persons who make that creative, enjoyable effort. To make the effort because of the artists' dependency is to turn it into a form of slavery.[2] The proposition that culture is the enjoyment of the effort to meet individually and socially determined needs helps us understand workers' resistance to scientific management and automation, and also the creativity in national liberation struggles as in Nicaragua, Mozambique, etc.

I turn now to mass culture, in which all the arts—fine and other—are applied in increasingly scientific ways to the mass production and mass marketing of consumer goods and services. Consciousness Industry (hereafter CI) forms this output with the unique imprint of the directing set of institutions: the giant transnational corporations—the Fortune 400 (hereafter TNCs). I need not remind you that Canada's economy is dominated by branch plants of these TNCs and has been for many decades. The dominance of giant monopolistic corporations in the U.S. is greatest in the most dynamic sector: communications, transportation, and public utilities. Here, one-fourth of one percent of the firms hold 88 percent of total assets in that sector. Next most monopolized is manufacturing, where one-fifth of one percent of the firms hold 73 percent of sector assets.[3]

How does CI relate to consciousness and ideology? Consider the mass media, which are its leading edge. The news in the media is substantially managed—through corporate and government press releases, off-the-record briefings, the timing of government actions to manipulate public opinion (a bombing raid on Libya is timed for the eve of a congressional vote on Reagan's Nicaragua policy) and through TV and radio addresses by our leaders. CI also produces our consumer goods and services. These products in different ways are teaching machines, forming our consciousness. Their appeal to sensuous, personal and technical pleasure pervades our marketing system. With their packaging and point of sale advertising, these products cultivate individual possessiveness and associated ideology.

The principal product of the advertiser-supported mass media is audience-power. Though there had been newspapers and periodicals before the last quarter of the 19th century, there were no *mass* circulation media until CI created them then. The mass media produce audience power and advertisers buy it because it does an essential service for CI. It performs the mass distribution of mass produced commodities. The results of audience-power at work are, first, that audience members market consumer goods and services to themselves. Second, they learn to vote for one candidate or public issue rather than another in the political arena. The difference between the first and second result gets increasingly blurred as political candidates and issues are marketed with the same techniques as other commodities. And, third, audience members learn, generation after generation, belief in the ideology of capitalism. Just how audience members reach these results is very unclear and needs research—research which economists (neoclassical and Marxist) have not yet begun to do. Here I can only say that audience-power is a very peculiar kind of commodity. When labour-power is produced and used in what is usually regarded as production and trade, the worker gets paid something for his/her labour. The exceptions where productive work is done and is not paid for are: audience-power at work—probably more than half by women—and work performed in and around the home, again mostly by women. (An oral footnote here: the relevance of understanding audience-power to the women's movement seems so great that I wonder why the women's movement has failed to take it seriously.) And the third exception is slavery.

What is the relation of the advertising to the ostensibly non-advertising component of the mass media? It is no secret that the policy of media enterprises on the so-called program or news content is a prime concern of advertisers. Media enterprises frame their broadcast "program" policy or print "editorial" policy to produce the kind of audiences (as measured by their demographics and psychographics) which they know advertisers will want to buy. Indeed in the 1950s and 1960s major TNCs told the media and writers: "In general, the moral code of the characters in our dramas will be more or less synonymous with the moral code of the bulk of the American middle-class. ... There will be no material that may give offense either directly or by inference to any...organizations, institutions, residents of any state or section of the country, or a commercial organization of any sort. ... There will be no material for or against sharply drawn national or regional controversial issues. ... Where it seems fitting, the characters should reflect recognition and acceptance of the world situation in their thoughts and actions, although in dealing with war, our writers should minimize the 'horror' aspects. ... Men in uniform shall not be cast as heavy villains or portrayed as engaging in any criminal activity. There will be no material on any of our programs which could in any way further the concept of business as cold, ruthless and lacking all sentiment or spiritual motivation."[4] Since then the guidance has been less strident but similar. And as Applebaum-Hébert said:

> Without any direct intervention by sponsors in production or programming decisions, producers make programs and broadcasters schedule them with a view to achieving the real purpose of commercial broadcasting—namely, the delivery of large audiences to paying advertisers.[5]

The conclusion is inescapable that there is no real separation of the advertisements from what lies between them. The commercial mass media product is *entirely* advertising.

Some have criticized my *Dependency Road* analysis as being economic determinism, suggesting that it shows CI as irresistible. On the contrary, it is analysis of a dialectical struggle in which CI is resisted by people and their older institutions. The dominant side today is that of capital, working through CI. But while alienated from each other by the ruling ideology, people daily resist CI as individuals, as members of families, labour unions, churches, political parties, and government (most often local government, as when nuclear free zones are proclaimed). My analysis argues that this popular resistance has the potential to take back the hegemony which CI seized over the past century. But in reality CI now is clearly the stronger side.

It helps to grasp the size of the reorganization of policies and structures, which is required to ask: "Who are the players in CI?" The leading edge is the advertising/market research agencies plus the mass media. Backing them are the educational system, photography and commercial art. In the next rank are professional and pre-professional sports, comic books, parlor games (such as Monopoly), recorded music, tourism, restaurants, hotels and transportation. In the next rank are the other consumer goods industries—the Homogenous Package Goods (soap, soft drinks, etc.) and the consumer durables (such as household appliances, motorcycles and automobiles). As backdrop for CI are the industries which bind together the whole Monopoly Capitalist system: the Military-Industrial Complex, telecommunications, banks, insurance, finance, real estate, the gambling industry, and crime, both organized and unorganized.

How are the arts related to CI? Dialectically. Suppose a TNC decides to create a fast food chain. It employs people from dozens of arts, ranging from architects to clowns (to publicize the chain near elementary schools). All of these artists are constrained by policies scientifically determined to be most efficient—productive of highest profit. And while the individual artist working in mass culture production may struggle against capital, the latter is the principal aspect of the contradiction.

Where does Canada's national policy stand on culture and "technology"? The extent to which a country has autonomy may be judged by whether it *practices* a common body of culture as expressed in its values, artifacts, institutions and policies. I call this the *cultural realism* of a country. It gives coherence to the people's consciousness. When a country's cultural realism is highly developed (as in Sweden), it doesn't need royal commissions to assert the need for cultural identity: it already has it. In Canada frequent royal commissions and government policy statements keep telling us that we need to do certain things in order to establish our elusive identity. Why don't we have an identity?

Our population contains streams of cultural realism from many sources: the conquered cultures of our indigenous peoples; the dominant elite culture from Britain; the Francophone culture from France; substantial (and largely folk) streams from other European countries, from Asia, and from Central and South America. They could have been and still could be nurtured together to create a unique and vibrant Canadian cultural identity. To accomplish this would have required a conscious national policy. A variety of measures, which I call collectively a "cultural screen" would have been used to protect a small country's cultural realism. Sometimes a language barrier is its anchor, as in Finland and Quebec. To counter the homogenizing effect of anglophone mass culture, much more would be needed. A wide range of protective measures to shield pursuit of unique Canadian values by writers, performers, and producers has been available for the print media, TV, and motion pictures, but never implemented.[6] Why not?

In order for a country to develop materially, capital is needed for producers' goods. Capital can be obtained in two ways. The most culturally secure source is savings from current income, enforced on its citizens and their domestically owned corporations. Or, it can be obtained from external sources, and again there are two ways. Capital can be borrowed from abroad, and when the loans are repaid, cultural security is possible. Alternatively, foreign capital can be invited to come in and to own the enterprises it builds. This is the route taken by the Canadian ruling class and the result is that our economic and political institutions have policies determined by the TNCs. As Trudeau said in 1968, Canada is no more independent of the United States than is Poland of the Soviet Union. We both have 10 percent independence.[7]

After our dependency on foreign owners was established, the Aird Royal Commission in 1928 was the first of a long line of commissions to search for our non-existent national identity and propose measures to protect its remaining fragments. These commissions were composed of well-intentioned people. But they focussed their concern unduly on the politically safe area of high culture and tended to ignore both the threat to Canadian autonomy posed by CI and the track record of other medium-sized countries which have successfully used cultural screens to protect their cultural autonomy. The history of the CBC validates this analysis. Following the Aird Commission's recommendation of a publicly owned broadcasting system, the struggle led by the Canadian Radio League from 1930 to 1936 came closer than any other Canadian movement to erecting a pivotal element in a Canadian cultural screen against the onslaught of CI. Canada should be proud of it and of the CBC down to the end of World War II. Then, with the advent of TV and private cable systems, the roof fell in. What was the flaw in the movement for the CBC?

Dr. Augustin Frigon was a member of the Aird Commission and he argued that "you cannot mix up the interests of the man who wants to make money out of the equipment and the man who wants to render service to his country."[8] Our policy was to try to mix those contradictory interests. While seemingly facing takeover by the public system, the private broadcasters never gave up. Aided by the fact that the CBC was forced to seek advertising support, CI appears to have won their objective to have a commercially-oriented Canadian broadcasting system.

Canada has not taken the necessary steps to achieve cultural autonomy because we lack the political will to do so, with the costs it would entail. We have a severe if not terminal case of political schizophrenia! I offer a recent example. The Applebaum-Hébert report (1982) made eleven proposals aimed to inhibit commercial radio-TV from further damaging Canadian cultural autonomy. Prominent on that list was a proposed new Broadcasting Act. That Act would establish total political independence for the CRTC from the end-runs from the private sector to the government, which have eroded the CBC and CRTC. It would mandate the CRTC to do what it already had the responsibility to do: enforce license obligations by private stations to serve the public. The new Act would direct the CRTC to require private stations to allocate substantial proportions of time and gross revenues to new Canadian productions; and to require cable operators to increase the proportions of Canadian programs on their several tiers; to require cable operators to commit significant proportions of gross revenues to facilities and programming of community channels, etc. That was in 1982.

But the CRTC's policy and actions reveal it as an agency devoted to advancing the interests of CI and to opposing steps like those proposed by Applebaum-Hébert. Under its statute, the CRTC is supposed to take an arm's length relationship with both the private businesses and the CBC, to which it grants licenses, and the groups representing the public interest. A review of the CRTC's posture and actions since 1984, however, shows it as maximally identified with the private sector and distanced from the latter groups. We are always told that the reason U.S. broadcast programs must be imported is that Canadian broadcasters cannot afford to produce programs to compete with them. Yet private broadcasting in Canada is fabulously profitable. André Bureau, as chair of the CRTC, told the Montreal Association of Financial Analysts recently that by comparison with other sectors of the economy, it did "extremely well." The average return on investment of private TV broadcasters, year after year, is about 50 percent per annum, for private radio, about 40 percent, and for cable more than 20 percent. It is a familiar fact, noted by the Fowler Commissions of 1956 and 1965, and the Special Senate Committee in 1970. But, as Bureau told the financial analysts, "Broadcasting and telecommunications must be seen and treated as *industries* [sic] like any other and not simply as cultural forces or vehicles." Shortly after moving to the chair of the CRTC from the private sector, Bureau told the Broadcast Executives Society (8 March 1984) the CRTC's first priority is the "financial viability of proposed undertakings," in other words, protecting and increasing its profitability. Accordingly, it recently proposed regulations which would cut out any limits on advertising on private AM broadcasting, and loosen limits on FM advertising (19 March 1986). Its second priority is to take a "supervisory," not a regulatory approach, to the industry—following Washington's lead where it is called "deregulation." Priority 3 is "flexibility in aiding the industry to respond to changes in technology, the economy, or public taste." Lest anyone suspect that an arm's length relationship still exists, Bureau assured the cable industry, "The Commission has been swift to act when structural changes have been necessary...changes which the market told us were needed." Indeed, he boasted, "we are moving to respond as quickly as possible to your concerns; often even before you formally make them known to us" (9 April 1985). Priority 4, Bureau calls "strategic planning" by the private broadcasting industry. Here is where the CRTC deals with the issues involved in Canadian content rules. "Strategic planning" means that the CRTC has invited the industry to formulate an agenda of proposals which are then informally discussed, jointly with the CRTC. Out of such meetings come CRTC proposals for formal hearings. Bureau describes these sessions as "executive brainstorms." To further assure the licensees they could trust the CRTC, they were told, "Insisting on knowing where the industry wants to go will also help us determine our own priorities and get the structures in place. ..."

It would be wrong to think that the CRTC is totally indifferent to the public, simply because its first four priorities are the welfare of the industry. The concerns of the public are the fifth and last priority of the CRTC. However, the agency's posture toward them is passive and formal. Mr. Bureau speaks of "*concerns* coming *from the public*" and underlines the words. There is no mention of "brainstorming," informally, with Canada's creative artists (unions or associations) in connection with Canadian content. And, as if in an afterthought, Bureau warns the industry: "However, the objectives and solutions we have described cannot be examined in a vacuum. Political realities and government objectives must also be brought to bear." He confirms the CRTC role by saying, "The challenge for all of us is indeed significant, but with mutual understanding and concentrated planning, it is certain that your successes will be maximized."[9] What about the CBC? In this context the CRTC's relationship to the CBC seems to be at arm's length in contrast to its cozy relationship to the private sector. To discuss the CBC's present and potential cultural role would require another speech.

The split between our Canadian need for cultural autonomy and our policy and actions which move us to greater dependence on foreign TNCs is currently bound up with the illusion that "high technology" and the law of comparative advantage will magically confer autonomy on us. In fact they will have the opposite effect. The establishment uses the term "technology" as a talisman as if it referred to some autonomous, exogenous force to which people must submit. While this determinist notion, "technology," is a myth, there is a kernel of fact buried in it, namely, the art of designing, producing and using tools and machines. The present notion of "technology" indeed originated with the TNCs which in the last quarter of the 19th century combined capital, science, engineering, bureaucracy, ideology and propaganda to create a one-word slogan more compelling than the terms modern industrialism, or monopoly capitalism. Two Canadians (Harold Innis and Marshall McLuhan), helped popularize the myth. E. G. Mesthene, of Harvard's Program on Technology, defines technology as "the organization of knowledge for practical purposes. ..."[10] Federal and provincial government policies push "high technology" as an export to help us to autonomy. This is a delusion which assumes that Canada can compete with the U.S., Japan, etc. in the world market. This delusion rests on the supposed advantages of free trade, or the law of comparative advantage. According to it, specialization according to the relative cost of using resources in every country results in the most efficient division of labour possible for world-wide markets. The key word is "efficient," meaning that it results in the largest possible profit. But profit for whom? Profit for those enterprises and countries which are major players in world markets. But when Britain was accumulating the capital and other resources for the development of the factory system (from the 15th to mid-19th centuries), it practiced the opposite of free trade. Its Mercantile regulations were an effective screen to protect its cultural realism. Only when Britain's economic and military might gave it monopoly power for its basic industries in the world market, about the middle of the 19th century, did it talk about the law of comparative advantage. And weaker countries (such as Britain before then, and Japan until recently) always defy it and erect economic and cultural screens if they hope to reach autonomy.

Also closely related to the myth of "technology" is the "Information Age" slogan. This refers to the application of sophisticated electronics, arts and scientific management to both the production and consumption "fronts" on which people confront capitalism. Through it, information is now commodified in a new way: as a resource input into the production system. Information age policy follows Charles Babbage's 1832 dictum for the expansion of capital, the sense of which was: Increase profits by breaking down traditional jobs and substituting machines for their simpler, repetitive functions. Today, the TNC's practice of it has two targets. On the production front, it is to substitute machines for people. It does this by eliminating paperwork and workers up to and including the level of executives (and their staffs) at branch plant levels. On this front complete automation (including robotic factories) is the goal. On the consumption front, the target is to create a new market structure resting on new equipment in the home—to encompass "entertainment" plus banking, home security, etc. On both fronts its effects are to increase the wealth of the few at the cost of the many.

But this Information Age offensive involves a dialectical process of struggle. On the production front, people resist through unions, political parties, spontaneous demonstrations and sabotage. And on the consumption front, the drive of monopoly capitalism collides with the results of its successes on the production front. With unemployment, lower incomes and inflation in the cost of living, middle class, white collar and blue collar people simply do not have the buying power to buy the "wired city" electronic goodies. Thus in the United States in the six months ending in March 1986, videotex service was stopped by the Knight Ridder firm to 20,000 subscribers, the Times-Mirror to 3,000, and Centel terminated 1,000. Why? The stated reason was lack of consumer interest. Simultaneously sales of home computers have fallen.

Organizationally, the "Information Age" is causing mergers in industry and trade sectors, with lay-offs of redundant executives and professionals. It means further convergence of giant TNCs which previously worked different markets, e.g., telecommunications by the Bell companies and computers by IBM, et al. Now they are rivals in the same market; the teleprocessing of information, and further mergers (with resulting lay-offs) will come. A simultaneous merger process in advertising agencies signals the effect of the Information Age on CI. Already in 1985 the ten largest

U.S. agencies, with about $27 billion in advertising billings, accounted for nearly 17 percent of the world total billings of $162 billion. On 12 May 1986, *Time* reported that "Merger mania is turning Madison Avenue agencies into mega-shops with clients in almost every business and bases in every world market" with three huge mergers in the preceding month. One of these, combining BBDO International with two smaller agencies, produced a super-agency with nearly $5 billion in billings—the world's largest agency. Among the reasons given is "the increasing international needs of advertisers. As U.S. businesses seek a stronger foothold in foreign markets, the agencies are under pressure to offer these clients full-service global marketing operations." At the same time, mergers among investment bankers and stock brokerage firms presage further TNC integration, which is currently diminishing the scope for Canadian-owned financial institutions.

A spin-off from the slogan of free trade, which is particularly relevant to Canada's communication and cultural policy, is the "free flow of information." Like its cousin, "free trade," the free flow of information policy assumes that in the real world there is substantially perfect competition. Because monopoly is more common than competition in both trade and information exchange, both slogans are used by the dominant empire to justify its market control. In the peak period of British empire, the globe-circling Cables and Wireless submarine cables linked with the Reuters News Agency, and the similar partnership between French cables and the Havas News Agency, provided a "free flow of information" essential to the hegemony in global markets enjoyed by their empires. Shortly before World War II, the head of the Associated Press and the Chairman of the Federal Communications Commission attacked those monopolies of the flow of information. As Kent Cooper, President of the AP, put it:

> In precluding the Associated Press from disseminating news abroad, Reuters and Havas served three purposes: (1) they kept out Associated Press competition; (2) they were free to present American news disparagingly to the United States if they presented it at all; (3) they could present news of their own countries most favorably and without it being contradicted. ... This was done by reporting great advances at home in English and French civilizations, the benefits of which would, of course, be bestowed on the world.[11]

These are among the arguments that Third World countries today use against U.S. dominated free flow of information. Put simply, free trade and free flow of information are like one-way streets down which you are free to drive bulldozers, if you have them.

What can Canada do in this situation? About the end of World War I, when Canada was emerging from British colonial status, it could have played off British as against U.S. influence to achieve a modest national autonomy, analogous to that of Finland. Our ruling class, however, from the beginning has preferred to manage Canada as compradors, serving colonial masters. Therefore, it increasingly shifted our dependency to the United States after 1918. What are our broad alternatives, culturally, politically, economically now? Looked at logically, there seem to be two viable alternatives, though they are starkly different. The first alternative is to negotiate with the United States to accept ten or twelve new states into its Union. Then, like California or Oregon, we could continue to have our distinctive flags, and the limited autonomy enjoyed by the several states. If effected, this union would offer material advantages, over time. It is a realistic if unattractive option.

The alternative would be to make the effort necessary to gain and maintain a modest but substantial Canadian autonomy in cultural, political and economic terms. This alternative might have as a first step the analysis of the nature of our predicament and possible policies to cure it. Would it be possible that people in the cultural/communication area might take the initiative? We might explore and develop the enormous potential of our diverse peoples for enjoying the act of meeting our needs of all kinds. Would Canadians then make the effort needed to get a working consensus on strategies and tactics to be persuaded? Even this preliminary stage might free us from the terrible inferiority complex which prevents us from being self-reliant and self-sufficient—a complex which will only be cured when the prospect of being a star in Hollywood or New York (or Harvard or Chicago) no longer hypnotizes us. If such a cultural program were to be viable, it would have to be based on a progressive withdrawal from our dependence on the U.S. economic system. We would have to abandon the fantasy that our success depends on our subsidized private sector's entries in the "high technology" sweepstakes in competition with the U.S., Japan, et al. We would have to buy out our present branch plants, progressively. We would control our own industries, paying for them through our own savings or through borrowing abroad—but never through allowing new direct foreign investment. We would take back control of our own military, as well as our own communications institutions. We would withdraw from Norad and NATO and pursue a foreign policy designed by Canadians for Canadians. We would preserve and extend our public sector, and its expenditures would serve Canadian interests. In short, we would adjust our national goals to realistic possibilities. But it would be naive and foolhardy to begin such a planning process (much less to put it into effect) without facing the fact that it would cost us heavily in material standards of life during the transition stage, and perhaps later. What is involved is a basic redirecting of government and private sector policy. It would require reorganization of structures which we have come to take for granted over the past century. While in principle realistic, this alternative would be immensely difficult. Of course, the development of public opinion to support such a social reorganization is a necessary basis for accomplishing it. The policy of Canadian mass media has served CI to bring us to our present politically schizophrenic condition. And I wonder how the ideology of our mass media now relates to a policy which would make Canada modestly autonomous. For example, the leading editorial in the *Vancouver Sun*, 3 June 1986, "Shooting oneself in the head," criticized the Mulroney government's use of a tariff on books and periodicals as being like "committing intellectual suicide." I am not now concerned with the merits or demerits of that tariff, but with the ideological position from which the editorial made this attack, namely: "It is not only economic nationalism, it represents cultural nationalism at its worst and most damaging." I think we should face that ideological position squarely. How can Canada attain substantial autonomy if our mass media propaganda treats the cause of economic nationalism and cultural nationalism as "stupid" and "suicidal"?

Why is the second alternative so drastic, calling for deep structural reorganization of our ways of living and our means of communication? Why don't we have a third option: to let the status quo continue and work to reform it? Because the record of the past century shows that piecemeal reform doesn't achieve its professed objectives. Because if the status quo continues, the public sector will continue to be eroded by the market. Because the gravitational pull of the U.S. will pull us closer and closer to it. A continuation of royal commissions, as those from Massey-Levesque to Applebaum-Hébert show, fail to confront the whole scope of Canada's dependence on the U.S., including our complicity in the U.S. Military-Industrial Complex. By and large such royal commissions offer a show-and-tell opportunity for our creative artists. Their testimony is tidily summarized; then well-meaning, minor recommendations are based on them. The usual result is titillation of our artistic sensibilities, and promises without performance to back them up. In fact, there is no static status quo. If we try to maintain it, Canada's cultural identity will remain an unapproached goal. We will increasingly exhibit the symptoms of political schizophrenia: talking pretty idealism, and practicing a less worthy materialism. We know that fence-straddling is not a long-term viable option. Indeed, fence-straddling is no more healthy for a country than it is for an individual: it damages the means of production and reproduction of both.

Personally, I am convinced that the cure for our political schizophrenia is to be found in either alternative one or two. As between them I would struggle for the pro-autonomy alternative. It may now be too late for the autonomy course to succeed. But it is certainly not too late to *try* to make it work.

Notes to "Culture, Communication 'Technology,' and . . ."

1. William J. Baumol and William G. Bowen, *Performing Arts—The Economic Dilemma* (New York: Twentieth Century Fund, Inc., 1966).
2. Wolfgang Fritz Haug, "Some Theoretical Problems in Discussion of Working-Class Culture," in A. Mattelart and S. Siegelaub (eds.), *Communication and Class Struggle, Vol. 2.: Liberation, Socialism* (New York: International General, 1983), pp. 95–100.
3. Edward S. Herman, *Corporate Control, Corporate Power* (New York: Cambridge University Press, 1981), p. 189.
4. "Madison Ave.'s Program Taboos," *Variety*, October 26, 1960, p. 28.
5. Louis Applebaum and Jacques Hébert, *Report of the Federal Cultural Policy Review Committee* (Ottawa: Minister of Supply and Services, 1982), p. 278.
6. Dallas W. Smythe, *Dependency Road: Communications, Capitalism, Consciousness and Canada* (Norwood, NJ: Ablex Publishing Company, 1981), pp. 241, 133–135.
7. Smythe, *Dependency Road*, pp. 91–102.
8. Smythe, *Dependency Road*, p. 165.
9. Cable Association, 9 April 1983.
10. Quoted in A. H. Teich (ed.), *Technology and Man's Future* (New York: St. Martin's Press, 1972), p. 152.
11. Quoted in Herbert I. Schiller, *Communication and Cultural Domination* (White Plains, NY: International Arts and Sciences Press, 1976), p. 27.

17

"The theory of self-reliance begins with an affirmation of the failure of the Western capitalist theory of development"

Editor's Note: "High-Tech: Who Wins, Who Loses?" was presented in 1987 at a labor congress in Mexico, one of the very few times Dallas Smythe spoke to a workers' organization. Given the orientation of Smythe's research and his progressive sympathies, the infrequency of his contact with labor groups might seem rather strange to the casual observer, who would think a closer affinity should have existed. Smythe felt, though, that the North American labor movement (with some small exceptions) had sold out to capitalism, so it is understandable that he had little rapport with mainstream labor. As well, mainstream labor was not especially interested in what he had to say—the message threatened labor's cohabitation with capital. But Third World labor was a different matter because, along with other groups, it had the potential of working toward "decentralized decision-making," as Smythe calls it.

Through his years of public speaking, Smythe talked to just about anybody who would listen. As we have seen, that included the religious establishment, which might seem distant from, if not hostile to, his message. Yet for him it was not so much a question of an unlikely audience, as it was the disposition of the audience to be open to what he had to say.

In "High-Tech," Smythe returned to one of his favorite subjects—the meaning of "technology," how technology originates, and how it is used. In a novel expansion of the theme, Smythe points out almost casually that technology is not just "modern industrialism" but also "all the organizations *and people* who make the system work" (my emphasis). The notion that technology includes people might seem shocking, even ludicrous, at first. Yet when we remember that, to Smythe, technology was industrialism and that industrialism was a way of organizing production, it makes sense to see humans as part of the structure.

In this paper, published here for the first time, Smythe situates the problem of technology in the context of Third World development and shows how communication technology, rather than liberating some nations, could actually become an instrument of further oppression. He points to Integrated Services Digital Network (ISDN) as one example of technology that could deprive many countries of the ability to control their own communications networks. If ISDN is installed, he says, the debate about the New World Information Order could be over, because such countries will not be able to have a communications policy of their own. Their sovereignty will vanish as they are folded into a global network controlled from outside by business interests and government allies. Contributing to this impotence, Smythe points out, is the small role played in the International Telecommunications Union by Third World countries, whose lack of finances and expertise puts them at a severe disadvantage. A parallel problem is that the private sector is "against the public sector," leading to an erosion of the public communication system through privatization.

In the previous paper in this collection, Smythe urged Canada to disassociate itself from U.S. capitalism and to pursue an independent, albeit difficult, course of national development. This is the same position Smythe outlines in "High-Tech." Drawing on arguments from Armand Mattelart, Smythe calls on Third World countries to practice self-reliant development that stresses qualitative change for *everyone.* Self-reliance, Smythe says, means cultural identity and cultural diversity, protected by cultural screens. Those who believe things such as portable video equipment and VCRs can produce decentralized democratic communication are wrong, he says, because that is the trap of "technological determinism." Decentralized democratic communication depends on the network of decentralized, democratic social organizations "into which such tools may or may not fit."

As in the paper on Canada, Smythe rejects a middle course based on reformism. He says the struggle over high-tech electronics can have, for the Third World, only two possible outcomes—"either the oppressive power of international capital will be vastly increased or self-reliant peoples will make leaping progress toward controlling the terms of their

own lives." As Smythe argues in the introduction to the paper, it is a contest between international capitalists' need for profit and the vast majority of the people's need for human dignity and development.

Although Dallas Smythe continued to write into 1992, "High-Tech" was among the last public presentations he made.

High-Tech: Who Wins, Who Loses?

[Seminar on Socio-Economic Impact of New Communication Technologies, Labour Congress, Mexico, November 1987]

LIFE IS A STRUGGLE, with winners and losers. The principal contradiction in the world is between the vast majority of the population (mostly in the Third World) and giant transnationals' (TNCs') capital. The people need food, clothing, shelter, health care and democratic decision-making, which are the conditions for human dignity and development. International capitalists need profits. Capital is now the principal aspect of that contradiction, but the conditions are ripe for genuinely self-reliant peoples to take control of their own lives.

1.

What does "technology" mean? It means simply modern industrialism—capitalism in action. For example, TV technology is much more than the TV set and the transmitter. It includes all the organizations and people who make the system work, from repairman to actress in the TV commercial. The word "technology" is a propaganda term. It has, however, very real elements. First is capital, which initiates and invests in the whole project. Second is science, which is harnessed to capital to invent the technique. Third is engineering, which actually designs the material parts of the project. Fourth is bureaucracy—both private and public—which houses the project. Fifth is the ideology of possessive individualism, which nourishes and is produced by the project. Sixth is the publicity which makes the project acceptable to the public. And seventh, the general population—the expected collaboration with the project. "Technology" is nothing but modern industrialism.

"Technology" does not drop from outer space; it is the result of human institutions. It is not neutral in its political effects. It is idealist nonsense to speak of "technology" as if it were a blank page which would be used for "good" or "bad" purposes. It will serve the systematic purpose of its innovators.

To accept the latest "technology" because it is the newest is to accept the inevitability of the domination of capital over people.

What should be clear by now is that self-reliant national cultures can only modernize *on their own terms.* I mean High-Tech should be challenged—and filtered through a country's cultural screen. This will reject or modify impacts of High-Tech—I elaborate this later.

The "Information Society" (or High-Tech) has two targets. First, to eliminate labour intensive operations—the service operations *inside* and *between* business organizations.

High-Tech requires much investment in new labour-saving equipment. It produces massive structural employment. Its effect is to redistribute income. Those who already get high incomes get even higher incomes. Workers in the service industries get lower incomes.

The High-Tech offensive is making rapid progress in the core toward this target. In the Third World labour intensive practices are common and this is for good social, economic and political reasons. In the Third World High-Tech is, or ought to be, unacceptable *in general.*

The second High-Tech target is to create new markets for hardware and software in the home: for shopping, banking, etc., as well as "entertainment." This wing of High-Tech has had much less success either in the core or the Third World.

2.

The basis of the High-Tech information offensive is Integrated Services Digital Network (ISDN). What is it all about? From their innovation in the 19th century until the 1950s the telephone and telegraph each used its own transmission channels (on land or underwater). With the coming of the transistor, coaxial cable, microwave relays, satellite channels, and fibre optic cable, the quantity of transmission channel space available expanded greatly. The various telephone and telegraph services could now be *combined* on the *same "broadband"* channels, *if the whole network were digital.* However, telephone service had been based on the analog mode. The industry committed itself to conversion of the whole telephone network from analog to digital. The Integrated Services Digital Network (ISDN) is the result: It is simply the end-to-end connection of broadband digital networks.

The project for the creation of the ISDN *only* makes business sense if the system can be global and substantially universally adopted. This is necessary in order to pay for the enormous investment required and provide the desired profits. To achieve this objective decisions must be made *on a global basis* for *all* aspects of the operation. For example:

- What engineering standards will be employed?
- Where and by whom will decisions be made to manage and maintain the system?
- Who decides who gets access to use ISDN? Where are they?
- What are to be the terms governing *information storage and forwarding database retrieval—protocol conversion and encryption—telemetry—connections between networks?* Who will decide, where will they be, and what will be their jurisdiction?

As Dan Schiller puts it, the ISDN, as now planned, will: (1) speed up reduction in the use of human labour, the quality of work and real wages; (2) enable intracorporate transborder data to flow more abundantly; (3) allow capital to move across borders in search of profits more easily; and (4) strengthen new military and intelligence activities aimed to protect the markets in which TNCs buy cheap labour and sell their products.[1]

Most Third World countries will find the cost of building their segments of the ISDN system very high indeed. Even those Third World countries which do install ISDN will face grave dangers. It is technically possible and cheaper for the global ISDN network to be built so that the most basic decisions regarding its use will be made in a few nodal points rather than in every country (decisions like: How will it be programmed? Who will have access to it to send or receive every kind of service?).

If yours turns out to be a country *without* such a nodal point you will be subject to external control. In such a country the debate about the New World Economic Order or the New World Information Order will be ended: your country could not have a communication policy of its own. Third World country sovereignty is at stake.

The development of policy for ISDN is riddled with contradictions between the players now in the struggle at the ITU [International Telecommunications Union]:

1. PTTs and private corporations which provide broadband services.
2. Manufacturers of telecommunications equipment.
3. Computer manufacturers.
4. Computer service firms (value-added)—such as Tymshare.
5. Business *customers* who buy broadband services.
6. Militaries and the industrial complexes associated with them.
7. Civil governments of all countries.

Mostly absent from the struggle in the ITU are Third World countries. And totally absent are the most important players: people represented through their own voluntary organizations (including labour unions and churches).

Each of these groups of players is to some degree in conflict with others over the technical and organizational aspects of ISDN. Moreover, rivalries within each group of players for markets and power make possible alliances with members of other groups—if Third World countries were actively present in the ITU discussions.

One cleavage between the players, however, is clear. That is the private sector as against the public sector. When broadband services are switched now it is with computers. Public policy permitted the Private Automatic Branch Exchange (PABX) to become the breach in the monopoly of telecommunications providers (whether the PTTs or private, e.g., ATT). Every PABX on a customer's premises provides the means for the customer to operate his own private telecommunications system, connecting head with branch offices, customers, etc. Since 1959 the private sector has grown immensely in size in telecommunications, relative to the PTTs. Britain and Australia are examples. I give one example of the gains by the private sector: a seemingly neutral decision in planning ISDN at the ITU would seem to be the designation of calling codes. Now, when I telephone to Mexico, the code is 52—there is one to each country. Already by 1984 the ISDN planners had decided to change the calling codes so that *multiple* vendors of service would get calling codes. So with ISDN, Mexico will probably have more than one code number. This will divert some users from the present Mexican PTT or "recognized private operating agency." And the U.S. stated in 1984 that "this is but the first step in movement toward implementation of ISDN in a manner which actually promotes a multiple-vendor environment."[2]

The forum where the fate of ISDN is being decided is the International Telecommunications Union (ITU). The ITU was created by national governments more than a century ago to regulate international telegraph (later also telephone and radio). The ITU produces treaties between *countries* which govern telecommunications standards (including operating practices) and allocation of radio frequency use for the globe. Since the 1970s about two-thirds of the country members are in the Third World. After the Non-Aligned Movement was founded in 1955 in Bandung, it coordinated the struggle for equitable shares of the radio spectrum. The central issue in sharing the use of the spectrum is whether such use is to be planned or not. If it is planned, small countries can be assured a share. If not planned, it is left to the capitalist market to determine. So successful were Third World countries in the struggle that after the 1982 Plenipotentiary Conference, the core countries' strategy shifted. From crude attempts to block Third World demand, the new strategy is an offensive aimed to co-opt Third World initiatives and convert them into new, large and profitable markets for high-tech equipment—ISDN is the vehicle. How is this being done?

Policy decisions in the ITU come from Plenipotentiary Conferences and/or Administrative Conferences (to which issues are referred by the Plenipotentiaries and where decisions in principle are administered). There are two types of Administrative Conferences: "Radio" and "Telephone and Telegraph." Radio Administrative Conferences concern mostly issues about the allocation of the radio spectrum to particular service classes of users and the standards to be used by such service classes. However, the scientific and technical standards and operating practices for telecommunications are developed in the second type of Administrative Conference: the Telephone and Telegraph Conferences (CCITTs). Planning for each type of conference is organized under a Consultative Committee.

Third World progress in the ITU has been in the Plenipotentiaries and the Administrative Radio Conferences. For this there are two reasons. The Radio Conference issues are more politically visible and immediately sensitive (i.e., the issue of allocating orbital slots). And the sheer weight of numbers of Third World countries can be mobilized more easily around such issues. The second reason is that the Third World countries have not participated effectively in the determination of standards by the CCITT. On Japan's initiative in 1980 the ITU delegated the ISDN project to the Telephone and Telegraph Consultative Committee where the core countries have three great advantages. One is the enormous lead which they have in expertise about electronics.

The second advantage is the method of work in the CCITT. It uses technical committees, subcommittees and working groups which meet frequently and which feed scientific reports to the CCITT Plenary meetings. Third World countries lack the funds to send representatives to all those meetings. They also lack the depth and range of expertise to staff delegations large enough to cover all the committee meetings while retaining enough experts to conduct normal operations at home. The CCITT in 1979 had 17 committees. Of the 117 Third World countries eligible to attend only 15 attended one or more study groups and ten of those attended only one. By contrast, six developed countries attended all 17 committees and 13 additional developed countries attended a majority of committees.

A third advantage of the core countries is the privatization of decision-making in the CCITT. Almost from its beginning the ITU has permitted private enterprises which operate telecommunications in certain countries to participate (without a vote) in the work of the CCITT. In 1979 there were 36 private operating entities from 20 highly industrialized countries which did just that. Of the 36 entities, 15 came from the U.S. (including Puerto Rico). An additional 12 recognized private operating agencies came from eight Third World countries. Another privatizing influence in the CCITT is its "Scientific or Industrial Organization" members. This category includes *non-operating entities.* These are giant TNCs interested in telecommunications. So we find IBM, Xerox, Hughes Aircraft, Rockwell International, Honeywell, Hewlett-Packard and General Electric officially taking part in planning ISDN. The amazing total of 131 such entities (in 1979) is larger than the total Third World countries in the ITU! Of these 131 TNCs in the CCITT, 35 come from the U.S., 25 from France, 17 from the U.K., and 15 from Italy.[3]

How do these core country advantages work? According to Codding and Rutkowski, these private organizations:

> are given a wide opportunity to affect the work of the study groups where the basic research takes place. ... The non-administration participants...were in a majority in all of the CCITT study groups except for two.[4]

So when the committees make reports:

> In theory, they are simply statements of the Committee's position on the subject. However, because they represent a consensus on the part of the key administrations, operating authorities and major manufacturers, they enjoy considerable force and effect—often more so than regulations adopted by treaty.[5]

When the reports from the Consultative Committee will be submitted to the World Administrative Telephone and Telegraph Conference in 1988, the options related to ISDN and telecommunications development which would be in the interest of the Third World will have been severely narrowed or closed.

Regardless of which type of ITU Conference it is, the Third World is handicapped. Careful research by Codding has established that the most important factors which determine a country's influence in the ITU is "size of delegation," followed by "pages of proposals submitted at the conference."[6] Even at WARC–79, where Third World countries had a large majority of votes, five core countries sent a total of 300 delegates, while

74 countries with less than seven delegates each, sent a total of 284 delegates.

Earlier I offered two reasons why the Third World is not more effective in the ITU: lack of funds to field delegations, and lack of skilled experts. Codding and Rutkowski's research suggests that there is a third reason: Third World countries do not need high-tech, such as ISDN. "Many developing countries tend to refrain from active participation in the real work of the CCIs"[7] because they need intermediate and less expensive technologies rather than the most advanced and usually most expensive, and it is harder to get loans to finance the former than the latter. To the extent to which this reason for Third World ineffectiveness in the ITU is true, I believe that, while the reason is very understandable, it is wrong. Protection of national sovereignty in the Third World against the threats embodied in ISDN calls for an *active* defensive strategy, *not a retreat.*

In their drive for a global market, the core countries in 1982–85 grafted on to the ITU a marketing agency for ISDN-related high-tech electronics. They created (through ITU) the Maitland Commission to produce a global program to improve telecommunications, especially aimed at the Third World. That Commission urged that ISDN digital components should be pushed by the ITU with the aid of a catalog of suppliers and systems. Sales to Third World countries should be financed through development assistance programs and loans from the usual national and international agencies. Further, the ITU was to create a Centre for Telecommunications Development which would advise developing countries, help them to prepare plans and financing proposals, provide assistance in management, training and research. Swiftly the ITU held the "First World Telecommunications Development Conference" in Arusha in May 1985. It duly created the Centre, supervised by an Advisory Board including ATT and Hughes Aircraft.

In a cynical nod to reality, the Maitland Commission's report did admit that "data communications or even broadband communications is not as significant at the moment in the Third World as is transmission of telephone signals. ..."[8] It also conceded that:

> when telecommunications networks in the developing world are extended to provide advanced data communication facilities, entities in industrialized countries who would normally operate such facilities may gain advantages with respect to information on trade and market conditions.[9]

However, you should not worry! For the Commission said that this result might be avoided by "closer co-operation between industrialized and developing countries in the data communication field."[10] This was supported by another recommendation (which would make such "co-operation" easier) that Third World countries which operate their own telecommunications facilities (usually by PTTs) should turn them over to private enterprise.[11]

This is the grim reality which high-tech presents to the Third World.

3.

What policies might Third World countries pursue to protect themselves from subordination to the "high-tech" offensive of which the tap-root is ISDN? It seems that desirable policies develop from the practice and theory of self-reliant development in Third World countries (and also in the core countries). Armand Mattelart and I argue that the theory of self-reliance begins with an affirmation of the failure of the Western capitalist theory of development which focusses on *quantitative* growth in GNP and assumes that benefits will "trickle down" to the masses of people from that growth.[12] In the Arusha declaration of 1967 the Third World urged that *qualitative* criteria be used to judge development.

Self-reliance comes from recognition of the value of solidarity—the basis for *participation* by everyone—and *development* in favour of everyone—not only the elite or middle class.

Self-reliance is tied to the demand for cultural identity and cultural diversity, protected by what I have called "cultural screens."[13] Culture is not merely objects or artifacts. It is also *an aspect* of all areas and things. It is the aspect of enjoying the effort to meet human needs. And the ends to be pursued must be defined by the groups and persons who make that creative, enjoyable effort. To make the effort because of dependency is to turn it into slavery.

It is in this connection that what people call High-Tech produces a sort of slavery. High-Tech thrives on splintering group relations, and accelerates such pulverization. Instead of chains of movements expressing the solidarity of groups and individuals, we get monads, isolated from one another by competition and individual consumption. Self-reliance calls for *appropriate* machines and software designed to meet the basic needs of the population. Super 8 cameras, portable video recorders and VCRs are often said to produce decentralized democratic communication networks. Wrong: that is the trap of "technological determinism." Decentralized democratic communications depends not on tools but on *the network* of decentralized, democratic social organizations into which such tools may or may not fit. But such democratic decentralized organizations must be seen in relation to national and global problems. A viable *local* action requires a truly democratic *national* structure and any genuine *national* development draws its strength and relevance from self-reliant *local* communities which it supports and promotes. This is a continuum. It is also a dialectical process which links the local community ultimately with the world community.

At its roots the local community's actions are in the community's collective *knowledge*. The *nurture* of this knowledge is the first active step toward self-reliant development. Uncounted hundreds of thousands of "base communities" and "base Christian communities" in Latin America, Africa, India and southeast Asia are organizing such knowledge among the desperately poor of the Third World, probably more in rural than in urban areas. In the towns and cities of both peripheral countries and the core, the trade union movement, working class political parties, Christian groups, environmental movements, human rights organizations, women's organizations and consumer organizations press toward decentralized decision-making. By their actions more than their rhetoric, these movements and loosely-knit organizations assert their fundamental need and right to establish a democratic development path. They reject the claim of governments and big business to be the only or main decision-makers. This pro-democratic tide is rising at the same time that the old political parties, labour unions and movements are being eroded where they have not accommodated to the fact that democratic development may require a multiplicity of interconnected but independent organizations based on communities.

How does Self-Reliance relate to high-tech (e.g., ISDN)? It would resist it through its own organizations, strategies and tactics. Such a struggle amounts in fact to making revolutionary changes. A strategically vital part of that struggle is, or ought to be, located in the ITU. That is where electronic standards, practices and radio allocation is determined. The use of the radio spectrum—a tap root of political power—is at stake. While the difficulties Third World countries face in the short-run in working in the ITU are obvious, it is a serious error in the long-run to fail to work in the ITU.

Depending on the outcome of the struggle over high-tech electronics either the oppressive power of international capital will be vastly increased or self-reliant peoples will make leaping progress toward controlling the terms of their own lives.

Notes to "High-Tech. . ."

1. Dan Schiller, "The Emerging Global Grid: Planning for What?" *Media, Culture and Society,* vol. 7, no. 1, January 1985, pp. 105–125.
2. Schiller, "The Emerging Global Grid," pp. 118–119.
3. George A. Codding, Jr. and Anthony M. Rutkowski, *The International Telecommunications Union in a Changing World* (Dedham, Massachusetts: Artech House Inc., 1982), pp. 344–390.
4. Codding and Rutkowski, p. 102.
5. Codding and Rutkowski, p. 95.
6. George A. Codding, Jr., "Influence in International Conferences," *International Organization,* vol. 35, no. 4, Autumn 1981, pp. 715–724.
7. Codding and Rutkowski, p. 105.
8. International Telecommunications Union (Maitland Commission), *The Missing Link* (Geneva, 1984), p. 33.
9. International Telecommunications Union, p. 33.
10. International Telecommunications Union, p. 33.
11. International Telecommunications Union, p. 38.
12. Armand Mattelart, *Transnationals and the Third World: The Struggle for Culture,* translated by David Buxton (South Hadley, Massachusetts: Bergin & Garvey Publishers, Inc., 1983), pp. 24–26, 139–142, 151–157.
13. Dallas W. Smythe, *Dependency Road: Communications, Capitalism, Consciousness and Canada* (Norwood, New Jersey: Ablex Publishing Corp., 1981), chapter 10.

Eulogy

THOMAS GUBACK

EDITOR'S NOTE: On October 17, 1992, at Simon Fraser University, there was a memorial service for Dallas Smythe that was attended by family, friends, and colleagues. The same day, there was a mass said for him at Emmanual Memorial Episcopal Church in Champaign, Illinois, the Rev. Fr. Alan Herbst, ossje, officiating. I read the following encomium.

TODAY WE REMEMBER DALLAS WALKER SMYTHE. You may have known him personally, as I did for more than 30 years. You may have known him through his writing, teaching, and speaking. Or you may have known him only by reputation as a scholar and activist—two terms that some people would think are incompatible, since they feel that scholarship should be value-free, objective, impartial, and neutral. Dallas did not agree with that. To him, there was no impartiality. "Value-free" anything was nonsense. Commitment, openly declared and fiercely supported, was what counted. He knew which side of the line he was on, and he never stopped speaking about it, and he never stopped struggling for it, right to the end.

I spent several days with Dallas in December last year, since I am editing a book of his papers and speeches. I asked Dallas what radicalized him. As a young man trained in economics, what had made him take sides, what had made him speak up for the exploited, the oppressed, the destitute, the homeless. He said it was the Okies and the Arkies who started it. You see, after Dallas received his doctorate in economics from Berkeley in 1937, he worked with the Wage and Hour Division of the Department of Labor in Washington—and in 1939 he was assigned to the House Committee on

Migration and Destitute Citizens. As he explained it to me, his job was to study the consequences of and reasons for their condition and to draw a lesson from it. That lesson he did draw—a lesson that shaped the remainder of his life. About that same time, he also did the studies that helped enforce those Wage and Hour laws that applied to workers in interstate businesses. It was another experience that showed him the brutality of oppression and exploitation.

Dallas was a radical, a progressive. His name was in files. He was investigated. Only by a fluke did he not become a victim of McCarthyism and blacklisting. He left the government in 1948—he was with the Federal Communications Commission then—to join the faculty of the University of Illinois. When he came here, his loyalty was questioned again. The accusers didn't bother to ask "loyalty to whom? loyalty to what virtues?" The answer was that Dallas had stuck up for the people on the bottom. Dallas had stuck up for democracy. He had stuck up for justice. And those are the virtues that Power doesn't like. At the University, Dallas never ceased getting us to recognize abuses and never ceased showing us how to correct them. When you come to think about it, that's what education should be.

In my years working with Dallas, I never knew him to attend a church service. But his association with churches stands out boldly on his record. In 1951, he was asked by the Broadcasting and Film Commission of the National Council of Churches of Christ to co-author a study of the effects of broadcast programs and films produced by churches. Did they become a substitute for going to church? Did they build Christian character? Did they reach non-churchgoers? Did they faithfully convey the Christian Gospel? That study was housed at the Divinity School at Yale and drew on a population sample from New Haven. The results were published in 1955 in a book called *The Television-Radio Audience and Religion.* It led to Dallas serving on committees of the National Council of Churches, speaking before church groups, and writing about religion and the mass media. Even into the early 1960s, he still was addressing seminaries in Kentucky and New York and church groups throughout the United States.

The 1950s, you might remember, were not glorious times for liberals, and certainly not for radicals. Yet Dallas found, in lecturing at Divinity Schools, that—as he put it—theologians were not afraid to discuss capitalism, socialism and communism frankly and with enthusiasm. In the late 1950s, when Dallas began speaking out against the arms race and nuclear weapons, when he began speaking out for peace and understanding during the Cold War, he said he found a ready and sympathetic audience in the religious community. He told me that theologians he met "were quite openly considering the role of religion as an opponent of oppressive authority" and that "they were delighted to find someone who was willing to talk about the ideological aspects of the Cold War."

I asked Dallas, when I saw him last, whether he thought there was a much closer connection—than would be superficially apparent—between radical and Christian points of view. His answer was unequivocal: Yes. Although his current work was in other areas, I think he would have approved the growing links between radical political economics and Christian theology, between economic justice and religion, between the struggle to end oppression and a Christian economic ethic.

I discovered when I read Dallas's unfinished autobiography that as a youngster he had been confirmed in the Anglican Church of Canada, which, with the Episcopal Church in the United States, is part of the worldwide Anglican Communion.

That is why today—here—we remember DALLAS WALKER SMYTHE.

Regina, Saskatchewan, March 9, 1907.

Langley, British Columbia, September 6, 1992.

May light perpetual shine upon you.

DALLAS SMYTHE, 1991, in his home office. (*Courtesy Thomas Guback.*)

About the Book and Editor

Dallas Smythe, deceased on September 6, 1992, at the age of eighty-five, was the Renaissance scholar, teacher, policy adviser, and activist generally credited with founding the field of the political economy of communications. For almost fifty years he participated in most major policy developments in broadcasting and telecommunication in the United States and Canada, as well as in many international policy developments. When he died, he left a wide range of published and unpublished works, an incomplete manuscript, and more than sixty books to be returned to the library.

For Smythe, the primary purpose of research was to develop knowledge that would be applied in policies and practices to improve the human condition, especially that of the disenfranchised and powerless. His emphasis on action and implementation has left us with a large volume of unpublished papers and speeches. Although a prodigious researcher, he was always more concerned with researching the new issues that lay ahead than with writing his completed work for formal publication. This volume contains most of Smythe's seminal papers and talks that have escaped publication to date, have stood the test of time in terms of relevance and insight, and remain important contributions to the field of the political economy of communications today.

Thomas Guback, a former student of Smythe's, a collaborator on some of his early research projects, and a leader among the current generation of scholars in the Smythe tradition, has selected and introduced each of the papers to place them in context for readers.

Thomas Guback is research professor of communications at the Institute of Communications Research at the University of Illinois at Urbana-Champaign.

Index